EUGENICS AND

MODERNIZATION

IN INTERWAR

ROMANIA

Pitt Series in Russian and East European Studies

Jonathan Harris, Editor

EUGENICS AND

MODERNIZATION

IN INTERWAR

ROMANIA

Maria Bucur

UNIVERSITY OF PITTSBURGH PRESS

Published by the University of Pittsburgh Press, Pittsburgh, Pa., 15260

Copyright © 2002, University of Pittsburgh Press

Manufactured in the United States of America

Printed on acid-free paper

10 9 8 7 6 5 4 3 2 1

Text photos are from Francisc Rainer, *Enquetes anthropologiques dans trois villages roumains des Carpathes* (Bucharest: Monitorul Oficial, 1937).

Library of Congress Cataloging-in-Publication Data

Bucur, Maria, 1968–
    Eugenics and modernization in interwar Romania / Maria Bucur.
        p. cm. — (Pitt series in russian and east european studies.)
    Based on the author's thesis (Ph. d.—University of Illinois at
    Urbana-Champaign, 1996) presented under the title: Disciplining the
    future, eugenics and modernization in interwar Romania.
    Includes bibliographical references and index.
        ISBN 0-8229-4172-4
    1. Eugenics—Romania—History. I. Title. II. Series in Russian and
    East European studies
        HQ755.5.R6 B8 2002
        363.9'2'09498—dc21

                                                            2001003341

CONTENTS

ACKNOWLEDGMENTS

This book could not have been written without the support of many individuals and institutions. My deepest gratitude goes to Keith Hitchins, who guided me with personal and intellectual generosity through the early stages of this project. Peter Fritzsche, Sonya Michel, Kenneth Jowitt, Gale Stokes, John Lampe, Madeleine Levine, Ellen Dwyer, Matei Clinescu, David Ransel, Carl Ipsen, Jeff Wasserstrom, Nancy Wingfield, and Sorin Antohi all provided useful comments at various points along the way. The final choices made in the manuscript are, however, my responsibility. I am also indebted to many people in Romania, without whom I would never have come across some of the most interesting material for this book: Cornelia Bodea; Pompiliu Teodor; Vasile Puşcaş; Meda Bârcă; Doru Radosav; Romeo Lăzărescu; as well as the patient and friendly staffs at the National Archives in Cluj and Sibiu, at the Library of the Romanian Academy, and at the University Library in Cluj. I am also thankful for the financial assistance provided by I.R.E.X., the University of Illinois, Indiana University, the Woodrow Wilson Center, and the American Association of University Women. Finally, this book could not have been finished without the help of two people—my husband, who patiently supported my progress and read through countless drafts of the manuscript; and my grandmother, without whom I could not have survived the loneliness and cold in Romania. She was the spirit that kept me going through many months of research in unheated archives and libraries. It is to her that I dedicate this book. Sărut mâna, buni.

INTRODUCTION

The military-bureaucratic state ... provided the crucible and target for
nationalism ... ; its utilitarian assumptions and norms of efficiency
became the most suited to the increasingly rationalist temper of the
products of its educational institution, the intelligentsia.

Anthony D. Smith, *Theories of Nationalism*

I N T H E middle of the twentieth century, Romanian geographer and education reformer Simion Mehedinţi wrote: "Through Mendelism, modern biology
has given us the key that enables each nation to gain access if not to Heaven, at
least to its gates. . . . The birth of children with superior gifts can be for each nation a source of scientific, ethical, artistic, and social creativity, that would increase the potential of that entire ethnic group."[1] Daring to imagine humans as
masters not only of their individual lives but also of their collective present and
future—this was the initial eugenic utopia. Since its rise as a scientific discipline
in the late nineteenth century, eugenics has fascinated and repelled biologists,
doctors, social reformers, politicians, and historians. More recently, interest in
the relationship between heredity and behavior has found a parallel in the
growth of historical analyses focusing on eugenics.[2] Many of these analyses
have shown how eugenic assumptions were once widely shared in countries as

dissimilar as Hitler's Germany and Roosevelt's United States. Discussion of Eastern European interest in eugenics is, however, almost entirely absent from this prodigious body of work.[3]

My study seeks to shed light on this heretofore neglected aspect of the international reach of eugenics discourse by focusing on a particularly intriguing case study—twentieth-century Romania. The notion that the quality and quantity of the human species could and should be controlled found many adepts in this country. Between 1918 and 1948, a growing group of professionals, initially mostly doctors, set out to change Romanian health care, society, and the state according to the gospel of eugenics. My study focuses primarily on the interwar period (1918–40). The complicated questions of Romania's involvement in World War II and the potential links between Romanian doctors and the Holocaust render the 1940–45 period a separate chapter in Romanian history. For instance, the overt and aggressive racism of some of the more radical eugenicists, such as Iordache Făcăoaru, points to potential connections between their ideas and some of the racist anti-Semitic and anti-Roma policies of World War II and the Holocaust. However, this question cannot be assessed properly yet, because of lack of access to essential archival resources.[4] Two recent in-depth studies that touch on the relationship between the Romanian Holocaust and public health policy makers and doctors arrive at diverging conclusions.[5] This book brings these issues into discussion but cannot fully explore them.

The three main organizations supporting eugenics were the Royal Eugenics Society, the Eugenic Section of the Romanian Social Institute, and the Biopolitical Section of the Transylvanian association Astra. Their active membership was not large.[6] Yet among their members were some of the most illustrious doctors in interwar Romania: Iuliu Moldovan, the leader of the movement in Transylvania; the endocrinologist Gheorghe Marinescu; Gheorghe Banu, the leader of the movement at the Medical School in Bucharest; Mihai Sturdza; and others. Active supporters of eugenics came also from other academic and professional disciplines, among them famous and respected personalities: Emil Racoviță, at one time the president of the Romanian Academy and a speleologist of worldwide reputation; Dimitrie Gusti, the most important sociologist of the interwar period; Sabin Manuilă, the most prominent interwar demographer; Simion Mehedinți; Alexandru Ștefănescu-Goangă; and Iuliu Hațiegan. The last two were also rectors of the University of Cluj during the interwar period.

Two monthly publications, *Buletin Eugenic și Biopolitic* (1927–47) and *Revista de Igienă Socială* (1930–44), were dedicated primarily to eugenics. Many other publications also featured articles on eugenics. These publications ranged from professional journals, such as *Ardealul Medical* and *Revista de Medicină Legală*, to popular periodicals, such as *Societatea de Mâine, Transilvania,* and *Calendarul Asociaţiunii*. Discussions of eugenic ideas became so commonplace that even newspapers like *Universul* and *Adevărul* occasionally published articles on eugenic sterilization and birth control.

In addition to familiarizing the Romanian public with eugenic ideas—in effect generating a eugenic culture, itself an important contribution to shaping interwar Romania—eugenicists attempted to enact public health and education reform. They introduced eugenic notions in schools, from the primary level to university medical education, and tried to restructure selection of pupils according to hereditary aptitudes. This last endeavor was largely unsuccessful. Eugenicists also crafted the most comprehensive piece of legislation prior to the post-1945 period regarding state responsibility and authority over public health. The Moldovan Law of 1930 included measures that ranged from the training of doctors, infant care, and regulation of venereal diseases to industrial hygiene and local fund-raising for public health. However, because Romanian eugenicists overall did not favor sterilization as a tool for generating eugenic betterment, this law did not include any such measures. Instead, the Moldovan Law and other policies placed faith in education and the power of persuasion —in changing people's behavior by informing them about their biological limitations and eugenic responsibilities.

Under pressure from supporters of eugenics, some restrictive measures were also passed in the mid-1930s. Abortion was criminalized, with one exception— when eugenic prerogatives dictated the need to prevent reproduction (if the parents suffered from hereditary defects). Yet even in this case abortion remained voluntary. Another restrictive measure was designed to prevent ethnic Romanians from marrying non-Romanians. No general law was ever passed, but army officers and government officials were pressured against miscegenation. A limited measure regarding the intermarriage of army officers was finally passed in 1938. More serious restrictions were passed in 1940, under the dictatorship of Carol II. As far as I could find out, the eugenics movement had little direct influence on the anti-Semitic laws of August 1940. The eugenicists' most significant role was in introducing and popularizing eugenic culture. In doing so, they contributed to destabilizing the fledgling political life of Romania and making illiberal tendencies appealing to educated professionals, academics, and even Orthodox and Uniate priests, who considered themselves pillars of stability and morality.

Eugenics was an important force in Romanian culture during the first half of the twentieth century. It helped shape state institutions as well as public debates about the relationship between individuals and the state, playing a different role than did similar movements in Western Europe and the United States. Romanian eugenicists presented their theories as offering a path toward modernization that would conserve vital elements of the past while embracing the future through a combination of state-controlled policies and grassroots volunteerism. At the same time, their synthesis of tradition and modernization helped them to negotiate the apparently irreconcilable interwar debates of the Romanian educated elites between traditionalist conservatives and their opponents— the Europeanizing modernists.

This book explores the main themes at the heart of the eugenic arguments and programs. It does not attempt to provide a complete history of eugenics in Romania. While an institutional or purely intellectual history of the eugenics movement would be valuable in aiding understanding of the development of science in Romania, such an approach would offer limited insights into larger historical processes. My analysis focuses instead on the impact of eugenics discourse beyond the scientific community and the role of this discourse in shaping national identity. I look at the relationship between individual rights and the needs of the nation and at the role of the state in embodying the nation's vital interests. For while Romanian eugenics never played an important role in scientific research, it was nonetheless a vital force in reconceptualizing the terms of the debate about individual and collective rights and responsibilities during the interwar years. Like Frank Dikötter, I consider eugenics "not so much as a clear set of scientific principles as a 'modern' way of talking about social problems in biologizing terms."[7]

This study also analyzes the ways in which eugenic ideas were put into practice. My discussion brings to light the gap between the unbounded faith of reformers in the ability of the state to mobilize and control human resources, on the one hand, and the actual limitations in the effectiveness of state institutions in carrying out ambitious eugenic plans, on the other. Although the implementation of policies fell short of the eugenicists' aspirations, legislative and educational measures did have long-term consequences that we may find hard to grasp at first but that are felt even today.

One of the goals of eugenic policies was the reconstruction of the public sphere, and eugenicists were successful in this regard. Not only did they urge greater personal voluntary involvement in the public arena, but they also helped expand the responsibilities and powers of the state over individuals' social welfare. Eugenicists' ideas and legislative measures provided tools for future emissaries of the state (whether the 1940 fascist regime or the post-1947 communist one) in their attempts to justify the importance of controlling and politicizing social actions that previously had not been considered concerns of the state, from marriage to reproduction.

I seek to discuss the eugenics movement in Romania with intellectual dispassion rather than to condemn it. Although I view as reprehensible the increased control exercised by the state and elite social groups in defining the meaning of individual lives in purely utilitarian terms, I am not interested in identifying the villains and victims in this process. Rather, I aim to understand the motivations of various groups and individuals who supported such measures. My work stands both as the first thorough study of eugenics in Eastern Europe (outside of Russia) and as a contribution to some prominent themes in the historiography of the period, from the antithesis between modernization and traditionalism to the nature and significance of anti-Semitism for the growth of the extreme right in particular to the shifts in the parameters of the public sphere in general.

Historiography on Eugenics

Over the last two decades the historiography dedicated to the issue of eugenics has developed into a veritable industry.[8] The growth of this literature has been shaped both by questions of intellectual history regarding the development of science and medicine over the last century and by current ethical and moral considerations. The various implications of biological determinism in politics and social welfare are as much an issue today as they were a century ago, especially with the publicity generated by books such as *The Bell Curve* and more recently by genetic cloning.[9]

This body of work has moved from attempts to distance eugenics (as pseudoscientific) from the mainstream development of science to explorations of the wide appeal of this theory among doctors, biologists, and other educated professionals and social reformers across the political spectrum.[10] Historians initially focused on eugenics and the extreme right, especially on Nazi policies toward Jews and other "biologically undesirable" populations. Over time, this historiography has shifted toward a more nuanced analysis of eugenics, which reflects the broad spectrum of interpretations and agendas to which eugenics lent itself.[11] From middle-class fears about overpopulation of the poor in England to fears about migration among politicians and the white public in the United States, eugenics drew support especially from educated professionals and social reformers. Some—such as the Fabians in England—had leftist leanings, and others— for instance many supporters of eugenics in the American South —had staunchly rightist views.[12] Over the past decade, in the historiography of the modern period, eugenics has emerged as an important science and social-reform movement, no longer identified as simply an aberration of fringe right-wing movements.

The historiography of eugenics grew within the national narratives of the various Western countries where eugenics had developed most prominently—Great Britain, France, Germany, and the United States. It concentrated on these developed industrialized nations because they had long scientific traditions, large middle classes, and publics well acquainted with the language of science and in particular with the controversies that arose out of Darwin's evolutionary theory. These industrialized countries also displayed the problems of societies that had begun to pay too high a price for material progress and civilization in terms of future health—the squalor of large cities, the spread of tuberculosis, alcoholism. By focusing on these issues, historians were themselves reinforcing the claim that eugenics was a reaction to the unprecedented scale of the social problems that industrialized nations faced in the late nineteenth century rather than a radical way of recasting the relationship between individuals and the community and between private and public concerns.[13]

These works also constructed their own norms and expectations about certain aspects of eugenics. As Nancy Leys Stepan has argued, in this literature Lamarckian eugenics often became identified with left-wing politics or with an outdated hereditary theory and was regarded as weak or soft eugenics.[14] However, as Stepan's work on Latin America has shown, some eugenicists remained proponents of neo-Lamarckism neither because they came from underdeveloped regions, with access only to outdated knowledge, nor because of any left-wing political leanings. Eugenicists in Latin America read Lamarckian ideas in their own political and cultural context and found them more persuasive than Mendelian ideas because of particular religious, public health, and medical training traditions. This layer of the debate between neo-Lamarckian and

Mendelian eugenics remained invisible to historians who focused on Western Europe and the United States. My own analysis adds a new dimension to the comparison between neo-Lamarckism and Mendelism by examining these ideas in the Romanian context.

The tie between eugenics and racism was central to most of these works of historiography, whether focused on the professional development of eugenicists, on the validity of their scientific claims, or on their political allegiances.[15] Many historians have focused predominantly on the ways in which eugenicists defined racial identity and aimed to "cleanse" their states of unwanted populations as the most significant aspects of eugenic theories. In some analyses the racial dimension is an implicit general undercurrent that surfaces in the discussion of particular aspects of eugenics. This could hardly be otherwise, because of the connections made between biological determinism and race selection in the early part of the twentieth century. Subsequently, the painful memory of the Holocaust transformed every discussion of eugenics into an ethical and moral one, whether the subject was the role played by German doctors in reaching the Final Solution or the American Eugenics Society.[16] The legacy of the Holocaust served to project culturally specific concerns on the historiography of eugenics in a universalistic way.

Over the last decade studies of eugenics have problematized this picture of eugenics as primarily a theory that represented a racist reaction against the growing negative effects of uncontrolled industrialization. Stepan's book on the eugenics movement in Latin America calls into question many of the assumptions of previous historians, both about the preconditions for interest in eugenics—an industrialized society with a large educated middle class—and about the ways in which previous historians linked eugenics to a conservative, even reactionary political agenda. My work follows in the footsteps of Stepan's approach, which seeks to "normalize" eugenics. To normalize is not to make an apology for eugenics; rather it represents an attempt to evaluate this movement in its appropriate historical context, "prospectively rather than retrospectively."[17]

Stepan and German historian Atina Grossmann have pointed out that eugenics also focused on limiting and controlling gender roles, especially women's, rendering this aspect crucial to understanding the meaning of eugenics.[18] My own analysis underlines at various points the ways in which gender and race are concepts essential to eugenic constructions of the public sphere. However, these two aspects of eugenics are not the end point of my discussion. Rather, I consider eugenic notions of race and gender as part of a Weltanschauung whose implications range beyond defining and controlling women's reproductive capabilities and the racial homogeneity of the nation. Setting gender and ethnic/racial differences as the foundation for enforcing a eugenic social hierarchy was a way to renegotiate the relationship between individual and communal prerogatives over legitimate actions.

These measures worked to destroy the autonomy of "normal" individuals at the same time as that of "degenerate" ones.[19] Undoubtedly there were great qualitative differences between the actual treatment of these two categories of individuals. Yet eugenicists wanted decisions about treatment left to the professional technocratic elite (especially the hygiene doctors) and the representatives of the state. Thus, neither the healthy nor the ill were to have individual recourse to action in defining their status; a "normal" individual could become part of the "degenerate" community without having committed any particular action, and the reverse—in principle, at least—could also occur. Various forms of individual empowerment came to depend strictly on two fundamental principles: collective (i.e., national) interests, especially of a multigenerational nature, always took precedence over individual ones; and it was the responsibility of the state to protect these interests.

The Romanian Case

For those familiar with the literature on eugenics movements elsewhere, Romanian eugenics may at first seem to replicate some of the same dynamics active in the development of eugenics in other countries.[20] However, most historiography has focused on countries in which interest in eugenics did not develop concomitantly with a great political change such as the formation of Greater Romania, when a new nation was patched together practically overnight, beyond the aspirations of its constituent parts.

In France, Germany, England, and the United States, eugenics addressed perceived crises of development within populations with an already well-defined sense of national identity. If they sought to reconstruct this identity, eugenicists participated in a debate over issues that the public easily recognized. This was especially the case in Germany, where a general sense of malaise dominated the public discourse about German identity after World War I.[21] There, however, eugenicists sought to address crushed expectations rather than to construct a sense of identity filled with the promise of the unknown, as Romanian eugenicists did right after the war.

In this regard, Romanian proponents of eugenics engaged in a politics of identity building that was closer to that of the Soviet Union than to that of Western countries. During the interwar period Soviet eugenicists attempted to construct the new Homo Sovieticus according to the laws of hereditary determinism and evolution much as Romanians attempted to construct an entirely new model for a typical, healthy Romanian. The Romanian and Soviet versions of eugenics differed radically, however, at the level of scientific theory and in their politics.[22]

The other significant difference between the development of eugenics in Romania and in the West was Romania's lack of industrialization. While eugenicists in England, the United States, and Germany constructed their reform discourses around a rhetoric of crisis regarding the terrible costs of industrialization, Romanian eugenicists focused on the problems of a rural, agricultural economy. Romanians believed they could learn from negative experiences elsewhere and thus avoid the great social costs of industrialization in their country, from alcoholism to syphilis and malnutrition. Their solutions to the perceived crisis of industrialization were closely tied not only to the biological determinism of eugenics but also to the specific features of the Romanian context.

In 1918, over 77 percent of Romania's total population lived in the countryside. The country had a staggering illiteracy rate; frontiers that encompassed 40 percent more territory than before 1914; and a fragmented, irregular administrative infrastructure. Romania's population also comprised great ethnic and cultural diversity. In the interwar period Romania confronted problems very different from those of France or Germany at the turn of the century, when the latter countries became interested in eugenics. As a result, the Romanian case involved more than a modification or adaptation of Western eugenic ideas for an Eastern European context. Romanian eugenicists recast these theories and strategies for social mobilization to serve different ends than those pursued by their Western counterparts. Studying Romania provides the basis for a more nuanced understanding of the appeal of eugenics in different cultural and developmental contexts.

Another prevailing claim among historians of eugenics in Western Europe has been that eugenic scientists and reformers were "fundamentally conservative in nature." William Schneider, a historian of French eugenics, defines "conservative," through Garland Allen's words, as a desire to "return to the good old days."[23] Schneider and other proponents of this view have failed, however, to look beyond the face value of the eugenicists' rhetoric of normalcy. While this rhetoric appears to reflect a conservative outlook, the ideas these eugenicists espoused—particularly their call for mobilizing the biological capital of the nation—represented a radical departure from any preexisting views of individual identity in society, especially regarding the powers and responsibilities of the state.

My analysis focuses on the eugenicists' fundamentally modernizing view of the state, especially as it emerges from Iuliu Moldovan's *Biopolitica* (see chapter 3). The emphasis on expanding the prerogatives of the state was particularly strong and appears clearly in the language of reform in German and Romanian eugenics because of these countries' well-established traditions of state involvement in social welfare, public health, and other public activities proposed by eugenicists. In France, Britain, and the United States, alternative nongovernmental institutional support for such activities offered a substitute basis for experimenting with eugenics projects. Yet it was precisely because of these alternatives, as well as a more entrenched political culture of individualism, that eugenic attempts to propose legislative change and the expansion of state responsibilities in matters of public health, social welfare, and other endeavors had only limited success in these countries.[24]

Eugenics and the Historiographic Debates about Interwar Romania

My analysis also employs eugenics to reexamine the antagonism between traditionalist and modernist forces in interwar Romania. The historiography on interwar Eastern Europe has focused significantly on the polarized debates that developed in this region over trying to find the best path of development.[25] Romania offers possibly the clearest illustration of this trend.[26] Whether focusing on writers, economists, or politicians, scholars have sometimes reinforced this dichotomy even when attempting to critique it. Embedded in their analyses are specific assumptions regarding modernization and development, modernism and traditionalism.

The position of eugenicists does not fit well within the current models that analyze development and modernization in interwar Eastern Europe. For instance, sociologist Daniel Chirot has recently posited the opposition of "secular western" values and "anti-secular nativist" ones as an important axis for understanding development. Such a model identifies the West only with post-Enlightenment rationalism and the nativist anti-Western position as exclusively anti-secular. But the eugenics movement in Romania defies such categorization and shows the limited explanatory power of such models. How does one explain Gusti's support for eugenics along the ideological divisions identified by Chirot when Chirot claims that Gusti "concentrated on empirical studies and refused to cave in to the mystical irrationality of [the] time"?[27] Precisely because eugenics defies easy categorization as either traditionalist (i.e., anti-Western and anti-secular) or modernizing (i.e., rationalist and democratic), it seems to offer a means to overcome this dichotomy. In order to better situate my arguments, I will begin with a definition of these notions.

In defining "modernization" and "modernism" I prefer to distance myself from what is presumed, in many other analyses of this period, to be their implicit antithesis: backwardness and traditionalism. In some of the literature focusing on the political and economic history of the nineteenth century, modernization has been described as implicitly progressive.[28] I question this unproblematic association and want to focus only on the structural-institutional changes subsumed under the broad label of modernization in the last century in Eastern Europe: the growth of state institutions meant to subordinate local practices to a unitary system; the development of modern political parties; the secularization of political and social authority; industrialization; the growth of cities; and the development of occupations tied to the new state institutions.

I define "modernism" as the attempt to grapple with the challenges of the modern condition, the challenges brought about by the above-mentioned institutional developments.[29] This is not a term that eugenicists used to identify themselves; instead, they reserved this term for their critique of the literary avant-garde that placed the self and existential angst at the center of its concerns. This is not to say that eugenicists rejected the need to confront industrialization or the development of modern political parties. What distinguished their approach was their adamant rejection of liberalism as a response to these challenges, in part because of the liberal emphasis on equal individual opportunity. Eugenicists considered this liberal attitude to be out of touch with the challenges of modernization. In this context, I define "traditionalism" as the position of rejecting modernization and its challenges—as a longing for the past, a form of cultural nostalgia. Eugenicists do not fit well in this camp, because of their emphasis on *mobilizing* traditions rather than preserving them.

The irreconcilable gap between the modernizing Europeanists and the anti-

Western traditionalists is less clear than the participants in the debate over modernization claimed in the 1920s and 1930s. By pointing out the paradoxical blending of new and old, rationalist and subjective arguments, individualist and communitarian ideas in Romanian eugenics, I want to bring out the complex and often ambiguous nature of the dialogue on modernization in Romania between the two world wars. Modernism was not always progressive, nor was traditionalism always reactionary. Hence, I want to suggest rethinking the labels frequently applied to actors in the public sphere during the interwar years.

Finally, over the past few years the "Jewish question" has gained prominence in both the historiography of interwar Romania and in current efforts to reconstruct Romanian identity. Many historians of interwar Romania have distanced the Romanian intelligentsia from any ties to anti-Semitism and the extreme right by depicting the general intellectual discourse during the interwar period as modernist, cosmopolitan, and pluralist.[30] An opposite camp has focused on the presence of extremist strands of anti-Semitism and xenophobic nationalism among some of the educated elites.[31] These historians identify such currents as reactionary or traditionalist and tie their ideas and actions to the tragic fate of the Jews during World War II.

By drawing such unambiguous lines of demarcation, historians have obscured the extent to which a rhetoric of progress, modernization, and scientific objectivism can be antiliberal and imply the growth of the state's prerogatives at the expense of citizens' rights. A few comments are in order with regard to the relationship between the extreme right and eugenics between 1918 and 1940. There is certainly some affinity between some of Nichifor Crainic's ideas of the ethnocratic state and the type of biopolitical state Iuliu Moldovan imagined.[32] There are parallels between the exclusivist racism and anti-Semitism in the writings of A. C. Cuza and many of the writings authored by Iordache Făcăoaru and a few other extremist eugenicists—even Sabin Manuilă (though only in 1940). Yet the eugenics movement did not seek explicit ties with these intellectuals and their movements, nor were the ideas of eugenicists (with a few exceptions) explicitly and directly employed by Cuza, Crainic, Octavian Goga, or Corneliu Zelea-Codreanu in their own writings. Therefore, a direct and unequivocal link between the Romanian extreme right and the eugenics movement cannot be established. That is not to say that important indirect links did not exist between eugenics and the Romanian extreme right. It was particularly because eugenicists took care in presenting their ideas as rational and moderate, in the

language of science and objectivity, that they were successful in offering an attractive vision of controlled progress to the Romanian educated elite without
connecting this vision to the extreme right. At the same time, this eugenic critique of liberal democracy was not inextricably tied to an anti-Semitic ideology.

This phenomenon helps explain why many educated professionals in Romania were willing to accommodate growing right-wing extremist groups and state
power in the late 1930s without thinking of themselves as perpetrators of racism.
They did not succumb to forceful extremism but rather responded to what appeared to be a more secure and moderate solution in a period of ideological and
intellectual fluidity, in a polity without deep roots in liberalism or democratic
civic culture. The results of this process did, however, prove to be tragic during
the war for many Romanian Jews.

Theory and Methodology

My approach to eugenics in Romania has been shaped especially by my interest in discourse analysis and in gender and class as analytical categories. My
work has been influenced by the approach of scholars who have used post-
structuralist theory in their analyses—among them Judith Walkowitz and Paul
Rabinow.[33] I embrace the notion that historical artifacts are fluid texts, whose
value rests in their multiple readings by historical actors and researchers alike.
As such, I do not see my own analysis as a "privileged" vantage point but rather
as a *particular* one, situated in a specific theoretical and methodological context.
My analysis is thus an invitation to an intellectual dialogue with other historians of Eastern Europe, science, and gender, rather than an attempt to provide
a definitive interpretation of eugenics in interwar Romania.

This methodological approach has also driven the organization of the book.
Although I have followed the changes in eugenicists' views and in the effects of
their ideas and actions, my intention is not to provide a continuous straight
narrative of these processes. I consider that such a strategy would have limited
the readers' exposure to the parallel conflicting meanings present in the texts
and actions analyzed. My approach is thematic and stresses the complex nature
of the production of knowledge and of political and intellectual discourse. Like
other scholars, such as Rabinow and Walkowitz, I find the Foucauldian emphasis on the dynamic nature of the networks by which knowledge is produced,
embodied, read, and renegotiated a particularly fertile approach to understand-

ing historical processes.[34] In my analysis I underline the ways in which cultural norms are constantly negotiated and played out in various forms by both the producers and the consumers of knowledge as an intellectual artifact.

At the same time, I do not want to suggest that all historical actors have the same weight in constructing meaning and effecting change. On the contrary, my discussion of the relationship between the educated Romanian elite and the peasant population, for instance, problematizes the claim of eugenic reformers to objective rationalism and patriotic altruism. My analysis underlines the particular stakes and privileged position of eugenicists in trying to mobilize the "biological energies" of the peasant population, yet it does not exclude the voices of these peasants as active agents in the making and implementation of reform policies.

A similar vision of unequal power relations emerges from my analysis of debates over gender roles. As will become apparent, women were not simply objects of the debates over gender roles and political rights but were also active participants. At the same time, women's choices in engaging in this debate were much more limited than those of women in the United States or Western Europe, where women's associations had been an integral part of the public sphere since the mid-nineteenth century. In Romania, the marginal representation of women's issues in the political and intellectual discourse of the interwar period provides a radically different context for interpreting the motivations for and meaning of women's participation in eugenic organizations and projects.

In my attempt to offer different readings and meanings of eugenic ideas, I opt for three particular methods. First, I use the technique of literary critique elaborated by intellectual historians such as Dominique LaCapra to show how eugenic ideas were constructed in a particular language, with metaphors, comparisons, and even an analytical logic that were culturally specific, in spite of eugenicists' claims to a universal objective foundation.[35] In order to assess the impact of eugenic theories and reform ideas among producers of knowledge in interwar Romania, I follow the spread of these tropes among doctors, lawyers, journalists, educators, biologists, and social scientists. I start my search by examining texts that were prominent signposts in the intellectual and political debates over reform in interwar Romania. In rereading such "standard" works of the interwar period I discover arguments advocating liberal reform and progress in the language of biological determinism. For example, although hailed as one of the most adamant of the "Europeanizing" modernists, Eugen

Lovinescu also used "race" as an immovable category in his discussion of fostering progress:

> In order to evolve, a people needs malleability along with stability. In our people, we consider only the fixed element of our race and national life as a [valuable] patrimony.[36]

Eugenic theories introduced a particular paradigm and language for defining social problems. At the same time, the local political and general cultural context helped mold the meaning of this theory. Consequently, the solutions to social problems constructed within the eugenics discourse were limited both by the language of biological determinism and by the cultural context in which eugenicists operated. For instance, although concerned with the quality of reproduction and professing a Mendelian approach to eugenics (i.e., focusing overwhelmingly on the genetic rather than the environmental forces that shape biological characteristics), many Romanian eugenicists focused their efforts on puericulture, which emphasized the need to control environmental factors in order to improve the health of newborns. This interest in educating young mothers in matters of child care was not a "misreading" of Mendelian eugenics but rather a deliberate choice to shape genetic concerns to the local context. This conscious decision is evidenced by the language used in the projects for infant and maternal care, which emphasizes the significance of puericulture for the well-being of the nation's biological capital rather than of individual mothers and their offspring.

Following eugenic echoes in the language and arguments about reform and modernization in interwar Romania allows me to arrive at a comprehensive picture of the important role played by eugenicists during this period. My analysis follows these connections to show that eugenicists helped change the concepts of social organization and reform, of public health and education, of the role of science in generating social reform, of women's roles, and of the state's responsibility for social welfare. Furthermore, eugenicists generated a series of important legislative measures regarding public health, from the Moldovan Law in 1930 to the legalization of abortion on the basis of eugenic criteria. They also played a prominent role in reforming education at all levels.

Another important methodological tool in my work is gender analysis, as my discussion of recent historiography on eugenics indicates. In Romania's case, this analytical framework offers valuable new insights about the debates regarding reproductive control, women's social and political rights, and the gender dimensions of the separation between the public and private spheres during the twentieth century. My analysis seeks to show how discussions of gender roles in relation to issues of citizenship, marital choice, and education played into larger eugenic theories about individual versus collective rights and strategies for social reform through a "total" state.

Finally, I focus on the intersection of class, gender, and ethnic identities in Romanian eugenics. My approach is particularly indebted to the insights opened up by the work of Kathleen Canning on German labor history and by the work of Marion Kaplan, who has illustrated the ways in which class, gender, and ethnic difference blended in Jewish-German women's identity as members of the middle class.[37] In my discussion of the social hierarchy envisioned by eugenicists I show how arguments about hereditary differences became a vehicle for the newly emerged professional middle classes to assert more power in society and to claim legitimate control over the fate of the lower classes. I also discuss the ethnic dimensions of the eugenics discourse that sought to secure the authority of the ethnically Romanian professional middle stratum as the technocratic leadership of the future eugenic state. Eugenicists did not openly advocate a quota system to secure the predominance of ethnic Romanians in government, education, and the liberal professions. Nonetheless, their discussions of intermarriage and urban development frequently alluded to the prominence of middle-class Hungarians in such positions of authority as a social problem for the health of the nation at large.

Organization

This book is divided into two parts, the first discussing eugenics discourse and the second eugenic reforms. Chapter 1 discusses the backgrounds of the important actors in the eugenics movement, providing a historical context for understanding both how eugenicists recast social relations in a biologizing discourse and what ideological directions these ideas followed in the interwar period. Having introduced the main protagonists of the eugenics movement, my study continues by exploring their ideas. Chapter 2 focuses on the most influential intellectual currents and their impact on efforts to reconstruct the role of science in society. I contend that eugenicists played an important part in the spread of a scientific paradigm based on biological determinism among Romanian intellectuals. As a result of a gradual shift from a Weltanschauung dominated by religious values to one dominated by the laws of biology—heredity, evolution, and differentiation—eugenicists played a role in the secularization of Romanian society.

Chapter 3 discusses in detail the impact of eugenics discourse on the relationship between individuals and the state, showing how Romanians gave meaning to these ideas according to their particular political and cultural context. The analysis focuses most prominently on Iuliu Moldovan's *Biopolitica,* which became the most important text of the late 1920s and 1930s for proponents of eugenics and other reform-minded intellectuals. This chapter shows the multifaceted implications of applying biological determinism to concepts of political organization. As will become apparent, however, various thinkers took the same ideas and used them differently to reconfigure the body politic. Therefore, the political aspects of eugenics in Romania emerge as a shifting, often contradictory phenomenon rather than as a coherent and monolithic vision.

Chapter 4 concentrates on the impact of eugenic political ideas on social relations and hierarchy, especially regarding the middle classes and the peasantry. My analysis highlights the ways in which eugenicists reconstructed gender identities, politicizing them and obscuring the boundaries between the private and the public. Finally, I address the ways in which eugenicists drew the distinction between the "acceptable," healthy community and the "other" in order to control social relations. As in their discussions of other social categories, they used (presumably) hereditary identifiers to construct these communities. The discussion here emphasizes the different definitions of "self" and "other" used by eugenicists and right-wing extremist groups such as the Iron Guard. My analysis also brings out important divergences between Romanian eugenicists and their counterparts in Western Europe regarding social hierarchy.

The second part of the book examines the role eugenicists played in education and public health legislation. Chapter 5 focuses on educational reforms, the aspect of Romanian eugenics that resembles most closely the interest of the German movement in education in scope, depth, and overall impact, but not in some of its anti-Semitic excesses. Eugenicists' involvement in education policies ranged from general issues of pedagogy and selection of students to specific measures such as shifts in the core secondary curriculum. Eugenicists' concepts of gender differences also played an important role in shaping these reforms. In the final analysis, the attempt to modernize education—the cornerstone of the eugenic vision of progress in Romania—was torn between mobilizing the intellectual and physical energies of all ethnic Romanians by liberating them from ignorance and directing the unleashed energies toward eugenic aims.

This desire—to both mobilize and control human energies—pervaded eugenicists' public health reforms, which are the subject of chapter 6. Although eugenicists, in particular Moldovan, created comprehensive public health legislation in the interwar period, their contributions in this area were not without shortcomings. They attempted to expand the access of the general public to basic measures of public health, such as immunization and regular medical checkups, but with an eye to controlling the population doctors were to serve. Doctors became the guardians of the general public, not only in terms of freeing them from illness but also with regard to their freedom to choose a spouse or to reproduce. The choices of the "healthy" came to be regulated as closely as those of the "dysgenic" population. Thus, measures of public health sought not only to expand the responsibilities of the state toward its citizens but also to increase its regulatory powers as the guardian of the nation's health.

My conclusion is also something of an epilogue, for it suggests that there were important continuities from the interwar period into the communist years and that there is reason for concern regarding the appeal of biological determinism in postsocialist Romania. Indeed, scientists and social reformers continue to ask the same questions that eugenicists posed about the relationship between individuals and communities in the modern state, about heredity and progress. Today we remain uncertain about the extent to which the modern welfare state should regulate the lives and reproductive rights of its citizens. The association of "eugenics" with the Nazi policies of sterilization, euthanasia, and mass murder has served both to damn this term and to disassociate it from the progress-oriented measures of the post-1945 welfare state. A closer analysis of eugenic ideas and programs such as those in Romania shows, however, that we have not gone that far beyond these ideas. Many scientists and policy makers today ask questions similar to the ones eugenicists did; they have the same general concerns and even a similar approach vis-à-vis the issues of modernization, social organization, and progress through control of reproduction.

CHAPTER 1

FROM CULTURAL DESPAIR

TO NATIONAL REBIRTH

> We are in the unpleasant situation of having to admit that we are feed-
> ing ourselves too much with the illusion of our ancestral ethnic vigour
> and we don't want to recognize that the Romanian people are not
> prospering according with their natural qualities. . . . The Romanian
> people deserve a better fate, . . . to fulfill their historic role in Europe, as
> an avant-garde of civilization and Latinity.
>
> Project for Public Health and Welfare Law, 1930

B E F O R E 1918 there was no organized effort in Romania to introduce eugenics into academic study or policy making. However, scientists and doctors
were familiar with Charles Darwin's and Francis Galton's works. For instance,
by 1900 Darwin's theory of evolution had entered the high school curriculum.[1]
Some publications focusing specifically on the meaning of heredity had made
their way into the public discourse.[2] Yet these theories about evolution and
heredity did not play a central role in the formation of public health or social
welfare policies.[3] By contrast, between 1918 and 1947, a wealth of monographs,
scholarly journals, conferences, and newspaper articles documents a vigorous
debate about eugenics that went beyond theoretical discussion and extended to
political ideology and many programs for normative social change and public

health. This chapter focuses on the origins of this movement and traces its development in the broader Romanian context by examining the professional lives of some of the most prominent supporters of eugenics.

In Western Europe and the United States eugenics had been well known in the social and medical disciplines, especially biology, medicine, and anthropology, since before World War I. In the United States, Germany, and Great Britain eugenics had also enjoyed increasing institutional support and authority among the wider public from the turn of the century. In France, similar support began to develop after World War I. Historian William Schneider links the growth of French eugenics to the outspoken support of a few prominent doctors at the École de Medicine and to eugenicists' embracing of puericulture.[4]

In Romania, interest in eugenics developed initially out of the educational experiences of a few doctors who studied abroad and in connection with specific regional professional, political, and—more broadly speaking—nationalist interests, especially in the case of the Cluj-based eugenics movement. From the beginning, political ambitions and differences helped shape both the extent of institutional support from the state and the eugenicists' own choices about allies and funding opportunities.

Romanian Politics before 1918: Nationalism, Liberalism, and Institutional Modernization

The institutional and political background of the rise of eugenics parallels the lives of Romanians on the two sides of the Carpathians from the mid-nineteenth century through World War I. After 1866 the Romanian Principality to the southeast of the Carpathians (to become an independent kingdom in 1881) underwent a process of institutional and political modernization. During the same period Transylvania became part of the Hungarian share of the *Ausgleich* settlement in the Habsburg Empire.

Romanians in the Regat (the Romanian Kingdom) began to use the tools of constitutional rule and developed a party system dominated by two groups— the conservatives and the liberals. The struggle for power between these two parties, neither of which was very interested in politics for the masses, ruled political and public life in general. The important interests at stake were of an economic nature. Conservatives considered traditional agricultural production the most important wealth resource for a country like Romania, which had not yet experienced significant industrialization. Over time they became interested in modernizing some aspects of Romanian economic life, but with particular concerns about maintaining their own economic advantages. Meanwhile, liberals argued more aggressively on behalf of the modernization of agriculture and especially greater industrialization. Both parties wanted the state to offer special protection for their economic sectors, as well as structural support in the form of banks, a strong currency, and railroads. Actively protecting the welfare of the general population was a low priority for either party.

The development of public concern in Romania for health and social welfare issues differed greatly from that evidenced in England, France, and Germany, where the bourgeoisie and increasingly the working classes had begun to tie social identity to participating in philanthropic or mutual-aid endeavors. A similar culture of charity did not begin to develop in the Romanian Kingdom until the late nineteenth century.[5] Even then, volunteerism was limited in size and scope, as most efforts were locally and socially bound.

Social welfare and public health activities in Romania bore little more than apparent similarities to the German case as well. There, *Kulturkampf* policies had been largely a response to pressures from liberal, Catholic, and socialist reformers, who had themselves staked a claim to legitimately representing the public interests of the German population. The *Kaiserreich* took into account these alternative forms of social welfare and sought to eliminate this competition for public authority by outdoing these programs. No such pressures developed in Romania before 1918. Therefore, programs for social welfare and public health remained limited to the initiative of a handful of reform-minded liberal professionals in the service of the state, with little support or pressure from either within or outside of official channels.

The one populist issue that did get attention was the fate of Romanians outside of the Regat's borders: in Transylvania, Bukovina, southern Dobrudja, and Bessarabia. Carol I, Romania's first king (1881–1914), used this issue successfully to muster mass support for government policies on several occasions, such as the Balkan War of 1913. Less official forms of nationalism and irredentist agitation, such as the work of the Cultural League and the efforts of intellectuals such as Nicolae Iorga, kept the public interested in this issue and willing to mobilize for the sake of their brothers across the border.

The peasant rebellion of 1907 forced new questions of social welfare and health into public debate. The rebellion devastated any notion of social stability in the countryside, making the political elite aware of the power that rested in numbers. Furthermore, it provided an impetus for the politicians and thinkers already involved in discussing the peasant problem to provide solutions for what appeared to be a systemic problem. For some, change meant modernization of the agricultural economy (e.g., introducing new technologies); for others land redistribution and enfranchisement of peasants; while still other intellectuals simply wanted to keep this vital force intact, untouched by the forces of modernization, which seemed to corrupt rural life and culture.[6]

The enemies singled out by propeasant factions ranged from latifundia owners to the National Liberal Party (its tariff policies in particular), from Jewish estate managers (*arendaşi*) to Jewish village tavern owners. While all the different critiques shared a harrowing representation of the current living conditions and health of the rural population, it took the experience of World War I and especially the menacing Bolshevik Revolution across the border to persuade the Romanian regime to address these problems in a substantial way. The result was universal male suffrage and a comprehensive program for land reform between 1921 and 1923.[7]

Romanians in Transylvania faced a different situation. Here the foundations of a modern political system and economy were laid during the 1848–49 revolutionary year. In 1867, Hungarian liberals saw their opportunity to build institutions that would embody aspirations that had emerged two decades earlier, from a constitutional parliamentary political system to a rational, efficient administration and a modern economy.

Romanians in Transylvania had to pay a greater price than their Hungarian conationals for access to these new opportunities, for this ethnic group was not one of the "received" nations under Hungarian law. As a result, Romanians were treated as subjects who were in effect Hungarian by virtue of their place in the monarchy and could not receive government funds for schools and other public institutions that used the Romanian language. Nonetheless, Romanians did receive some benefits from the post-1867 reforms, including greater access to education, albeit in Hungarian or German; more participation in politics; and increased economic opportunities for professionals and entrepreneurs. At the same time, important restrictions remained, for Romanians were still second-class citizens. Thus, along with the promise of growing opportunities, educated Romanians began to experience a sense of frustration.

Their inability to avail themselves of the growing opportunities came to dominate the political experience of Romanians in the Hungarian parliament, where their grievances often seemed of no consequence to the dominant political parties. During this period, the leadership of the Romanian population in Transylvania gained much experience in parliamentary political practices and legislation. However, their particular angle on this experience was dominated by their marginalization by the Hungarian majority. Hence, the members of the Romanian National Party came to identify both the system of parliamentary politics and the political factions that dominated it—Hungarian liberals in particular—as tools of self-interest. They grew distrustful of the claims made by this system to serve the greater good of all citizens. This combination of growing understanding of parliamentary politics and frustration at the hands of governmental institutions was essential to the attitude that Romanians in Transylvania carried into the union with the Romanian Kingdom in 1918.

At the same time, Romanians were able to benefit—again with a growing sense of disappointment on the side—from the educational and economic opportunities offered by the *Ausgleich,* in particular from the programs for the modernization of Austria-Hungary. More Romanians than ever before were able to pursue a secondary education, some in the few private Romanian schools made possible by the new prosperity of Romanian entrepreneurs and professionals. During this period, the economic vitality of the Romanian population grew to the point at which a vigorous cultural life could develop under the auspices of a privately funded institution that became the heart of the Romanian nationalist movement: the "Asociația transilvană pentru literatura și cultura poporului român," or Astra.

Astra provided an infrastructure for both cultural and political networking among Romanians in Transylvania, since it stretched from the village grassroots to the national level. Eugenicists would recognize this valuable tool for promoting their ideas after 1918, turning it into the largest nongovernmental Romanian organization with a coherent eugenic program. Before 1918, however, Astra became a focal point for constructing Romanian identity and the meeting ground for various intellectuals and professionals who had a common perspective and background and shared a resentment of the Dualist Settlement based on their unfulfilled expectations and growing political frustrations. These common points became as much a part of these Romanians' national identity as the language they spoke or the patriotic hymns they sang.

Medical Education and Public Health Institutions before 1918

Before turning to the proponents of eugenics, a brief incursion into the development of medical education and public health institutions in Romania before 1918 is necessary. During the first half of the nineteenth century interest in the natural sciences was modest at best in educational institutions. A humble school that provided rudimentary training in basic surgery did open in Bucharest in 1841.[8] Nevertheless, one can speak of significant efforts only after 1859 and especially after the War of Independence (1877–78). In the second half of the nineteenth century a significant number of Romanians began to pursue an education abroad, not only in humanist studies but also increasingly in scientific fields, from medicine to chemistry. It was only during this period that scientists became prominent figures in the construction of knowledge. Romanian schools also began to encourage a shift in the curriculum to include various forms of science within a system that was still overwhelmingly shaped by the German classical education, focusing on humanist theoretical studies.[9] In 1869, under the leadership of Carol Davilla, the modest medical school in Bucharest became the first national School for Medicine. A similar school opened in Iaşi in 1879, although that city had already become an important center for medical practice and training through hospitals and other public health projects. The achievements of these schools were limited, however, by comparison with the flourishing medical and biological research and teaching in Germany, France, England, and even Austria-Hungary, Romania's western neighbor.[10] Still, a few brilliant individuals, doctors whose research became recognized internationally, rose from the ranks of these first generations. Among them was Victor Babeş, whose research on rabies vaccines brought him European notoriety.

Romanian doctors and biologists formed self-conscious autonomous professional groups rather late by comparison with their counterparts in Western Europe. The first professional medical organization was created in 1884. Its membership had grown to twelve hundred by the turn of the century, twenty of those members women.[11] This was a small number indeed, as the population of the Romanian Kingdom was at the time approximately six million.

Another important element related to the development of the medical profession was the early dependency of individual physicians on second incomes derived from state jobs teaching or working in state institutions of public health.

Thus, although they were interested in developing professional institutional autonomy, doctors were also interested in maintaining and increasing state funding for public health and education from a purely self-interested perspective.[12] Their dependency helps explain the increasingly statist positions of many doctors during the interwar period, especially in the face of economic instability starting in the late 1920s.

Before 1910 public health institutions received modest support from the state. The budget of the Ministry of Internal Affairs provided some funding for private organizations (hospitals, philanthropic societies, orphanages, and asylums) that focused directly on taking care of public health problems. The state played a minimal regulatory role in dealing with matters of public health. Between 1874 and 1910 it passed a series of legislative measures that initially left local administrators (regional prefects and mayors) in charge of administering basic public hygiene measures and notifying medical authorities about any public health problems, including epidemics.

The ineffective implementation of these regulations and resulting health problems prompted doctors to lobby for more forceful legislation, which was passed in 1910 as the Cantacuzino Law, named for its main promoter, Ioan Cantacuzino. This law created a state-funded institution, the External Health Service (*serviciul sanitar extern*), which was to be run entirely by a medical staff and would oversee the standards of professionalism in public health. This law was an important step in generating state-funded public health institutions and raising the professional visibility and social prominence of doctors to a much higher level.[13] It also represented an important precursory move in reshaping the control and responsibilities of the state vis-à-vis public health. Furthermore, Cantacuzino's view of social plagues and public health was already sympathetic to the biological-determinist ideas that flourished in the interwar period.[14]

In Transylvania during the same period medical education did not develop very much, as students interested in medicine attended schools in Budapest or Vienna. The few historical works that mention in passing the development of the medical profession in Transylvania after the *Ausgleich* emphasize the growing gap caused by opportunities for ethnic Hungarians and discrimination against ethnic Romanians.[15]

Iuliu Moldovan: His Education and Career in Public Health

After World War I Greater Romania rose from the ashes of two dead empires. At the peace talks Romania was awarded a settlement beyond the expectations of most of its inhabitants, enlarging its borders by 40 percent, with acquisitions from the defunct Russian Empire and Austria-Hungary—Transylvania, the Banat, Bukovina, and Bessarabia. Like other newly created European states, Romania was at the crossroads of fulfilled nationalist dreams and future challenges. Intellectuals and politicians searched for the means to integrate their country into Europe and create a modern state without losing the particularities of their traditional national culture, with its rural and Christian flavor.

Out of this background of opportunity and of the frustration experienced by Romanians following the *Ausgleich* arose the most important Romanian promoter of a new science-based nationalist discourse: Iuliu Moldovan, who founded and led the eugenics movement in Transylvania until 1948. Moldovan (1882–1966), son of the local Uniate priest, was born and spent his childhood in the village of Bogata, in the Mureş region of Transylvania. This upbringing helped shape his later focus on rural life and his appreciation for the important intellectual and moral role played by village priests. After graduating as valedictorian from the Medias gymnasium in 1900, Moldovan departed for the Vienna Medical School, then one of the most renowned medical institutions in Europe. Between 1900 and 1918, Moldovan spent most of his time in Western Europe studying, researching, and practicing medicine, focusing on preventive medicine and in particular on epidemiology.[16]

After graduating from Vienna, he worked for two years as an assistant at the Institute for Pathological Anatomy in Prague, where he obtained the title of Doctor in Education in 1906. He returned to Vienna and worked first as a medical officer at a military garrison and then as an assistant in the Central Bacteriology Laboratory in Vienna, under Dr. Robert Döerr. His affiliation with the army proved fateful, for it allowed him to experience hands-on the effectiveness of new preventive vaccines used on the Austro-Hungarian troops. His long-term stay in the army may have alsó had an impact on Moldovan's concept of order, hierarchy, and responsibility, for he spent twelve of his most important formative years (from twenty-four to thirty-six) as a medical officer in the Austro-Hungarian army.

Some of his work during this period included fighting cholera among troops in Dalmatia and Montenegro and doing research, first at the Institute for Tropical Disease in Hamburg and then at the Pasteur Institute in Paris. Moldovan's research took him to the zoological station in Naples and to a related institute in Rome. Yet his familiarity with hereditary determinism and eugenics came especially from his experiences in Vienna and Hamburg, where these ideas had already become fairly popular. In 1915 Moldovan obtained his Ph.D. in general pathology from the Vienna Medical School; he was the first Romanian to do so. During World War I he served on the Eastern front as a medical officer in the Austro-Hungarian army, administering the anticholera vaccine program for the army in Galicia. By 1918 Moldovan had proven himself to be a valuable specialist on epidemiology and preventive medicine.

At only thirty-six, after Austria-Hungary's defeat in the war, he became the General Secretary for Social Welfare under the Romanian Directing Council, the interim government in Transylvania.[17] Between 15 December, 1918, and 2 April, 1920, Moldovan had ministerial authority in the area of health and social welfare in Transylvania, now under Romanian rule. This early work laid the foundation for some of his later comprehensive programs. It was during this period that he had the opportunity to start from scratch and create a series of institutions and programs that reflected his already strong convictions about the importance of combining curative and preventive medicine and about the need to make basic preventive medical services and hygiene education accessible to the rural masses. In this position Moldovan had a free hand to pass a number of important decrees. Thus, for a brief period he was able to experience firsthand the kind of technocratic power that would become one of the centerpieces of his later writings.

In this capacity Moldovan created a new administrative infrastructure that divided Transylvania into seven hygiene inspectorates. In addition, he founded three hospitals—one in Abrud, one in Reghin, and one for women in Cluj; a tuberculosis sanitarium in Aiud; an Institute for Nursing in Cluj; several centers for children's assistance in Beiuş and Orlat; and a program for mobile medical laboratories (*ambulatorii*) for the rural areas—virtual traveling clinics for preventive medicine and basic medical aid.[18]

In 1919 he also helped found the medical school in Cluj and the Institute of Hygiene and Social Hygiene, continuing to act as its director until the occupation of Northern Transylvania by the Hungarian army in August 1940.[19] The latter institution became the most important site for the continuous support of eugenics in Romania. Several generations of doctors received training there in both eugenic theories and in the application of eugenics in laboratory and field research. The curriculum and specific projects for public health and hygiene developed at this institute grew out of the general focus on eugenics by its faculty and staff. Moldovan was the main force directing these activities, but other supporters of eugenics, such as Aurel Voina, Petre Râmneanțu, and Iordache Făcăoaru, played important roles at the institute as well.

Because the medical school in Cluj was started under Moldovan's leadership as General Secretary for Social Welfare, its organization reflected from the start his vision of combining research with praxis and preventive with curative medicine. In addition, questions of specialization, which were just emerging in the older Bucharest school, were a prominent concern from the beginning. Moldovan was adamant in making social hygiene not only a basic component of medical training but also a prominent and respectable specialization. Even after he lost his other official positions and remained only the director of the Institute of Hygiene, Moldovan continued this campaign with the school's subsequent deans. Thus, the imprint of his eugenic vision was inscribed from the beginning in the institutional setting of the medical school in Cluj and continuously reinforced until after the communist takeover.

Between 1918 and 1920 Moldovan came in direct contact with many of the health problems in Transylvania, some of them apparently of epidemic proportions. Until then, no comprehensive effort had been made to understand the general standards of health in Transylvania, let alone address some of the problems. The nineteen traveling medical clinics Moldovan founded in 1919 provided the perfect means for collecting significant data from various regions, processing this information at the Institute of Hygiene in Cluj, and then returning to the same locations with practical measures. This method of combining research with praxis was new in Transylvania and certainly unprecedented in scale for the whole region, including the older parts of the Regat. Moldovan applied his experiences in the army to understanding the causes of an apparently disastrous standard of public health and formulating solutions for this critical situation. This technique was not inherently eugenic by any means. However, the particular analysis of public health problems that emerged from the collected data, the resulting measures, and the long-term goals of these measures were linked closely to a broader eugenic vision.[20]

Moldovan's later focus on specific "social plagues" dated from this period.

He observed the spread of syphilis to epidemic proportions in the countryside, an unlikely place for a venereal disease that seemed particular to large cities and their promiscuity.[21] The mass draft and the participation of many peasants in the war helped explain this phenomenon, in Moldovan's eyes, for he had already observed this problem at the front. Prostitution became a related issue, for Moldovan and most other public health officials considered it to be one of the major causes of the spread of syphilis both in the army and subsequently among the civilian population. From statistics drawn up by the traveling medical clinics, several other important issues emerged as critical problems for the organization of public health in Romania. Alcoholism and tuberculosis seemed important because they affected not only the individual suffering directly but also his or her family.[22] Fertility, although high in most areas, barely kept pace with mortality, which was distressingly high among infants. Moldovan made it his life's work to understand the causes of this situation, which he believed a threat to Romania's future, and to correct it.

In his sixteen months at the helm of public health administration in Transylvania, Moldovan believed he had laid the foundations for a new form of health care, one that devoted equal attention to preventive and curative medicine and combined research with praxis, guided by a focus on the health of ethnic Romanians. In 1920 his position was incorporated into the Romanian Kingdom's older administrative framework, as the Directing Council was dissolved. In the following five years Moldovan tried to continue implementing his earlier programs and ideas as General Hygiene Inspector for Transylvania. From his published work and private correspondence from this period, it seems clear that—in spite of historians' silence on this issue—Moldovan found this change very frustrating: "A whole series of laws and regulations [were passed from Bucharest] after November 1920, without any preparation, any written proof of the laws, without sending a single expert from the center to guide us, although we had requested [them]."[23]

The growing friction with Bucharest was compounded by a scandal that erupted in 1922, in which Moldovan was accused of squandering state funds. The investigation that followed proved all allegations false but served nonetheless to further embitter Moldovan, who became convinced this had been a campaign of the liberal regime in Bucharest to taint his reputation.[24] Thus, in the aftermath of Transylvania's effective union with the Romanian Kingdom, Moldovan came to view Ion I. C. Brătianu's National Liberal Party as dishonest,

opportunistic, and disinterested in the general welfare of the nation and especially in the vital regional problems of Transylvania. This early disenchantment
with the union was typical of many other young professionals who had harbored great ambitions in 1918 but were quickly disappointed by the increasing
centralization after 1920.[25] Such experiences also served to reinforce strong regional loyalties at the expense of furthering links with doctors from the Regat
who were also interested in eugenic ideas.

Moldovan instead found a more trusting and genuinely interested ear in the
sphere of public health policy making among the more familiar leadership of
the National Party in Transylvania and subsequently of the National-Peasant
Party (NPP)—in particular its leader, Iuliu Maniu. Moldovan's sympathies for
the NPP did not become apparent until 1928, when he was named General Secretary of the Ministry of Health and Social Welfare under the Maniu government, though they undoubtedly existed prior to that date. Maniu, in particular,
was by then already familiar with Moldovan's eugenic ideas. As early as 1926 the
platform of the NPP had contained specific references to the need to implement comprehensive public health reforms, references expressed in a language
that came very close to the eugenicists' own manifestoes for public health:

> The Service for public health will have to be reorganized as an independent techni-
> cal service, which will encompass all problems related to maintaining the health and
> vigor of the present and *future generations*. . . . A rational education will have to
> guarantee the indispensable harmony between the physical, the intellectual and the
> moral, as an essential foundation for the validity of our nation.[26]

This alliance between eugenicists and the NPP was somewhat inconsistent
with their respective guiding principles, for the Peasantists aimed to represent
the rural constituency as individual voters within a democratic parliamentary
system, while eugenicists sought to protect collective interests in a corporate
setting. It is likely that both groups saw this as a somewhat pragmatic alliance.
Eugenicists needed a political ally that would respect their notion of technocratic control over social welfare and public health reform. The NPP did not
seem concerned with the authoritarian, antiparliamentary tinges of eugenicists' ideas. To Peasantists, Moldovan and his movement represented a pioneering effort in caring about the rural population not only as a workforce but
also as a vital resource for the Romanian nation. The focus of both of these
groups on the problems and positive potential of the rural population, as well

as their similar regional interests in Transylvania, helped bridge the gap caused by their important differences. Furthermore, the utopian ethos and moral values of the leadership of the eugenics movement echoed Maniu's own vision of social order and progress.

This alliance with a party that stood for tradition but in fact sought to reconstruct politics through its populist appeal and its focus on the rural population illustrates the fundamentally modernizing nature of the eugenics movement in Romania. In England, France, and Germany, most eugenicists identified themselves with either a socialist party, if their ideas were tied closely to notions of expanding social welfare programs, or a conservative party, if they believed in cutting down wasteful expenditures on public health and welfare. In Romania, however, eugenicists chose to ally themselves with a party created after 1918, which had no ties to either the conservative or the liberal parties in the Regat and in effect stood for "a third way" (not to be confused with the similar language used by fascist factions at that time).

Later, eugenicists seemed to part ways with the NPP, for in 1938 Moldovan and Iuliu Haţiegan—another well respected figure in the Romanian medical and academic world—became members of the Superior Council in Carol II's Front for National Renaissance, with which Maniu had a very antagonistic relationship.[27] This separation was probably linked to the inability of the NPP to carry out the platform with which it came to power in 1928. The short-lived Peasantist government was as inefficient in its administration of power as the previous liberal regime had been. This inadequate performance did not help Moldovan's already shaky trust in parliamentary politics. At the same time, his own corporatist ideas better fit the rhetoric of Carol's dictatorship.

Moldovan's acceptance of the position in the Superior Council was also likely connected to his trust in Dimitrie Gusti's integrity and support. The Superior Council had little actual authority in political life, but its members did benefit from some financial leeway in pursuing projects such as the new Social Service. As a prominent member of the council and head of the Social Service, Gusti intervened on several occasions to help Moldovan's efforts on behalf of eugenic reform through state subsidies for Astra's activities.[28] By that point Moldovan had given up his efforts at making a difference at the national level through comprehensive legislation, continuing his pursuit of eugenic education and programs for public health reform at the regional level, through the Institute of Hygiene in Cluj and through Astra.

Moldovan and Astra

It is unclear whether Moldovan had close ties with Astra before 1918. None of his biographies or even his one surviving short autobiography mentions anything on this subject. However, he became a vital voice in this organization during the interwar period, especially in the 1930s. In turn, Astra played a central role in translating the specific interest of active eugenics supporters into a broader concern for the health of ethnic Romanians and a nationalist discourse in the language of hereditary determinism.

In the early 1920s, after the effective union of Transylvania with the Regat had been accomplished, Astra found itself at a dead end. The aim of this organization had been to keep Romanian identity and culture alive in Transylvania under conditions of marginalization after the *Ausgleich*. Its most ambitious goal had been for Transylvania to become united with the "mother" country. Once this occurred, Astra's leaders found themselves without a clear view of their organization's role. They all believed Astra was as important as ever for Romanians in Transylvania, but they were at a loss about formulating some realistic aims and programs that would persuade both their members and the government in Bucharest about Astra's vital role in Romanian society and culture.

The problems of this organization were compounded by other factors. A host of other patriotic organizations from the Regat began to spread their wings into Transylvania after 1918, while other autochthonous organizations started mushrooming in the region as well. From Bucharest, Transylvania appeared as a new frontier—as a territory and population that awaited incorporation into the successful institutions that had grown up in the Romanian Kingdom, such as Nicolae Iorga's Cultural League, the most important cultural organization with irredentist aims before 1918. Thus, with so many competing organizations around, Astra found its membership dwindling and also its funds. In some villages by the mid-1920s there were as many as three different cultural organizations that lay claim to representing the link between the grassroots and the national level.[29] Furthermore, most of these organizations drew their funds and ability to function from their connections to various political factions and thus carried political overtones along with their cultural agenda.

Therefore, Astra's leaders became acutely aware of the need to confront this competition by reasserting their primacy in Transylvania by virtue of their proven leadership; their cross-party interests; and their focus on local and regional needs, while keeping wider national ideals at heart. Starting in 1925, a new element emerged in Astra's statutes alongside the older principles of enlightening the masses and keeping national identity alive: "promotion of the physical, moral and intellectual prosperity of the Romanian nation."[30] The Medical and Biopolitical Sections of Astra were also created at this time.

The architect of both of these changes was Iuliu Moldovan. A year later, at Astra's annual meeting in Zalău, Moldovan was able to push through another set of changes. The voting members of Astra approved the introduction of a new item among the goals set forth in its statutes: "[to] organize a working program based on the *biological-national* principle, ensuring that this program would emphasize the sociological orientations that go along with this principle regarding the development of the individual, the family, and the nation."[31] In addition to this change in Astra's aims, Moldovan and his colleague Iuliu Hațiegan helped pass resolutions that laid the foundations for two new organizations—a Feminine Section and a Subsection for Physical Education—under the guidance of the Medical Section of Astra. With the help of Astra's new statutes, these organizations gradually became some of the most important venues for articulating and implementing programs of eugenic orientation in Transylvania. Since these measures preceded any state-sponsored efforts, Astra's leaders continued to cling to their autonomy of action with regard to eugenics programs and drove a hard bargain in terms of cooperating with later governmental programs that sought to build upon Astra's proven expertise in such matters.[32]

The impact of this shift in the focus of Astra's activities for the eugenics movement was tremendous. Although the active membership of the Biopolitical Section numbered only seventy in 1936, the activities of this organization touched a much broader audience.[33] Astra conferences were always well attended by the local Romanian population, whether members of Astra or not. And the Biopolitical Section of Astra was extremely active in popularizing eugenic ideas through such conferences. Its most important program was a series of lectures organized in 1927 entitled "The Biology of the Romanian People." The speakers included Emil Racoviță, Dimitrie Gusti, Alexandru Tzigara-Samurcaș, Constantin Rădulescu-Motru, Simion Mehedinți, Ioan Bologa, and Alexandru Vaida-Voevod.[34] These were all renowned figures in the Romanian cultural and political public arenas, virtually household names among the educated middle classes; the lectures attracted great crowds, either because of the fame of the speakers or because of the topics discussed.[35] Each lecture addressed a different aspect of the nation's biology, connecting the speaker's discussion to the notions of hereditary determinism that eugenicists were forcefully promoting. That these important figures agreed to participate in such a program indicates not only some degree of familiarity with the eugenics movement in Romania but also a certain level of approval of eugenic ideas; if these figures were not wholehearted collaborators, they were at least passive supporters.[36]

Moldovan continued to make eugenics an important focus for Astra in the 1930s, especially after his election as president of this organization in 1932.[37] This event marked the recognition of Moldovan's efforts within Astra since 1918 by a broad group of Romanians from all social strata. (Astra's elections were democratic, every active member holding the right to vote.) And since these efforts had focused overwhelmingly on eugenic education and on programs for public hygiene and pre- and postnatal care along eugenic principles, Moldovan's election represented an endorsement of his ideas and his well-publicized eugenic goals. His election and his continued leadership of Astra until 1947 suggest a genuine interest in and approval of eugenics among the rank and file of this large institution.[38]

Astra also became one of the essential sources for funding a new periodical publication, *Buletin Eugenic și Biopolitic*, which was initiated by Moldovan in 1927. The organization also provided the initial market for this publication. During its twenty years of publication, *Buletin Eugenic și Biopolitic* became the most important source of information for those interested in eugenic ideas, organizations, legislation, and programs abroad and in Romanian polemics regarding public health, reproductive control, the role of doctors in the countryside, and biological dangers to the nation's health. Several other publications funded by Astra, especially the annual *Calendar* and the journal *Transilvania*, also published articles that popularized eugenic ideas and gave reports on the activities of Romanian eugenicists.

As mentioned earlier, Moldovan had held the position of General Secretary for Social Welfare under the Directing Council—a position akin to being Minister of Health—and had subsequently become General Hygiene Inspector for Transylvania between 1920 and 1925. Disenchanted with the politics of the bureaucracy of which he was a member, he turned toward Astra and his academic responsibilities at the medical school in Cluj and the Institute of Hygiene as more fruitful avenues for his ambitions. In 1928, however, when the NPP briefly came to power, Maniu brought Moldovan into his cabinet, presumably with the assurance of backing up Moldovan's plans for comprehensive public health reform.[39]

In his two years as General Secretary at the Ministry of Health, Moldovan was able to draw up a law project that would have radically changed not only active programs of public health but the whole concept of health care and the institutions relevant to it in accordance with eugenic principles. Although the law was passed in 1930, it was a watered-down version of Moldovan's project, some of its more radical eugenic parts having been eliminated during preliminary debates. Furthermore, following the 1931 cabinet change in which Moldovan lost his post, the Moldovan Law was not put into practice to the extent its author would have liked.[40] The Moldovan Law, however, stayed on the books with little change in its ideological foundations until 1948, after the communist takeover, and played an important role in the development of public health institutions and programs until that time.

Moldovan's collaboration with the government did not resume until 1939, when he became a member of the Superior Council of the Front for National Renaissance. In addition to this position, which guaranteed little authority and did not designate precisely any responsibilities under the new regime, Moldovan secured a more important gain for himself and Astra. Dimitrie Gusti, a renowned sociologist, had been named head of the Social Service, a new project underwritten by Carol II's regime that aimed at promoting greater social mobilization behind the Front by establishing new links between young urban professionals and intellectuals and the rural masses. The law that gave birth to this new program designated Astra as the institutional basis for implementing the Social Service in Transylvania, with great autonomy in its structure and administration of the program. Furthermore, Astra's president would hold the one permanent seat among the five members of an executive board responsible for making crucial decisions about the goals, general guidelines, and funding of the Social Service. Thus, Moldovan became again a powerful figure in creating and implementing a program for social change and mobilization. For the brief period during which this law was in force, until August 1940, the Social Service provided another important institutional framework for popularizing eugenic ideas and programs in Transylvania.

After the start of World War II and the cession of Northern Transylvania to Hungary, Moldovan moved his Institute of Hygiene to Sibiu, where it continued to operate on a much smaller scale until 1945, along with the University of Cluj at Sibiu and Astra. It seems that during this period Moldovan did not have any direct relations with the short-lived legionary regime in 1940.[41] He became, however, a member of the Commission of Social Hygiene under Marshal Ion Antonescu's authoritarian regime, an institution whose workings remain unclear because of the unavailability of the Ministry of Health's archives for the 1940–44 period.[42] At the same time, Moldovan was allowed to continue his work at the university and at the institute without any harassment by the authorities, who were enforcing much stricter control over similar organizations, such as Gusti's School for Social Monographs and the Romanian Social Institute. It appears that although it may not have necessarily solicited Moldovan's close collaboration, the wartime regime at least tacitly endorsed his work and preoccupation with eugenics. Nevertheless, the support of the wartime regime for such work never reached the level of endorsement enjoyed by the Munich faction of the German eugenics movement during World War II.[43] Although Moldovan's basic projects remained in operation between 1940 and 1944, they did so on a reduced scale and with little direct impact on policy making and implementation. It was with other eugenicists that the legionary movement and later the Antonescu regime worked directly.[44]

Moldovan was forcibly retired in 1947 and soon thereafter sent to prison at Sighet, where he spent six years as an ex-member of a "bourgeois" government cabinet.[45] After his release he returned to Cluj, where he continued to do some research and writing on epidemiology and public health matters with help from some of his younger collaborators. In 1967, shortly before his death, his doctorate was recognized by the communist regime—an important step toward his rehabilitation—and he was made a member of the Romanian Medical Academy.

Moldovan's Epigones: Petre Râmneanțu

Moldovan skillfully selected several generations of collaborators and students who followed in his footsteps and helped spread eugenic ideas and programs, whether at the University of Cluj and its medical school, within Astra, or in other public forums. His two closest collaborators were Petre Râmneanțu and Iordache Făcăoaru, both of whom had been his students. Râmneanțu began working as an assistant under Moldovan at the Institute of Hygiene in 1931 and continued to tie his work to Moldovan's eugenic concepts until his death in

1980. During his long career, Râmneanțu published an impressive number of studies, many of which constituted attempts to use statistical analysis and various bio- and anthropometric measurements to establish the hereditary background and potential of the population of Transylvania along ethnic divisions.[46] Like his colleague Iordache Făcăoaru, Râmneanțu was most influenced by German eugenics.

His studies of the hereditary identity of the Szekler population in southeastern Transylvania received continued recognition in the form of prestigious prizes into the post-1944 period.[47] His career, unlike that of his mentor, continued after 1948, albeit on a smaller scale and with great restrictions imposed on his ability to publish works on hereditary pathology. However, Râmneanțu carried Moldovan's torch until the end of his life through public lectures at the Union for Medical Sciences and a very generous biography he completed one year before his death.

Râmneanțu is a significant figure in the eugenics movement not only because of his numerous publications and academic recognition during the interwar period but also because he was able to make a successful transition into the communist regime and lead a full professional life, enjoying access to research and intellectual information until his natural death. Although harassed by the Romanian secret police (the Securitate), according to some of his close friends, Râmneanțu read, wrote, and published with no more imposed censorship than anyone else during this period.[48] Furthermore, his personal writings —following the debate over the connections among eugenics, racism, the Nazi regime, and the Final Solution—betray no sense of guilt. Indeed, Râmneanțu was at peace with his support for eugenics until the end of his life.[49]

Iordache Făcăoaru

Iordache Făcăoaru was another of Moldovan's close collaborators. He was an uncompromising supporter of coercive eugenic measures throughout his life, more interested in the most efficient solutions for ensuring the nation's future health (as *he* defined this health) than in adapting such solutions to the limitations imposed by the local traditions and mentality of the Romanian population. This intransigence may have been due to his personal background, but it was likely fostered by his years of study in Berlin, where he completed a Ph.D. in sociology with a dissertation entitled "Soziale Auslese." Făcăoaru also liked to practice what he preached and decided to marry a German woman of healthy Aryan stock. Indeed, he was very thorough in checking the genealogical purity and health of Tilly, his future wife, before he decided to marry her.[50]

Făcăoaru worked for Moldovan at the Institute of Hygiene throughout the 1930s and also did a lot of anthropometric field research, first with the monographic research teams led by Dimitrie Gusti. After World War I Gusti had initiated a school for sociological research that would be based first and foremost on fieldwork and that sought to incorporate all aspects of human relations—biological, social, cultural, and moral—into sociological analysis.[51] This new school became a training ground for many young intellectuals and sought to bring them back in touch with the realities of rural life and its riches through the fieldwork they had to undertake. It appears that Făcăoaru began to work with Gusti's teams as a specialist in biological, medical, and anthropometric issues sometime in the late 1920s.[52] He undoubtedly perfected some of his field-research methods during this period and even had a chance to explain at large his version of applying eugenic theories to sociological analysis while teaching Gusti's annual seminar at the university in Bucharest. Through Făcăoaru's teaching many of the ideas already well articulated among his colleagues at the Institute of Hygiene in Cluj became publicized in the academic circles in Bucharest. Gusti himself was clearly interested in eugenics and extracted from this theory his view of the biological register of social relations.[53]

Făcăoaru then went on to direct his own field research in Transylvania with funding from Astra. His studies were entirely shaped by his view of social relations as a function of hereditary traits. He focused on families and their genealogy rather than on individual statistics. In addition, the type of data he collected revolved much more around anthropometric characteristics than around environmental factors, such as literacy or occupation. Issues of education and economy interested him only insofar as they could be tied to hereditary characteristics.

Făcăoaru used these studies to sketch the profile of the normal authentic Romanian in order to separate this population from the impure "others" that lived in Romania. His emphasis on purity and "weeding out" inferior groups and individuals in order to strengthen the nation was close to the German emphasis on cleansing the Aryan race—a view popularized by Julius Friedrich Lehman starting in the late 1920s that became the official ideology of the Nazi regime after 1933.[54] Most other proponents of eugenics, Moldovan included, did not place as much emphasis on racial/ethnic purity as Făcăoaru did. This is evidenced especially by eugenicists' lack of support for sterilization measures and their reluctant approval of eugenically mandated abortions.

Făcăoaru had unabashed rightist political leanings; he became a member of the Iron Guard. This movement had grown up in Romania in the late 1920s from a student-based anti-Semitic extremist group to an organization that commanded significant support among a broader base, from intellectuals to peasants. Făcăoaru had wholeheartedly praised the efficiency of the German eugenics programs during the early 1930s and had made his anti-Roma and anti-Semitic feelings public.[55] In 1940, under the short-lived legionary regime, he held an important government position, controlling the implementation of public health measures. He became, in a sense, the ideologue of that regime in matters relating to health, biology, and race purity, using eugenics as the basis for his arguments and programs of action.

After January 1941, when the alliance between the Iron Guard and Antonescu ended with the ousting of the legionaries from government, Făcăoaru maintained his privileged position. He stayed on as an adviser, albeit in a less conspicuous position. His work behind the scenes continued, however, at full speed. During the war, with the financial help of Transnistria's Romanian military governor, Gheorghe Alexianu, Făcăoaru undertook an extended field-research trip to Transnistria in order to establish the "authenticity" of the Romanian population living there.[56] The study involved a large number of people from various parts of Transnistria and presumably authenticated the fact that this region rightfully belonged to Romania on the basis of objective, scientific, biological proof—which amounted to a series of anthropometric measurements.[57]

It is unclear whether Făcăoaru's experiences there involved contact with or research on the Jewish population that had been forcibly exiled to this region. However, since his contacts were at the level of the governor, it is safe to assume that he had knowledge of the fate of the Jewish population there. It is also likely that, in an indirect manner, he was able to influence the officials' view of the Jewish "problem" along the lines of his well-published anti-Semitic opinions, which advocated coercive negative measures, such as sterilization, against this population.

With his well-documented relationship to the Romanian right and to the occupation of Transnistria, it is hard to imagine how Făcăoaru was able to survive the transition to the communist regime and the early years of Stalinist oppression. Somehow, however, he managed to live through this period until the late seventies.[58] Like his friend Petre Râmneanțu, Făcăoaru was untouched by any feelings of guilt for his support of eugenics, which in his case had been much closer to Nazi race-purification programs.

What relationship can be established between Moldovan and his disciples, especially with regard to Făcăoaru's open embrace of the extreme right? Moldovan did attempt on several occasions to distance himself from these ideas, most prominently in an article published in 1943—the text of a speech he gave at the opening of the University of Cluj at Sibiu, in which he emphatically stated that "the concept of race cannot ever be a forceful idea and a goal [for Romanians]."[59] He continued by asserting that "biopolitics is not rightwing, nor leftwing, but rather contains such tendencies in their constant antagonism and within the parameters necessary for adapting them."[60] Yet Moldovan continued to open the pages of the Buletin to Făcăoaru, who was one of the main contributors to the journal during the war. One cannot speculate about any private criticisms he may have leveled against his former student, but such criticisms are irrelevant. Moldovan, in fact, did not live up to his self-avowed role as leader of the eugenics movement by establishing forcefully and reinforcing this role vis-à-vis his collaborators, especially when he had been so central to their training and their participation in research and writing about eugenics. By the same token, this failure does not suggest that he should be identified with the extremism of Făcăoaru in more than an indirect fashion.

Other Eugenicists from the Cluj School

Other important collaborators in the eugenics movement in Cluj included Iuliu Hațiegan, one-time Rector of the University of Cluj, who conducted his efforts on behalf of eugenics within the framework of Astra, as head of its Subsection for Physical and Moral Education; and Gheorghe Preda, another important figure in Astra and a leading specialist in mental health. Among Iuliu Moldovan's students-turned-collaborators at the Institute of Hygiene was Aurel Voina, a renowned specialist on venereal diseases and prostitution who joined the Iron Guard and became active in the legionary regime in 1940. Sabin Manuilă, who later became the foremost demographer in Romania, was another of Moldovan's disciples. Although his personal relations with Moldovan became strained in the late 1930s, Manuilă's work reflected respect for his mentor's ideas. His wife,

Veturia Manuilă, also pursued interests that incorporated eugenic ideas. She helped found and run the first School for Social Work in Romania and incorporated notions of eugenics as a mandatory part of the school's curriculum.[61]

Some of Moldovan's collaborators made the transition to the communist period very successfully, adjusting their interests in controlling the health of future generations according to the new egalitarian communist ideology. Mihai Kernbach, who specialized in the hereditary nature of mental pathologies and criminality, returned to Cluj after 1944 as the dean of the medical school. Iosif Stoichiţia also succeeded in maintaining his position of authority as Sanitary Inspector in Transylvania after 1944, overseeing the implementation of public health programs and the rebuilding of institutions after Romania reacquired Northern Transylvania. Salvator Cupcea, another of Moldovan's prominent collaborators, held the position of Minister of Health in 1946.

Eugenics in Bucharest

In a letter to Râmneanţu from 1978, Făcăoaru complained about the lack of support for their ideas in Bucharest and Iaşi. He was speaking in particular about the lukewarm efforts in these academic centers to encourage teaching and research in anthropology, but implicitly Făcăoaru was referring to eugenics as well.[62] In reality, Bucharest intellectual and professional circles included quite a few individuals interested in eugenics. Several institutions supported eugenics in Bucharest, but it was especially through the work of a few individuals who directed publications or were temporarily at the helm of important institutions that awareness of and interest in eugenics spread in the Regat.[63]

One of these prominent individuals was Dimitrie Gusti, whose school for monographic research proved a fertile ground for informing a significant number of college students about eugenics. This school has been considered in both Romanian and Western historiography as an important site for progressive sociological research.[64] The courses taught here included notions of hereditary determinism broadly speaking, eugenic theory, and anthropometry. Gusti also opened the pages of his renowned *Arhiva pentru Ştiinţa şi Reforma Socială* to proponents of eugenics and went so far as to help create an Anthropological and Eugenic Section at the Romanian Social Institute, headed by Sabin Manuilă.[65] The great intellectual reputation of Gusti's institute helped give legitimacy to the Eugenic Section and attract a wide public to its well-publicized series of lectures on eugenics. Later, the activities of this section merged with Astra's Biopolitical Section.

Gusti continued to show his support for eugenics in his capacity as Minister of Education from 1933 to 1934, for under his leadership a number of textbooks that included notions of eugenics were published and a series of eugenics-inspired reforms regarding pedagogical principles and methodologies was passed.[66] In the late 1930s, as head of the Social Service, Gusti also enlisted the help of Astra and its leadership, Moldovan in particular, in helping to build this organization in Transylvania. The ideas behind the Social Service and its principles for action were greatly inspired by Moldovan's own concept of eugenics.[67] In spite of never explicitly identifying himself as a supporter of eugenics, Gusti did, in fact, play an important role in making eugenics known and in translating this theory into social programs.

One of Gusti's closest collaborators in implementing the Social Service program was Gheorghe Banu (1889–1957), one of the central figures who supported eugenics in the academic and professional communities in Bucharest.[68] His most important venue for promoting eugenics was *Revista de Igienă Socială*, a monthly that focused on issues of public hygiene from a eugenic perspective. This journal was an important source not only for discussions of current health problems in Romania but also for information about similar issues abroad. It featured regularly a section that reviewed relevant books published in the United States, England, Germany, France, Italy, and even the Soviet Union and provided reports about any important congresses and new public health legislation abroad.

Although some of Moldovan's collaborators published articles in this journal (Aurel Voina in particular), Banu's publication seldom mentioned the achievements of Banu's colleagues in Cluj, just as Moldovan's *Buletin Eugenic şi Biopolitic* very rarely acknowledged the supporters of eugenics in Bucharest.[69] The reason for this apparent unwillingness to work together, given a similar interest in eugenics, can likely be explained by different regional interests, both political and—especially—professional.

Banu also published a large number of lengthy studies on eugenics, focusing in particular on pre- and postnatal care and puericulture, the new science of healthy and nurturing parenting.[70] His work focused especially on the impact of hereditary characteristics on a child's early development and on the relationship between mother and child. His professional sympathies appeared to be Francophile, as he published several of his works in Paris and often wrote in French. The sources of his inspiration also point toward affinities with the French eugenics movement, for he focused greatly on puericulture and often made reference to works by French-speaking proponents of eugenics, such as the Belgian René Sand.[71] However, his writings also made many references to German eugenicists, especially Alfred Grotjhan.[72]

Banu undertook his most important actions on behalf of eugenics during his leadership of the Ministry of Health in 1932–33, a position he held again in 1937–38 as a member of Octavian Goga's and A. C. Cuza's short-lived right-wing regime. It is unclear why he accepted this position, as he did not publish any works overtly endorsing the racist ideology or radical anti-Semitism of these two politicians. However, the choice itself suggests that Banu did not find this position problematic or at odds with his own ideas, although some of his writings do critique the racist ideas of some of the writers Cuza celebrated.[73] Banu was at best inconsistent in his own scientific claims and at worst a tacit supporter of the ideas advocated by Goga and Cuza. However, it is presently difficult to ascertain whether Banu openly supported these politicians' extremist views, as documents pertaining to his work in the Ministry of Health during this brief period do not offer any clear proof in support of this position.

Most of his work did, in fact, follow in Moldovan's footsteps by trying to place an important part of available state and nongovernmental resources in the service of preventive medicine programs.[74] Banu also decided to keep alive a section of the ministry started by Moldovan—the Bureau for Mental Hygiene and Eugenics—but integrated it into the exterior services of the ministry, placing it further away from the center of decision making.[75] He later continued some of this work of putting his eugenic ideas into practice as subdirector of Gusti's Social Service in 1939. He continued his activities teaching and acting as director of the Institute of Hygiene and Public Health in Bucharest during the war. He was forcibly retired in December 1948 and died of cancer in 1957.[76]

Other well-known and respected doctors in Bucharest were actively involved in eugenics as well. The most wholehearted proponent was Gheorghe Marinescu (1863–1938), a renowned endocrinologist. Marinescu began publishing articles on normal and pathological heredity before World War I, but his most important publications on eugenics date from the interwar period, when he slowly introduced ideas about the need to control hereditary characteristics to sophisticated audiences, including the members of the Romanian Academy.[77]

Marinescu's presentations were highly praised and firmly supported by the academicians and his colleagues at the medical school in Bucharest. In 1935 Marinescu decided to put his money where his mouth was and founded the Royal Society for Eugenics with the implicit endorsement of Carol II. This organization was to become a source for educating the intelligentsia and later the wider public about the principles of eugenics and the need to create a "eugenicist consciousness."[78] After a short period this society merged with the Anthropological and Eugenic Section of Gusti's Romanian Social Institute and continued its educational activities within this new institutional framework. Both finally merged with Astra's Biopolitical Section in 1937.[79]

One of Gusti's students, the sociologist Traian Herseni, became another prominent supporter of eugenics and a collaborator in Moldovan's publications. Along with Făcăoaru, he offers the best example of unabashedly going from full support of eugenics to membership in the Iron Guard and then successfully making the transition to the communist regime. While in the late 1930s and during the war Herseni published openly racist studies, he later became a prominent member of the Communist Party and wrote officially endorsed sociology textbooks in the new Marxist-Leninist normative discourse.[80]

Another prominent proponent of eugenics in the Regat was Francisc Rainer, the anthropologist and anatomist who practically built single-handedly from the ground up the specialization in anthropology at the medical school in Bucharest. He is well known for his vast collection of craniums and skeletons, which the renowned French anthropologist Eugène Pittard praised on several occasions. Rainer participated in Gusti's monographic endeavors in his capacity as an anthropologist and undertook his own anthropometric field research, the results of which he later published in a well-received book, *Enquetes anthropologiques dans trois villages roumains des Carpathes*.[81] His interests included not only academic research but also policy making. In 1929 he published an article entitled "The Amendment of a Man of Science," attacking Ion Mihalache's land reform of 1923 as eugenically unsound legislation.[82] Rainer's otherwise little-publicized support for eugenics comes through very clearly in this essay.[83]

Along with doctors and anthropologists, some lawyers also became interested in eugenic theories and their implications for reconceptualizing the very foundations of civil and penal law. One issue in particular, the legalization of abortion in accordance with eugenic principles, preoccupied many members of the legal profession. Ioan Vasilescu-Buciumi, a lawyer from Craiova, was one of those who ardently pursued the question of a eugenics-based penal code in his discussions of the basis for legalizing abortion and the possibility of reforming criminals.[84] His political sympathies came to light in 1940, when he assumed an official position in the legionary government.

■ ■ ■

A F T E R 1918, interest in eugenics spread from a small circle of doctors and social scientists to a much broader audience of professionals. A few institutions, such as the Institute of Social Hygiene in Cluj, Astra, and the Social Service, played an important role in this development. However, it was particularly through efforts of committed individuals in these institutions that eugenics became a priority. Just as important for the popularization of eugenics were periodical publications. Several specialized titles, such as *Buletin Eugenic şi Biopolitic* and *Revista de Igienă Socială,* and some periodicals with a broader readership, among them *Calendarul, Transilvania,* and *Arhiva pentru Ştiinţaşi Reforma Socială,* played an essential role in making the language of hereditary determinism and eugenic ideas familiar in the debates over current crises and reform. They helped generate a "eugenic culture" that encompassed different intellectual, ideological, and political orientations. The political directions embraced by proponents of eugenics varied from support for Maniu's National-Peasant Party to alliances with the Goga-Cuza anti-Semitic regime and full membership in the Iron Guard. These various links will be explored further in chapter 3. First, however, this discussion turns toward the intellectual foundation of Romanian eugenics.

CHAPTER 2

THE EUGENIC SOLUTION

A New Scientific Paradigm

> Man has not found in science a talisman, with which to penetrate all
> the mysteries of his being. He has only obtained a good tool to guide
> himself and especially adapt himself to the social world.
>
> Constantin Rădulescu-Motru, "Valoarea științei"

> The main agents for strengthening and guiding a national state on the
> path of progress are culture and science.
>
> Grigore Antipa, *Problemele evoluției poporului român*

I N 1906 the philosopher Constantin Rădulescu-Motru showed skepticism
about the role of science in fostering positive change. By 1919, the speleologist
Grigore Antipa was expressing great confidence in science as one of the main
forces behind progress in the modern age. After World War I science grew in
significance in Romania as a fundamental way of understanding the world and
mapping out a path toward modernization. This chapter focuses on the important role played by eugenicists in this process.

This discussion begins by investigating the intellectual sources of the new
gospel of eugenics, focusing on the ideas, individuals, and institutions abroad
that were most influential in shaping the vision of Romanian eugenicists. What

is interesting, first, is how these eugenicists arrived at the synthesis best illustrated by Iuliu Moldovan's *Biopolitica* and George Banu's *Tratat de medicină socială* and why they considered it important to build their arguments about social reform in the language of science, particularly biological determinism.[1]

The eugenicists' language and arguments helped create particular solutions that shifted the discourse about individual identity and social organization from the realm of religion and spirituality to that of science. Most eugenicists were not explicit about these far-reaching implications of their ideas, yet their writings reveal a paradigmatic shift in the construction of social relations and the body politic, displacing the emphasis on the afterlife and spiritual salvation with a focus on health and the human body at the center of the social contract. The acceptance of eugenics among the intelligentsia and in the academic community shows its success in speaking to already existing concerns. In fact, eugenicists were an influential group in bringing over and adapting contemporary Western language and scientific arguments, firmly implanting them in the Romanian academic community—an achievement that outlasted their movement.

A note of clarification is in order at this point. Various terms are used here to discuss attitudes linked to eugenics: "biological determinism," "hereditary determinism," "race hygiene," "social hygiene," and "biopolitics." These notions are related on a broad spectrum—of knowledge about and support for eugenics —but they also embody important differences, which should be delineated briefly. The broadest of these terms is "biological determinism," which is here defined as a general tendency in science, intellectual debates, and policy making to focus predominantly, if not exclusively, on the biological aspects of causation when analyzing sociopolitical phenomena. This attitude does not necessarily imply full support for eugenics, but rather a familiarity with and acceptance of biological theories regarding the relationship between physiological forces and social ones. During the interwar period, this was a mainstream position among many doctors, social scientists, and policy makers in Western Europe, and it became common in Eastern Europe in the 1930s.

"Hereditary determinism" connotes a more specific type of biological determinism, in that the focus here is specifically on *hereditary* factors that play a role in shaping social change. This notion is here defined as an attitude with strong eugenic tendencies, even when its proponents do not identify themselves as eugenicists, because this position presupposes embracing the idea that hereditary traits have an essential role in shaping behavior. Hereditary determinism, however, often focused on animals and plants as living beings, without making explicit associations with the development of human beings. This is one important distinction between hereditary determinism and eugenics.[2] In addition, some individuals using arguments of hereditary determinism in their writings did not necessarily think through some of the possible implications of this position in terms of policy making, especially in relation to the state's authority over reproductive control. Therefore, they cannot be considered full-fledged eugenicists, but only implicit supporters of eugenics.

"Race hygiene," the term employed by some German proponents of eugenics to define their theories, appeared in the writings of Romanian eugenicists as well, but only infrequently, and then usually framed as a reference to German eugenics. The term "social hygiene" appeared more frequently in Romanian writings. One of the most important periodical publications with a eugenic outlook was the *Revista de Igienă Socială*, edited by Banu. "Social hygiene" connotes a specific focus on social policy as a site for enacting reform, from education to public health and social welfare. When using this term, most writers identified their support for eugenics, if only implicitly, by the types of solutions and goals they singled out in their calls for specific policies.

By contrast, those using the term "biopolitics" when addressing specific reforms focused their attention on the state as a site of change and were interested overall in more comprehensive types of reform. Use of this term also implicitly indicated that proponents considered eugenics an undisputed normative scientific position.

The references in this text will be overwhelmingly to "hereditary determinism," to suggest the general acceptance of the theoretical premises of eugenics without an implicit commitment to it as a movement, or to "eugenics," to indicate the conscious embracing of this theory with all of its intellectual, ideological, and policy making implications.

The Scientific Paradigm

The turn toward a theory about social rights, responsibilities, and limitations imbued with the language of science had already taken place in Europe before 1914. Since the eighteenth century science had become an important way of constructing knowledge in Western-Central Europe and later in the United States. During the following one hundred years and especially after the Darwinian

Revolution in the natural sciences, scientific discourse spread beyond the laboratory and the drawing board to influence the conceptualization of social relations and politics.[3] Rationalist yet increasingly organicist empirical methods were used to explain social developments through parallels between the physical world and human society relating to the causes and effects of various phenomena. Biological metaphors and explanations came to dominate this discourse at the expense of other sciences, such as physics and mathematics.

The focus on hereditary determinism grew as part of this general trend in the sciences and as a particular response to social problems developing in the industrializing world. Eugenics developed in the late nineteenth and early twentieth centuries from the fanciful theory of Francis Galton about the heredity of genius into a full-fledged international movement for social change. Virtually every Western European country boasted its own eugenics society, from France, England, and Italy to Germany and Finland.[4]

Eugenicists in Western Europe argued that the nineteenth century had produced a series of chronic epidemics, from venereal diseases—most prominently syphilis—to mental illnesses such as hysteria. Crime seemed to spread like wildfire in the cities for reasons that seemed unaccountable, other than a general social malaise.[5] Eugenicists identified this situation as a crisis that was not simply moral but also biological and hereditary.

Across the Atlantic, the American Eugenics Society and other such organizations made the United States the avant-garde location for eugenic research and programs. For instance, the United States was the first country to take the issue of sterilization very seriously by legalizing it in some form or another in twenty-nine states by 1939, the first state being Indiana (1907). Eugenics held an appeal for some public health and social reformers in South America as well, most prominently in Argentina. It comes as little surprise, then, that after 1918, in their efforts to become "European" nations, social reformers in the newly created states in Eastern Europe became interested in this allegedly avant-garde scientific theory and social reform movement. Eugenics societies sprouted in Poland, Czechoslovakia, Hungary, Yugoslavia, and last but not least, Romania.

This delay in interest in eugenics is not difficult to understand. In Romania, science-based arguments (rationalist approaches to understanding physical and social phenomena based on empirical, inductive methods) about prescribing social and political change were late in coming. Throughout the eighteenth and nineteenth centuries historical and linguistic debates stood at the center of defining social and political rights among the Romanian population in the three main Romanian provinces, Wallachia, Moldavia, and Transylvania. In Wallachia and Moldavia, knowledge was constructed and controlled primarily from within the Orthodox Church, whose interests lay elsewhere than in science.[6]

With an overwhelmingly illiterate rural population and weak urban centers, the Romanian church did not experience challenges to this authority from the lay population as did religious authorities in England, France, and Germany during the same period. In the midst of two multiethnic and multidenominational empires, Romanian intellectuals competed for socioeconomic power and political rights in a nationalist-cultural vein. In these territories nationalism gained ground in the late eighteenth century as a cultural concept tied to literary, linguistic, and religious characteristics. Only in the second half of the nineteenth century did politicians and intellectuals begin to tie nationalism to legal issues and the notion of a nation-state.[7] Even when focusing on the rights of individuals, most Romanian intellectuals and politicians did so by talking about collective national rights and making reference to historical precedents from medieval treaties to archaeological remains and linguistic particularities. Notions of free will and individual unalienable rights, as well as concepts such as the "social contract," did not have high currency in this nationalist intellectual and political discourse.

This nationalism was representative to some extent of the entire Balkan region and even of some of the ethnic groups living in the Habsburg Empire. There, the Catholic Church's hold on institutions of education and knowledge also constricted the development of secular challenges to its authority. However, the larger educated urban population and a greater interest on the part of the Habsburg crown in the imperial schools did provide the groundwork for an earlier and greater focus on the natural sciences. It was no coincidence that an important number of scientists and doctors who became closely involved in creating and implementing public health reforms in Romania after World War I came from Transylvania, a province of the Habsburg Empire until 1918.

Secularization also came late to these lands, as the Orthodox Church retained tremendous social, administrative, and economic power in Wallachia and Moldavia until 1864, when it lost most of its lands and legal privileges. In Transylvania this church enjoyed great prestige among the entire Romanian population, since it had been the primary institution for constructing and preserving cultural identity and protecting the interests of this ethnic group since the eighteenth century.[8] Science remained marginal in this discourse, although, with the gradual secularization of Romanian society and intellectual life over the nineteenth century, the stage was set for greater openness to such arguments. Still, with the Orthodox Church's legacy of extensive intellectual and institutional authority, there was little interest in the natural and physical sciences among educators and students. Even when young men began to travel to Berlin, Saint Petersburg, Vienna, and Paris for studies in the early nineteenth century, they focused overwhelmingly on humanist disciplines. Therefore, an established scientific discourse and an institutional basis for the development of the natural sciences, including eugenics, did not develop in Romania during this period as it did especially in England and Germany.

It was not until the end of World War I that the language and arguments of science became familiar to a wide audience among the educated elites. Between the two world wars the use of biologically deterministic language and eugenic arguments spread not only in academic publications but also in newspapers and other popular publications. This development bears testimony to a shift in intellectual paradigms in interwar Romania and, in particular, to the increasing acceptance of a science-based mode of analyzing and organizing society and knowledge. This constitutes one of the important differences between eugenics in Romania and elsewhere in Western Europe and the United States. While eugenic ideas in those countries were shaped by interaction with competing scientific discourses, in Romania eugenicists were able to make universalistic claims without great opposition from an already well-established scientific community.[9]

Hereditarian Thought in Romania before 1918

As early as 1876 some Romanian doctors were concerned with the impact of heredity on health and disease. A short study published that year by Dr. Petrini (de Galatz) describes the disastrous effects of choosing a mate with no regard to hereditary potential and the illnesses that may result, from tuberculosis to syphilis.[10] This book is remarkable because, although published before Galton's work, it prefigures many of the concerns and ideas Romanian eugenicists would incorporate from the English thinker half a century later. Petrini's argument, however, is not based on rigorous research and scientifically constructed empirical evidence. Petrini had no clear sense of the differences between inborn and acquired characteristics. Rather, his conclusions are based on "common-sense" clinical observations. Similarly, his style of writing and argumentation rarely incorporates references to well-defined and respected sources or to specific works. His study thus falls under the category of "medical philosophy" rather than scientific research.

A few other important Romanian intellectuals of the time also explored the meaning of heredity for understanding progress and human relations. In his *Teoria ondulaţiunii universale* (1876–78), philosopher Vasile Conta (1845–82) developed a personal vision of evolution and heredity. Clearly knowledgeable about both Charles Darwin's and Herbert Spencer's writings on evolution, Conta created an original vision of the laws that govern change. His theory of waves implies that no one hereditary characteristic can remain prominent permanently in future generations. Geniuses represent not only the apogee of a particular "wave" of positive heredity but also the moment that signals inevitable regression into mediocrity to make room for another "wave."[11] Permanent hereditary improvement is impossible. This view directly contradicted Galton, who claimed that careful planning and control over reproduction could help prevent the degeneracy of genius and hence of any hereditary characteristic.

A series of other important late nineteenth-century Romanian thinkers, such as historian Alexandru D. Xenopol, mulled over the significance of heredity in trying to analyze human actions and long-term historical changes.[12] The fundamental question they posed was whether heredity actively produced permanent change or was simply the repository of tradition in a situation in which environmental and manmade factors played the central role in producing long-lasting progressive changes. The question of development posited in this form resembled, in effect, the argument that developed in the first decade of the twentieth century between Lamarckians and Mendelians.[13] It is unclear whether Xenopol was familiar with these debates, but his concerns were certainly similar to those of scientists engaged in discussing the cause and site of hereditary determinism. What outside influences did play a role in the development of interest in hereditary determinism in Romania, and with what effects?

Influences from Abroad

In England, since 1883 interest in eugenics had been sustained by several groups among the educated middle classes with political leanings ranging from liberal and socialist to staunchly conservative.[14] Eugenics grew from a small faction of the science community into a popular movement for social reform in response to the perceived negative effects of industrialization and urbanization, from the decreasing standard of living among the working classes to a decreasing birthrate among the beneficiaries of this process—the middle class. One particularity of the eugenics movement in England was support for Mendelian heredity at the expense of Lamarckian notions regarding the heredity of acquired characteristics. Although overwhelmingly Mendelian in their leanings, Romanian eugenicists did not look toward the British movement as a role model.

France had a somewhat more timid eugenics movement, which started only in the early twentieth century. French eugenicists have been described as "soft," for they were far more concerned with the absolute than with the qualitative decline of the birthrate. Thus, the French were interested in "regeneration" rather than "degeneracy" and focused more efforts on improving environmental factors that would help the process of regeneration.[15] Neo-Lamarckism was held in greater regard in this country than in England or Germany, and puericulture became the main focus of French eugenicists starting in the 1920s. Most of their policies and studies reflected concern for the negative effects of industrialization and a desire to regenerate especially the working classes. Most Romanians viewed neo-Lamarckism as an outdated theory, although they were influenced by French puericulture. Banu looked more favorably upon French eugenics and adopted some of its concerns with working-class women's health and welfare as eugenic priorities.[16]

Germany had a vigorous eugenics movement even before the creation of the Weimar Republic.[17] During the Wilhelminian period, German proponents of race hygiene—as they named their version of eugenics—were concerned with the illnesses of their industrializing society and focused on creating effective and efficient programs of public health and social welfare, much as their Romanian counterparts later did. There was no strong anti-Semitic component to German eugenics at that time. The term "race hygiene" did not consciously refer to a biological and social hierarchy of human communities based on racial characteristics. According to historian Sheila Weiss, Wilhelm Schallmayer, the first important leader of the eugenics movement in Germany, "remained staunchly opposed to the plural form of the word *Rasse* [in *Rassehygiene*] because it excluded what for him was the more important meaning of race, . . . the sum total of hereditary traits of an individual or a population."[18]

Another school of thought developed simultaneously among a group of German social thinkers who were interested in defining current problems within racially constructed parameters. Some of the most prominent representatives of this group, who had a great impact on eugenic concepts in Romania as well, were Alfred Ploetz, Ernst Rudin, and Friz Lenz. They sought to solve social problems by separating healthy populations from degenerate ones along racial rather than social, educational, or purely medical lines.[19] Furthermore, they shared a negative opinion of the effect of uncontrolled material progress during the nineteenth century and used the new science of eugenics as a tool for criticizing laissez-faire economics and liberal politics.[20] Eugenics became an avenue for many discontented intellectuals and professionals to attack liberal democracy through science. Several of the most important figures in Romanian eugenics, such as Moldovan and Făcăoaru, came in direct contact with these writers during their studies in Germany, some at the turn of the century and others after World War I. Their own ideas would subsequently be influenced more by the German than by any other model, especially with regard to applied eugenics.

The United States also served as a prominent example for the young Romanian eugenicists.[21] By 1918, the United States had gained the reputation of having the most forceful eugenics movement and legislation. The American Eugenics Society had the image of a solid, scientifically grounded organization. It enlisted the financial support of important benefactors such as Andrew Carnegie. Charles Davenport had founded his eugenics laboratory on Long Island. This research center provided statistics upon statistics about the hereditary aspects of public health issues and made recommendations about the reforms needed to correct the problems it identified and helped construct.

Most significantly for eugenicists in other countries, American eugenics had successfully made the transition from a scientific, academic movement that merely observed and advised to an authoritative voice in making policy, such as anti-immigration legislation.[22] Also, eugenicists in America had been successful in convincing twenty-nine state legislatures to legalize some form of sterilization. While these were accomplishments to which eugenicists in other countries turned as a powerful example, the success of eugenics in the United States had to do with the country's unique history, demographics, and civic culture. European eugenicists were closer to each other than to their American colleagues, with regard to both academic-professional ties and the general socio-economic and cultural context in which they operated.

Nonetheless, after 1918 Romanian eugenicists made a continuous effort to follow the developments in eugenics across the Atlantic. They traveled to the United States to gain knowledge from their American counterparts and tried to emulate—as far as the Romanian context permitted—what they perceived to be the admirable civic-minded volunteerist spirit of the Americans.[23] In the Romanians' commentaries on their U.S. counterparts, there is a conspicuous absence of any discussion about the racist and xenophobic aspects of some strands of American eugenics.

Though arising out of contact with these well-established eugenics movements, the Romanian one was not simply an imitative outgrowth of the general European trend during the interwar period in search of a third way between liberalism and socialism.[24] While this may have been the case in Germany and France, in Romania the intellectual context in which eugenics developed was very different. In particular, by 1918 a scientific discourse about social organization and evolution had not yet become a widely accepted paradigm among the educated Romanian public, let alone among the newly emerged mass constituency of peasant and urban lower-class voters. Natural sciences such as biology were not part of the regular curriculum taught in secondary schools. Instead, education still bore the imprint of nineteenth-century humanist pedagogy, focusing on culture, history, and the abstract sciences, particularly mathematics.[25]

Most importantly, Romanian society had become secularized only to a limited extent, among some of the educated strata. The lifestyle of the urban upper classes had become similar to that of the middle classes elsewhere in Europe and was marked by increased secularization. "Making it" into the social upper strata in Romania was signaled by the same types of material possessions that marked success in the West, from large homes adorned with all the available comforts to an education in Paris. The vast majority of the Romanian population lived, however, either in rural or in semiurban communities, at the center of which the church towered more prominently than the school or town hall.[26]

With the changes brought about at the end of World War I, the lines of communication between the upper strata and the masses underwent a process of reevaluation. Both religious beliefs and secular values came under scrutiny. Many among the intelligentsia questioned the Western secular values that seemed increasingly to be taking over urban public spaces. Others were appalled by the backwardness of the peasants who had gained the vote in 1918 but who had no political education and no clear notion of their rights and obligations as citizens in the modern state.[27] The loyalties of these newly enfranchised peasants were still much closer to the village and its local authority—most often the priest—than to any public figure.

In this emerging debate over secularization, few intellectual currents in Romania went so far as eugenics did in boldly claiming that society, state, and human relations in general should have the scientific laws of life as their basis rather than the divine laws inscribed in the Bible.[28] To be sure, Romanian eugenicists did not identify themselves as atheists or agnostics. In fact, many openly acknowledged their religious affiliations. However, their ideas radically challenged the deeply established Weltanschauung based on religion and the authority of the church.

The Romanian Mendelian Synthesis

Before World War I, most scientists and doctors in Romania did not consider heredity an active force in producing long-term social change.[29] In contrast to those in Germany, England, or France, most policy makers and scientists in Romania did not express a sense of imminent crisis about the future of the country on the basis of its diminishing human capital. There were, however, some voices that expressed similar fears, especially with regard to the "infiltration" of Jews in Romanian society. After the Congress of Berlin (1878) these fears were fueled even more by the Great Powers' lobbying that Jews be granted citizenship.

A. C. Cuza, whose own views of hereditary determinism were indebted to those of Alexandre de Gobineau, was particularly vitriolic in his accusations that Jews were a plague for the Romanian nation. Cuza became the most adamant Romanian proponent of aggressive anti-Semitism, based on the notion that Jews were a separate, extra-European, and inferior race.[30] Cuza's racist views about Jews did not change much over time, and they provided the ideological foundation for his League of National Christian Defense and later the National Christian Party.[31] Cuza's views about the need for national purification through the exclusion of Jews bore some similarity to those of some of the more aggressive eugenicists, such as Iordache Făcăoaru. Yet even such eugenicists shied away from embracing the arguments and sources Cuza used in supporting his position, deemed maniacal even by some of his contemporaries.[32] Făcăoaru and other supporters of the far right still tried to preserve some appearance of having a scientific foundation for their ideological positions. Other writers, among them the well-respected historian Xenopol, also embraced an anti-Semitic rhetoric of crisis.[33]

However, even at the end of the calamitous World War I, most Romanian intellectuals celebrated or critiqued progress in the cultural and social realm with little concern for the biological aspects of the matter. For instance, historian Vasile Pârvan's view of progress was inextricably linked to the ability of man to conquer his material constraints.[34] His theory of historical change was greatly indebted to the still strong positivist school of thought, which stressed the boundless possibilities for progress on account of human reason and the ability to overcome environmental limitations.

For some intellectuals and politicians, this faith in progress was enhanced by the outcome of World War I. Although Romanian troops had suffered great losses during the war and the country itself was ravaged by the occupation of over half of its territory, the rewards reaped by the Romanian Kingdom during the peace negotiations surpassed the dreams of even the most adamant nationalists. Yet this very outcome provided the ground for the debate that ensued after 1918 about how progress manifested itself and whether the changes undergone by Romania recently were indeed progressive. This issue has been the subject of a rich historiography that has focused on the debate between "modernists" and "traditionalists" in literary, philosophical, and related political circles.[35] However, to date there has been no investigation of the extent to which this debate developed within the scientific community and of how it shaped the development of a more widely accepted scientific paradigm during the twentieth century.

After 1918, while some intellectuals reaffirmed the positive qualities of material progress, other individuals began critiquing these developments. They identified degeneracy and a growing social crisis as the hidden effects of increasing material well-being and civilization. Some of these critics took their cue from the cultural analyses of writers such as Oswald Spengler and Friedrich Nietzsche, who also remained popular throughout the interwar period in Western Europe.[36] Others, however, offered a critique of material progress that focused on heredity as a vital yet long overlooked element in fostering change—

as both a positive force and a potentially destructive one. By taking the issue of progress from the cultural and economic realms into the realm of biology, these intellectuals reconstructed both this problem and its solution, introducing science as a new and essential component for understanding the problems of modern society.

What they proposed was "going back to the basics." In view of the increasingly sophisticated factors at play in modern society, they sought to reevaluate the meaning of all appendages of progress according to a presumably objective paradigm—the universal laws of biology.[37] This vision was inspired by the debate over progress and its impact on humanity's biological foundations that was taking place in the West during the same period. Coming to terms with the conflicts between Lamarckians and Mendelians helped Romanian eugenicists situate themselves within the larger international movement and present their position as a progressive attitude toward current social problems.

The Lamarckian-Mendelian debate had developed in the first decade of the twentieth century.[38] The Lamarckian school claimed that characteristics acquired during a lifetime could be passed down to the next generation. Nurturing environments produced progress for all who benefited from them. The responsibility of individuals making reproductive choices thus appeared small in comparison to the greater responsibility of securing a positive environment for all offspring. This view made Lamarckian theories an attractive platform for advocates of increased welfare measures for the poor. In turn, many historians have identified Lamarckian ideas with "soft" eugenics and left-wing politics.[39] However, some aggressive and conservative eugenics movements, especially in Latin America, also found Lamarckian ideas appealing.[40]

In the early decades of the twentieth century, Mendelians became a more forceful faction in the debate over heredity versus environment. With the publication in 1906 of Gregor Mendel's discoveries, research into the causes and effects of heredity had taken a radical turn, for the Austrian monk's experiments suggested that heredity was independent of environment and, furthermore, played an active role in long-term genetic changes.[41]

By 1918 Lamarck's ideas had fallen into disfavor among many eugenicists, especially in Germany and England, partly because of their perceived lack of scientific support and partly because Lamarckians were perceived as left-wing reformers who wanted to increase the responsibilities of the state toward the urban "degenerate" poor.[42] Still, Lamarckism did not lose its appeal in France and even retained some followers in England throughout the interwar period.[43]

The conflict between Lamarckians and Mendelians went beyond the scientific credibility of their arguments. Several historians of eugenics have shown how this controversy became a vehicle for debating the different approaches to public health in industrializing nations.[44] For instance, according to Loren Graham, in Germany Lamarckism became the theory favored by the "soft" Social Democrats, while Mendelism was favored by professionals and academics with a more right-wing political outlook.[45] In the 1930s Mendelian heredity came to dominate German eugenics. In the United States, research by Thomas Morgan seemed to point toward the greater scientific soundness of this view as well.[46] The impact of this focus on heredity rather than environment as a propellant of change (i.e., progress) was far-reaching. It shifted the emphasis of programs for improving the "human stock" away from wide social issues, such as adequate nutrition, housing, and education for the economically disadvantaged, toward individuals and their genes. Thus, many proponents of eugenics came to identify progress with controlling reproduction and, implicitly, marital choices, access to birth control, and the very ability to reproduce.

Most Romanian eugenicists embraced a Mendelian view in the Lamarckian-Mendelian controversy, while at the same time stressing the importance of environmental factors in their eugenic programs.[47] This position was influenced to a great extent by the exposure Romanian doctors had while studying abroad, predominantly in schools with a Mendelian outlook, especially in Germany and Austria. In particular, it seems that the Munich school, with its stricter Mendelian outlook and emphasis on race hygiene, rather than the Berlin school, which focused on welfare issues, provided the paradigm that eugenicists in Transylvania tended to follow.[48]

Romanian eugenicists made a conscious choice in embracing Mendelism and felt the need to defend this position vis-à-vis neo-Lamarckism on many occasions. The Buletin Eugenic și Biopolitic published in its first few issues a series of articles that attempted to lay out the scientific foundation for the relationship between hereditary-determinist theories—both Mendelian and Lamarckian—and eugenics. The author, Val Pușcariu, first presented the debates between Etienne Geoffroy Saint-Hilaire and Lamarck in the nineteenth century without critiquing Lamarck's theories.[49] He went on, however, to identify the Mendelian position as more accurate by describing the processes by which biological, psy-chological, and intellectual characteristics were passed from one generation to the next.[50] A few years later, Marinescu made an even clearer statement before the Romanian Academy in rejecting Lamarckian notions regarding the hered-ity of acquired characteristics.[51]

Perhaps the most detailed discussion of these theories of hereditary deter-minism can be found in a course on eugenics published by Iordache Făcăoaru in 1935. Though acknowledging that environment had an impact on individual development over time, Făcăoaru asserted that hereditary characteristics would suffer alteration only if the "germinal plasma" (i.e., the genetic baggage) of two separate populations were mixed:

> The hereditary heritage does not change from one generation to the next and from one environment to the next without determining causes. The same laws, same ter-ritory, and no matter how many other *external conditions* would make up the unitary environment of several distinct ethnic groups' social life, over centuries or millennia these groups would remain different from each other. For how long? . . . As long as the network of circulation of the germinal plasma will not be linked to the network of the neighboring group. As long as "blood" will not be mixed through marriage.[52]

In defending their Mendelian position, Romanian eugenicists made recur-rent references to the latest scholarship of prominent figures in the German race hygiene movement, from Alfred Ploetz to Otman von Verschuer, Erwin Baur, Eugen Fischer, and Fritz Lenz.[53] The Romanians' close attention to these German authors shows their interest in following in the footsteps of this school of eugenics.

Another important source of the development of Romanian eugenics was the American eugenics movement. Romanians' interest in eugenics grew to some extent out of reading Charles Davenport's writings and the publications of the American Eugenics Society, which had been available in Vienna and Berlin for those pursuing an education in either place. However, just as important for evaluating the actions of American eugenicists was the opportunity to travel to the United States. Before 1918, the ties between the scientific community in the New World and that in Romania had been practically nonexistent. One organ-ization, however, helped change this picture radically: the Rockefeller Founda-tion. In an attempt to spread the wings of its commitment to "the advancement of knowledge," the foundation sent several representatives to Europe after

World War I to evaluate the state of public health and make recommendations for the foundation's further involvement in helping to modernize institutions that played a role in improving health care in various communities.[54]

During the interwar period, the Rockefeller Foundation greatly increased its involvement in Romanian public health. In fact, it became a cosponsor along with the Romanian government in developing a series of institutions that helped fundamentally to shape the direction of health care in Romania, from the Institute of Hygiene in Bucharest to the nursing schools in Bucharest and Cluj, and a series of laboratories and research stations, especially in Transylvania.[55] The scope and depth of the Rockefeller Foundation's involvement in Romania was shaped by its relationship with Iuliu Moldovan. Having identified him as the most progressive supporter of public health among Romanian doctors and politicians, the foundation kept a close personal relationship with him and the Institute of Hygiene in Cluj until 1947. For instance, the institute's subscriptions to foreign professional journals (among them several prominent eugenics periodicals, such as the American Eugenics Society's *Eugenics Review*) were almost entirely subventioned by the Rockefeller Foundation.[56]

More importantly, the foundation started a program of travel grants for promising Romanian scholars.[57] The selection process was left in the hands of the local officers. The representatives of the Rockefeller Foundation in Romania were responsible for making the final nominations, which the trustees in New York would almost invariably endorse. These nominations, however, were made in collaboration with several Romanian specialists, among whom Iuliu Moldovan was always present. After the first generation of fellows returned from their grant period, they became part of this process, but many of them were also Moldovan's protégés. Thus, Moldovan was able to send many of his future collaborators, on Rockefeller grants, to undertake research in the United States.

Aside from Moldovan, Iordache Făcăoaru, Sabin Manuilă, Petre Râmneanțu, Aurel Voina, and Mihail Zolog—all on Moldovan's recommendation—each spent an extended period of time examining the research and academic debates over public health at Johns Hopkins University and in other places, such as Charles Davenport's laboratory on Long Island. Their travel itineraries also included ample opportunity to see eugenic concepts of public health at work by observing the various programs set up by different government institutions for social welfare and by private medical organizations. Sabin Manuilă's correspondence from this period and Iuliu Moldovan's detailed U.S. travel journal both document the admiration these men had for the modern programs of public health in the United States.[58]

It seems rather inconsistent that eugenicists in Romania would have looked toward both German and American eugenicists as their role models, for the contexts of these two movements were so different. In particular, American eugenicists operated in a liberal parliamentary democratic framework that they did not criticize as bankrupt. Their German counterparts, on the other hand—especially in the Munich school—based their normative concept of eugenics on the critique of individualism and of the negative effects of the Weimar Republic's parliamentary democratic experiment. Romanian eugenicists' own position was much closer to the German than the American example, by virtue of their own intellectual affinities and past political experiences with liberalism.

However, they did not desire to incorporate Western eugenics in Romania in a wholesale fashion, for they realized that the socioeconomic context in their own country greatly differed from that of industrially advanced countries. Rather, what emerges from their writings is a selective appropriation of ideas. Moldovan, Voina, and others admired the modern and effective system of studying public health issues and implementing useful programs in the United States and especially in Germany. They tried to emulate this efficiency in their own programs while addressing problems specific to the Romanian context. At a more personal level, the American spirit of volunteerism greatly impressed Romanian eugenicists, who saw in the examples of various private organizations in the United States role models for the type of responsible grassroots efforts they tried to foster in Romania on behalf of eugenics. They viewed the philanthropic works of the Rockefellers and Carnegies as models to be emulated by their Romanian counterparts.

Romanian eugenicists also kept up with the latest developments in eugenics and related public health programs from France and the Soviet Union to Finland and Italy. Romanian eugenics publications regularly featured reviews of newly published works in all Western countries, with a predilection for German publications.[59] Also, they kept their readers informed about the latest conferences and congresses as well as any relevant legislation. This conscious monitoring of Western eugenics was not a mere academic endeavor. Rather, such information was brought to the attention of the Romanian public as worth debating and, possibly, adapting to the Romanian context. This was especially the case with foreign eugenic legislation, which was amply discussed in Romanian periodicals, with clear hints about the examples Romania should follow. The legislation and programs that received the closest attention in Romanian eugenics journals were the German ones. The journals even compared German legislation with that of other countries, such as Finland, to show the greater effectiveness of the German laws.[60] Romanians were very impressed with the Germans' consistent, systematic thinking and thorough application of eugenic principles in all aspects of social life.

Beyond the German and American examples, Romanians did not express as much enthusiasm about eugenic legislation and programs in other countries, even though they followed, for example, the Lambrosian tradition in Italy and the ongoing debates there over the heredity of criminal types.[61] Also, Romanian eugenicists showed great interest in Nicola Pende's theories, especially with regard to reforming education in accordance with natural (hereditary) aptitudes and limitations.[62] However, Italy was not discussed very prominently in Romanian eugenics publications.

France constituted something of a special case in this regard. Clearly, eugenicists in Romania followed the latest writings by French proponents of eugenics and often made use of their works.[63] Many Romanian scientists and doctors had undertaken their studies in France and were greatly indebted to the ideas prominent among French scientists and doctors.[64] This was especially the case with Romanians living in the Regat, which counted among its academic elites a strong faction of Francophiles. By contrast, the educated elite in Transylvania looked toward Vienna and Berlin for their sources of intellectual and scientific stimulation.[65] However, even among the Francophile Bucharest circles, few eugenicists embraced the pronatalist view of French eugenics without criticizing its disregard for quality in trying to redress the problems of its human capital.[66] Most Romanians favored the increase in birthrate among the healthy population, while hoping to limit reproduction among potentially dysgenic populations (e.g., criminals, alcoholics, prostitutes, and non-Romanians). They criticized France's "softness" on the question of controlling the quality of reproduction—one of the important aspects of the neo-Lamarckian outlook of French eugenics.

Some proponents of eugenics focused, however, on the similarities between the French case and some of Romania's problems. In particular, the sluggish birthrate in the Banat, one of Romania's newly acquired territories, with a standard of living that surpassed that of any other region, seemed to parallel the problems faced by postwar France.[67] Those preoccupied with the decline in the birthrate in the Banat used this case both as a cautionary tale and as an example of how the state needed to start thinking about programs to solve such problems. French eugenics remained, however, a marginal influence on the development of eugenics in Romania, surpassed by the much greater impact of German and American eugenics. In fact, the birthrate problem in the Banat became the most prominent example used to stress issues of both quantity and quality in discussions of eugenic programs in Romania. France stood as the archetype of what could happen in Romania if both of these aspects of reproduction were not addressed at the same time.

The arguments and language used to construct a critique of post-1918 conditions in Romania appropriated a similar Western discourse about the crisis in human development and the need for normative biological solutions. Romanian eugenicists used this case to warn their compatriots about the dangerous side effects of embracing Western institutions, lifestyles, and infatuation with material progress.[68] Eugenics had been used in the West to correct the great damage already done by the massive processes of industrialization and urbanization during the nineteenth century. In turn, Romanians claimed they could learn from their Western counterparts how to rethink these processes and reorganize priorities regarding development and modernization.[69] Eugenicists did not advocate abandoning such important goals, for by turning its back on these processes, Romania would be unfit to survive in the modern age of competition for vital space. However, by protecting their human capital in accordance with biological prerogatives, eugenicists claimed that Romanians stood a better chance in this competition in the long run.

Similar arguments about balancing development with a greater regard for the biological limitations dictated by heredity had already developed in Western Europe.[70] In the Romanian case, however, this critique came before a genuine period of industrial "take-off" had occurred in Romania. Modernization was hotly debated at the time, with some factions advocating speedy development of important industries and modern Western-style institutions.[71] Others feared that Romania could not compete with the West on these grounds and furthermore risked losing its "authentic" traditions in the process of modernization.[72]

At stake in the debate between these factions was the very definition of "Romanianness," of the country's destiny. There seemed to be little ground for compromise between modernists and their traditionalist opponents, because they disagreed about such basic notions as the Romanian identity and sense of purpose. In this apparently irreconcilable debate, eugenicists offered a new way of constructing identity that accounted for both the need to preserve "authentic" Romanian traditions and the need to pursue modernization—inextricably related conditions for the successful integration of Romania into the modern European context. Thus, without being necessarily innovative, Romanian eugenicists gave Western European ideas about biological heredity a different twist, incorporating them as an integral part of the discourse about constructing Romanian identity in the twentieth century.

The Laws of Hereditary Determinism

In their discussions of modernization and tradition, eugenicists called for a "return" to the natural, universal laws of life as the most objective basis for organizing political, economic, and social priorities in the modern world. These universal laws represented a synthesis of Darwin's, Galton's, and Mendel's theories about heredity and evolution. Moldovan summed up this synthesis as follows:

> Life's course is subject to laws that may be contested only at the risk of unsettling or destroying vital processes . . . : heredity, variation, differentiation and integration, dynamic equilibrium, progressive specialization—these are some of the most important norms for deciding life's course.[73]

By calling for a *return* to these laws, eugenicists misrepresented reality and their own goals. For at no point in Romania's past had the laws of heredity, variation, selection, and evolution played a conscious role in social and political life. In fact, this was a hierarchy of meaning that eugenicists themselves constructed, using the authority of science as the objective truth that would legitimize their sweeping claims.

According to eugenicists, these laws provided irrefutable guidelines for understanding all of life's processes and for reevaluating the significance of humankind's progress over the past few hundred years, when these laws of biology had been constantly disregarded.[74] The trinity of the French Revolution—liberty, equality, and fraternity—had been the guiding principle of human actions in Western Europe and the basis for constructing both social and political institutions since 1789. These ideals constructed individuals as autonomous beings with inalienable rights, as citizens, focusing on their legal rights and obligations in the community at the civic level. In the eyes of eugenicists, the body had not become a site over which public debates about rights, obligations, freedoms, and limitations occurred. Certainly, the scientific community had been asserting an increasingly prominent public voice during the nineteenth century, with the growing interest in Darwinism and other evolutionary theories. Yet this attention had not been translated into attempts to reconstruct the very basis of political and social life around the body.[75]

Recently, Michel Foucault and a number of other historians have questioned this view. In light of their work, social reform and policy making *had* begun to focus on the subtle ways in which the human body became a significant locus for affecting public behavior and mentalities throughout the period criticized by Romanian eugenicists.[76] The critique of these eugenicists operated, however, at a more obvious level of policy making: they complained about the liberals' lack of spending on public health standards, for instance. Furthermore, the type of discourse described by Foucault, Thomas Laqueur, and others developed precisely out of the increased rationalization of European culture since the Enlightenment.[77] The process they describe was not typical of the development of the public sphere and culture in Romania until the late nineteenth century.[78] The rationalist paradigm that developed during the Enlightenment in Western Europe did not lead to challenging traditional authority in Romanian lands and reinventing the basis of its legitimacy through reason. Furthermore, an educated, critical public developed in Romania only as a marginal stratum among the social elites, unable to generate the type of thorough, systematic critique that developed in Western Europe during the eighteenth century. Only by the mid-nineteenth century did such challenges begin to play a significant role in Romanian culture and politics. Thus, eugenicists' reconceptualization of social relations and politics around the body introduced a novel vision of human relations in Romanian intellectual and sociopolitical discourse.

Eugenicists' insistence on making universal biological laws the foundation of understanding and reevaluating human action in all of its aspects in fact shifted the focus from the individual as an agent of free will to the individual as the agent of an intergenerational link of hereditary characteristics. The site of the individual's significance in the greater community was the body. This was a revolutionary claim, for the primacy of the laws of life called into question the definitions of liberty, equality, and fraternity.[79] The individual's liberty came to be limited inevitably by the ties each individual had to previous and future generations.

The aim for equality was recast as antiprogressive, for it contradicted the very basis of evolution, which eugenicists claimed rested upon increasing differentiation of individuals' functions for the benefit of the greater unit.[80] Fraternity alone seemed to fit into the eugenicists' new hierarchy of meaning. Yet this was a fraternity based on biological laws; it incorporated the community of cultural tradition only insofar as tradition did not contradict the more important prerogatives imposed by the laws of heredity and selection. Eugenicists wanted to foster fraternity in creating a healthy community for the future rather than a sense of collective identity among free individuals in the present.[81]

The critique of the ideals of the French Revolution was a recurrent theme in illiberal circles in Romania after 1918. The Romanian historian Zigu Ornea has identified a similar common thread among intellectuals with direct links to the extreme right—Nichifor Crainic, Nae Ionescu, and Mihail Manoilescu, among others.[82] At the same time Ornea makes the broader claim that overall most intellectuals and politicians supported parliamentary democracy and the liberal ideas criticized by the extreme right.[83] In other words, illiberal critiques were not the norm but the exception. The position of the Romanian eugenicists challenges this confidence in the support for democracy in interwar Romania. While a few of these individuals did identify directly with the extreme right, many more eugenicists considered themselves moderates and did not join Cuza or Codreanu's movements, rather remaining supporters of the NPP. The spectrum of illiberalism was broader and less clearly identified with a marginal radical rightist position than Ornea suggests in his study.

According to Moldovan and his colleagues, the most important force among the laws of life was heredity.[84] This emphasis reflects a Mendelian outlook, for most Romanian eugenicists identified environmental material improvements as marginal forces in evolution. Although they did not deny that the environment had some impact on individual and collective development and even progress across several generations, Romanian eugenicists insisted that the role of the environment was to help or hinder hereditary characteristics and inborn potentialities somewhat, but never to modify these traits.[85] Through such an argument eugenicists could claim the imperative need to act upon certain environmental factors, such as public hygiene, at the same time that they insisted on controlling individual bodies—controlling their ability to reproduce and the development of their hereditary characteristics.

By focusing on heredity as the most important force in fostering human development, eugenicists were able to make a series of far-reaching claims. To begin with, they presented eugenics as the most solid basis for evaluating what had been "authentic" Romanian traditions. They shifted the criteria for analyzing these traditions from the cultural grounds used by most other contemporaries to biological grounds.[86] Eugenicists did not deny the importance of cultural artifacts and symbols as important markers of the hereditary patrimony of the Romanian people. However, they placed them in a secondary position vis-à-vis biological data that could demonstrate with greater scientific certainty specific features of Romanian identity.

By focusing on heredity rather than cultural traditions as the basis for defining "Romanianness," eugenicists were engaging in another issue hotly debated at the time, especially in Transylvania. For almost a century, Hungarians and Romanians there had battled over the question of "who arrived first" as the most powerful basis for claiming undisputed rights to rule over the region.[87] Historians were prominent actors in this debate, unearthing, manufacturing, and disputing one record after another from the early Middle Ages on. Their arguments sought to prove either that a Romanian ruler had established control over Transylvania first and then had his authority usurped by the Hungarians or that Hungarians had simply been more successful in securing rights over this region in a legitimate fashion—through armed struggle and a peace agreement. Linguists explored the Latin origins of the Romanian language in order to show the continuity of the Romanian population in Transylvania as its oldest inhabitants and the heirs to a great civilization, the Roman Empire.[88] Archaeologists pointed toward the artifacts left by Roman conquerors in the region as proof of the direct connection between the Romanian people and this great civilization.

During the nineteenth century Romanian nationalism had developed in keeping with these historic-linguistic arguments, which had been challenged at every turn by counterexamples put forth by Hungarian historians, linguists, and lawyers.[89] They pointed toward different yet equally valid (or shaky, depending on how one looked at the evidence) examples that the Hungarians had successfully defeated the Romanian small states (*voivodate*) in the early thirteenth century and had gone on to create their own great culture. They claimed that their rights over Transylvania were inscribed in many legal acts and treaties signed and recognized by the major powers in Europe.

The eugenicists' emphasis on the overwhelming significance of heredity in determining the identity of an individual or a nation attempted to circumvent this ongoing debate by suggesting that such issues should be discussed only within the parameters of a scientific, biologizing discourse. The basis of legitimate rule in Transylvania could only be decided dispassionately, they claimed, by looking at the objective reality of how heredity had operated in this region and whom it had favored rather than by using manufactured or easily manipulated historical, linguistic, and cultural arguments.[90]

Eugenicists described the differences between Hungarians and Romanians in biological hereditary terms even when discussing moral or intellectual characteristics. In fact, they went so far as to argue that some of the Hungarian-speaking population in Transylvania, the Szeklers, who had been identified as historically and culturally Hungarian, were in fact "authentic" Romanians on the basis of their biology.[91] With these arguments Romanian eugenicists hoped to prove once and for all to any Hungarian revisionists that Transylvania was inhabited overwhelmingly by Romanians, whose specific biological hereditary traits, as the country's greatest human capital and source of future vigor, dictated certain goals for this region and for the Romanian state. Thus, the emphasis on the law of heredity served as a basis for making aggressive nationalist claims that reached beyond science into the realm of territorial acquisition.

This intense preoccupation with the authenticity of the population in Transylvania and the historic rights over this region was a particularity of eugenicists around Moldovan's circle in Cluj. The underlying political-cultural concern was their struggle to carve out a legitimate claim for acquiring more power in regional affairs and a sense of identity that would support such claims for empowerment. Such pains were generally not so close to the heart of eugenicists in the Regat, where struggles for empowerment were anchored in a different network of institutions, social relations, and cultural codes.

The law of variation—the second fundamental principle of evolution emphasized by eugenicists—served as the objective proof that equality was not a natural (i.e., normal) mode of organizing relations among persons in society and the polity.[92] Rather, life showed that progress meant increased variation among individuals, not only in their various talents and aptitudes but also in their intelligence and general biological potential. No one was responsible for having been born with a certain hereditary wealth or burden, but this baggage was the basis on which each individual developed. To deny such differences would be an unnatural, futile attempt to ignore the very basis of the human condition. Instead, according to eugenicists, the modern protecting force of human progress, the state, needed to correct the egalitarian tendencies within its polity and to reorganize its institutions so that it might make efficient use of all its human resources—from each according to the needs of the nation, to each according to his or her eugenic potential.[93]

The principle of variation as both the outcome of and the condition for evolution became well accepted among the medical and scientific community. Marinescu, the prominent endocrinologist, helped familiarize his colleagues in the academic circles in Bucharest with this notion through a series of articles and presentations before the Romanian Academy on the subject of heredity and variation and their connection with eugenics.[94] His work and that of other prominent figures in the scientific community—such as Emil Racoviță, a speleologist of international reputation and president of the Romanian Academy—did not necessarily turn every Romanian doctor and biologist into a wholehearted supporter of eugenics.[95] However, such work did play an important role in introducing these theories about evolution and heredity into the accepted science curricula at the university level. Some of the more prominent examples, beyond Moldovan's and Banu's work in academia, are the work of Francisc Rainer in Bucharest and of Victor Papilian in Cluj. Both were interested in eugenics, although neither was a prominent collaborator in the publications led by proponents of eugenics. However, both Rainer and Papilian used notions of hereditary determinism in evolution to define the parameters of their own scientific discipline, anthropology.[96]

Intellectuals and scientists with a more liberal-positivist outlook about evolution criticized the validity of these concepts to some extent. Some critics were those who still embraced a neo-Lamarckian view, even though they did not identify themselves as such. They believed that one could best generate longterm change by operating within the environment—by addressing present material inadequacies, as these had a negative impact on each individual, and by working to improve each person's chances for development in a similarly nurturing, progressive environment.[97] Yet proponents of eugenics offered a strong argument on behalf of paying more attention to hereditary determinism, backed by the authority of prominent names in the world of science abroad, from Alfred Ploetz to Thomas Morgan and from Charles Davenport to Gregor Mendel. In the course of the interwar period they succeeded in gaining acceptance beyond the narrow professional circles for their vision of progress and evolution based on the irrefutable laws of heredity and variation as a legitimate paradigm for scientific philosophy and research.

Their impact is dramatically illustrated by the work of Petre Andrei, a prominent sociologist at Iaşi University. In his 1936 synthesis, *Sociologie generală*, Andrei offers a harsh critique of organicist theories of social organization, constructing in fact a veiled indictment of fascist ideologies and their racist, antiprogressive aspects. Andrei's own leanings were clearly more liberal, proparliamentary, and individualistic—closer to Durkheim and Weber than to Spengler. He feared the power of Romania's mysticist right wing, the possibility that they might sap the willpower of the youth and use them as puppets.[98] However, at the same time Andrei embraced eugenics as a scientific theory that offered valid critiques of present problems and indicated sound solutions that could correct such problems and prevent future ones: "The directing principles of eugenics are very daring today and go very far in demanding vigorous measures which, although harmful to some individuals, are both useful and necessary for the collective unit."[99]

He accepted both the Mendelian principles of heredity and the notions of variation and inequality as basic features of progress. Andrei was never an active supporter of Moldovan's eugenics school, but like other Romanian intellectuals and scientists, he incorporated eugenicists' theoretical scientific arguments about heredity and evolution into his own analysis of social relations.[100]

Andrei's attitude toward eugenics illustrates eloquently the attraction many other educated Romanians felt for this theory. For although eugenics offered a very powerful critique of the liberal democratic ideas that many Romanian modernizers saw as the foundation for future progress in the country, this theory also offered solutions to social problems in accordance with scientific arguments that many of the same modernizers found hard to refute or even outright appealing. In fact, like Andrei, many other Romanian intellectuals, from geographer Simion Mehedinţi to endocrinologist Gheorghe Marinescu, found in science a way out of the more mundane and unresolved debates over the extent to which the political and economic arenas should be democratized and liberalized, with all the attendant sociocultural implications. Thus, what may appear to the contemporary reader to be a paradoxical, inconsistent pairing of eugenics with liberal democratic ideas in Andrei's case was in the eyes of that thinker and other contemporaries an unproblematic progressive outlook.

Eugenics and Secularization

The science-based arguments and language used in the eugenic critiques of Romania's problems acted as an important force in accelerating the secularization of Romanian society beyond the academic community, particularly in Transylvania, where the movement was strongest. Before 1918 public culture had become secularized to some extent within a thin layer of Romanian society. The mentality of the middle classes, which helped set the tone for public culture and tastes, had become less closely related to the values and institutions of the Orthodox Church during the nineteenth century. In art and literature realist and later naturalist currents developed, reflecting similar movements in Western Europe.[101] To be sure, interest in religious spirituality had seen a revival around the turn of the century, similar to the attempts to reappropriate folk and religious motifs among some modernist circles in the rest of Europe.[102] Yet currents such as *sămănătorism* did not reflect the spirituality of peasant culture but rather reconstructed it in an already secularized cosmopolitan medium. In fact, the rural population did not play an active role in public culture beyond acting as a backdrop for an increasingly urbanized official culture. The image of the pious peasant was an abstraction, the object of much contemplation over the modern condition, but peasants did not have an active, autonomous voice in this discourse.

After 1918, with their sudden emergence as a massive public presence as a result of universal male enfranchisement, peasants forced a shift in the focus of public mentalities toward a more religiously based culture. Certain literary and political movements initiated in the Regat, such as Nichifor Crainic's Gândirism and the League of the Archangel Michael, viewed this element as the source of a new vitality for Romanian culture and the body politic and attempted to tap into this resource of potential supporters.[103] They viewed Orthodoxism as a vital part of the Romanian identity, placing the Orthodox Church at the center of their ideas for social reform.[104] Other factions, such as the Peasantists, sought to represent the economic and political interests of the peasantry as independent, rational, individual producers. Although they acknowledged the emotional ties of the rural population to their religious traditions, Peasantists did not address this as a potential source of conflict with the secular-rationalist aspects of their ideology.

Eugenicists, especially of the Cluj school, also focused their attention on the peasantry as the group most important to their activities. Unlike many of their contemporaries, they confronted from the very beginning the issue of the peasants' overwhelmingly religious mentality when trying to turn this massive population into a well-integrated functioning part of the national community and the modern Romanian state. Eugenicists did not reject the importance of the church in the local rural community as a source of both spiritual and administrative authority.[105] They realized that if reformers sought to bring about effective change in the values and behavior of peasants, they needed to turn the local priest into a potential ally or at least a friendly observer. In the eyes of the rural population, the authority of other important local figures, such as the mayor, the policeman (*jandarm*), and the schoolteacher, was more often than not subject to the local priest's sanction. Eugenicists understood this important issue and actively tried to rally the support of religious authorities for their programs, from the Patriarch to the parish priest.

At the same time, from early on in the discussions about the need to transform Romanian society according to the universal laws of life, eugenicists identified the church as a potential obstacle because of its disregard for issues pertaining to the physical well-being of its followers.[106] Indeed, the Orthodox Church did not boast of important voluntary associations fostered by priests or church authorities that attempted to address problems of social welfare through a "good Samaritan" philosophy. If philanthropy existed at the local level, it developed in a very informal way, without public sanction or consistent help from the church. Communities took care of their sick and poor without more than a very basic Christian commitment to helping the needy.

The Orthodox Church had played an essential role in establishing and running many of the hospitals that existed in Romania prior to 1918.[107] Indeed, without its help, public health would have been practically nonexistent in Romania. However, these institutions were run less in the spirit of helping to maintain the health of the general population and more as spaces for putting away the sick. Furthermore, the church did not seek to enlist the active help of the wider population in the work undertaken within these hospitals. Therefore, the significance of these institutions remained somewhat marginal in the lives of the general population.[108]

In Transylvania the picture is slightly different, because both the Uniate and the Orthodox Churches were involved to some extent in the nationalist movement. This included a focus not only on language, cultural traditions, and political representation but also on actually caring for the welfare of the Romanian population, including its health. Still, resources here were very limited, so most efforts concentrated on schools and cultural associations.

This picture contrasted greatly with the much better organized voluntary associations that had developed in Western Europe through the official channels of various Protestant denominations and the Catholic Church. By the late nineteenth century such organizations provided important networks for addressing issues of public health and social welfare at a national level and helped to create a culture of civic duty to undertake good works in the community. The Orthodox Church in Romania had not fostered such a culture. Instead, philanthropy had been guided by a spirit of pity (*milă*), something much closer to Orthodox Christian theology than the notion of "good works" as a path toward salvation.[109]

Eugenicists sought to transform the focus of the Church's social work from charity toward its unfortunate outcasts into a more progressive sense of care for the community as a whole.[110] In their view, religious authorities from the local level to the highest echelons were to carry to their flocks the eugenic message concerning the need to respect the laws of life in their behavior and to act with a greater sense of responsibility toward the community, present and future —and not only in the afterlife but in the life of future generations on earth.

It seems problematic that eugenicists did not perceive a great inconsistency between their belief in the universality of the objective laws of evolution and heredity, on the one hand, and the creationist beliefs that lay at the foundation of Christianity. Clearly they were aware of such potential problems, yet they chose to view the basic beliefs and function of the church as compatible with their own theories and goals. Gheorghe Preda, one of Moldovan's close collaborators and a specialist in mental health, gave voice to this view in an essay published in 1925.[111] Here he attempted to reconcile the apparently contradictory bases and functions of religion and science by focusing on the importance of faith and tolerance as the foundation of both of these worldviews.[112]

However, if eugenicists were ready to acknowledge the importance and validity of religion in modern Romania, they also sought to control this important force in their programs rather than work with it as an autonomous factor. Their efforts in this direction eventually contributed to diminishing somewhat the authority of the church at the local level and incorporating other secular institutions in the social structure of the village. This can be seen clearly in the kind of institutional setup eugenicists proposed for refocusing the local community around common ideals. Instead of making the school, the church, or the town hall the most prominent institution for bringing the community together, eugenicists imagined a new space—the Cultural Hearth (*Căminul cultural*).[113]

This place would become the symbolic repository of "authentic" cultural traditions, a museum of the village's history and culture, and the place where knowledge about traditions would become "scientifically" reconstructed to fit the present and future needs of both the local and the national community.[114] Although all members of the community were called upon to make their voices heard in this process in a very direct, democratic fashion, the vital decisions were to be made by the authoritative figures in the community—the mayor; the teacher; the priest; other local officials, such as the policeman; and the local doctor, with the help of his staff.[115] No longer would the church be the space for creating cohesion and order within the community. No longer would the priest be *the* great authority figure. On the contrary, article 11 of the Law for Social Service—which provided the institutional framework for building the Cultural Hearths—stated that "priests, members of the academic corps, administrative employees, as well as any state-paid professional were obligated to frame their work in the community within the Cultural Hearth."[116]

Thus, through eugenicists' efforts in building these new institutions, the doctor was to become the most important figure in the local community. Eugenicists made a persuasive case for this change, for, in their view, doctors promised to alleviate suffering in a more visible and effective way than the priest. Doctors also had the scientific expertise to advise the village council on vital issues regarding the present and future interests of the community, from questions of nutrition and food storage to the hygiene of the local water supplies and the strength of the village's future workforce.[117] With their increased presence in rural Romania, doctors offered a successful secular alternative to the well-established authority of the church. Eugenicists, as promoters of both increasing the presence of the permanent medical staff in the countryside and establishing new institutions for controlling the human potential of every community, in fact contributed very effectively to creating a new secular network of social mobilization and control and a new source of authority in rural society—social medicine.[118] To be sure, eugenicists were not the sole proponents of greater medical help in the countryside. However, at least in Transylvania they played a very important role in educating secondary medical staff, such as nurses, for practice in rural areas. For instance, Moldovan helped set up the medical school in Cluj in 1918 and remained involved in its curriculum and job placement for its graduates during the interwar period.

Eugenicists also offered doctors financial incentives and other means of gaining prestige in order to entice them to opt for a practice in the countryside.[119] For instance, several important research projects conducted at the Institute of Hygiene in Cluj called for prolonged field research. Moldovan was very skillful in enticing his students to participate in such endeavors by taking up prolonged residence in rural areas in order to gather the data necessary for the research on specific projects. While stationed in the countryside, these doctors were encouraged to perform other duties as local doctors, from routine checkups to various talks on pre- and postnatal care and marital counseling. They were also encouraged to recruit potential students for the positions of sanitary agent and nurse, as well as to bring other doctors and secondary medical staff into these areas as permanent residents.[120]

Most importantly, eugenicists provided an alternative to the prevailing perception that medical practice in the countryside was a dead end. Instead, doctors were offered an opportunity to see themselves in a position of authority and prestige and encouraged to publish their experiences, observations, and professionally relevant ideas in the pages of various medical and social reform journals.[121] As with other practical measures, the Cluj group was by far the most active in this regard and had a greater impact in Transylvania than elsewhere. *Transilvania, Buletin Eugenic și Biopolitic, Revista Institutului Social Banat-Crișana,* and *Ardealul Medical* all published articles written by such doctors and repeatedly reinforced the importance of their role in the service of the nation's health.[122]

Romanian society was forcibly secularized to a much greater extent after the communist takeover. Critics of this process have, perhaps, overemphasized the degree to which in 1944 Romania was still overwhelmingly dominated by an Orthodox Christian mentality. Eugenicists were one of the forces that had challenged the authority of the church and religious thinking by subtly incorporating religion into eugenic programs and hence displacing it from the center of authority, especially in rural communities. Thus, by the rise of the communist regime, the image of the church as the central pillar of the community had already been shaken to some degree.

■ ■ ■

M A N Y critics of eugenics have divorced this movement from any significant contributions to "real" scientific thinking by labeling this theory a pseudo-science. Whether scientifically sound or not according to late twentieth-century standards, eugenics clearly had an important impact on the scientific and wider intellectual discourse of the twentieth century. Many excellent scientists were persuaded by the arguments made by eugenicists about the importance of heredity in understanding human behavior, and many were enthralled by the possibility of controlling this process, with little regard for some of the darker aspects of this theory. As scientists, they trusted their own spirit of objectivity and responsibility without serious self-doubt. This attraction continued to be strong among some Romanian scientists and doctors—sometimes because of the theory's antiliberal critique, other times in spite of it. Whether proponents, observers, or critics, by the end of the interwar period many in the scientific community had incorporated eugenic notions of hereditary determinism into their own arguments. Eugenicists had helped shape the very development of the scientific paradigm of organizing knowledge about human behavior.

Furthermore, they had contributed to the secularization of Romanian society, especially among the professional educated elites, the primary audience for their ideas. Eugenicists also challenged the authority of the church at the local level in the countryside. In Transylvania, where they were most active, they effectively replaced the image of the priest as the most important authority figure in the village with that of the doctor as a healer for the individual and the community. Eugenicists portrayed the technical knowledge of a doctor as much more beneficial for the average peasant than the spiritual insights of the priest. To be sure, theirs was not a thorough, all-out campaign against the church. However, eugenicists helped introduce heretofore nonexistent medical services into the countryside and raised the consciousness of the Romanian rural population about matters of health, while subtly shifting images of authority from religious to secular figures and values. In this sense, also, eugenics played a modernizing role in interwar Romania.

CHAPTER 3

THE BIOPOLITICAL STATE

> Public health can no longer be considered the sum total of the citizens'
> physical health. At the same time, . . . the state cannot be defined any
> longer as an association of individuals and a simple defender of indi-
> vidual interests, but rather as a form of life of the ethnic community,
> the nation [*neamul*].
>
> Iuliu Moldovan, *Tratat de sănătate publică*

EUGENICISTS were not satisfied simply with criticizing the problems
in Romanian political and social life. In spite of the persistent assertion of their
apolitical nature, eugenicists also desired to create state institutions that could
serve as vehicles for eugenic policies. In fact, several of the more prominent eugenics proponents, Moldovan in particular, went so far as to imagine an ideal
total state, whose every institution and action would be based on eugenic prerogatives. No other eugenics movement in either Europe or the Americas was
as bold in its claims and ambitious in its political goals. Moldovan named this
vision "biopolitics" and relentlessly promoted it until 1948, when he was dis-
credited by the new communist regime.

While specific attributes of this ideal state varied from one eugenicist to the
next and over time, generally eugenicists sought to reshape the relationship be-

tween citizens and the state by expanding the government's powers and responsibilities and limiting individual freedoms for both healthy and "dysgenic"
populations. Following these developments allows for an exploration of the
eugenic conceptualization of important political issues in the interwar period.
These issues ranged from the need to create a common set of civic values out
of the multitude of traditions incorporated into Greater Romania in 1918 to the
problem of how best to modernize agriculture and rural life and develop a viable industrial base in the midst of economic uncertainty.[1] These problems
were almost all different from those that helped shape the particularities of eugenic discourse and solutions in Western Europe and the United States. The
Romanian responses present a useful comparison with these other movements,
as Romanian eugenicists—Moldovan in particular—worked out more explicitly than some of their counterparts abroad the implications of Mendelian
heredity for political life and social relations. Moldovan's writings offer a useful framework for discussing the implications of eugenic thought in shaping a
normative political and social discourse. This analysis focuses on the language
and arguments used by Moldovan and his supporters to frame the vision of a
biopolitical state.

What is of interest is how these thinkers imagined solutions for their contemporary problems, as well as how these solutions compared to better-known
totalitarian ideologies that took shape during the same years.[2] For while eugenicists in Romania offered solutions similar in some ways to those of their
German counterparts, the Romanian social and intellectual context produced
a biopolitics different from the Nazi race hygiene. The two most important differences were the Romanians' less persistent emphasis on race purity and their
more persistent emphasis on education and on voluntary rather than coercive
measures as tools for effecting eugenic betterment.

What set apart the eugenic ideology of the new state from other attempts to
come to grips with modernization in Romania was its claim to be rational and
to offer scientific, irrefutable proofs of its theories. The eugenic alternative introduced an unfamiliar way of viewing politics in the Romanian landscape, where
the discourse of science had not yet entered the intellectual mainstream, let
alone the political arena. The extent to which eugenicists succeeded in making
their ideology accessible to a wide audience and even introducing a biologically determinist discourse into political and social debates is a more remarkable feat than German eugenicists could claim. For in a Romania that was still

over 78 percent rural and overwhelmingly illiterate, this ideology offered a brand-new paradigm for organizing political and social institutions: eugenicists helped introduce science as a fundamental mode of observing, evaluating, and organizing contemporary Romania.[3]

Furthermore, eugenicists identified themselves as belonging to a modernizing school of thought in the ongoing contest between modernists and traditionalists. Thus far, most historians have focused on this debate in connection with several literary and related political currents.[4] However, the debate over modernization was broader and included members of the professional middle class, from Ștefan Zeletin to Simion Mehedinți, Iuliu Hațiegan, and Mihail Manoilescu.[5] In this discussion eugenicists attempted to strike a balance between the wholesale borrowing of ideas and institutions from the West, something they accused liberals of doing, and turning their backs on the realities of the modern condition in the ongoing competition for vital space in Europe.

This chapter explores how eugenic views of the ideal state combined authoritarian and welfare notions, as eugenicists wanted to expand greatly the programs for social help through state institutions. This was a synthesis unlike those promoted by eugenics in the United States, England, and France, for in those countries individualist antiauthoritarian discourses were an important component of political culture. In Germany, the welfare part of the scheme fell out of favor in the late 1920s, opening the path toward authoritarian politics. In Romania, on the other hand, most eugenicists maintained that a "third way" could be reached—a balance between state control over and care for individuals as members of a larger unit, the nation. This third way did, however, help destabilize parliamentary politics and contributed significantly to the already rising tide of illiberalism in Eastern Europe. Moldovan was the most influential writer on this subject, as he traced a comprehensive picture—indeed a manifesto —for biopolitics. All thinkers and reformers interested in or supporting eugenics would subsequently refer to Moldovan's early writings as *the* standard for eugenic thinking in the interwar period.

Moldovan's Early Political Writings: Biopolitics as the Third Way

Moldovan's earliest synthesis was a small book entitled *Igiena națiunii* (1925), followed shortly thereafter by *Biopolitica* (1926). The first described imperative eugenic measures, based on Moldovan's critique of industrialization and urbanization. Moldovan's analysis did not reject these developments per se, but their excesses. In the author's view, such individualist and materialist approaches had derailed scientific and technological progress from its natural course of development, rendering industrialization dysgenic. Thus, Moldovan concluded, "we are not, and cannot be against industrialization, just as we don't oppose labor; but one serious postulate has to become established—that this industrialization should not debilitate but rather biologically enhance the human capital."[6] Hence, he called for educational measures and "a conservatism when accepting the advancements of civilization."[7] Having learned from the mistakes of others in England and Germany, Moldovan was hoping to forgo the degenerative effects of industrialization in the West.

Already Moldovan had separated himself from his contemporaries in the debate over development and modernization by basing his arguments on the "biological enhancement of the human capital." Politicians such as Ion Mihalache and Ion I. C. Brătianu, economists such as Nicolae Manoilescu, and intellectuals such as Ştefan Zeletin and Eugen Lovinescu framed their questions about the merits of rapid modernization and the role of the state differently. Should the state encourage or even subsidize industrialization or, on the contrary, focus on agriculture and the rural areas? Did Romania need European-like institutions and political structure or a more "authentic" structure, based on ancestral traditions? Moldovan presented a different voice. He seemed to assume a posture of compromise between modernizers and traditionalists, arguing that "[o]ptimal evolution can result only by combining individualism with social biological principles."[8]

By portraying eugenics as a moderate approach to development, Moldovan aimed to respond to concerns expressed by many intellectuals and professionals like himself, who had become disenchanted with the existing political options but were just as dissatisfied with the extremist alternatives put forth by socialists, legionaries, and staunch conservative nationalists.[9] His language did not resemble the mystical tone of legionary prophesying and did not make angry proposals for radical change. Rather, Moldovan made use of "clinical" language —describing case studies and then making diagnoses based on his observations, as well as recommending the treatments that best suited a particular "ailment." Moldovan offered his educated audience a congenial solution to their frustrations, for it appeared to be rational and disengaged from the partisan "politicism" that characterized most other ideologies.

In addition, Moldovan's writing exuded middle-class morality with regard to the family and the separation of the private and public spheres. This type of argumentation would characterize his writings throughout the interwar years, while the tone of his prose would become increasingly fiery, alternating between concern and frustration. While a similar tone and argumentation could be found in the writings of eugenicists in Western Europe in the post–World War I period, there the eugenic rhetoric reflected and helped reinforce a sense of *crisis*. Eugenic texts stood as a bastion against the destructive tendencies of postwar developments. Moldovan's language, on the other hand, proposed creating a new order rather than maintaining already existing institutions. Biopolitics offered a discourse that resonated with newly emerged professionals' search for values and institutions that would embody their ambitions.

Moldovan's early work, however, made only a few specific recommendations. It reiterated the need to induce biological consciousness (i.e., responsibility toward the present and future generations), especially among the professional middle stratum, and proposed legislation that would control marriage licensing, eugenic abortion, and sterilization. Moldovan did not go into great detail about the institutions that would help enforce these measures or the specific social questions his proposals raised. *Igiena națiunii* remained a tentative approach to the social problems at which Moldovan hinted. This work was a testing ground for ideas that were in the process of forming but had not yet been pushed to their logical conclusions.

Biopolitica: Toward a Total Eugenic State

In *Biopolitica,* however, Moldovan offered a full-blown description of the impact of eugenic prerogatives on every area of public life and state organization. The book was a slim volume of less than one hundred pages, published in a small format. In size and appearance it more resembled a pamphlet or extended essay than a scientific analysis. In prose style and organization it resembled a political essay. Moldovan did not use footnotes and did not provide a bibliography, though his ideas were in part borrowed from eugenicists abroad. The general format of *Biopolitica* suggests that the author intended it as a work of popularization rather than as a treatise for the scientific community.

A series of journals reviewed this book after its publication in 1926. Most reviewers were close collaborators of Moldovan, such as Aurel Voina, and extolled the qualities of the book. During the next decade and a half, Moldovan's biopolitical ideas found their way into texts written by others, including Dimitrie Gusti, the most important sociologist in interwar Romania; Emil Racoviță; Simion Mehedinți; and Alexandru Vaida-Voevod. The wide echo of Moldovan's ideas in the work of such varied disciplines shows that *Biopolitica* and the eugenic texts that followed it reflected the interests and outlook of many other members of the Romanian educated elite. The positive response also calls into question the assumption that liberalism and pluralism constituted the "norm" in the debates over modernization and progress in interwar Romania, while illiberal populist movements that looked toward the past or tried to foster an undemocratic future represented "outside" or fringe challenges.[10] The acceptance of Moldovan's critique of and solutions for the current situation showed that many among the Romanian educated public also harbored a basic distrust of the liberal political institutions established by the Romanian Constitution of 1866 and reaffirmed in 1923. Even if they did not consider joining more overtly extreme right-wing movements such as A. C. Cuza's League of Christian National Defense (LANC), these critics played an important role in reducing the chances for political pluralism and stability.

Biopolitica was in effect a manifesto that called for a total eugenic state based on biological principles—an entirely new way of organizing politics in Romania. Moldovan built his argument on the scientific laws of heredity, yet he used a language of common sense accessible to any educated reader. With this strategy he was able to introduce a series of revolutionary ideas, whose implications in terms of state organization reached into every corner of public and private life. Much of Moldovan's argument will be examined here in detail in order to emphasize the all-encompassing, explosive implications of a text that professed to speak with the authority of scientific objective truth and became a well-respected, even revered text among Romanian intellectuals.[11]

The basic premise of *Biopolitica* is the validity of the eugenic argument that human life, social and individual, is governed by certain objective laws—heredity, variation, adaptation, and selection. For Moldovan this also meant that any modern state that wanted to promote the general well-being of its population should follow these laws as its foundation. He stated from the start that "the Constitution will have as its exclusive focus biological evolution."[12] Therefore, political life would be defined by the hereditary nature of human physical, intellectual, psychological, and moral characteristics and obligations.

Furthermore, the constitution would take into account the natural inequality among individuals—not by trying to overcompensate for it but by creating avenues for all individuals to become useful to the nation within their inborn limitations. His ideas attacked directly the principle of equality that was one of the cornerstones of almost all European constitutions at that time, the Romanian one included. The business of the state would be to "control the maximization of individual value for the common good," a statement in the tradition of utilitarian philosophy.[13] This notion of placing biological evolution at the foundation of political life and the legal framework of the state went further than any other eugenic writings of the time in revolutionizing the definition of the state's prerogatives over public life. In 1926 even German eugenicists were still operating within the established state framework, with no overt ambition to explode it. In fact, although the resemblance was unintentional, this statement was quite similar to the communist principles of the Soviet Union.

Moldovan went to great lengths to show that biopolitics differed from the liberal concept of the state as a body regulating the civic rights of individuals as autonomous beings; that biopolitics parted from the socialist emphasis on the need to even out inequality; and that biopolitics differed from the traditionalist nationalism that professed that Romania could focus on preserving its authentically peasant traditions and social organization—its vitality—only by turning its back on Europe and modernization. Nonetheless, this early eugenic vision shared some notions about the public sphere with the ideologies it sought to replace. Eugenicists' faith in man's ability (the gender reference is intentional) to design progress through artificial selection was akin to arguments set forth by liberals that competition was essential to growth and that humanity had unbounded possibilities for progress. At the same time, Moldovan's biopolitical principle that the state was obligated to ensure basic standards of health and well-being bore similarities to socialist arguments on behalf of increasing the responsibilities of the welfare state. Finally, eugenics was close to the traditionalist-nationalist view of the nation as a living, organic being and of the village as the source of its authentic, real qualities.

In the end, however, a principle fundamentally different from all others grounded eugenic concepts of the ideal state and of public life. What legitimated the ideal was not the Declaration of the Rights of Man, historical and legal precedents, cultural and political traditions, or the principle of means of production ownership. Rather, Moldovan identified the very laws of life as the legitimizing principle of eugenics, a basis that appeared so solid that he and many others came to see it as irrefutable.

At the level of historical analysis, this also demonstrates the inadequacy of splitting the ideological scene in interwar Romania along a clear left-right axis.[14] In fact, the novelty of ideology, of mass politics, and of the new context, Greater Romania, rendered the picture of political affiliations very complicated. Eugenicists were both observers of this phenomenon and participants in redrawing the boundaries between private and public, between civic and personal. Their ideas of where state prerogatives ended and where personal responsibility began challenged the left-right divide. Moldovan's position in *Biopolitica* can be described as a modernist stance, radical in its far-reaching implications in spite of its clinical language and conservative appearance (e.g., its emphasis on preserving the peasants' biological capital).

Biopolitics as a Corporatist Solution: Citizenship—Rights and Obligations

Moldovan's philosophical grounding in organicist thought was linked to certain prominent figures from the nineteenth and twentieth centuries. He referred on many occasions to the German philosopher Oswald Spengler's description of civilizations as organic beings that followed life courses—birth, growth, maturing, aging, decay, and death. Moldovan approved of this organicist language and felt that many of Spengler's metaphors inspired by biology were accurate. He disagreed, however, with the German philosopher's depiction of a civilization's—and hence a nation's—inevitable decline and with Spengler's consequent grim predictions for the West.

For Moldovan, the laws of heredity, variation, adaptation, and selection offered a solution to Spengler's despair. Decline, Moldovan contended, was not an inevitable natural process but rather a phenomenon of degeneracy as a result of dysgenic forces. Civilized nations possessed the scientific knowledge about these processes—gained from Darwin's, Galton's, and most recently Mendel's, Morgan's, and Pearson's works—to analyze them in the light of the objective truths of science. Moreover, in Moldovan's optimistic interpretation these civilizations held in their hands the means of controlling evolution through eugenics. Therefore, "decline" was the fate only of those who failed to analyze degenerate phenomena and follow eugenics. For those who assumed responsibility for these negative developments and acted, the future held the promise of "regeneration."

This critique of Spengler's ideas was not uncommon among eugenicists abroad as well. Moldovan, however, credited none of his contemporaries. He was more interested in helping to prevent a Romanian version of the situation in the West described by Spengler. As Moldovan saw it, Romania had a very healthy hereditary potential, still largely unspoiled by materialist civilization. This was especially the case in Transylvania, with its presumably unspoiled and isolated Romanian peasants. Thus, one could take the tools offered by eugenicists elsewhere to repair the damage done in the course of the nineteenth century and turn them into *preventive* measures in Romania, in order to secure a more biologically aware modernization of the state.

Moldovan's particular vision of modern Romania focused on the importance of defining *all* attributes, actions, and goals of the state in terms of national identity—a form of totalitarian nationalism. He identified the nation as a naturally created unit, which evolved as an organic, living being, governed by the same laws of heredity, variation, and selection that also defined individual lives. The needs of the nation superseded those of the individual, and the attributes of the state derived from the need to protect the progress of nation. In Moldovan's vision, state institutions, legislation, and actions would slowly be molded in accordance with the particularities of the nation and would reflect closely its biological destiny. The state would become the tightly fitting armor of the nation rather than a conglomerate of institutions and policies meant to protect citizens individually, sometimes simultaneously supporting competing claims.

Many historians have viewed this type of organicist nationalism as conservative and somewhat backward looking, for it is usually encoded in a language that celebrates the past, focusing on restoring past glories.[15] In Romania, even in the 1920s, Eugen Lovinescu defined the Junimea group, for instance, as conservative and even reactionary because of its organicist nationalism.[16] Though considering nationalism a product of the modern age, historians such as Eric Hobsbawm have also focused a great deal on the conservatism of this ideology.[17] Some theorists of nationalism, Anthony D. Smith most prominently, have also stressed the continuities in the rise and spread of nationalism from the perspective of ethnicity as a sociological element.[18] John Hutchinson has challenged this evaluation in his analysis of cultural nationalism. He claims that "cultural nationalists should be seen . . . as moral innovators" because of their integrationist tendencies regarding different camps of nationalists.[19] Romanian eugenicists can be described as such only with the specification that they were also radical and destabilizing of traditional morality in their goals, even when their language was rationalist and clinical. The language and goals of Romanian eugenicists were future oriented, bent on constructing new political and social structures in accordance with the organic needs of the nation in the modern age, even when their metaphors celebrated images from the past.

Moldovan had a teleological understanding of the nation and state. Both had a naturally established reason for existing, which he explained in terms of scientific laws of causality. The universality of these laws implied that one could use them not only to understand the present but also to reconstruct the past and *predict* the future. In fact, Moldovan stressed throughout his work that his efforts to shape state institutions according to the laws of biological determinism were driven by the desire to rationalize social organization and "artificial selection," so that the state would ensure "the biological prosperity of the human capital."[20] This view of the state related directly to the eugenic crisis he saw growing in the West as a result of the great comforts offered by modern civilization, which he hoped to prevent from taking shape in Romania. With the rise of institutions that protected the weak, the progress of civilization and culture meant a decrease in the biological capital of the nation. Moldovan's alternative was to reorient all state actions toward the rational increase of biological capital. This discourse substantiates John Breuilly's claim that nationalism seeks to politicize all idioms and practices by collapsing "the distinctions between culture, politics, society and state."[21] The twist added to Breuilly's discussion by the case of Moldovan's biopolitics is Moldovan's insistence on using hereditary-determinist categories as the key to questioning these distinctions.

The practical side of this ideology was closely connected to Moldovan's concept of who would be a part of the nation and who would have to be excluded on the basis of organic, biologically hereditary differences. The widest common element was ethnicity, understood as a "community of blood, tradition and destiny."[22] This definition implied that cultural ties—"tradition"—were not enough for someone to claim allegiance to a nation. He or she would need to prove blood ties to the ethnic body and, furthermore, a commitment to fulfilling responsibly the future destiny of the nation.

This relationship with the nation's future may seem redundant after

Moldovan's emphasis on the biological dimension of ethnicity ("blood"), but it was an essential component of his vision. The individual had to assume consciously his or her identity—the present role in society and responsibilities toward future generations—in order to claim the right to membership in the state. Again, Moldovan struck a different chord than traditionalist nationalists, for "assuming" an identity meant, in fact, consciously constructing a role within the nation in accordance with its needs and present context—as a community irrevocably grounded in the modern experience.

This emphasis on individual responsibility toward the national community as a means for building the biological capital at the grassroots level was unlike that of most eugenicists in Western Europe and the United States, whose rhetoric reinforced their own role in acting to control degeneracy. The existing historiography does not suggest that eugenicists in these countries were keen on engaging the masses as more than recipients of eugenic programs. Moldovan's call for a sense of responsibility and mobilization went further than eugenicists in Western Europe did, reaching out to the entire population, implicitly understood as ethnic Romanians.

This eugenic definition of the nation and of its constituents carries tacit implications about who could *not* be part of this organic body. It also suggests Moldovan's conscious attempt to link eugenic theories with practical venues for political empowerment along ethnic lines, with an implicit emphasis on separation from other ethnic groups in Romania and possibly disempowering these groups at the same time. If Romanians by blood, language, and traditions were the natural components of the Romanian nation, then non-Romanians seemed to be automatically excluded. In practical terms, this would mean that Hungarians, Germans, Jews, Roma, Bulgarians, Ukrainians, Russians, Turks, and all the other ethnic groups that made up 30 percent of the population of Greater Romania were alien, parasitic communities within the greater organic unit.[23]

However, Moldovan was as much a pragmatist as an idealist. He realized the implications of such an assertion at a point in the development of interwar Romania when the state needed to mobilize all its available internal human and material resources in order to create a functional framework for civic and economic life. Hence, he added as a corollary to his strict definition of the nation the "natural" inclination of the Romanian people toward tolerance. In other words, he seemed willing to allow other ethnic groups to coexist inside Romania, although he was not inclined to have the future eugenic state cater to the specific needs—cultural or biological—of minority groups. He found even this limited claim for tolerance increasingly harder to sustain over time, as some of his collaborators (especially Făcăoaru and Herseni) began to praise the natural anti-Semitism and conservative traditionalism of the Romanian people in the late 1930s. By then, it had become clearer that an exclusivist and even racist direction had developed among some followers of eugenics, closer in their rhetoric of exclusion to the Iron Guard and other right-wing political movements than to the clinical-rationalist position Moldovan still hung on to. In 1926, however, the discourse over the future of the Romanian state was still inclusive of non-Romanians in some ways.

Nonetheless, Moldovan made it clear that Romanians would have a superior position, as the majority "authentic" population. According to his view of natural social hierarchy, this would be a rational policy—to the greater biological capital would go the greater resources.[24] Moldovan claimed this to be an equitable position, as minorities would also benefit from public resources. He never explicitly called for excluding minorities from state programs of public health or social welfare on the basis of ethnicity. Rather, he proposed reducing the state's spending on programs and actions that would cater to the specific organic needs of each of these communities. For instance, if the problem of infant mortality was extremely widespread among Roma, the state would need to address this problem and enforce solutions among the Romanian population before it turned toward the Roma. According to Moldovan's corporatist outlook, the destiny of the Romanian state would be tied to that of the Romanian national body, not to the needs of the competing groups that existed within it.

It is important to note that in *Biopolitica* Moldovan passed over in silence any reference to the citizenship rights of the Jewish population. In 1926 the debates over granting citizenship to Jews were still intense within Romanian politics. A. C. Cuza's League of National Christian Defense and even Nicolae Iorga's National Democratic Party predicted disastrous effects for the Romanian population as a result of this constitutional reform after the war.[25] Around the same period (though after the publication of *Biopolitica*), the anti-Semitic Legion of the Archangel Michael was becoming increasingly vociferous in its apocalyptic descriptions of the impact of the "degenerate" Jewish race on the indigenous population. At the same time, a vigorous anti-Semitic current, with which Moldovan was undoubtedly familiar, was gaining strength in political debates in Italy and Germany. Overall, anti-Semitism was considered a mainstream position in Romanian politics during this period.[26]

It was clearly not for lack of general interest that there was no mention of a "Jewish problem" in Moldovan's *Biopolitica*. It seems, however, that Moldovan was more sensitive to the particular problems he noticed around his native Transylvania. The presence of a significant Jewish population there was less obvious than in the Regat, because many Jews in Transylvania had assimilated voluntarily to Hungarian nationality over the course of the preceding half century. Thus, although Cluj and Oradea both had large numbers of Jews, these populations spoke Hungarian and many had converted to various forms of Christianity. Moldovan was more impressed with the potential revisionism of the large Hungarian minority, especially in the important centers of public and administrative life in Transylvania—from Cluj to Tîrgu Mureş, Oradea, and Arad—than with the presence of a Jewish population in this region. And he displayed openly his fears of Hungarian revisionism and the degenerative effect of this population on the health of ethnic Romanians. Still, he did not express explicitly a desire to deny nonethnic Romanians citizenship on the basis of these apprehensions.

Gender and Citizenship

Moldovan's corporatist nationalism was also reflected in his view of gender with regard to citizenship in the modern state. *Biopolitica* devoted a whole chapter to "The Problem of Feminism" and eugenic solutions to it. This interest in women's issues stood in sharp contrast to other contemporary analyses. His faith in the preparedness of Romanian women for participation in political life was great in 1926. He declared his support for extending enfranchisement to women as a necessary modernizing measure. At the same time, he emphasized the need for women to take charge of this process themselves by organizing and becoming more active in social welfare in order to achieve voting rights.[27]

This is a remarkable and unique attitude in comparison with that of eugenicists elsewhere, particularly in Britain, France, and the United States. Although in these countries women were an important constituency affected by eugenic ideas and programs, their empowerment in the public sphere was not actively sought.[28] Some proponents of women's rights, from Margaret Sanger to Beatrice Webb, had used eugenic arguments to claim control over access to birth control. Yet in Western Europe and the United States women had already been involved in social activism since the early nineteenth century and had gained full political rights after World War I (save in France); their interest in eugenics developed from this self-assured foundation.

In Romania, eugenic arguments on behalf of women's empowerment promised more radical change in gender roles in the political arena in the context of a smaller and less institutionalized women's movement. Yet Moldovan's enthusiasm for women's rights may appear more wholehearted than it really was. At first glance, his analysis seems almost feminist. However, his discussion of women's issues was in fact a preemptive move designed to displace the appeal of feminist groups' rhetoric.

Feminists did not represent a mass movement in Romania. Yet they had made themselves noticed through certain remarkable figures such as Calypso Botez, a social reformer who had persuasively lobbied on behalf of women's enfranchisement since 1918 and had even managed to put the issue up for serious debate in a well-attended series of lectures on the shape of the constitution, organized in 1923 by the well-known Romanian Social Institute.[29] Feminists such as Botez had depicted themselves as *the* authoritative voice of women's grievances and had forcefully argued that women should receive voting rights based on the equality of all human beings, a principle included in the new Romanian Constitution.

For his part, Moldovan viewed feminists in Romania as archenemies of eugenics, a stance he would later articulate more clearly.[30] In his eyes, feminism was a form of individualism that ran against women's eugenic destiny—one of the unhappy results of the irresponsible excesses of individualism and materialism in the process of modernization and industrialization in the nineteenth century. He perceived this movement as a threat to the larger interests of the community, for feminists emphasized women's potential to succeed in every area of public life, if given a chance. This would mean a woman could choose any profession at the expense of being an obedient wife and raising a family. Thus, feminists encouraged women to become assertive, even combative, and to seek recognition of their individual potential talents and abilities by men, even if that meant exacerbating conflicts between the two sexes. Moldovan characterized this attitude as dysgenic, for it fostered the use of creative forces for social and political conflict and thus contributed to tearing apart any notion of solidarity, undermining common interests.[31]

Furthermore, these feminist claims threatened to blur the separation Moldovan sought to construct between the public and private spheres along gender lines. His notions of eugenic value and moral virtue were closely tied to separation between the public and private spheres. This attitude rings a familiar chord for historians of gender in nineteenth-century Europe.[32] The difference between the European picture and Moldovan's stance, however, was Moldovan's pioneering position in Romanian discourse about gender roles. He was the first to draw the distinction between public and private spheres along the lines of gender differences based on hereditary traits and at the same time to show persistent support for women's enfranchisement.

Still, if Moldovan approved of women voting, it was to make better use of their nurturing qualities for the common good, not to allow them access to any occupation and means of empowerment in the public sphere and thus increase competition with men for these public resources. The implications of this attitude were far-reaching: at the same time that they wanted to separate the public and the private arenas of social action, eugenicists still sought to politicize both of these realms and place the state in control of this process. Moldovan's approach to extending voting rights to women while at the same time attempting to control their empowerment illustrates very well the ways in which he sought to reconstruct citizenship rights and the powers of the state according to a corporatist vision.

By the late 1930s, Moldovan and other eugenicists who believed women should be mobilized for the greater well-being of the nation had changed their arguments and rhetoric. Discussions of emancipation faded at the expense of emphasizing that women had virtually achieved civic equality with men, except for voting rights.[33] Therefore, eugenicists argued, focusing on achieving this one last step seemed almost frivolous when other issues, such as increasing the quantity and quality of births, demanded urgent attention. At the same time, arguments about women's rights and roles in the state began to emphasize the negative aspects of women's participation in the public sphere and the need to limit or even exclude this participation.[34] Women were to remain subjects of the total state, rather than full members with voting rights, while the prerogatives of the state grew increasingly paternalistic. Later discussions of policies to control marriages and reproduction revealed more extreme measures to reconfigure women's roles from full participants in the eugenic state to silent subjects of a paternalist regime.[35]

Hereditary Justice

The state envisioned by Moldovan in *Biopolitica* went beyond any previous discussions of organizing and managing public life. The new eugenic state would reach into every area of public and private life and establish ways of social interaction based on a new hierarchy of values—biopolitics. Moldovan went into detail to show how every existing ministry and all other subordinate state institutions would be reorganized and why new forms of bureaucracy needed to be created. He also outlined how these institutions, endowed with both legislative and executive power, would be vital organs of the greater state organism:

> The biopolitical program will establish specifically the general organization of the State, and thus, the essential content of the Constitution, focusing exclusively on biological evolution. It [the program] will indicate precisely the activities of the central departments of the exterior services and of society [at large].[36]

The tasks allocated to the Ministry of Justice in effect reconceptualize the definitions of "law" and "justice" by shifting the focus from protecting the rights of individuals to defending the interests of the nation—not only as a present entity but also as a hereditary one, with a predictable future. Moldovan put it plainly:

> The Reform . . . must start with a complete revision of the contemporary foundations of [public] law and must place the biological interests of the family above those of the individual and the biological integrity of the human capital above the interests of material property.[37]

The last part of this statement may appear to be an almost humanitarian vision of justice—placing people's lives above material interests—but Moldovan was more interested in conveying the scientific grounding of the new concept of biopolitical law. He was quick to stress that only such a reform could ensure that individuals would assume biological responsibility and begin to evaluate their actions and those of others against biopolitical prerogatives, rather than on the basis of a "sentimental fiction dictated by pity."[38] Clearly, humanitarian ideals were not Moldovan's priority. He also did not address thorny questions such as the specific criteria for evaluating the worth of "human capital"—along ethnic or gender lines, for instance.

Another important component of this view of justice was the notion that individual worth in a eugenic sense (focused on hereditary qualities and health in general) would play an essential role in evaluating the gravity of criminal actions. Citizens were to become so many cogs in the great machine that would drive the state forward. Their actions would be judged according to the biological interests of the nation and each individual's eugenic potential. The same criminal act—for instance, abortion—would be judged in accordance with the eugenic potential of the woman who had this operation; the healthier her genetic capital, the more severe the punishment. This concept sought to reconstruct the very basis of the justice system, which until then had judged *acts* rather than *actors* and had considered everyone equal before the law. Eugenicists believed this system to be basically flawed, for it disregarded fundamental biological differences and natural social hierarchies. However, the new system would not reward its "superior" citizens by scrutinizing them less than the "inferior" population. In fact, Moldovan wanted to bring about a judicial system that would control the lives and actions of the eugenically superior population as much as those of the "dysgenics."[39] This concept of justice situated the individual as an object of legal restriction and empowered the state and its representatives at the expense of individual citizens in a totalitarian manner.

Medicine and Political Order

At the center of the reorganizing process stood the Ministry of Health, rendering doctors as the most authoritative technocratic elite in the new state. The general organizing principle of this institution would be to shift the definition of "medicine" from a stopgap or curative discipline to a preventive one. Also, "health" would have to be defined not as the mere absence of any noticeable illness but rather as a complex notion that took into account hereditary potential —latent dysgenic characteristics or special talents—that could be transmitted to the next generation.

Starting from this premise, the whole medical profession would gradually change. In keeping with Moldovan's Mendelian outlook, doctors would start looking at patients in a different light and tie various phenomena to hereditary characteristics rather than to environmental conditions. Diagnoses and therapeutics would also change radically in accordance with the health needs of the greater body, the nation. Thus, if a patient needed prolonged, expensive treatment for an ailment such as cancer, the decision to prescribe it would be weighted in terms not only of the individual's chance of survival and financial capabilities but also of his or her eugenic potential and the needs of the state. It might very well be decided that such a curative effort would work to the disadvantage of the greater well-being, and the treatment would not be prescribed. On the other hand, an individual who seemed normal might become the subject of mandatory medical treatment, if a certain latent hereditary, hence dysgenic, ailment were discovered in his or her body. Moldovan viewed state expenditures for such preventive endeavors as an important, albeit costly, prerogative over curative medicine.

Doctors would gain immense power over the life and death of all citizens within an institutional framework that entrusted medicine with the authority to protect and construct present and future well-being.[40] They would be the technical advisors and the protecting forces of the nation's future health. Moldovan's view of medical education and practice certification took this issue into account, as he stressed the need to balance this powerful position with a rigorous selection of doctors based on their sense of responsibility toward the eugenic priorities of the nation.

Public Works: Environmental Factors and Biological Progress

If the Ministry of Health was the centerpiece of biopolitical reform in all other areas of public life, Moldovan also emphasized environmental hygiene as a priority for the Ministry of Public Works. Although he rejected Lamarckian theories, Moldovan believed environmental factors could have a debilitating influence, especially on individuals with latent hereditary pathologies. Therefore, it would be imperative to ensure a healthy environment and a standard of public hygiene that would allow healthy heredity to take its course, thereby facilitating eugenic progress.

The Ministry of Public Works would focus on enforcing the availability of a clean water supply, light, heat, and a modern sewage system in public civic and commercial spaces. Future building contracts for private residences would also have to follow a standardized procedure set up by this ministry and make available the same public facilities as well as sufficient living space.[41]

This view of public hygiene and urban planning was remarkably comprehensive for that time in Romania, when Bucharest and other cities were growing by periodic additions of a *mahala* to their peripheries.[42] Moldovan's call for rationalizing such processes echoed ideas of planning developed by Henri Prost and other architects engaged in the replanning of urban spaces in France around the turn of the century.[43] Moldovan clearly embraced modernization, as did these French architects. However, his goal—maximizing the biological capital of the nation—separates his ideas from those of his French contemporaries. At the same time, no eugenicists abroad tied the rationalization of urban planning so closely to securing genetic health. Mendelians abroad, in particular, had become more critical of such Lamarckian approaches to environmental reform. Moldovan reframed these welfare concerns to emphasize their significance for the health of the future community. Ironically, it was the communist regime that finally accomplished this goal.

Economics, Development, and Labor Relations

On the basis of the eugenic priorities established by specialists in the Ministry of Health, further general organizing guidelines and specific changes would be recommended in virtually every aspect of public life. For example, the Ministry of Labor would regulate labor organization and pass legislation to maintain the "biological equilibrium . . . between man and the external environment." Limiting child labor and the employment of women were two such regulating measures. The socialist movement was struggling at that time for the same types of legislation. Yet Moldovan's language struck a less radical and threatening chord with the anti-Bolshevik atmosphere in Romania. This ministry would use as its guideline the maximization of "individual productive capabilities" within a presumably positive spiritual, psychological, moral, and intellectual environment. Moldovan mentioned labor regulation in the United States as the most progressive approach to this issue and sought to adapt such regulation to the Romanian context. In this area, as in others, he appropriated Taylorist concepts of modernizing production to the Romanian context by shifting emphasis from efficiency for the sake of the market or individual producers, workers, and consumers to the need to keep the nation on a healthy, harmonious track of development while supporting industrialization.[44]

The state would also regulate industry and commerce by "rationalizing industrialization" in terms of a biological conceptualization of this endeavor. The provisions for change in the Ministry of Industry and Commerce constitute the weakest section of *Biopolitica*. It seems that Moldovan had a rather crude understanding of all the issues involved in evaluating the pros and cons of industrialization and the development of commerce. He did agree almost grudgingly that it would be impractical to argue against industrialization, but he was not very clear on the specific measures that needed to be taken in order to facilitate industrialization in accordance with biopolitical prerogatives.

Moldovan's critical opinion of state actions under the current liberal regime comes out most clearly in his analysis of the changes needed in the Ministry of Agriculture. Since he viewed the rural population as "the generator of energy" within the nation (i.e., its engine), this ministry had huge responsibilities vis-à-vis peasants.[45] Moldovan thought that the 1921 land reform had disregarded this issue completely, since it did not follow as a guideline the need to favor "the elements with superior or intact biological qualities" above others in order to lay the foundation for the flourishing of eugenic families.[46] The egalitarian distribution of land on the basis of simple quantitative calculations was "irresponsible from the biological point of view," according to Moldovan, for it disregarded the qualitative aspect of land redistribution—the difference in eugenic potential among various recipients.[47] His hope was that agrarian reform could be revised with biopolitical prerogatives in mind.

Biopolitica did not discuss in any detail who had been the dysgenic beneficiaries of the land reform and, implicitly, who would be deprived of their land under a eugenic regime. Later studies by Moldovan and a related open letter to Ion Mihalache, the leader of the NPP, signed by one of Moldovan's supporters, Francisc Rainer, the prominent anthropologist and professor of anatomy at the medical school in Bucharest, shed some light on this important, if concealed, aspect of the eugenic critique of land reform.[48] As with other measures of redistributing national economic resources, Moldovan followed the guidelines discussed earlier when defining the "nation." In particular, Romanian communities "of blood, tradition and destiny" should have been favored above other populations in this process of land redistribution. Roma, in particular, would have to be sought out and dispossessed as a parasitic entity that was encroaching on the limited resources of the healthy national organism. Also, women were not to be counted as autonomous individuals but rather as dependents, since their eugenic role would be limited to human reproduction rather than economic production. Similar arguments about the need to protect the well-being of the nation and state developed later in a more aggressive manner, when measures for the "Romanianization" of economic life and the interdiction against Jewish ownership of property were discussed and enacted in August 1940 under Carol II's dictatorship and during the war under the Ion Antonescu regime.

State Finance and Biopolitics

Moldovan's reshaping of the Ministry of Finance was nothing short of revolutionary. His vision radically changed the concepts of generating and spending state revenues. He believed these two activities were among the strongest weapons available to the state in shaping the behavior of its citizens. Therefore, lawmakers had to proceed in a very deliberate manner in rethinking taxation, starting from the basic premise that the state's priorities were to encourage not only economic development but also biological evolution. Higher taxes for some would be a means of punishing dysgenic behavior. For instance, bachelors and childless couples would pay extra taxes compared to families with children.[49] Today, such a view of taxation does not seem particularly new or eugenic. But Moldovan articulated his plan for such a system of taxation by arguing not about its benefits to individuals or the economy but about its benefits to the nation as a whole and to the state as protector of the "biological capital."

The new system of taxation would also be a means of redistributing wealth in society, so that the state would help directly those with eugenic potential without having to take any money away from other necessary expenditures. Although this thinking may strike the contemporary reader as extremely illiberal and even reactionary, in the Romanian context this concept of taxation represented a departure from both traditionalist conservative thinking and liberal ideas.[50] The state would no longer be the broker of economic interests among more powerful strata in society or of its own bureaucracy but would, instead, become the protector of the community's welfare at large. This conceptualization of the state was clearly grounded in an acceptance of the modern condition with all of its opportunities and limitations.

During World War II, a similar view of taxation—but one that was overtly racist and specifically anti-Semitic—led to dramatic restrictive policies directed against the Jewish population. Through various general and also very specific measures regarding Jewish property and wealth of any sort, the Antonescu regime extorted immense amounts of money from the Jewish population and utilized these funds both to finance the war effort and to provide essential revenues for social help that was to benefit the ethnic Romanian population exclusively.[51] The Patronage Council, whose activities were praised by Romanian eugenicists, was one of the important recipients of these funds, while its humanitarian help was never extended to nonethnic Romanians. Moldovan did not participate in drafting these anti-Semitic policies. But in an indirect manner, his view of rethinking state finances and especially of placing the state in a more powerful, coercive position vis-à-vis individual citizens did pave the way for more exclusivist, even racist interpretations of his ideas.

Another aspect of state finances on which Moldovan focused was the salaries of state employees. The starting premise of his discussion was the imperative need to hire these employees along biopolitical criteria: (1) an individual's inborn intellectual and physical aptitudes should be suited to the specific responsibilities of the job occupied; (2) all state officials needed to have a high sense of responsibility toward the nation's future; and (3) implicitly, all employees would have to be ethnically Romanian and male. With this "healthy" basis, the state would then need to ensure that the salaries of its employees would not lead to a reduction in their standard of living and eugenic potential. Moldovan considered that those who were educated and committed to working for the well-being of the state needed to be able to perform their assumed public (i.e., eugenic) responsibilities without having to worry on a daily basis about feeding their families.[52] Also, he hoped that higher salaries and other benefits added to the basic pay—such as monthly family and dependents' allowances and decreasing taxes with the increased number of dependents—would work to encourage this elite group to reproduce, greatly enhancing the biological capital of the nation.

This vision of the state sought to improve the social status of the Romanian professional strata, implicitly punishing any other groups in society as a result, for access to state resources was a zero-sum game in interwar Romania. Discrimination against non-Romanians and women would clearly be a part of this new social and political hierarchy, yet it remained an unstated feature, unlike the aggressive anti-Semitic ideology of A. C. Cuza's or Corneliu Zelea-Codreanu's parties. Such silence enabled Moldovan to present his ideas as more rational and moderate than those of the far right, in spite of the radical implications of his proposals. Furthermore, this new state would not privilege *all* Romanians, for access to the security of a government position was predicated upon a strong sense of responsibility for the nation's future and on technical specialization in the particular field in which a technocrat was to operate. Efficiency was ostensibly a more important attribute in Moldovan's imagined technocratic leadership than ethnic or racial purity.

Using taxation and state finances to refigure the body politic was an entirely new concept in Romania. Until then, the greatest priority had been defense, while issues of subsidizing the development of industry and modernizing agriculture had only recently come under discussion. Moldovan did not want to decrease the prerogatives of the state in these areas but rather to add others, organizing all of these means of controlling the wealth and development of the country into a coherent whole, rather than allowing them to be piecemeal, as they had been before. His view of the state's use of public revenues came closer to the welfare state than to the ideas of contemporary liberals or conservative nationalists. However, the *goals* of the state's greater expenditure on public welfare resembled ideals embraced by fascist theories during that period.

Education, Culture, and Eugenic Progress

With regard to education, Moldovan wanted to revise the general concept of pedagogy, from equal theoretical studies for all students to a differentiated education on the basis of individual inborn talents and limitations. The new Ministry of Education would organize pedagogical resources to make the best use of every individual's capabilities in the interest of the nation on the basis of science rather than philosophy or history, as had been the case before. This system of education would help create and reinforce a new hierarchy—based on hereditary natural endowments, as well as on social and state priorities, rather than on universal humanist ideals. Education, therefore, would be aimed at helping to fulfill each individual's potential for the benefit of the community, rather than simply enabling each individual to make choices according to personal goals.

The Ministry of Art and Culture would take its cue from biopolitics as well, reorienting its resources toward mobilizing the eugenically superior and educating all Romanians about this new ideology. Moldovan stressed in particular the need for the church to imbue its rhetoric with the spirit of the age and promote the primacy of spiritual and moral values such as selflessness and responsibility toward *this* life above abandonment of oneself for the afterlife.[53] During this early period in his writings, Moldovan was apprehensive about the negative role of the church in reinforcing a fatalist view of health and hygiene in the countryside. He still saw in the church a powerful enemy of science and progress. Later on, he recognized more fully the strategic value of using the authority of the church, especially in rural areas, and sought to co-opt rather than criticize it.[54]

Internal Administration and External Affairs

The Ministry of Internal Affairs, the institution most closely associated with the police state during the twentieth century, actually appeared nonaggressive in *Biopolitica*. Moldovan focused his discussion on the need to decentralize administration by placing more authority over decision making and spending at the local level, a measure also favored by the Peasantists in reaction to the centralizing policies of the liberal regime.[55] The key issue here was replacing the current staff—most often political appointees of questionable qualifications and sense of civic responsibility—with technocrats. These specialists would not only be able to perform their duties and make decisions wisely but would also be free from political clientelism.[56] Later discussions of law enforcement reflected this hope that technocrats stood a better chance of administering the law successfully by getting the general population to cooperate willingly. Most eugenicists did not seem bent on using coercion in order to enforce the new eugenic order. Their belief in the power of persuasion and education underlay this view of reorganizing the Ministry of Internal Affairs.

Moldovan's other unstated grievance in his discussion of decentralization may have been his personal disappointment regarding the way in which the administrative union of Transylvania with the Romanian Kingdom had been handled in Bucharest. He and many others believed that regional concerns and expertise had been ignored in this process and that as a result the efficiency of local administration had suffered greatly, especially in the newly added provinces.[57]

The Ministry of War would also need to reconceptualize the notion of national defense and its use of biological capital. Since World War I had depleted the number of the eugenically most able individuals in all participating nations, Moldovan concluded that war as a means of solving conflict was, overall, dysgenic. The task of this ministry would be to cultivate not only the physical vigor and preparedness of Romanian youth for combat but also a spirit of sacrifice that would strive for peace rather than aggressive action.[58] This pacifist element of *Biopolitica* contrasts strongly with Moldovan's background as an officer in the Habsburg army and with the aggressive embrace of violent state action among the radical right-wing movements in Romania—A. C. Cuza's LANC and the soon-to-be-founded League of the Archangel Michael. This pacifism is not surprising, however, when the staunchly antirevisionist perspective of Moldovan and most other Romanian intellectuals and politicians from Transylvania is taken into consideration.

A corollary to this call for peaceful resolution to conflicts was Moldovan's direction for reforming the Ministry of External Affairs, which would have to keep biological prerogatives as its guiding principle when conducting foreign negotiations. One of the specific measures *Biopolitica* mentions is "assuring ahead of time the necessary space for the development and biological self-fulfillment of the nation."[59] Moldovan did not go into detail about this goal, which bore a striking similarity to some contemporary right-wing extremist ideologies about the need to secure a nation's vital space, most prominently Hitler's ideas of Lebensraum. However, it is unlikely that Moldovan had in mind extending Romania's frontiers at a time when politicians were still having difficulties creating a functional unit out of the various provinces recently incorporated into the kingdom. Rather, he was concerned with reinforcing the protection of the present borders, especially since he and many other Romanians of the professional strata perceived an ever-present threat of Hungarian revisionism.

Moldovan's addition to the state bureaucracy was the Ministry of National Vigor. This new institution would be a think tank for biopolitical policies. It would combine the expertise of specialists from the fields of biology, medicine, demography, anthropology, sociology, law, and other related professions to research the current situation of the country from a eugenic standpoint. These specialists would organize a eugenic census every few years and analyze it and would regulate specific measures undertaken by other state institutions in order to ensure that general biopolitical guidelines were followed and eugenic goals were fulfilled.[60] The Ministry of National Vigor would have the power to make decisions and undertake action in a wide array of areas, from physical education and nutrition to immigration and the growth of the birthrate.

The Biopolitical State as a Totalitarian Order

Moldovan sketched out, sometimes in broad strokes and at other times in minute detail, a state whose institutions would regulate public life in all its aspects and would combine legislative and executive powers, unlike the current parliamentary system. In this discourse there was no place for political debate and contests among parties and their respective programs to set the course for managing the welfare of the country. Biopolitics, as a scientifically based objective set of principles, would preclude the need for any such debates. Instead, progress would result from discussions among specialists regarding the meaning of variations in heredity and the merits of specific corrective measures along eugenic lines. Competition would still exist in society, but it would focus on receiving state resources for development rather than simply on ensuring a free market, and it would be structured by the state in a hierarchy of eugenic merit. This type of paternalist, authoritarian view of the state seemed familiar to Romanian audiences, whose civic education in parliamentary practices was very limited. However, eugenicists offered a new way of organizing the body politic based on biological prerogatives and placed stricter responsibilities on the state, turning it from a benevolent father into a supreme guardian of the nation's future.

This view of the state as the entity best suited to protecting the well-being of the nation and the progress of society appears steeped in Hegelian thought. Moldovan did not make direct references to Hegel's philosophy of history and his vision of the state, but he undoubtedly became familiar with the ideas and writings of the German philosopher during his studies in Vienna. In a later work (1943), Moldovan gave his view of the state an expression that came very close to Hegel's: "The state is a people organized in an organic tie with its land, so that, by mastering its destiny it may ensure its existence, independence and perfection."[61]

As significant as Moldovan's intellectual background is for evaluating the novelty and impact of his ideas in the political discourse of interwar Romania, so is a comparison with other contemporary alternatives to the existing organization of the state and public sphere. The most prominent challenges came from the Italian fascists, the Nazis, and the Soviet communists. Recently, Abbott Gleason has analyzed the similarities among the ideologies of these political movements and developed a general profile of totalitarianism. The elements that compose this profile appear similar to those of Moldovan's biopolitical state. Both were presented as antitheses to the existing liberal state and to the pluralist structure of political life via parliamentary practices.[62]

Totalitarian ideologies sought to control private life and mobilize all social forces in the service of their ideals. To this end, the state could use any and all means to control its subjects. Here Moldovan repeatedly stressed the importance of educating all citizens and stimulating their sense of biological responsibility. However, in *Biopolitica* Moldovan did not imagine developing an infrastructure that would control every aspect of private behavior and would seek social mobilization by all possible means. Moldovan had faith in the power of persuasion to bring about change and in the willingness of most citizens to comply with eugenic principles, once they understood them. If eugenics was to succeed as an effective program of comprehensive reform of the state, it would do so less through coercion than through acts of will and the voluntary commitment of all individuals to the welfare of the national body, albeit in a public sphere that limited individual choice on the basis of biological priorities and eugenic principles.

Another radical difference between Moldovan's biopolitics and totalitarian ideologies was Moldovan's emphasis on lawfulness. At no point during his career did Moldovan openly endorse violence—whether overt or covert—by the state against its citizens. It may be argued that proposing measures of sterilization was equivalent to legitimizing state violence. However, Moldovan presented this measure as an extreme form of preventive action, always a last resort behind education, finding a cure for any latent hereditary pathologies, and voluntary abstinence. The style and substance of his arguments about the need to protect the health of the nation were a far cry from the fascist celebrations of aggressiveness and open violence. Here Moldovan displays significant differences from some of his followers, such as Făcăoaru.[63]

Moldovan's biopolitical state came closer to the concept of the total state held by the German philosopher Carl Schmitt and, in the Romanian context, to the corporatist vision of the economist Mihail Manoilescu. Gleason's study of totalitarianism describes Schmitt's philosophy as a precursor of later, more developed and policy-oriented totalitarian ideologies.[64] He considers Schmitt's vision static, authoritarian, and even reactionary, compared to later aggressive efforts to destroy existing liberal structures and unleash national ("vital") energies through the fascist movement or, in the Romanian context, the Legion of the Archangel Michael. Schmitt's vision, however, perhaps cannot be so quickly defined as "reactionary."[65] Although Schmitt expressed nostalgia for the ways in which hereditary aristocracy had ensured social stability in the past, his illiberal philosophy envisioned state institutions that had not existed under the leadership of the old aristocracy to reconstruct social stability. The state would secure stability and orderly growth through a network of public institutions that would preclude a return to the preliberal age that he may have longed for in terms of social hierarchy and stability. As a scholar of Schmitt has recently argued, "the political alternative suggested by his critique is not a revival of a neomedieval estatist notion of representation, but rather the very modern notion of plebiscitary legitimated executive rule."[66]

Moldovan's view of the biopolitical state drew similarly upon some past forms of social organization but was, in fact, bent on reordering them to fit the problems and the goals most suitable for the modern age. In fact, his synthesis came closer to a doctrine that had been recently formulated in Romania—corporatism.[67] Moldovan's emphasis on the need to place state institutions in control of managing access to resources and modernization while eliminating free competition for political power from the public sphere was akin to Manoilescu's vision of neoliberalism and state-subsidized development. Furthermore, Manoilescu formulated his arguments in a language of biological determinism that showed awareness of and interest in the same laws of heredity that stood at the basis of Moldovan's biopolitics. Moreover, the two men knew each other, and although they were not close collaborators, they were never harsh critics of each other, but rather a sympathetic, if passive, mutual audience. By 1941, however, Manoilescu had become more interested in Iordache

Făcăoaru's eugenic outlook, praising his work on the racial structure of the Romanian population, especially Făcăoaru's discussion of the superiority of the Aryan race.[68]

Moldovan's ideas also resemble those of Nichifor Crainic, especially his doctrines of ethnocracy and Orthodoxism. Writing in the late 1930s, Crainic may have been, in fact, influenced by Moldovan's ideas and language.[69] Crainic's program of a "Romania for all Romanians and only Romanians" defined ethnicity in part in terms of biology. However, he also stated that "the concept of the ethnocratic state is spiritualist" and that its laws should be based on fundamental Christian principles, as interpreted in Orthodox theology.[70] In this regard, Crainic's founding principles differed radically from Moldovan's science-based corporatism. In addition, Crainic's language and specific measures of "purification" were explicitly anti-Semitic and xenophobic, while Moldovan's fears of Hungarian revisionism were only implicit in his writings.

Changes in Moldovan's Biopolitical Vision

Throughout his career Moldovan remained generally faithful to the ideas he expressed in *Biopolitica*. After 1932, when he became the president of Astra, Moldovan began to use the institutional basis and social network of this organization as a vehicle for creating and enforcing comprehensive programs of eugenic education and public health.[71] Astra's annual general conference became the highest pulpit from which he could address a national audience. His speeches offer a good indication of the changes in the language and arguments used to construct Moldovan's vision of the eugenic state. During the first two years his addresses reveal a deep sense of distress about the lack of effective implementation of his 1930 Public Health Law, Moldovan accusing politicians and other professionals of a lack of eugenic responsibility. In 1936, with Carol II present, Moldovan chose instead to focus on the imperative need for the state to assume responsibility for controlling and improving the nation's biological capital, a role that he depicted in grave yet positive terms:

> The state must assume the main duty of basing its entire organization, in all areas, on the realities and needs of the human biological capital to prosper within its natural course; [the state] must know [the nation's] evolution, its surrounding environment, and it must improve this biological capital prudently, keeping it at a safe

distance from all that could diminish its value or compromise its future. The state has the obligation to place at the center of its permanent attention not the individual, but the healthy family, . . . and to increase its active biological forces from generation to generation, so that it [the state] may defend its patrimony through its own powers.[72]

By the mid-1930s, Moldovan seemed less ambitious with regard to immediate comprehensive goals than he had in his works from the late 1920s. The reality of Romania's financial problems during the Great Depression had by then shown him that it would be impractical to expect or even to attempt to design programs of eugenic reform with the hope for immediate comprehensive change. What is remarkable in his discourse from the mid-1930s is the absence of a rhetoric of crisis, of negative images about the threats faced by Romania. At that time, both politicians and the intelligentsia at large had begun to turn toward such negative arguments, both in Romania and abroad.[73] Moldovan, on the other hand, while staying on the same path of advocating a biopolitical state, spoke from a perspective that appeared more moderate and prudent than that of his contemporaries.

Direct references to ethnic purification—to biological threats from inside and out—were entirely absent from his discourse. The closest he came to hinting at negative measures was the phrase "keeping at a safe distance from all that could diminish its value or compromise its future." Even if such a phrase could be interpreted as a call for segregation from those deemed ethnically or biologically undesirable, it was certainly a very muted one, a far cry from the aggressive discourse of the Goga-Cuza National Christian Party or Crainic's ethnocratic state.

Over the next decade, Moldovan kept reiterating the need for the state to reorient its priorities toward protecting the biological capital, but he scaled down the magnitude of his programs from creating a total state to focusing on providing basic preventive medicine, eugenic education, and marriage and puericulture counseling for the rural populations:

The foundation of the ethnic state is, undoubtedly, its peasantry, rooted in the country's soil. . . . The nation [neamul] rules through this basis. . . . The destiny of the nation results from the interaction between this biological foundation and the environment.[74]

His ambivalence regarding Lamarckian notions of hereditary determinism also comes through in this statement. Moldovan, like many of his counterparts in Western Europe and the United States, was unwilling to dismiss the significance of the environment over the development of hereditary traits.[75] Throughout the 1930s he remained a faithful admirer of eugenic programs in Germany, whose efficiency he considered a worthy role model. However, in 1934 he consciously stressed the essential differences between Romanian eugenics and its German counterpart, in which racism played an important role:

> Racist doctrines place one's own race as the most distinguished one in the world; in this case the Nordic, blond, tall, doliocephalic race . . . distances itself from other races and inferior peoples. . . . Will this [concept] be able to revive the biological forces depleted through industrialization, urbanization, and advanced materialist civilization? . . . It is improper for us to interfere in establishing other nations' leading concepts about life. However, it is certain that this doctrine [racism] fits neither with our nature, nor with our national aspirations.[76]

The "natural" attributes of Romanians included modesty, Christian values, and the readiness to assimilate what was superior around them, while limiting their own aspirations to the nation's natural endowments. Moldovan's cautious discussion of racism in Germany may have reflected the uncertainties of a foreign observer early on in the course of the Third Reich's anti-Semitic policies. But this also situates Moldovan at a distance from the unabashed praise of the same theories in the writings of Cuza, Manoilescu, and Codreanu.

However, by 1943 Moldovan had had sufficient time and information to provide a more assertive discussion of German eugenics' anti-Semitism, while still unabashedly praising German efficiency. His comments in a public address on the "ethnic state" sound more like an apology for racist ideology than an attempt to distance Romanian eugenics even more clearly from its German counterpart: "Such an ideal [race purity] was needed in order to bring Germany out of its decay and the shameful state in which it had fallen because of a leadership accused of bowing down to foreign powers." Moldovan continued his exoneration of Germany by noting that race purity had, after all, not played a very important role "in education policies, in economics, eugenics, demography . . . , which were all shaped not so much by racial politics, as by an ethnic policy, or rather a policy of biology."[77]

Moldovan's comments seem implicitly to legitimize racism as a harmless aspect of eugenics. It is baffling, however, to see this cautious attitude in endorsing Germany's anti-Semitism when Romania had several laws on the books denying Jews citizenship rights on the basis of their blood—in other words, their racial identity. At the time that Moldovan wrote about the racist undercurrent in German eugenics, there were no powerful opponents of anti-Semitism in Romanian public life to take into consideration. His cautious evaluation of German racism was likely driven by an effort to prove that his own ideas stemmed from a sense of responsibility and regard for science rather than from desire for power. In the end, his public record was not one of anti-Semitism. Moldovan did not openly underwrite proposals for anti-Semitic eugenic measures. However, his lack of clarity on this issue at a time when the state drew some of its power from the ability to manipulate vague fears among ethnic Romanians shows Moldovan to be less than the responsible intellectual and technocratic leader he believed himself to be.

Moldovan was more consistent in his continued call for the need to place the laws of heredity and concern for the nation's biological capital at the foundation of organizing a modernized and competitive state structure. Formulations almost identical to his ideas in *Biopolitica* can be found in works published as late as 1947. In the midst of drastic political and social changes at the hands of the communist regime imposed by the Soviets, Moldovan wrote:

> At the basis of any form of government must stand the politics of life . . . and it must add greater value to the national biological patrimony.[78]

This quote illustrates, however, not only persisting ideas but also significant changes in Moldovan's vision and strategies. "Biopolitics" and "eugenics" no longer found their way into his texts, an absence made more conspicuous by the prevalence of these two terms in Moldovan's earlier writings. Instead, undoubtedly aware of the harsh criticism of eugenics after 1945 and of the already emerging identification of eugenics with Nazi ideology, he adapted his ideas to the times and switched to the euphemistic notion of the "politics of life," a rather transparent but significant mask for his persisting belief that eugenics was still a normative theory that needed to be incorporated into the process of creating the new postwar state. The fact that his ideas were not considered threatening by the emerging communist regime but rather a significant addition to the body of knowledge published during the early years of transition and consolidation (the voluminous *Tratat de medicină socială* went through three printings in 1947) bears witness to the widespread acceptance of eugenics as a valid and even authoritative theory and strategy for analyzing and constructing the body politic.

The Impact of *Biopolitica*

Moldovan's students and collaborators at the Institute of Hygiene in Cluj followed in his footsteps, sometimes reinforcing his arguments for constructing a total eugenic state, other times leading their own crusades for a comprehensive eugenic reform of state institutions and of the body politic. One of Moldovan's most loyal disciples, Iordache Făcăoaru, who started as an assistant at the institute, went on to more important positions, such as teaching a course in eugenics at the medical school in Cluj. Although this course focused primarily on the biological notions needed to understand genetic heredity, variation, and selection, Făcăoaru interspersed his description of these phenomena with evaluations of the impact such developments were having on the political arena in interwar Romania. In his final section of the course he dedicated a whole chapter to "Practical Eugenics," in which he rehearsed some of the points made by his mentor in the works discussed earlier. Făcăoaru did not offer an overview of the eugenic state but rather focused on precise measures for social selection in the process of achieving such a state. By mixing the description of objective biological phenomena with an evaluation of Romanian politics, Făcăoaru intentionally obliterated the line between critical thinking and normative ideology. He politicized biology at the same time that he reconstructed the issues of development and modernization at the level of biological heredity and evolution.

Among other measures, his course mentioned the need to control marriage and reproduction, implying that the state should create medical and legal institutions that would counsel and supervise eugenic marriages and would reward eugenic births while punishing dysgenic ones. One unstated implication was that the state should create special revenue funds for such programs, since matrimonial offices and puericulture clinics would be a long-term development at the national level. Făcăoaru also described what amounted to a comprehensive education reform in terms of creating schools suited to different levels of intelligence and different hereditary talents.[79]

From a eugenic perspective, this reform in education would contribute to wider changes—the state's active social selection in all areas of public and professional life.[80] This selection would be not only horizontal, across all occupations, but also vertical, at all levels of a profession, and ongoing throughout a person's lifetime. In order to implement such a vision state institutions would have to undergo comprehensive change. Făcăoaru did not expand on this issue, however, but rather incorporated Moldovan's already well-articulated view. He was more interested in seeing social roles and organization change according to eugenic prerogatives than in working out the numerous necessary steps to bring about long-term institutional change.

As he was more pragmatic than Moldovan, Făcăoaru spent more time on economic incentives, both positive and negative, to induce eugenic change. He picked up on his mentor's critique of the 1921 agrarian reform and pushed it further, singling out the dysgenic families who had wrongfully been given land at that time:

> The land redistribution was done without any regard for criteria of national interest. . . . [Politicians] should have taken into account the ethnic origins, foreign from our own, of a community of an inferior extra-European extraction, which for centuries had not allowed these people to rise to a standard of living comparable to that of European agriculture, a rise that could not be produced in the past few years. The preoccupation to assimilate Gypsies into our rural population is a crime and betrays the lack of any respect and concern for the biological integrity of our peasant masses, which constitute the life source of our nation.[81]

Făcăoaru's indictment identifies more clearly than Moldovan's writings the unwanted populations and renders a more imperative sense of crisis about the eugenic problems in Romania. This position reveals Făcăoaru's deeply racist view of the relationship between ethnic Romanians and other inhabitants of Romania.

His fears about this crisis and desire for immediate, drastic action translated into a step-by-step assertive call for the implementation of coercive eugenic measures. Făcăoaru developed a brief, yet all-encompassing system of control and punishment, which rendered a picture of the eugenic state much closer to a totalitarian police state than Moldovan's discourse did. Făcăoaru favored using violent means to induce change and endorsed such methods as legitimate state policies. Above all, in his opinion, sterilization was "one of the means unanimously indicated by eugenicists."[82] He did not mention the critiques of other Romanian eugenicists on this issue; he stood alone as a staunch supporter of forced sterilization.[83]

If this would be the primary way to weed out future dysgenic populations, other methods included the prenuptial health certificate, with the personal eugenic file (set up at birth, with any pertinent details about one's eugenic state added gradually) as a corollary. Other negative measures included segregation in work camps, the death penalty for repeat offenders of crimes that could be related to inferior heredity, limiting immigration to eugenically superior races, reforming naturalization policies (measures aimed primarily against Jews), controlling urbanization, limiting access to university education by ethnic quotas and hereditary vocation (another measure with strong anti-Semitic undertones), and limiting women's access to public life to assure the fulfillment of their eugenic roles as wives and mothers.[84] For Făcăoaru, who had completed his Ph.D. in anthropology at the University of Munich in 1929, the Third Reich stood out as the most successful role model in the implementation of what he held to be normative eugenic programs.

Făcăoaru went much further than any other Romanian eugenicists in endorsing coercive eugenics in a way that identifies his ideas more closely with those of Nazi eugenicists than with those of some of his counterparts in Romania. Făcăoaru was a firm believer in the importance of placing race inequality at the center of the eugenic state's organization and policies. He had no patience for appropriating such ideas to the particularities of the Romanian nation, as Moldovan had attempted. Făcăoaru was interested only in what would work efficiently in the interest of the nation's eugenic future and of the state. In 1937, at the Seventeenth International Congress of Anthropology and Archeology, held in Bucharest, he stood out among many other eugenicists as the staunchest supporter of state-controlled sterilization. Făcăoaru's proposal to vote that "sterilization practiced from a eugenic standpoint should be made obligatory and coercive" was voted down by a majority of participants.[85] Most of his colleagues, except for a lawyer with sympathies for the legionary movement, favored a voluntary approach to this measure.[86] Făcăoaru was firm, if in a minority, in sustaining his view that only state coercion could bring about eugenic amelioration.

In 1940 he was finally able to push his ideas more aggressively when he joined the legionary government. He identified his views on eugenics with the "Captain's testament"—the ideology of the Iron Guard—and thus with the fundamental priorities of the legionary state that was coming into being.[87] In fact, it is difficult to find explicit connections between Corneliu Zelea-Codreanu's writings and eugenics. This radical right-wing political leader constructed arguments about the need to regenerate Romanian politics and society on the basis of vaguely defined Orthodox cultural traditions and a mystical mission of the Romanian nation. His language was replete with apocalyptic Biblical images rather than with a discourse emphasizing the scientific laws of life.[88] Most importantly, where Codreanu accentuated the need for members to submit to Christian ideals of devotion and to follow the Captain with little regard for the means necessary to achieve salvation, eugenicists spoke of rational, objective truths that demanded a sense of responsibility and biological self-control. While at first glance eugenics may appear to have been a useful tool for this profoundly anti-Semitic ideology, in fact Codreanu's fascism spoke from a completely different paradigm than eugenics and did not make a conscious attempt to incorporate eugenic analyses in order to provide an "objective" argument for its anti-Semitism.

Făcăoaru constructed this connection only in 1940, tying the two ideologies together in a personal manner without explicit endorsement from most other Romanian eugenicists. (Traian Herseni was an exception.) Făcăoaru's writing reiterated his support for the restrictive measures discussed earlier, but in a more aggressive manner. Most of his calls remained without a great echo in policy making, especially with the onset of World War II. The legionaries' ousting from the Antonescu regime in January 1941 reordered the priorities of the state toward the war effort. Făcăoaru maintained his prominent position as an advisor on public health matters, but the new regime paid less attention to eugenics and consequently devoted less financial support to such matters, without which any plans for mandatory sterilization or prenuptial health certificates carried little weight. Nonetheless, the scathing critique of liberal democracy and praise of Germany as a role model that Făcăoaru delivered from the height of his academic pulpit does suggest that he may have had an important, if indirect, impact on legitimizing, if not promoting, the ideological orientation of the younger generation—his students—toward xenophobia, racism, and right-wing extremism.

Făcăoaru never mentioned Iuliu Moldovan by name in *Cuvântul*, the official paper of the legionary regime, although he made references to other collaborators from the Institute of Hygiene in Cluj, such as Aurel Voina. However, most of the eugenic ideas Făcăoaru publicized were in fact Moldovan's. Furthermore, while making his direct ties with the legionaries public, Făcăoaru continued to publish in Moldovan's *Buletin Eugenic și Biopolitic*, uncensored by his mentor. Făcăoaru respected Moldovan's authority and wisdom beyond any personal feelings. Moldovan may have been afraid of being singled out as an enemy of the legionaries just as Nicolae Iorga had been.[89] However, other prominent members of the intelligentsia had stood up to the legionaries' challenge and racism in general, among them Eugen Lovinescu, P. P. Negulescu, Garabet Ibrăileanu, and Constantin Rădulescu-Motru.[90] Furthermore, Făcăoaru would have probably deferred quietly to his mentor, whom he placed "among the canonized saints, . . . [or] as an icon in the golden list of the nation's great benefactors," rather than expose him to the Iron Guard.[91] Yet here again Moldovan fell short of his self-asserted leadership role in the eugenics movement in his relationship to Făcăoaru and his extremist views.

Other Eugenic Views of the State

Other proponents of eugenics unaffiliated with Moldovan also explored the potential of eugenics for reshaping state institutions and the meaning of citizenship. Ioan Manliu was another doctor interested in constructing a state based on eugenic priorities. He published a few works in the 1920s, before Moldovan's doctrine of biopolitics appeared. Yet, in spite of the similarities between Manliu's ideas and his own, Moldovan did not mention his name in his later works. As early as 1921, Manliu offered a normative picture of the need to implement eugenic programs in all areas of public life, in accordance with a new definition of the state:

> Race hygiene must lead to researching all the factors that can influence favorably or unfavorably the racial physical qualities and the mental faculties in the future generations. . . . Our state must carry out its eugenic actions in accordance with the axiom that any human being has the right to be born healthy, and thus, to inherit a healthy intelligence in a healthy body. Both are conditioned by a good hereditary mass and need a favorable environment.[92]

Thus, the state needed to mobilize all of its resources and institutions—the intelligentsia, public health programs, economic policies, science education, art, legislative and administrative institutions, communications, education, the church, the army, war, and international relations—in this direction.

His ideas with regard to the eugenic programs that needed urgent implementation were similar to Moldovan's. However, Manliu's analysis focused on the effect of such policies on the hereditary potential, health, and eugenic fulfillment of *individual* citizens rather than on the nation as an organic unit:

> The supreme goal of schools should be an education toward happiness. To achieve happiness, however, one needs harmoniously developed personalities. We must shape harmonious human beings. . . . By favoring the development of one's pre-formed center, one's talents, we will obtain . . . great artists, persons with a vast culture and morality, individuals of erudition, lovers of art and humanity.[93]

It seems that for Manliu eugenic progress represented the sum of all individuals' betterment in valorizing hereditary talents. This vision differed radically from Moldovan's notion of the individual as valuable only as a subunit of the greater organic being—the nation.

If Manliu aspired to emulate any outside model of eugenic policies and a healthy state organization, it was not the German or the French one, both of which he openly critiqued.[94] Rather, he looked upon the United States as a worthy example, from its individualist ideological foundations to its Fordist fixation with efficiency, its immigration and sterilization legislation, and its phenomenal great men—Carnegie and Rockefeller, most prominently.[95] In short, he urged: "Let's be Americans!"[96] As Manliu's ideas show, not all Romanians read eugenic theories the same way. They had different visions of what Romania should become and what tools and role models it should use in its quest for modernization.

Manliu's writings did not attain the popularity that *Biopolitica* enjoyed during the interwar period, perhaps because Manliu did not hold any official position of authority and could not use an institutional basis as a springboard for his ideas. It is more likely, however, that his embracing of what he identified as the individualism and entrepreneurial spirit of eugenicists in the United States did not find great echoes in Romanian society. By contrast, Moldovan's legalistic rhetoric, his language of moderation, and his nationalist overtones all struck a more familiar chord, especially among the other new Romanian professionals. However, Manliu continued to publish some articles in a Bucharest-based periodical that rose to greater significance in the 1930s, *Revista de Igienă Socială*. The soul of this publication was Banu, also the mentor of the largest eugenic group in the Regat.

Banu was a prolific writer and, in many ways, a more scholarly figure than Moldovan, whose syntheses read more like militant manifestoes and pamphlets than in-depth analyses of the theoretical foundations, history, and policy implications of eugenics.[97] Moldovan's only work that equals Banu's in depth and breadth is his last one, *Tratat de medicină socială* (1947). Banu offered on many occasions his view of how eugenics should ideally help shape all aspects of the state. Although he also proposed a solution that combined modernization with respect for tradition, his works placed emphasis on different issues than Moldovan's, reflecting his preference for questions pertaining to puericulture and social welfare rather than to education and a focus on the peasantry. Still, like Moldovan, Banu had a Mendelian outlook and used the same German scholarship and legislation as examples for Romanian eugenics.[98]

Banu first presented a synthesis of his ideas about the imperative need to place eugenics at the basis of reorganizing the state in a series of lectures that took place at the Carol II Foundation at the beginning of 1935. His first lecture framed the biology of the Romanian people as a "problem of social politics," based on the "right to have access to social welfare and public health."[99] He dutifully mentioned that such rights were inscribed in several European constitutions as a hint that they represented fundamental measures needed in Romania.

The principles he placed at the foundation of such a reorganization differed, however, from Moldovan's natural laws. These factors were "social solidarity, humanitarianism, egotism placed in the service of the community, and the economic equivalent of health capital," all in their positive and negative aspects.[100] Banu's understanding of the forces at play in fostering biological stability or imbalance was more closely related to environmental and social aspects of eugenics than Moldovan's vision, which emphasized the overwhelming importance of hereditary factors. Although a Mendelian, Banu did not separate hereditary factors from their social embodiment. For him, the value of "health capital" was essentially tied to the ways in which a particular state and society defined the rights of individual citizens vis-à-vis the collective whole. Banu was more consciously involved in defining principles for viable public policies than in formulating ideal, utopian visions of how the Romanian state and society should be structured according to the universal laws of life and heredity. He was critical in this regard of Moldovan's utopian ideas as reflected in the Public Health Law of 1930, seeing this law more as a reflection of Moldovan's readings of foreign scholarship on eugenics than of the Romanian realities.[101]

Banu's initial lectures defined the problems related to biological capital but offered little more than hints of a comprehensive program for the eugenic reorganization of the state. In November 1936, however, Banu held a conference at the Academy of Medicine in Bucharest, in which he outlined his "Principles of a Program for Race Hygiene," adopting this time the current German terminology for eugenics. He suggested that this program was an imperative measure by depicting an image of "brutal competition" among nations in an era of "racial egotism."[102] The state would become the central authority in controlling the implementation of this program: "The responsibility to pass all the measures needed to protect the family and the home belongs primarily to the State."[103] What was needed first and foremost was to centralize state institutions and mobilize private institutions behind state efforts.

Banu's program focused on "normalizing" the eugenic population at the same time that it would help identify and eliminate dysgenic elements. He seemed more keen than Moldovan on maintaining the possibility that individuals who seemed dysgenic could be reintegrated into the "normal" fold of society. With regard to repression of delinquents, Banu maintained that "repressive action must be replaced almost entirely by an action of social hygiene that would be translated into the creation of correctional institutions."[104]

Banu's focus on empiricism rather than theory was reflected in his methodology when outlining race hygiene problems. He often employed statistics about the quantitative and qualitative aspects of Romania's health, comparing it with the situation in other European nations. His use of graphics and numbers provided a more solid basis for his claims (in the scientific discourse of the day) than Moldovan's dramatic yet rather unsubstantiated depiction of the dysgenic situation in post–World War I Romania.[105] His style of rigorous academic writing was not yet the norm in Romanian publications and was certainly not followed by Moldovan very closely. In this respect, Banu seemed more concerned with integrating his personal work and the periodical under his editorship into European standards of academic scholarship. His greatest success was the publication in 1939 of a study that expanded on the ideas laid out in the 1936 article. The book appeared in Bucharest and Paris under the title *L'Hygiène de la race: Etude de biologie héréditaire et de normalisation de la race.*

Banu set up this study as a scholarly analysis, governed "strictly by a scientific spirit" rather than political considerations. To some extent, his study lived up to this claim. He offered, for instance, the arguments for and against sterilization, framing the discussion in terms of effectiveness and probability of proper implementation rather than in terms of identifying and isolating a deadly threat to the nation's health. He did, however, consider that "arguments of a biological [scientific] order justified" sterilization.[106]

Banu presented an apparently disengaged view regarding race theories, rejecting Chamberlain and Rosenberg as racists and unscientific but accepting a "somatic definition of race" as a collection of particular, stable (hereditary) biological characteristics, such as blood type.[107] Banu seemed interested in an "objective" definition of race in order to overcome any potential accusations that his work was racist. *L'Hygiène de la race* did not devote much attention to defining racial characteristics and their moral implications. This position seems disingenuous, however, if one takes into consideration Banu's choice to be part of the Goga-Cuza government in 1937.[108]

Banu focused more explicitly on class than on racial difference as an important site for defining eugenic state programs. Since modern society was already clearly stratified by class, he stressed the need to analyze the eugenic potential of each class and offer solutions suited to the problems posed by each group. For instance, rather than legalization of eugenic abortion across the board, Banu advocated a policy of stricter negative control over middle- and upper-class women's access to abortions, since they represented superior eugenic potential for the nation. On the other hand, since the working class seemed comprised of more dysgenics and had very limited resources to offer a healthy environment even for eugenically normal offspring, Banu considered the liberalization of working-class women's access to abortion as a positive eugenic measure. Overall, he favored focusing programs and resources on maintaining the great majority of average citizens within the limits of eugenic "normalcy" rather than concentrating too much effort and money on reducing dysgenic populations or increasing the numbers of the biological elite.[109] He seemed a true believer in the bell curve.

Yet Banu differed in one important regard from most British, American, and French proponents of eugenics concerned with the degeneracy of the working classes. Rather than placing all the burden for "normalizing" the biological capital of the working class on the shoulders of individual mothers, as most eugenicists in these countries advocated, he wanted instead to introduce some measures of *state* welfare to help improve environmental health factors, such as public hygiene, access to immunization, nutrition, working conditions, and economic power (e.g., control over the minimum wage). In this regard, Banu's view of the state's responsibilities went beyond Moldovan's basic and vague notions of guarding the interests and health of the nation to include some practical and direct forms of involvement; the state would serve not only as a powerful arbiter of health but also as a provider of better eugenic conditions for its citizens.

Banu was no socialist, however. He still wanted to limit these measures to ethnic Romanians, condemning intermarriage (*metissage*) as dysgenic. Still, he was more sensitive than Moldovan to environmental, practical factors that could influence the present and future health of the nation and to the social realities of an industrializing society and economy. Therefore, his programs appeared more reasonable in terms of practical measures as well as expectations. Banu made explicit references to the constraints imposed on his programs by the limited availability of state revenues. His solution, similar to Moldovan's intimations but more directly stated, was to cut down on administrative costs and programs for curative medicine and use such funds in programs of preventive medicine.[110] In the end Banu was much more focused on the attributes of the state, with less regard for individual citizens. He viewed the state as a monolithic entity that needed to control eugenic betterment, the subject of his concerns, while individuals remained simply objects of such policies:

> The problem which is imperative for the future protection of the healthy qualities of the population should concern the leadership of the State, which . . . should step in to ameliorate the organization and guidance of social reforms and, in the light of public health interest, initiate a vast program of propaganda for the hygiene education of the masses.[111]

It is unclear whether Banu's views of the state's responsibilities toward its mass of "normal" citizens had an impact in the post-1945 period. The new institutions of public health erected by the communist regime bore, however, greater resemblance to this vision of protecting the biological capital than to

Moldovan's biopolitics. Only in 1967, when abortion was made illegal for all practical purposes, did the communist state take a turn toward more restrictive measures of actively controlling the health of its citizens.

■ ■ ■

A LT H O U G H eugenicists claimed to be interested in the health of the nation and not in politics, some of their writings constituted attempts to reorganize the body politic and the very basis of the state according to eugenic priorities. This theory became the foundation for a political ideology that in some cases, as in Moldovan's *Biopolitica,* proved quite revolutionary. While emphasizing different aspects of the relationship between the state and its citizens, Moldovan, Făcăoaru, Manliu, and Banu all identified the state as the most powerful instrument in controlling social behavior, yet limited itself by universal hereditary laws. According to their writings (especially Moldovan's), the eugenic state emerged as a natural outgrowth of the nation's organic needs during the modern age.

Nonetheless, eugenicists also emphasized the need to build such a state on rational foundations. This view, blending organicism with rationalism and power with responsibility, represented a departure in Romanian political ideology during the interwar period. Other actors in the political arena strove to identify themselves either with an organic ideology, such as traditional nationalism or Nichifor Crainic's mysticist Gândirism, or with a rationalist Weltanschauung, to which liberals and, to some extent, Peasantists (especially Mihalache's wing) aspired. Eugenicists attempted to reconcile these two tendencies by rendering the conflict between them obsolete. Their solution was to shift the debate from competing philosophies of individuals' political rights to the body as a site for potential future strength, based on the unquestionable universal laws of nature.

Eugenicists in Romania may have admired their counterparts in Nazi Germany, but most of them were not ready to commit themselves to a wholehearted acceptance of fascist ideology and state organization for the sake of the eugenic future. Făcăoaru alone appeared fully committed to following the example of the Third Reich and made his sympathies explicit by accepting an official position in Romania's short-lived fascist government. There was much ambiguity on this continuum of political affiliations from the far right to the center, and it is difficult to locate each individual in a clearly defined niche. But the majority of Romanian eugenicists were reluctant to lobby aggressively on behalf of restrictive eugenic measures such as forced sterilization and did not condone the state's use of force as a legitimate tool for securing the future health of the nation. Throughout the interwar period, eugenicists overwhelmingly refrained from openly discussing the Jewish question from a racial or eugenic point of view. At the same time, not one supporter of eugenics criticized the 1940 anti-Semitic laws.

The eugenics discourse redrew the boundaries of the state, expanding its prerogatives and its powers within the community, especially at the expense of individuals' rights. However, eugenicists were also eager to expand the responsibilities of the state toward its members and especially toward the nation as an organic community. Their utopian totalistic vision contained some inconsistencies with regard to where responsibilities ended and coercive power began in the relationship between the state and its citizens. This vision also bore many similarities to the ideas espoused by the Italian fascists and many supporters of the Third Reich. Yet it was not a vision that embraced violence as a legitimate state tool or racism as a fundamental principle. It comes as little surprise then that the ambiguities that persisted in the biopolitical vision of a eugenic state were picked up and used differently by various eugenicists and politicians, from members of the National-Peasant Party to followers of Carol II and from proponents of the legionary movement to members of the post-1948 communist regime.

CHAPTER 4

NATURAL HIERARCHY

AND NATIONAL VALUES

The individual cannot be regarded as an isolated unit in the family or society, but as an element of the nation, an organism with its own biology and pathology. The present human material is not the final aim of our preoccupations; in it we have to see a laboratory for future generations, towards which we focus our attention with the same consideration as towards present human material.

Project for Public Health and Welfare Law, 1930

R O M A N I A N eugenicists focused not only on the state but also on reshaping social roles and hierarchies. The foundation of their vision was the concept that collective interests took precedence over individual ones. An individual's social role was, consequently, intrinsically related to the wider biosocial interests. The stress on the primacy of the community over the individual did not, however, represent an attempt to recover a long-lost form of social security. Rather, the principle of placing the interests of the community before those of the individual actor would lay the foundations of a new hierarchy of merit that, according to eugenicists, reflected better the needs and problems specific to the modern age. Such schemes in Romania were generally more comprehensive than those elaborated by eugenicists elsewhere.[1] Examining both the complexities and the inconsistencies of this vision of social hierarchy provides insight into how eugenic theories worked as vehicles for constructing and enforcing new social identities—individual and collective.

The new social hierarchy was premised upon the perceived biological strengths of the Romanian state and specifically ethnic Romanians. The overwhelmingly rural character of this population, the relatively small percentage of ethnic Romanians in entrepreneurship, the recent expansion of a constituency of Romanian professionals, and the emergence of mass politics with the granting of universal male suffrage after World War I were all important factors in shaping eugenicists' perceptions of the challenges ahead and the solutions needed to address them. At the top of the eugenic social structure stood a new "natural" elite, comprised of highly educated Romanian men of healthy biological stock who would also have to be apolitical and specialists in the technical professions. Along with them, peasants would also gain a privileged position in the new society, at the expense of many among the old elites, such as non-Romanian entrepreneurs, professional politicians, and members of the civil service, even if the latter two were Romanian males.

Eugenicists reworked gender relations as well, reinforcing traditional views of women's proper role in the home. However, the eugenic concept of this role added new, clear, legal dimensions to heretofore vague responsibilities for women and limitations on their behavior at home and in public. The question of urbanization and the dysgenic impact of the city on social relations and the nation's future health also preoccupied eugenicists. The issue of "authenticity" stood central to defining relations in the eugenic society as well. Only those proven to be "veritable" Romanians would constitute the backbone of the new hierarchy. This issue played into a broader strategy of creating a new sense of national identity along biological lines, rather than cultural-linguistic ones.

Like other normative social programs at the time, eugenics used concepts of the "other" to draw the boundaries of normalcy. What set eugenic strategies apart from ideas of other Romanians was eugenicists' insistence on the need to delineate the differences between the normal community and its outsiders by using scientific arguments about heredity. Although they made use of hard evidence to define the unwanted, eugenicists in Romania were much softer on the issue of separating the other from the healthy body of the nation than their counterparts in Germany. For Romanian eugenicists were willing to recognize the limited accuracy of their methods of singling out the outcasts and offered solutions for reintegrating some of them within the boundaries of normal society—from juvenile delinquents to prostitutes. Still, if they were soft on the issue of prostitution, they were much harder in defining and segregating the dysgenic other in terms of ethnicity.

Intellectuals and the Middle Class: Definitions and Debates

One of the main issues that gave rise to prolonged debates during the interwar period among the intelligentsia and political elite was the definition and significance of the middle class for the development of modern Romania. Along with some well-known texts, such as Ştefan Zeletin's *Burghezia română*, many other lesser-known essays and monographs focused on this issue, some in reaction to Zeletin's work.[2] More importantly, however, these texts illustrate the fundamental role that the question of the middle class in modern Romania played for all political theorists, economists, social scientists, and doctors who were trying to frame a successful path for Romania's future development.

One of the most important characteristics of all of these analyses (and one on which very few historians have focused) was their tendency to identify intellectuals as a separate group from the middle class. The difficulty of defining the social position of intellectuals has been reflected in many theoretical and historiographical analyses of class structure in the nineteenth and twentieth centuries.[3] Romanian intellectuals of the time, however, may be defined as part of the middle class if one considers the tastes, education, and especially the expectations of an elite and secure position in society that this group shared with the middle class. In this regard, the intelligentsia—be they writers, art critics, or members of academia—behaved similarly to the entrepreneurial middle class, from which they separated themselves self-consciously.[4]

As much as intellectuals and educated professionals had a tendency to analyze the middle class as somehow distanced from their own identity because of their source of wealth, the intelligentsia generally made social and political choices similar to those of the entrepreneurial bourgeoisie. They consumed many of the same cultural artifacts, from newspapers to highbrow literature. It was precisely because of these similarities that the intelligentsia attempted to construct a separate identity based on other attributes—especially moral and intellectual ones. Yet these were often unmarked. Eugenics seemed to offer clearer means for constructing and reinforcing the differences between the intelligentsia and the entrepreneurial middle class.

In eugenic analyses, the entrepreneurial middle class and the intellectual class appeared as two distinct groups, often at odds with each other, especially because of the important differences in the impact of their work and behavior on the health of the nation. The discussion that follows fleshes out these differences as they were perceived by eugenicists and measures their impact on conceptualizing social problems and solutions. There were constant tensions in eugenicists' attempts to separate intellectuals from entrepreneurs as distinct social categories in a eugenic hierarchy. In spite of these tensions, eugenicists persisted in their analysis, for at stake was the entire remapping of the social structure and social relations and, in particular, the authority that eugenicists themselves, as self-defined members of the intelligentsia, could claim in this new hierarchy.

As early as 1920 doctors interested in eugenics published essays that spoke of an "intellectual crisis" in Romania. In an essay entitled "The Laboratories and Intellectuals" (*Laboratoriile și intelectualii*) Gheorghe Marinescu, the future leader of the Royal Society for Eugenics, expressed deep worries about the impact of the war on the morality of Romanian society. The nouveaux-riches (i.e., the entrepreneurial bourgeoisie) of the war and political parties were, he declared, "paralyzing the good will of the youth who would like to dedicate themselves to laboratory research. . . ."[5] Intellectuals appeared to be victims of the new, materialistic, opportunistic wave that seemed to be sweeping through Romanian society, creating social conflict.

This analysis represented many among the entrepreneurial middle classes as agents of a dysgenic wave, because their enrichment did not seem to offer any positive effects for the larger whole but rather tore apart any sense of social solidarity. Furthermore, their values appeared to be divorced from any sense of moral responsibility toward the well-being of the nation. Instead, according to Marinescu, the entrepreneurial bourgeoisie was promoting the valuation of material goods and excesses over moderation, self-restraint, and dignity—moral values to which the new professionals laid claim.[6] Marinescu did not identify the entrepreneurial middle class along ethnic lines, nor did he associate their "dysgenic" role with their being nonethnic Romanians.

Marinescu's solution to this crisis was to call on intellectuals to organize themselves into associations or confederations (something like guilds) so that they might be enabled to play "the great role that their culture and moral value has bestowed upon them." Intellectuals would thus become the key force in ensuring "harmony among classes and a social equilibrium . . . between proletarians and capital. . . ."[7] Marinescu's analysis represents intellectuals and especially scientists as a group with inherent qualities that allowed them to stand above social conflicts and mediate them. Marinescu did not describe at any length what philosophy of social organization lay at the foundation of this view. He made his vision more explicit in later texts on eugenics. Nonetheless, this text already contains hints of a corporatist vision of social relations, according to which conflicts among different strata would be mediated from above by a technocratic intellectual elite.

This attitude of resentment vis-à-vis those who enriched themselves during the war was prevalent all over Europe in the early 1920s, especially among recently demobilized soldiers. In the case of Romania, this cry for change came especially from individuals who did not fight in the trenches but who believed they upheld superior values by virtue of their education and professional specialization. Marinescu and other proponents of this view sought in fact to build a niche for nouveaux intellectuals as the future leadership of the country. Elsewhere in Western Europe (e.g., in the veterans' groups in France and Germany) such cries more often attempted to *restore* positions lost during the war.

This view of the conflict between entrepreneurs and intellectuals found an echo among eugenicists whose writings explored other aspects of the intellectuals' roles in national, regional, and local communities. When *Buletin Eugenic și Biopolitic* and *Societatea de Mâine* first appeared, the two periodicals identified intellectuals—educated professionals—as the main audience for the information and specific eugenic analyses they offered regarding contemporary political and social problems. In 1925, Iuliu Hațiegan gave voice to this focus in an article about the new branch of Astra, the Medical and Biopolitical Section. This organization, he stated, would be dedicated to "preparing the groundwork among intellectuals [through] monthly publications, . . . a portable library . . . and a health calendar."[8] At the same time, these analyses identified the current economic and social problems with the irresponsible abuses of the entrepreneurial middle classes and professional politicians.

The view that intellectuals in particular held the key to educating the wider public about eugenic norms and values was particularly strong among eugenicists in Transylvania—Moldovan's disciples. The social, political, and cultural pre-1918 heritage of this region differed greatly from that of the Romanian Kingdom, and many intellectuals in Transylvania consciously emphasized the significance of these differences for the present and future fate of their region. One of the most important issues, as Ioachim Crăciun emphasized in an article written in 1939, was the recent creation of a Romanian intelligentsia, comprised predominantly of village priests and teachers, with few professionals and public officials among their ranks.[9] Even the highest dignitaries in the social and political hierarchy were but a step away from their rural origins, Moldovan being an example in point. Intellectuals appeared, thus, as the ideal group to mediate between eugenic priorities of the nation and the rural masses, with whom they had close contact and over whom they exerted a great deal of influence at the local informal level. The role played by teachers and priests in the pre-1918 period as powerful agents for educating and mobilizing peasants behind nationalist ideas offered solid guarantees to proponents of eugenics that local intellectuals would become the lifeline of the new order at the grassroots level.

At the same time, eugenicists in Moldovan's circle seemed rather ambivalent about the role of the middle classes in this new order. Their attitude was fueled by the history and present situation of most entrepreneurs, liberal professionals, and government employees in Transylvania. Before 1918 the business and bureaucratic strata had been overwhelmingly non-Romanian, because of long-standing traditions and more recent laws (post-1867) that made it especially difficult for ethnic Romanians to acquire official positions of power in the Austro-Hungarian Empire. After 1918, the Romanian state made efforts to compensate for what ethnic Romanians viewed as a gross injustice by systematically replacing ethnic Hungarians in government positions with Romanians.[10] This process developed slowly for lack of adequately educated and trained personnel. In fact, eugenicists believed the state proceeded dangerously slowly and repeatedly warned against the problems posed by this situation.

Eugenicists feared that a non-Romanian bureaucracy would not have the interests of the nation's health at heart and would not act as responsible overseers of eugenic norms. They went so far as to claim that these non-Romanian bureaucrats posed a direct dysgenic threat because they tended to marry Romanian women, whose national identity they suppressed, so that the offspring of such families would think of themselves and act as Hungarians or Germans rather than as Romanians. Thus, in their eyes, the social milieu that ideally should present the best eugenic potential proved in fact to be overwhelmingly dysgenic. Eugenicists suggested stricter control over state employees' marital choices and various positive and negative incentives to influence their reproductive decisions.[11]

This argument appealed to the Romanian intelligentsia in Transylvania because it promised them greater social status and security at the price of individual liberty, a reasonable exchange in their eyes. By asking members of the intelligentsia to give up their freedom to choose a non-Romanian wife in exchange for greater public responsibility and power, eugenicists did not in fact ask a great sacrifice of educated Romanians, for there was no long-standing tradition of intermarriage between Romanian men and Hungarian women. Furthermore, eugenicists provided scientific and "objective" tools with which many professionals could reevaluate their self-identity and prove that they were not second-class citizens, behind their fellow Hungarians. On the contrary, eugenics promised to validate the qualities of the Romanian middle classes through ethnic separation.

Entrepreneurs and liberal professionals among the Transylvanian middle classes were also overwhelmingly non-Romanian. Eugenicists could do very little to control the behavior of these individuals directly, since they had independent means of income, unlike government employees. Consequently, they distrusted these middle classes and tended to emphasize the dysgenic, threatening aspects of their behavior rather than attempt to rally their support behind eugenic ideas. When Moldovan's eugenicists attempted to mobilize Romanian entrepreneurs and professionals, they spoke to fellow countrymen rather than to businessmen and members of a professional group. By doing so, they avoided confronting an important site of anxiety in Romanian society and possibly resolving some of the tensions that developed between the intelligentsia and the middle classes during the interwar period. This accounts for some of the weakness of the eugenics movement in Romania, particularly with regard to securing more substantial funding. The counterexample of the United States, for instance, shows that the entrepreneurial classes could become great allies of eugenics, as the Rockefellers did in the early twentieth century. Try as they might, Romanian eugenicists proved unable to secure the interest of wealthy businessmen in their projects and had to rely almost exclusively on the state and on foreign aid from the Rockefeller Foundation.[12]

Eugenicists in Bucharest did not espouse the same fears regarding the inauthentic and hence dysgenic identity of the middle classes. Most bureaucrats and many entrepreneurs and professionals in Bucharest were Romanian. The largest group of non-Romanians among the middle class were Jews, about whom eugenicists did not express overt apprehension during the 1920s and early 1930s. Rather, a different fear dominated these eugenic analyses of the middle class—the irresponsible attitude of bourgeois families in making reproductive choices.

Here women appeared as the dysgenic agents. Eugenicists described in minute detail wealthy women's corrupt, immoral lifestyles, as such women organized their existence around aesthetic principles—keeping their bodies young and shapely, being seen in all of the fashionable places in town—rather than on the basis of eugenic priorities.[13] It seemed of no consequence to eugenicists that these women had very little legal control over the wealth of their families and that it may have been their spouses, in fact, who encouraged these women or even demanded that they remain "pretty things" on the arms of their husbands.

The birthrate decline among the middle classes was, as eugenicists pointed out, the result of a self-conscious decision facilitated by the rise in education among these women.[14] It was also greatly influenced by the desire of their husbands to preserve the wealth of the family intact. If their wives produced a healthy (male) heir, these bourgeois men were as reluctant as their spouses to have more offspring. Eugenicists, however, chose to point an angry finger specifically at women, describing them as dysgenic, irresponsible, or even criminal.

Most of these accusations indicate a desire to control middle-class women's reproductive decisions in order to tap into the eugenic potential of this class, which seemed to waste itself away at the expense of the future health of the nation. This was a familiar argument not only among eugenicists but also other reform groups in Western Europe and the United States since the middle of the nineteenth century, when the birthrate among the middle classes had begun to decrease steadily as the birthrate among the working classes remained relatively high. One important strand in the discourse about limiting access to birth control focused on both of these trends, attempting to control women's access to birth control according to the class-based definition of their biological worth.[15] In Romania, such arguments emerged only after World War I, and eugenicists played a leading role in constructing the meaning of gender roles based on both class and biological differences.

The Attributes of the New Eugenic Elite

Having focused on the intelligentsia as their army of "missionaries," eugenicists proceeded next to define the attributes this group needed in order to rise to the top as Romania's natural elite. The basic notion of the elite among Romanian eugenicists was molded by Galton's analysis of genius a half century earlier.[16] They believed that a selection of individuals with inborn superior qualities should be the basis for creating a eugenic elite. This selection would take into account both general health (lack of hereditary pathologies) and intellectual as well as moral characteristics. As Galton had a few generations before them, eugenicists in Romania believed that vocations were largely hereditary, as were special talents. The new elite would be selected from among the members of the human pool with superior hereditary talents and according to their special inborn attributes. Subsequently, they would have to undergo a special education and training commensurate with their future responsibilities in the eugenic state.

The most important question here is what particular human pool had the most promising eugenic potential. Opinions were mixed in terms of specific emphasis, but eugenicists agreed on a few basic issues: the members of this elite would have to be highly educated men specializing in particular fields of technical knowledge, from medicine to industrial hygiene and from pedagogy to nutrition analysis. Although they did not overtly state ethnicity as a criterion for selection, most eugenicists took this aspect for granted, for when faced with the alternative of non-Romanians in positions of authority, they reacted with alarm. This emphasis on ethnic purity went undisputed among the educated audiences who read and responded to eugenic articles in *Transilvania* or *Societatea de Mâine.* This public did not seem to make the connection between the eugenicists' ethnocentric aim and the violation of some basic principles of the current constitution, such as equal rights for all Romanian citizens regardless of ethnicity. The reason for this may rest in the memory of the frustration Romanian professionals in Transylvania had experienced under the Dualist regime. In addition, the eugenicists' moderate rationalist rhetoric appealed to the nationalist sensitivities of the professional middle classes more than the bombastic impassioned speeches about historical precedence and unjust past suffering that dominated the language of other nationalist groups, such as Nicolae Iorga's Nationalist Democratic Party.[17]

Thus far, the basis for selecting the new eugenic elite seemed to differ very little from the views espoused by most Romanian intellectuals and politicians at the time. The novelty rested in eugenicists' emphasis on the need to remove professional politicians from positions of authority, as these individuals presented no guarantees in terms of responsibility toward the future health of the nation. Eugenicists depicted politicians as inescapably corrupted by the party system, which fostered loyalty and a sense of responsibility only toward one's party members and constituency, rather than toward the greater whole.[18]

This was a veiled attack against the National Liberal Party in particular, because it had controlled the political process almost continuously during the 1920s and, in the eyes of the eugenicists, had made a mockery out of the notion of democratic elections or responsibility toward the common good. The political arena seemed dominated by the struggle for personal power rather than high ideals and well-planned programs for social action. Within this system of "politicianism" (*politicianismul*), appointments for all official positions changed with each regime. Thus, the critique went, there was no continuity in programs, and even individuals who had not been initially prone to corruption ended up behaving opportunistically, since the security of their positions was dictated by party loyalty rather than by fulfilling job responsibilities. Clientelism was replacing what in the eugenicists' view should have been a network of responsible nonpartisan technocrats.[19]

Eugenicists believed this endemic problem stemmed not only from the political and bureaucratic structure but also from the validation of the politician as an individual of high social standing in the public opinion. Thus, they went to great lengths in explaining the essentially dysgenic impact of such individuals on the whole nation and offered as an alternative an elite of biologically superior technicians. In the eugenicists' view, by virtue of their professional choices these new technocrats—doctors, anthropologists, engineers, and so on—had a closer allegiance to objective scientific truth and the well-being of the nation than any political ideologue could.

Therefore, the eugenicists' vision of natural social hierarchy was shaped not only by eugenic theories but also by the particular realities of post-1918 Romania. By using these theories of heredity, they offered a critique of political life in Romania unlike those of their contemporaries.[20] Their synthesis also differed from those of most eugenicists abroad in the connections they forged between heredity and politics and in their complete indictment of parliamentary politics.

In the United States and Britain, for instance, most eugenicists (with the exception of such individuals as anarchist Emma Goldman) leveled criticism regarding political institutions against particular parties of politicians, not against the entire system. Even in Germany, most supporters of the eugenics movement did not get on the antiparliamentary bandwagon until after the Nazi takeover.[21] The Romanians' adamant rejection of politicians as a socially respected group was born out of popular opinion and experiences particular to their country's political arena before World War I.

Another significant aspect of this critique was the recasting of moral and ethical questions in a biologizing discourse. Eugenicists did not simply appeal to their audience's old sense of morality but rather wanted to reconstruct the basis of this morality, for they defined "corruption" in terms of the harmful effects of certain actions on the biological well-being of the nation's future.[22] Eugenic rhetoric reworked notions of right and wrong and good and evil from their religious foundations into a highly secular and presumably scientific moral order, where health meant virtue and illness was evil. The new technocrats would replace the old guardians, the clergy, as the avant-garde of this new order. In eugenicists' eyes, these technical specialists possessed the necessary skills to identify the subtle yet important differences between long- and short-term ailments and their effects on the nation and could dispassionately administer the appropriate corrective measures.

This concept was new and offered a modernist alternative to both the conservative-aristocratic and the liberal views of elites and the basis of their authority. The essential difference between the traditional hereditary elites and those proposed by Romanian eugenicists was the rationalist criteria for selection, which appealed to notions of natural law and science rather than to the legally and religiously sanctioned tradition of privilege. Moldovan and his followers did not desire to return to a paternalist, hereditary aristocracy of blood, as conservatives during the preceding century had understood this notion. Rather, they saw this new technical elite as a dynamic force, whose powerful position rested not only on hereditary privilege (inborn superior qualities) but also on education and the demonstrated ability to act responsibly and impartially toward the future health of the nation. By the same token, according to eugenicists, the liberal view of establishing social status solely on the basis of individual achievement was also anachronistic in the post-1918 context. The time for catering to individual priorities at the expense of collective ones had passed, as had the process of selecting leaders on the basis of their material success rather than their hereditary qualities and technical expertise.[23]

One of the most remarkable aspects of this claim to a science-based social selection was the incongruity between these secular values and eugenicists' attempts to rally the support of the clergy behind them. Ioan Agârbiceanu, an outstanding writer and priest, published a number of articles on this issue. His loyalties were clearly behind the eugenics movement. Yet he did not see an inherent conflict between his own religious convictions and a theory that identified truth and moral values with the objective laws of nature:

> Life, ... reduced to the powers of traditions and of the inherited spiritual forces, can no longer suffice for maintaining our national patrimony and is even less adequate for ensuring the growth and strengthening of [this patrimony]. We must transform this static national energy into a dynamic, creative force.[24]

At another point he added more emphatically: "Our work must proceed according to scientific criteria."[25]

Although aware of the inherent tensions in their position vis-à-vis the church, many eugenicists chose not to discuss the incompatibility between the secular values they promoted and the older religious values of the population they addressed. Already in 1926 Moldovan had pointed out the dysgenic potential of the church in *Biopolitica*. Later, however, he chose to pass over this issue in silence, since it did not serve more pragmatic goals, such as mobilizing wider support for eugenic programs and teachings among village priests. Educating the rural masses about the need to lead healthy lives and make eugenically responsible reproductive choices appeared to Moldovan as a goal that did not violate Christian beliefs. He was successful in enlisting the support of a number of accomplished clergymen, who wrote on many occasions about the importance of the priest as a model and guiding force for greater health and eugenic awareness in the countryside. However, the unresolved tension between the claims of hereditary biology and those of Christianity may point to one of the reasons why eugenics did not have a greater echo at the grassroots level, where Orthodox and Uniate Christianity and not science was still the greatest pillar of popular faith and morality among ethnic Romanians.

Challenges to the Intelligentsia as a Hereditary Elite

By the mid-1930s, the intelligentsia had apparently become a problem in Romania. Numerous analyses discussed the issue of "university overpopulation" or, conversely, "intellectual unemployment." In a work focusing on this latter issue, Banu asserted that "as the rate of intellectual unemployment intensifies, the groundwork is laid for future social instability, the destruction of the family and propagation of extremist movements."[26] His concerns were most likely fueled by the growing adherence of university students and even faculty to the legionary movement. Banu viewed this situation as a problem, because it fostered "a particular psychology of intellectual workers without a stable situation, a class dominated by its instinct for revolt and revenge."[27] His solution was a reevaluation of the educational process that would gear secondary education toward more practical specialization rather than theoretical studies. He wanted to see a more rigorous professional selection, based on national eugenic prerogatives and a movement of young intellectuals back to rural areas, which needed an educated, responsible leadership. According to Banu, these measures were a responsibility of the state, since the class of unemployed intellectuals was a direct product of the democratization of the education system.[28]

It is remarkable that Banu identified this spirit of revolt and intolerance as a threat to Romania's interests. His analysis is a telling example of how eugenicists saw themselves as proponents of a moderate, orderly solution, distancing their critique of liberalism and parliamentary pluralism from its potential extremist interpretation by their audience. Although these negative analyses of democracy helped legitimize extremist, violent solutions to Romania's problems, many members of the educated elite still took refuge in the scientific, rational basis of these eugenic ideas as progressive and did not investigate the implications of these ideas beyond their immediate, explicit intentions.

Other proponents of eugenics did not see the growing number of intellectuals as a potential problem. For instance, Sabin Manuilă focused on the disparity between the great numbers of educated individuals in the liberal arts and the small numbers of technical specialists, be they engineers, chemists, or doctors. Furthermore, state institutions had been following a policy of hiring personnel with experience on the job rather than hiring better-educated and hence, in his view, better-qualified individuals. Manuilă, as Moldovan and

Banu had done previously, argued on behalf of a more effective professional selection process, so that the intelligentsia could play the leadership role appropriate to their education and moral integrity.[29] Analyses such as Manuilă's focused on the obligations of the state toward a better selection and use of human capital. This emphasis on the need to place responsibilities toward and control of this new elite in the hands of the government was an outgrowth of the eugenic view of the state as the natural protector of the nation's present and future health.

Other thinkers approached the issue of intellectual unemployment in a wholly different way, by focusing on the free will of these individuals to pursue a university education. *Destinul omenirii,* a well-known analysis written by the prominent philosopher P. P. Negulescu, exposed the problem of intellectual unemployment as a false one. The state had not tempted individuals to enroll in the university with false promises of secure, well-paid jobs in various government institutions. Rather, with the opening of the public sphere to the masses, educational "institutions had simply responded to the growing demands of those who wanted to make use of these new opportunities."[30] The expectations of these new intellectuals had far surpassed the limited resources of a young state like Romania to make use of this capital. However, Negulescu believed these intellectuals had to bear the responsibility for becoming integrated in society and finding a livelihood and fulfillment for their aspirations. The state offered opportunities, but it did not make—nor should it have made—any promises about every intellectual's financial security.

Negulescu's liberal critique emphasized the need to assume greater individual responsibility in an entirely different way than his eugenic contemporaries. He focused on each individual's control over his or her role in society and destiny, with the state as a basic frame for regulating interactions among autonomous individuals. In his view, intellectuals did not possess inherent responsibilities and privileges that were greater than those of other individuals. Their rise to positions of power depended on personal effort and was guaranteed only by superior performance in a particular position.

His eugenic counterparts, however, identified individual responsibility with biological limits, powers, and obligations toward the greater whole. Selection was to be made from the top down—individuals would be chosen and advanced according to the greater needs of the nation rather than through individual effort and ambition. By the end of the interwar period, it seemed that this latter view had come to prevail over Negulescu's with the founding of Carol II's Front for National Renaissance.

Peasants and the *Élan Vital*

Another important aspect of the eugenic social hierarchy concerned the peasantry. Although the eugenic elite would most likely come from among the educated intelligentsia, whose privileged social position proved their eugenic biological potential and nurturing qualities, the rural population appeared as the healthiest source, with the greatest potential, for rejuvenating this elite. All eugenicists seemed in agreement about their view of the village as "the great reservoir that feeds and refreshes the constructive energies of our country. . . ."[31] Peasants represented an untapped human resource, a repository of tradition and the key to the purity of the Romanian nation. Eugenicists used some basic facts about the past of the Romanian population in Transylvania to argue on behalf of this view. It was a widely accepted fact that, by the force of events or conscious choice, the peasantry had not intermarried with other ethnic groups in significant numbers in the past.[32]

This view was prevalent especially among eugenicists in Transylvania, while some prominent representatives of the Bucharest school, such as Banu, also focused on the rural underclasses. His study of the general health of the Romanian people concluded that the peasants demanded the most attention because of their untapped potential and vulnerability.[33] Thus, eugenicists managed to reconstruct what most historians had defined as the burden of an oppressed past into a biological treasure and a promise for future development. Their ideas about the peasantry attempted to construct a sense not only of pride but also of greater responsibility among the new elite.

This view appears idealistic at best and naive at worst. Depicting the peasant as an innocent participant in history or as a source of pure vitality was very much in vogue at the time, as writers from Nicolae Iorga to Nichifor Crainic depicted village life as a Paradise Lost.[34] Many eugenicists may have been touched by these idyllic descriptions of the village because of nostalgia, as most of them had been born, if not raised, in a rural setting. Moldovan, for instance, was the son of a village priest, while Petre Râmneanțu came from a peasant family in Gaiu Mare, a village in the Banat. Their urban experiences—from Vienna to

Bucharest and Cluj—were very likely shaped by the memories of their early years in a rural setting, as Moldovan's and Râmneanțu's autobiographical writings amply illustrate.[35]

However, eugenicists integrated this nostalgic view of the peasantry into a more aggressive, action-oriented outlook than did other contemporaries, such as Nichifor Crainic. They did not wish to keep these peasant energies intact, but sought instead to mobilize them in order to turn peasants into a real, rather than potential, asset for the nation's health. It seemed to them imperative to focus eugenic programs on the peasantry, not only to allow the potential of this population to materialize but also to counteract both the apparent tendency to migrate to the city and the growing dysgenic factors in the village—from alcoholism to tuberculosis and syphilis.

Another important eugenic concern had to do with the influx of corrupt professional politicians into the village, making false promises to peasants and taking advantage of the lack of political education among this newly enfranchised constituency. Many educated Romanians expressed fears about the uneducated use and abuse of political rights. This attitude betrayed a sense of ambivalence about the ability of peasants to participate in the political arena with the same rights as highly educated Romanians. At the same time, this mass of new voters represented a potential constituency for all parties. In this race to win over peasants, eugenicists struck a different chord than others did. In exchange for mobilization behind eugenic priorities, they offered peasants programs, from immunization programs to public hygiene measures, that claimed to directly improve their livelihood at the local level.[36]

Upon closer scrutiny, the eugenicists' view of the peasantry seems ambivalent at best. Eugenicists were interested in educating peasants about their eugenic responsibilities, most prominently through the Peasant Schools created by Astra in the early 1930s and, later, the Social Service founded by Dimitrie Gusti in 1936. However, eugenicists viewed education as potentially dangerous, for it often presented innocent peasant children with idealized tempting images of the city, corrupting them.[37] Thus, the peasantry would have to be held under control at the same time that it would be mobilized for the greater good. This issue of activating the power of the masses and at the same time holding it in check was the great dilemma of all populist parties during the interwar period. The eugenics movement tackled this problem by proposing programs and a social structure that placed technical specialists—a natural elite—in charge of reconciling these opposing goals. Peasants, as the "natural reservoir of biological vitality," would remain just that—a source for eugenic selection from above and the recipients of eugenic programs.

Another aspect of eugenic analyses of village life concerned the recent trend toward urbanization. Overall, eugenicists seemed quite alarmed about this phenomenon as a dysgenic process, since it tended to corrupt peasant values and the general health of the peasant population. The city offered peasant migrants the prospect of a life of toil in unhealthy conditions and more exposure to social dysgenic illnesses, such as venereal disease, alcoholism, and tuberculosis. Eugenics movements in Western Europe already emphasized that work in the urban industrial setting broke down healthy families into dysfunctional ones, endangering the health of future generations. This grim analysis did not point toward any viable solution, save a forceful prohibition against migration to cities. Such a policy was unrealistic because one could not hope to control individual behavior so closely and extensively.[38] Furthermore, most eugenicists recognized the forces of industrialization and some of its effects as inevitable. Therefore, they looked upon this problem pragmatically and were willing to concern themselves with urbanization as an inevitable phenomenon.

One of the most outspoken individuals on this issue was Sabin Manuilă, who in 1929 produced a work entitled *The Demographic Evolution of Cities and the Ethnic Minorities in Transylvania* (*Evoluţia demografică a oraşelor şi minorităţile etnice din Transilvania*). Here he identified the urban population as "the element of progress, of production"—as the embodiment of modernist ideas.[39] Urban dwellers represented the pinnacle of the nation's creative potential, its "source of human enrichment and, thus, the future of the nation."[40] Having depicted the positive aspects of urbanization, however, Manuilă turned to a more grim discussion of the dysgenic effects of city life, focusing on the decreasing birthrate among the urban upper classes and, in Transylvania, on the danger of having an overwhelmingly non-Romanian urban population. To ignore such a danger meant turning one's back on a vital problem of national interest.

His solution to this problem was to "create a scientific basis for a complete system" that would educate rural populations about their eugenic responsibilities at the same time that it would harness the positive energies of urban dwellers.[41] To a great extent, Manuilă encouraged urbanization in Transylvania as a "progressive" measure to bring some ethnic "balance" to the overwhelmingly non-Romanian population of Transylvanian cities, a long-standing phenomenon. Whether motivated by concerns about ethnic purity or economic progress, eugenicists did acknowledge the need to accept urbanization as an important phenomenon and to address it not only as a dysgenic aspect of modern life but also as an inevitable effect of modernization. Controlling this phenomenon, rather than eliminating it, became the focus of the eugenic attitude toward urbanization.

The Family and Gender Roles: Women as Dysgenic Factors

One topic preoccupied eugenicists more than any other aspect of social relations in the modern age—the family. In a sense, the relationships between husband and wife, parents and children, were at the heart of eugenic visions of social and political relations within the nation and state. The greatest worry among eugenicists was the imminent break-up of the traditional family unit as a result of the negative effects of modernization and industrialization—from growing individualism to rampant postwar materialism. The change in the economic system brought about by industrialization pushed both parents out of the house, rendering the idea of home obsolete.[42] Furthermore, urbanization pushed peasants into the cities, causing them to abandon their family ties and traditions. Since eugenicists looked at the family rather than the individual as the basic social unit, this change appeared disastrous to them, as the very fabric of society seemed to be unraveling before their eyes. How could the health of future generations be guaranteed if one lost the very building blocks of social continuity?

If the family was a victim of the general process of modernization, eugenicists did not condemn this *whole* process as a threat to the nation's health. Rather, they singled out specific enemies. Their favorite scapegoats were feminists and, in general, women who had seized the opportunities presented by modernization in order to evade their motherly eugenic responsibilities in the home.[43] At fault were not industrialization, economic insecurity, and the market for cheap, unskilled labor that pushed women into the workforce, but rather women's ambitions or their shortsighted vision of current economic problems. Instead of looking for solutions that would first and foremost ensure the health of their families and especially of their offspring, women responded to economic needs by taking up employment outside of the household. Practically no eugenic analysis I have come across even mentions the issue of men abandoning their families or, in general, the active role played by men in creating illegitimate and unstable couples. It seems that eugenicists identified women so closely with domestic responsibilities and men so closely with public ones that they could not see how the two spheres permanently overlapped.

This view of women as irresponsible actors in the household seemed modeled after a particular group of women with whom eugenicists often came in contact—middle-class educated women with feminist leanings.[44] Consequently, their critiques and their solutions for redressing the dysgenic effects of women's economic, social, and political emancipation addressed a very specific and restricted stratum of society. Furthermore, those writing the critiques lived themselves in a middle-class setting and harbored values specific to their status. In particular, the eugenicists' emphasis on the separation of the public and private spheres on a gendered basis grew out of their middle-class mentality and their exposure to middle-class culture in Romania or abroad.[45]

The eugenicists' vociferous antifeminist critiques seem somewhat out of place in the Romanian context. In Western Europe and the United States, where women had experienced a veritable awakening over the previous few decades in both economic and political life and posed an apparent threat to the established social order and gender roles, the negative attitude of eugenicists toward women's groups was part of the discourse of anxiety that dominated public life. In Romania, however, feminist forces were just coming alive since the turn of the century and especially after the war.[46] The eugenicists' aggressive critiques of feminism can be better understood not as reactions to a perceived crisis but through the prism of their emphasis on "preventive" measures. In particular, as eugenicists were very interested in stimulating women's participation in the new biopolitical order, they felt compelled to point out time and again the potential for women's misappropriation of their new empowered status. This particular strategy also separates the Romanian case from the British and American ones.[47]

As was the case with many reform movements in Western Europe and the United States, the solutions put forth by Romanian eugenicists with regard to the family and women's role in society did not necessarily correspond to social realities beyond the middle strata.[48] This is illustrated by eugenicists' view of peasant families. In particular, since agricultural techniques and tools had not yet become modernized in most areas, the economic system in the countryside was still largely based on full household participation in various aspects of agricultural production. Men and women, parents and children still labored—sometimes side by side, other times in different areas, but always closely integrated in an economic system based on the family wage. Therefore, when eugenicists called on peasant women to spend more time in the home, tending to household chores and raising healthy babies but did not offer any solutions for the obvious gaps that would occur in the production process, they were not being merely idealistic.[49] Rather, they were revealing an unrealistic, class-biased view of a problem that was more complex than eugenicists themselves were willing to concede and that they would only worsen by offering inadequate solutions.

If eugenicists wanted to secure a clearer division between the public sphere, which would be controlled by men, and the private sphere, which would become mainly women's responsibility, they also transformed the meaning of these two categories by politicizing the private sphere. Before World War I, both legislation and cultural practices had reinforced the separation of these two arenas. A civil code that copied most of the letter and spirit of the 1804 Napoleonic Code had been in place in Romania since 1866. Earlier legislation —the Caragea and Calimachi Codes, in particular—had defined family roles (spousal and parenting) in more gender-inclusive language and in a less rigid manner than the civil code adopted under the first Constitution of Romania (1866).[50] Yet both supporters and critics of this civil legislation did not actively discuss it in terms of its political implications, especially as pertaining to women's role in public life, but focused instead exclusively on the family.

Eugenicists wanted to subject this space to public surveillance. One might have sought intimacy in the home, but it was here that developments crucial to the future of the nation occurred, from choosing a mate to having children and raising them. Therefore, it seemed only rational to eugenicists to place the private sphere under a spotlight and seek to control private actions that had eugenic consequences. This proved to be one of the long-lasting legacies of eugenics in Romania, for other movements (most prominently, the right-wing extremists) also picked up on the issue of politicizing the private sphere. It was the communist regime that finally succeeded in placing all aspects of private life under public surveillance, through measures that came close to those advocated by eugenicists, such as individual genealogical files, forced divorces, and the criminalization of abortion.

This politicization of the private sphere seems to imply greater control over women's lives and, hence, more limitations over their social roles and author-ity. However, this was not necessarily the case, at least initially. Like women elsewhere (e.g., Margaret Sanger), some Romanian leaders of women's organi-zations—such as Maria Baiulescu, a leader in the National Society for Roman-ian Orthodox Women—embraced eugenic definitions of women's social roles as possible means for gaining greater social status, more power, and more recognition of their roles as mothers and wives than Romanian women had previously enjoyed.

In early eugenic writings women appear as the moral guardians of the na-tion's future, much like the "republican motherhood" model in Revolutionary America and France.[51] Eugenicists depicted this role not only as natural but also as the greatest fulfillment of a woman's feminine qualities—as a source of moral authority and one of the most important contributions to the future health of the nation:

> The family represents the hereditary tree on which the entire structure of the State rests; and the strength of the family rests in women's hands, for if this foundation were to crumble, it would bring with it the collapse of moral order and faith, and even the existence of a nation. The mother of this generation will have to be respon-sible and watch over her obligations with the conviction she is essentially needed, in order to bring tradition to life in the vulnerable souls of her sons.[52]

This passionate speech also illustrates the limits of women's empowerment. It essentializes women's social roles by using the singular in describing all Romanian women. In addition, when defining moral responsibility for future generations, it focuses exclusively on the sons of these moral guardians, im-plicitly excluding potential responsibilities regarding educating women toward more active public roles.

However, when women shifted their focus from asking for greater social recognition of their roles as mothers and wives to seeking enfranchisement on the basis of equality, the tone of eugenic analyses also changed. Instead of singing the praises of motherhood as a noble institution and of women as guardians of morality, eugenicists started focusing on the dysgenic actions of feminists, on the abandonment of the home by many women, and on the dangerous behav-ior of women in ethnic intermarriages. Some female proponents did not with-draw their support for eugenics after this change in tone, as they saw their own contribution to the eugenics movement as a vehicle for addressing women's issues in a more effective and appropriate manner, within the Romanian context, than that of any feminist organization. Another important factor accounting for their loyalty was the lack of other viable options for women with ambitions as reformers. In Transylvania, where support for eugenics was strongest, Astra maintained a better reputation than newer and smaller women's groups. Women who had become active in the Feminine Subsection at its inception stayed on, since the organization provided effective means for social action and reflected the strong nationalist feelings of its women members.

In the Regat, Veturia Manuilă's School for Social Assistance was a venue for the economic and social empowerment of women. Women had limited choices with regard to employment, as most female university graduates did not have much chance to compete with their male counterparts in most areas of employment, save, to some extent, within the budding areas of social work and public health. A virtual monopoly in this area, the School for Social Assistance combined professional training with inculcating eugenic notions of social hierarchy and health.[53]

Another aspect of gender relations, marital choice, was a constant preoccupation in the eugenic quest for a new social hierarchy. Many writers focused on ethnic intermarriage as a double-edged threat to the fabric of healthy social relations. Firstly, such marriages diminished the pool of eugenic human capital, for by marrying a non-Romanian one would parent children of mixed blood, diminishing their biological inheritance.[54] Secondly, these children would most likely grow up identifying themselves as non-Romanians. The reasoning behind this argument, as made by one writer, Petre Râmneanțu, was that once a Romanian woman married a non-Romanian, she would be lost to the nation and, in fact, become a traitor.[55] The weakness of her moral values and national consciousness, already evident in her marital choice, meant that she would raise her children in the traditions and language of her husband. In a sense, this appeared to be a natural, logical outcome of such a marriage, for eugenicists expected that women followed in their husbands' footsteps.

If this group of women appeared morally weak and hence unworthy of the trust placed in them to raise their children in a healthy, eugenic fashion, Râmneanțu depicted non-Romanian women who married Romanian men as powerful and dangerous. He focused especially on Hungarian women who married

Romanians, describing them as conscious agents of a revisionist plot to rob the Romanian nation of its healthy males and transform their offspring into Hungarians devoted to the revisionist cause:

> The enormous difference between the Romanian men who marry Hungarian women and the Hungarian men who marry Romanian women shows that the exogamy practiced [in Transylvania] is not due to a real state of cohabitation. The Hungarian women are executing a true seizure vis-à-vis the Romanian nation.[56]

Thus, women appeared as either unworthy of trust and social responsibility or as powerful, evil temptresses. The depiction of motherhood as a positive and important role for women in society became modified by these undercurrents of suspicion and fear. Eugenicists became more interested in controlling women's social roles than in validating their positive impact on the health of the nation.[57]

Defining the "Other": Social Deviance and Eugenic Normalcy

The ways in which eugenicists identified women as potential dysgenic actors in ethnic intermarriages exemplifies a wider strategy of locating individuals and groups whose vilification and exclusion from the healthy, normal social structure would help bring together the rest of society. This has been a recurrent feature emphasized in analyses of modern societies, especially among intellectual movements that attempted to construct normative models of social behavior. The definition of who could be included within the normal boundaries of society was always accompanied by the mirror image of who had to be excluded, this very exclusion becoming the condition for continued normalcy.[58]

In the case of eugenics, this became an important strategy for justifying the exclusion of various groups from what would ideally become the healthy nation and an important avenue for creating cohesion among the various social strata inside the nation. Of interest here are the criteria of selection and the rigidity of social boundaries. For while eugenicists identified several categories of individuals as dangerous to the health of the nation, they did not necessarily advocate the irrevocable exclusion and obliteration of these dysgenic groups. On the contrary, in many cases, since they still wanted to control the behavior of these individuals, eugenicists favored policies and programs—whether state-funded or private—that would help mediate the relationship between social outcasts and the rest of society. For instance, one eugenicist stated that "the prostitute must be protected and saved from the exploiting grip of her master and greedy boss, in order to take care of her health."[59] This attitude seems inconsistent with the general eugenic perception of what spending was effective in maintaining the health of the nation—for example, ignoring dysgenics such as prostitutes as recipients of public programs. After all, why invest so much effort and money in a population that was categorized as dysgenic?

It seems, however, that eugenicists were not as intent on keeping social boundaries rigid as it may first appear. At issue was the difference between acquired versus hereditary characteristics. As long as eugenicists did not possess the methods for unfailingly distinguishing between these two categories, they were aware of the risk of diagnosing and maybe permanently excluding from the nation's healthy body individuals who deceptively displayed the symptoms of degeneracy but did not in fact suffer from any hereditary pathologies. Presumably, one could still correct this behavior, eliminating its dysgenic characteristics and drawing some of these individuals back into the fold of normalcy, thereby enhancing the human capital.

Eugenics and Nonethnic Romanians

The largest group that became increasingly a focus of exclusion from the healthy nation was non-Romanians. Several eugenicists spent most of their research and writing trying to define authentic "Romanianness" in biological and anthropological terms, Petre Râmneanţu and Iordache Făcăoaru being the most prominent such examples. The former made it his life's work to try to demonstrate that the Szeklers in southeastern Transylvania were in fact Romanians. His claim rested on statistics regarding various characteristics, from anthropometric and blood agglutination measurements to blood groups. He compared the average blood agglutination figures for a sample of the Szekler population with averages for the Romanian population and then for the Hungarian population in Hungary proper, with the result that Szekler figures were much closer to those of Romanians than Hungarians. Râmneanţu used this as evidence to prove that Szeklers had much closer hereditary biological and anthropological ties with Romanians than with Hungarians and hence rightfully belonged to the Romanian Kingdom as authentic Romanians.[60]

The data he provided is based on a solid statistical analysis, yet this analysis rests on the shaky assumption that blood agglutination is a hereditary ethnic characteristic. It is true that such claims found some backing among scientists abroad as researchers still debated the scientific grounding of such claims. While mentioning these disputes, Romanian eugenicists chose without much difficulty to accept the theories that tied blood agglutination to ethnicity, because of the long-term stability of this characteristic in the process of evolution and adaptation. Blood agglutination seemed to represent the true, underlying essence of the communal identity, while other characteristics—such as anthropometric measurements of hair or bones—were more flexible and open both to alteration and to questioning by those ready to challenge the authenticity of the Szeklers' Romanian ethnic identity.

Râmneanțu insisted that Szeklers had been slowly Magyarized by Hungarian rulers in the Middle Ages and had thus begun to identify themselves linguistically, culturally, and ethnically as Hungarian. For Râmneanțu this presented the perfect example of how a population could appear as "other" than Romanian but in fact be a rightful part of the national unit. His study on the Szeklers was received with great interest and awarded the Oroveanu Prize by the Romanian Academy in 1936, carrying the substantial pecuniary value of 20,000 lei. Over the next four years Râmneanțu received two more such substantial prizes from the Romanian Academy and one from the General Association of Romanian Doctors for his work on the ethnic origins of the population in Transylvania.[61] It seems that his work was not only well known in academic circles but also highly regarded as scientific research. This response reflects the leaning of the Romanian scientific community at large toward an emphasis on hereditary determinism and a preoccupation with ethnic purity.

If Râmneanțu's work on the Szeklers shows how Romanian eugenicists attempted to reintegrate groups that seemed undesirable within the healthy body of the nation, other analyses placed more emphasis on the imperative to exclude "inauthentic" Romanians, especially Jews and Roma. The most outspoken eugenicist on the Jewish question was Făcăoaru. In an article published in 1938, he depicted Jews and "other extra-European populations" as "dead weight, . . . a mortal danger for the nation."[62] On the basis of the same "irrefutable" evidence of blood agglutination measurements that Râmneanțu had used, Făcăoaru aimed to exclude Jews completely from society by controlling marriages and by the sterilization of this unwanted population.[63]

Sabin Manuilă harbored a different opinion on the Jewish question. Although he also wanted more government control over this population, Manuilă believed that by the nature of their cultural and social traditions Jews had already segregated themselves and thus did not pose such a great threat to the Romanian population, in terms of "infecting their blood," as Făcăoaru had claimed.[64] After all, Manuilă argued, Jews married other Jews and rarely disguised themselves as "authentic" Romanians in order to become better integrated in Romanian society. This opinion is significant because of Manuilă's persistence in defining Jews as a biological and, even more specifically, a racial community. In Manuilă's opinion, the Jewish danger was economic rather than racial. Thus, he advocated greater control over this population's wealth and behavior in order to harness these resources for the greater needs of the Romanian state, a measure implemented by the Antonescu regime after 1940.

According to Manuilă, the Roma posed a greater danger to the Romanian social fabric, for they surreptitiously became assimilated into the healthy body of the nation, greatly diminishing its eugenic potential. A series of articles published in *România Nouă* at beginning of World War II exposes a side of Manuilă that has received no attention thus far.[65] In these articles Manuilă wrote in blatantly racist terms:

> The Gypsy problem is the most important and acute racial problem in Romania. . . . The anthropological Gypsy type must be defined as an undesirable one which must not influence our racial constitution. . . . The types who have reached leadership positions and have committed political crimes, completely foreign to the mental and moral structure of the Romanian soul, are obviously of Gypsy origin. . . . The Gypsy mix in the Romanian blood is the most dysgenic influence that affects our race.[66]

In a discourse that came to echo Nazi ideology, Manuilă shifted the focus in the eugenic quest for creating a natural elite from his earlier emphasis on replacing professional politicians—Romanian or not—with technical specialists to a focus on purifying the existing elite of its non-Romanian and especially Roma intruders. He identified the source of corruption and degeneracy not within the system but rather in the shape of these alleged impostors, whose exclusion would make it possible for the elite to become healthy again.

By 1942 Simion Mehedinți, who had already identified himself as a strong supporter of eugenics, had also shifted his rhetoric about the need for greater social control and selection toward an unequivocally racist tone:

> The time has come to put an end to this anarchy. . . . Not only the race hygiene, but also the social and cultural hygiene of all European countries demands the expulsion of Jews, Gypsies, and all other sartoide elements. . . . The modern state cannot live without a scrupulous order in all areas of activity.[67]

This attitude reveals an important shift in eugenics in the late thirties and early forties, away from a theory of dynamic change that encouraged greater responsibilities for the professional elite and a growth of state institutions with the help of these technocrats. In place of the earlier emphasis on increasing the positive biological potential in Romanian society, eugenicists shifted to a rhetoric of imminent danger that stressed the need to defend the healthy community by purifying it of "unwanted" populations. The onset of the war provided to some extent the context for this shift in emphasis toward restrictive eugenics. However, although this exogenous factor helps explain the greater appeal of this rhetoric of crisis, it does not diminish its fundamental racism.

Criminals as "Social Plagues"

There were other groups of social outcasts in which eugenicists invested attention. Two categories of criminals, in particular, occupied much of the eugenicists' attention: prostitutes and juvenile delinquents. The issue of criminality as hereditary pathology rather than individual action was a recurrent theme in eugenic discussions of social programs.[68] If criminal behavior were inherited, criminals could not be rehabilitated; instead it was necessary to focus on isolating criminals and preventing them both from inflicting their pathological nature on society and from reproducing themselves. Furthermore, any expenses in this direction were to be justified by the needs of the normal population.

However, if it could be proved that criminal acts were a result of environmental, negative forces rather than heredity, then eugenic programs for criminal rehabilitation could be justified.[69] In the case of prostitution, eugenicists carried on a debate that lasted through the interwar period on the question of whether there was a hereditary nature to prostitutes' behavior that meant they would inevitably go back to the streets or whether these women could indeed be saved and turned into functioning, if not perfectly healthy, members of society.

The debate over prostitution was not simply a battle between two philosophical points of view. Eugenicists tied prostitution to the rampant growth of syphilis in Romania after World War I and could see a solution to this problem only if prostitution itself, as a social problem, could be solved or at least kept under control. The focus on prostitutes themselves as the "other" served to draw attention away from their customers, who were in no way vilified and reprimanded. Some authors did mention in passing that men should behave more responsibly toward their wives, for they potentially endangered their spouses' health and reproductive systems.[70] But men were not singled out as the agents of this dysgenic phenomenon; rather they were viewed as victims of the prostitute.

Eugenicists were not alone in reinforcing this double standard regarding sexual behavior—active for men and passive for women. However, their arguments revolved not only around moral questions about corrupting young men's virtue and the proper norms for women's behavior but more emphatically around the question of infecting the healthy body of the nation with social illnesses that could become genetically debilitating. The charges brought against prostitutes thus became much heavier and used the language of science rather than ethics: prostitutes were a health hazard. With this image, eugenicists hoped to instill greater caution among men and to isolate prostitutes through a "*cordon sanitaire*" imposed voluntarily by the healthy members of society.

Solutions to the problem of prostitution ranged from abolition to regulation. The arguments in favor of these options replicated the debates held a century earlier in Victorian England.[71] Regulation finally won out as a more realistic approach, accompanied by attempts to rehabilitate prostitutes. Eugenicists concluded that women who were engaged in this practice could be brought back into the fold of normal society if only they would be willing to drop this habit. Again, eugenicists seemed to contradict themselves, for most of them had argued at one point that prostitutes were a type of degenerate criminal:

> Prostitution . . . appears as the feminine equivalent of vagabondage, of swindling and, to a certain extent, of criminality. . . . The exogenous influences, containing a combination of social, economic or chance elements, are not the determining factor [in this problem].[72]

At the same time, eugenicists perceived prostitutes not only as criminals but also as mothers or healthy young women who could become mothers. Moreover, they recognized that women often became prostitutes because of economic hardships or as victims of their professions, especially if they were servants. Therefore, some eugenicists proposed radical measures to ensure that lower-class women would not fall into prostitution, even if they had a latent propensity for it:

> We [should] ensure . . . equal pay for women and men; protection for pregnant workers and servants; . . . basic salaries for women working in restaurants, taverns, cafes; the recognition of paternity and of the obligation to raise one's child; [and] . . . the suppression of the rubric "illegitimate" from civil records.[73]

Thus, some eugenicists hoped to prevent prostitution to some extent and to reduce the existing problem through measures of social welfare that came closer to those proposed by their socialist contemporaries than to those of liberals, conservatives, or fascists. As in their other discussions that focused on women's issues, eugenicists favored a paternalistic role for the state in implementing such measures rather than a role that would allow women any choice in accessing welfare programs. This attitude betrayed a deeply engrained sense of distrust vis-à-vis the "second sex."

What marked the eugenicists' approach to this issue as distinctive, in addition to their biological-hereditary framing of the problem, was their insistence that the *medical staff* have the upper hand in regulating prostitution, rather than the police. They viewed the work of the police as heavy handed and insensitive to the intricacies of the wider public health implications of prostitution.[74] In regulating this occupation, the police only deterred prostitutes from cooperating, especially with regard to getting regular medical checkups. Eugenicists believed that providing a persuasive explanation of the health and eugenic issues at stake would provide more impetus for prostitutes to cooperate in programs of regulation and rehabilitation.

A similar distrust of the penal system defined the eugenic approach toward the issue of juvenile delinquency. Eugenicists attempted to walk the tightrope between determining the hereditary nature of youths' criminal actions and trying to rescue these individuals from becoming permanent outcasts.[75] In a sense, eugenicists regarded rehabilitation as a less costly solution for the healthy body of the nation, since dealing with these individuals as outcasts for the rest of their lives would impose greater expenditures on society. They were less willing than their counterparts in Germany, for instance, to impose drastic measures such as compulsory sterilization or isolation in labor camps. In a less aggressive fashion, Romanian eugenicists felt that the responsibilities of the healthy community extended toward these outcasts as well.

Făcăoaru alone made recurrent attempts to isolate such individuals. He repeatedly offered examples of degenerate criminal families and their cost to society—with excerpts from the factitious Kallikak family case to local ones in Transylvania—as a warning to his more lenient colleagues.[76] He was intent on extirpating all "unhealthy" elements from the nation's body without any compromise for the sake of traditional concepts of community. Individuals and groups alike should accept the needs of the nation as a law and abide by it, even when this meant renouncing traditional rights and privileges. His warnings, however, did not awaken similar fears among most Romanian eugenicists. In the case of prostitutes and juvenile delinquents, they remained more committed to attempts to control the boundaries between normal and outcast by means of both isolation and rehabilitation.

■ ■ ■

T H E eugenic vision of a new society tapped into some traditional views of social roles, such as women's mothering roles, at the same time that it sought to reorder the existing hierarchy according to different criteria and by using new technologies of social control. This synthesis contained some important inconsistencies. Tensions resulted in part from the questionable scientific basis of eugenicists' analyses, as in the case of identifying Szeklers as "authentic" Romanians. In other instances, eugenicists were unwilling or unable to recognize the ways in which their quest for a rational, moderate solution to the alleged problems of extremist individualism helped legitimize intolerant and violent xenophobia and racism.

In spite of these inconsistencies, eugenicists found enthusiastic supporters among the professional middle classes. Few were the voices raised against eugenics as scientifically false or inherently inconsistent with its own professed goals. The positive response among doctors, lawyers, social scientists, and even priests illustrates a wider ambivalence among the educated elite about the value of opening up equal opportunities for all as a guarantee of social advancement through personal merit. Many among this elite, although they had themselves risen from very modest backgrounds and achieved their positions of privilege through personal efforts, seemed to favor more control over social selection.

The privileged role played by the professional elite in eugenic texts, as the guiding force in creating the new eugenic hierarchy, was essential in rendering eugenic ideas attractive to the members of the Romanian intelligentsia, especially in Transylvania, where members of this group still suffered from an inferiority complex vis-à-vis their Hungarian counterparts. While implying they were bound by greater responsibilities toward the health of the nation, the new hierarchy promised a position of privilege and power for the Romanian professional elite. The quest for stability and status carried more weight than individual liberty in the mentality of the educated professional classes in interwar Romania.

The vision of the new eugenic society was fraught with tension, as it sought to resolve social friction by creating a strict social hierarchy according to biological priorities. This hierarchy was supposed to allow the development of a natural meritocracy, but eugenicists' insistence on control from above frustrated this goal. Another inconsistency concerned the desire to draw clear boundaries between the "healthy" body of the community and its "dysgenic" groups. These frontiers were hard to define—since eugenicists were not sure themselves of the infallibility of their definitions of normal versus dysgenic—and even harder to enforce. Finally the tension in this view of the eugenic society resulted from eugenicists' attempts to combine radical change in social relations with a desire to conserve certain existing traditions. This issue is best illustrated by eugenicists' reconceptualization of women's social roles. The following chapters will evaluate the effectiveness of various legal measures and other programs in resolving these tensions and will explore the impact of these actions on Romanian society during the interwar period.

CHAPTER 5

EDUCATION AND INBORN
CHARACTERISTICS

The closer a characteristic is linked to the hereditary structure, the
more important is the role of educational measures, for such a characteristic is very changeable. . . . We have to emphasize that the environment influences a given hereditary material but can bring about only
changes which are permitted by this hereditary material.

Alexandru Roşca, *Igiena mintală şcolară*

A nation . . . that maintains its health through eugenic measures and
knows how to select its valuable elements according to their inborn aptitudes has all the biological conditions for normal social development.

Dimitrie Gusti and Traian Herseni, *Elemente de sociologie cu
aplicări la cunoaşterea ţării şi a neamului nostru*

L I K E other contenders in the political and intellectual arena in post-1918 Romania, eugenicists recognized the power of education as a vehicle for trans-
forming Romanian society from a group of heterogeneous communities with
very different traditions and institutions into a homogeneous whole. In fact,
education was the cornerstone of most Romanian eugenicists' strategies for social mobilization and change.

This chapter focuses on the debates over education reform to reveal the hereditary-determinist thinking that ran through these arguments like a red thread. As will become apparent, the eugenic vision of intelligence, aptitudes, and talents as genetic endowments gave rise to a critique of the liberal, positivist, and theoretically oriented system of education that prevailed in Romania at the time. The solutions advocated by eugenicists for correcting the existing problems called for restructuring not only institutions but also basic notions of pedagogy and existing methodologies in accordance with the principles of biological determinism. According to eugenicists, the laws of heredity, variation, and selection would become the basis for the new pedagogy. The eugenicists' arguments and language permeated deeply the discourse over education reform, more than in any other area of social action. This chapter explores the eugenicists' impact on the restructuring of education by looking at various works about education reform as well as the resulting legislation, methodological guidelines, and textbooks published in the spirit of these suggested reforms. Finally, the discussion will focus on the ways in which eugenicists expanded the notion of education—from something that takes place in the classroom to a broader concept of social learning—and tried to address the need to educate adults continuously in order to transform them into responsible, well-adjusted "links" within the eugenic intergenerational chain. The discussion will also untangle some of the cultural and political implications of this aspect of Romanian eugenics. As will become apparent, the eugenicists' focus on education and the ability to persuade individuals to change their behavior, instead of on coercive measures such as sterilization, represents a unique reading of eugenic theories by their Romanian proponents, a reading that was different from those proposed by their German, English, or American counterparts.

Until recently, the question of how education was employed as a means of constructing particular visions of national identity has remained marginal for most historians of Romania, who have often viewed discussions of the shape of education in Greater Romania as illustrations of ideological differences within the greater context of cultural unity.[1] In an important study published in 1995, Irina Livezeanu focuses on the process of building educational institutions in interwar Romania as a contest over defining the identity and goals of this nation and its individual citizens in a homogenizing nationalist vein.[2] Livezeanu's book underlines the essential rifts that existed before 1918 or, in some cases, developed throughout the interwar period, especially between what Bucharest wanted and what the new regions of Greater Romania—Transylvania, Bukovina, Bessarabia, and the Banat—saw as their own legitimate interests in the process of creating new educational institutions or altering old regional ones. Livezeanu's emphasis on the importance of regional interests and their contest over building a larger infrastructure and, with it, a unified national identity sheds light on some of the stakes of eugenicists like Iuliu Moldovan in arguing for regional autonomy for educational organizations such as Astra.[3] Livezeanu's contribution is most valuable in identifying the ideological dimensions of these debates over institutional change, especially with regard to the rise of xenophobic and anti-Semitic policies.

The analysis here centers similarly on the illiberalism of educational ideas and policies, but from a different perspective—that of the assumptions and normative goals embedded in the language and arguments of Romanian eugenicists. By focusing on this level of analysis, my discussion shows that the contenders in this debate argued over more than access to revenue and regional interests; they tried to reshape individual and collective identity. At stake were conflicting philosophies about the function of education in this process and about the role of public, state institutions in educating individuals. The fact that biologizing arguments about these issues were reproduced in texts written by reformers who did not identify themselves as eugenicists speaks for the important role played by eugenics in constructing the language of the larger debate over education.

This point is especially significant when analyzing the later, more extremist measures taken against minorities—Hungarians and Jews in particular—with regard to their access to education and professional training.[4] The language of biological determinism became important in arguments about the need to focus all state efforts and revenues on educating the "authentic" Romanian population. It is also important to recognize the appeal of eugenic rhetoric when looking at discussions about the education of girls versus boys, in which the argument for biological differences, developed very aggressively by eugenicists, served as a means for reinforcing an essentialist, differential approach along gender lines.

By inserting the language and arguments of hereditary determinism and reifying biological differences along ethnic and gender lines in textbooks from the level of primary education to that of postgraduate courses, eugenicists acted as aggressive propagandists for their new gospel of biopolitics. It would be difficult to gauge the response of the general public to these ideas with any level of precision. However, by looking at the ways in which eugenic language and arguments were reproduced in texts by other education reformers, one can appreciate the significance of eugenics at the level of policy making in the realm of education. Furthermore, examining the eugenics-influenced textbooks used during the 1930s and early 1940s provides some clues as to why—even among educated professionals with no history of overt anti-Semitism—there was so much apathy toward, and, to some extent, tacit endorsement of, the more extremist rhetoric that began to permeate the popular press during this period. It may also help to explain why the radical anti-Semitic legislation of 1940 went largely unchallenged.

Eugenic arguments on behalf of thoroughly reforming the education system in accordance with the principles of hereditary intelligence, aptitudes, and talents more often than not did not make any overt suggestions about the hereditary differences between Romanians and Hungarians or Romanians and Jews on the basis of genetic characteristics. Yet in other published research, individuals like Petre Râmneanțu and Iordache Făcăoaru went to great lengths to prove the essential differences between ethnic Romanians and minorities living in Greater Romania with regard to blood agglutination and anthropometric measurements. These studies often made overt suggestions about the link between hereditary physical and personality- or intelligence-related characteristics.[5] Therefore, some implications about the relationship between ethnic purity and the heredity of superior talents and intelligence existed beneath the more general explanations about the hereditary basis of biological characteristics, even in hygiene textbooks for eighth graders.[6] More important, however, is the fact that the simplified arguments about the role of heredity in determining the health and progress of future generations became forceful tools for justifying biases against non-Romanians at every level of the education process and in other arenas of social and political interaction.

Education as a Eugenic Tool: Squaring the Mendelian Circle

From their earliest publications, Romanian eugenicists stressed the primacy of education as the most important tool for bringing about a eugenic consciousness among the Romanian population and, consequently, fostering healthier social organization and behavior. In 1926, Gheorghe Preda, a specialist on mental health and a strong supporter of eugenics, wrote:

> The problem of the nation . . . is an educational problem: the school and the church, science and religion must work together to respect our biological prerogatives.[7]

This early text emphasized the overwhelming role played by heredity in determining the personality and intellectual abilities of each individual. At the same time, the author carefully qualifies this claim by asserting that "heredity is not fatal. . . . Defects can be . . . redressed and even avoided through crossbreeding or abstinence."[8] Preda's choice of solutions to degeneracy does not mention sterilization—an important omission, which illustrates the reluctance among many Romanian eugenicists to propose coercive measures for eugenic betterment. Instead, he spoke of crossbreeding or abstinence, both of which indicate the author's trust in the ability of every individual to understand the stakes in biological heredity, if given the proper education. This rhetoric also suggests his belief that each individual would willingly change his or her behavior to fit the larger eugenic interests of the community. In his eyes, the key to this process was eugenically responsible education.

Another significant aspect of this text is its emphasis on the ability of an *environmental* factor, education, to "correct" heredity. In their discussions of hereditary characteristics, most Romanian eugenicists came down on the side of the Mendelian argument that acquired characteristics could not be transmitted from one generation to the next, as neo-Lamarckians asserted.[9] The Mendelian argument had been a weapon mostly of conservative-minded eugenicists in Germany and England, used to dissuade welfare reformers from pursuing programs that protected the disadvantaged and the poor in order to insure the well-being of the national community.[10] Mendelians made the argument that one had to be selective in implementing such programs and start with a "eugenically sound" population in order to yield the greatest benefits for the larger community.

Not surprisingly, in Romania the intelligentsia and the peasantry were most often singled out as the healthy groups. As shown earlier, on the basis of this Mendelian outlook, Romanian eugenicists tended to make a similar argument with regard to promoting selective welfare programs for the ethnically Romanian rural population. In one essay, Iordache Făcăoaru openly attacked Lamarckian theories of evolution and their implications for the possibility of modifying heredity through education:

> Not one of the experiments already carried out has confirmed the theory of heredity of acquired characteristics. . . . The effects of exercise, instruction and education are limited to the individual existence. . . . Improving the environment and living conditions remain without any effect on raising the biological level and perfecting human genes.[11]

Yet Preda's essay asserts that "the influence of the environment is decisive for changing one's genotype or the species."[12] How could this clearly neo-Lamarckian outlook be compatible with the Mendelian views of most Romanian eugenicists? Was Preda simply confused or in a fringe position? Not likely. Rather, it seems that like other Romanian eugenicists, he *had* to make this argument, in a sense, in order to construct an effective eugenic critique of the current system of education as degenerative. For if environmental factors could not have any impact on the quality of heredity, then it would not matter whether education was liberal and theoretical or more corporatist and practical. However, since most eugenicists were themselves educators and believed in the power of this tool to change behavior and foster progress, they found a way to get around the apparent contradiction between their Mendelian convictions and the seemingly neo-Lamarckian thrust of their faith in education.

Their main argument on behalf of emphasizing education was that although biological characteristics, including personality, moral character, and intelligence, were inherited to a great extent, they existed in each individual as "potentialities" rather than fully developed traits. In an extensive study on the heredity of mental and psychological characteristics published in 1944, Salvator Cupcea underlined the claim that "genes do not produce characteristics per se, but rather provide certain evolutionary guidelines."[13] This assertion allowed eugenicists to argue that although heredity was the most important factor in evolution, one had to give this force a helping hand by cultivating those hereditary characteristics most beneficial to the well-being of the community. In their eyes, the very notion of education became redefined as the process of selecting the most "eugenically sound" natural endowments and bringing about their optimal development. This view of education was all-encompassing and suggested that this process of selection and "grooming" of inborn aptitudes had to start at birth and extend into the adult years, well beyond the classroom walls. As a result, eugenic publications became a forum for an extensive discussion about the general principles and specific measures of education reform, from courses for young mothers to vocational trade schools and from reading and writing first-grade textbooks to new organizations for physical education.

The Debates over Education Reform: The Positivist-Theoretical versus Nationalist-Empirical Approaches

Having defended the effectiveness of education as a tool for eugenic improvement while distancing themselves from the Lamarckian school, where did Romanian eugenicists situate themselves in the larger debate about education reform? This issue attracted many prominent academic figures, some of whom were divided into two opposite camps—the Europeanists and the nationalists, a divide that was prefigured in the early debates of Junimea.[14] The Europeanists, with Ştefan Zeletin and Petre Andrei among their strongest voices, wanted to pattern Romanian education on the French model. Their positivist philosophy about pedagogy was driven by faith in reason and in the deductive method.[15] Zeletin in particular was critical of the ways in which, since the late nineteenth century, the Romanian education system had focused on producing bureaucrats who would fill the increasing number of positions created by the new institutions of the Romanian Kingdom.[16] Thus, all students had come to expect a great degree of economic security as a result of their education. Pursuing a degree in law, for instance, seemed the most secure way to land a job in the government or in an economy that otherwise did not present any guarantees for employment or any great promises for entrepreneurial growth for small businessmen. According to Zeletin, the education system itself fostered these false expectations and created a great degree of dissatisfaction among those who did not find employment afterwards.

Furthermore, Zeletin decried the inductive methodology used to prepare these bureaucrats, which he considered entirely inappropriate for Romania's needs at that time. This methodology had been adopted in the more highly industrialized nations, such as Germany, to create specialists in various productive professions, from artisans to engineers. In Romania, however, it seemed inappropriate to jump into an inductive methodology when more basic notions of mathematics, science, and ethics had not become common knowledge at the level of secondary education. The students would be unable to benefit from empirical methodology without an already good basis of shared fundamental notions.[17]

The Europeanists' analysis of Romanian education focused on socialization as a cultural process that developed within the limits of a particular social structure, level of economic development, and political system. They evaluated the quality of education only in relation to these factors. Their discussion about the effectiveness of the education system in addressing the specific needs of Romanian society did not engage the issues of biological limitations and inborn vocation. They did not even pay much attention to the issue of gender differences in creating institutions and developing specific curricula. Separate schools for boys and girls persisted in many places by virtue of their traditional development until 1918, yet they were not part of an aggressive policy to create two separate curricula for the two genders.

The nationalist camp included many illustrious names, such as Nicolae Iorga and Simion Mehedinți, as well as more infamous ones, such as A. C. Cuza. There were important differences among these various individuals, yet they all stood in relatively cohesive opposition to the positivist spirit of the Europeanists. Iorga's notions of education reform emphasized the need to inculcate a nationalist spirit, a sense of pride and loyalty, in all disciplines taught. In a more extremist version of this idea, A. C. Cuza sought to create a greater sense of Romanian identity through an education that would be overtly xenophobic and anti-Semitic.[18] Both of them, however, focused strictly on the curriculum rather than on reforming the general philosophy of education and the methods used to educate students or on the intellectual criteria for advancing through the various levels of education.

Toward a Eugenic Discourse about Education Reform

Simion Mehedinți, however, had a more all-encompassing view of what needed to be changed in Romanian education in order to address the important needs of the nation. He spoke not only about the particular material that would be taught in schools but also about creating different types of schools to fit the aptitudes and intelligence of various students. Furthermore, he defined education not only as instruction in school but also as a lifelong process in which society at large participated as a continuous pedagogue for each new generation—"the school of labor."[19] Mehedinți's contribution to reforming Romanian pedagogy toward a more practically oriented system of education has been the subject of several historical analyses.[20] However, no historian thus far has focused on the biological determinism that rests at the foundation of his ideas and on his specific praise for eugenics as the most solid basis for creating a system of education suited to Romania's needs in the twentieth century:

> With the help of modern science and technology, a great social genius could change the life rhythms of an entire nation in a very short time. . . . Through eugenic measures, a statesman could modify the very hereditary foundations of the nation and could become the First Pedagogue of the nation.[21]

Indeed, not only was Mehedinți very familiar with Francis Galton's studies on twins, which had focused on the heredity of intelligence and various aptitudes and talents, but he was also an avid supporter of Moldovan's biopolitics and often quoted Moldovan.[22] The basic reform advocated by Mehedinți had to do with creating a more individualized, more differentiated system of instruction and selecting students in order to make better use of the hereditary talents of each individual. His proposal for education reform raises the questions of criteria for selecting students and of the means for achieving a more efficient development of students' hereditary endowments—questions addressed more directly by Moldovan and his followers.

Eugenic Criteria for Selection: Intelligence versus Class, Ethnicity, and Gender Identity

Florin Ştefănescu-Goangă figured prominently among those who discussed the criteria for selecting students and curricula according to eugenic principles.[23] He claimed that mental superiority was closely tied to class identity. According to his figures, 70 percent of children with above-average and exceptional intelligence came from families of educated professionals.[24] Many other eugenicists, not only in Romania but also abroad, shared this reified view of class identity as an indication of inborn intelligence. In England, according to historian Donald Mackenzie, eugenicists used the rhetoric of hereditary intelligence as a form of bolstering the status of the liberal professions and enhancing access to elite educational institutions, as well as a form of social control over the poor.[25]

Although some sociologists, most prominently Max Weber, repeatedly argued on behalf of the cultural and social construction of class identity, many intellectuals and educated professionals readily embraced this new discourse that conflated hereditary intellectual superiority with class identity.

In Romania, however, this assertion posed an important problem to eugenicists, especially the Transylvanian group around Moldovan. If it were true that the middle class had the greatest intellectual hereditary capabilities, this would imply that the Hungarian and German populations in Transylvania, who made up the great majority of the urban middle classes, were in fact superior to the Romanian population, who constituted the bulk of the lower classes. No one in the Romanian community directly confronted the contradiction between eugenicists' fear of the non-Romanian urban middle classes and the claim that this social group embodied the greatest intellectual potential.

Ştefănescu-Goangă did not in fact mention ethnicity as an important criterion for setting up a hierarchy among students. Yet other eugenicists were undoubtedly aware of this issue, for many of them added an important corollary to their reification of the hereditary intellectual superiority of the professional middle classes.[26] They claimed that in the Romanian context the inferior position of the peasantry was not a sign of their hereditary deficiency but rather of the economic and social privations they had to suffer before 1918. In fact, peasants supposedly represented the "biological reservoir of all the strata that lay on top of it."[27] It remained unclear who would make up the lower slope of the intelligence bell curve, but according to these analyses, Romanians overall were located in the above-average portion.[28] Thus, education reform would focus on a more rigorous ethnic selection of the middle classes and on an increased effort to educate peasants across the board. Eugenicists constructed the criteria for student selection along ethnic lines as much as according to class divisions.

Gender was another basis for reforming education. The relationship between gender and the heredity of intelligence and specific aptitudes was, in fact, one of the issues about which eugenicists disagreed. In *Biopolitica* Moldovan had already emphatically stated that girls should receive a different education from boys, not only because of their gender-specific future social roles but also because of their different inborn intellectual and vocational characteristics.[29] Many other voices supported this opinion. Ovidiu Comşia, who wrote extensively on gender relations, asserted that "aside from the inherent biological differences that each individual manifests, there are also inherent differences between the two sexes. . . . Their biological structure is different, and their future mission is especially different."[30] He went so far as to assert that women in general were less prone to think analytically than men and that only biologically abnormal women were able to achieve intellectual excellence. Their "abnormality" had to do with their choice to remain unmarried or not to have children.[31]

There was no scientific proof that a genetic correlation existed between sexual characteristics and intelligence. Yet this argument, which tied gender identity to sex and to particular hereditary aptitudes and intelligence, acted as a powerful tool for controlling the polarized socialization of gender roles through the education system. It provided better guarantees for many reformers that the next generation would grow up identifying more closely with their biological limitations and potentialities along gender lines.

A different eugenic camp asserted that "there are no differences between boys and girls with regard to intelligence."[32] Alexandru Roşca, a psychologist at the University of Cluj, provided a sophisticated analysis of the cultural factors behind the apparent intelligence differential between men and women. He acknowledged that women were a small minority among the famous minds of the past. More often than not, Roşca asserted, women owed their place in historical memory to "their beauty, tragic fate, or philanthropic spirit."[33] However, he denied that these facts could be used as proof that women were genetically inferior to men. Rather, this gender imbalance illustrated the social and cultural practices, discriminatory education, and economic opportunities that traditionally provided women with fewer opportunities for intellectual achievement:

> The simple acknowledgement that the number of women geniuses is much smaller than that of men cannot constitute the proof that women are inferior. . . . This could be only claimed if we could prove that social, education, and other opportunities have been equal for the two sexes. . . . [But] girls' curriculum has been different from that of boys. . . . They've been given less scientific information. Women were barred from a great number of professions, . . . and even when admitted—they were badly paid.[34]

However, this group did not go so far as to insist emphatically that girls should be given the same educational opportunities as boys. In a sense, these critics were caught in a bind: on the one hand, they hoped to increase the level of education for women with superior intelligence, so that the nation at large would make more efficient use of this "human capital"; on the other, these eugenicists still insisted on defining notions of social utility in gendered terms. In other words, women of various talents and levels of intelligence should be selected without any bias regarding their intellectual abilities, but they should be placed in a system of education that would reflect the needs of the nation. For women, these needs were overwhelmingly identified with reproducing, educating, and taking care of the next generation of children, at home and in the appropriate public forums.[35]

This gendered view of education reform translated into different institutions and curricula for the two genders and into a selection process that clearly separated boys from girls as two groups with different levels of intelligence. Thus, the critique of the few opponents of this gender bias regarding intellectual abilities remained without an important impact on policy making.

Some eugenicists looked to other environmental dysgenic factors as a focus of their criteria for selection in the education process. They claimed that those with an immoral lifestyle (i.e., criminals and prostitutes) or suffering from alcoholism or syphilis were populations with a greater propensity for producing offspring of subnormal intelligence.[36] In this case, the selection would start not with the children, but with their parents. Eugenicists turned toward adults and used a rhetoric of shame to instill a greater sense of responsibility toward the next generation in terms familiar to the wider public: "How sad it is to know that your child, instead of inheriting intelligence, will probably end up in a homeless shelter or in an asylum for the mentally ill, or will become a criminal because of your misbehavior!"[37]

The issue of education reform on the basis of heredity thus became another opportunity for eugenicists to assert their role as a moral elite and to legitimize their desire for greater social control, especially over the lower classes. Some writings on this topic tried to increase the sense of crisis by showing how even seemingly normal families could be carriers of "dysgenic" characteristics such as alcoholism or moral degeneracy. Iordache Făcăoaru published a significant number of case studies in which he went to great lengths to tie behavioral patterns such as emotional imbalance to intellectual degeneracy in subsequent generations. His underlying goal was to increase the coercive powers of the state in controlling reproduction as a means of "preselecting" the next generation.[38]

Methods of Selection

Debates regarding the criteria for selecting students according to supposed inborn intellectual and vocational abilities were closely interwoven with discussions about the *methods* of selection and the refashioning of pedagogical priorities according to eugenic principles. One method would have been to use the health data of previous generations as an indicator of potential problems or resources that were latently "stored" inside each child. Throughout the interwar period Moldovan, Făcăoaru, and Râmneanțu pushed fervently for a systematic eugenic census—the creation of a "biological file" for each individual so that doctors and other eugenic specialists might follow the development of each individual from a wider intergenerational perspective.[39] These files would serve as the first database for selecting both those children with potentially subaverage intelligence and those whose "pedigree" recommended them as possible members of the intellectual elite. The two groups whose files would be most scrupulously followed were the Romanian middle classes and the peasantry, whom eugenicists deemed as having the greatest potential for generating individuals of exceptional intelligence and talents. This type of selection process was publicized as an incentive for all adults to act responsibly in their lives, since their behavior could have tremendous repercussions on their children's social mobility.

Aside from this "preselection," young pupils would be selected through various aptitude and intelligence tests. Some eugenicists considered the various intelligence tests given at the time to be measurements of literacy and erudition rather than of inborn intellectual abilities.[40] However, most others were in favor of using IQ tests as a reliable method for selecting students in accordance with their hereditary intellectual characteristics.[41] Various other forms of testing aptitudes would be added to this process to provide a complete picture of each student's gifts.

Physical health and an aesthetic appearance also played important roles in this process of student selection.[42] Pupils in good health and whose outward appearance resembled that of a "typical" Romanian received special consideration in this process of selection. Normative views of gender roles also played a role in imagining bipolar ideal bodies. Young women's bodies were especially scrutinized to find the signs of their reproductive potential and maternal instincts. Narrow hips, small breasts and the presence of dark bodily hair were all read as signs of a young woman's subnormal reproductive potential.[43]

Young men were not safe from such intrusive scrutiny either. Eugenicists recommended that their selection in school be based on normative criteria of masculinity, which included "a dynamic, vigorous, aggressive, and provocative demeanor."[44] Thus, a young man with narrow shoulders, without strong musculature, and with soft, thinning hair was branded as effeminate and stood fewer chances of being selected for elite schools.[45] By trying to control the construction of gender identity around the body, eugenicists aggressively helped polarize the meaning ascribed to many aspects of physical appearance in a feminine-masculine dichotomy.

Although eugenicists discussed at length the importance of reforming the criteria for student selection, they hinted only vaguely at *who* would be making the selection. Presumably the IQ tests could be given by anyone, for they were easy to interpret. Yet aptitude tests required specific training. Eugenicists mentioned in passing the important role teachers would play in this process but did not devise any proposals for training *them,* a crucial element in the greater scheme of making better use of students' inborn gifts. This oversight appears rather inconsistent with the eugenicists' otherwise comprehensive outlook on reform. It seemed that doctors would still play the most important role in this process, for they would periodically visit schools, examine students, and then have the authority to note down any relevant observation in each "biological file."[46]

Eugenicists seemed more preoccupied with the methods of selecting students according to their genetic endowments at the secondary and higher levels of education. Here, the entrance examinations would play the most important role. The measures proposed by eugenicists in an already very competitive academic system included a greater awareness of one's genealogy: if a student came from a healthy peasant family, he or she deserved special attention, for instance. The exams themselves would stress not only accumulated knowledge in certain disciplines but also "purer" forms of intelligence through special exams as well as aptitude tests. The first effort in this direction was a school for gifted children, founded in 1940 at the Dealu Monastery, which replaced the local military school.[47] Eugenicists praised this school as a pioneering example and encouraged the wartime regime to allocate greater resources toward creating such schools, which would then become the recruiting ground for the elite of following generations. Their requests remained without much effect, especially because of government focus on the war effort.

Some voices in the discussion about student selection in the education system had a different perspective on this issue. In 1929, one reformer wrote that only the democratization of the education system could guarantee that the brightest minds would rise to the top. He did not seem averse to negative selection, in the sense of denying access to elite schools to those with limited abilities—a notion he did not define sufficiently.[48] Yet he emphasized the need to let those with superior talents rise to the top through an equally nurturing and unconstrained environment. He considered a regimented system of selecting students from the start and tailoring education to the various levels of inborn intelligence and aptitudes as less effective. These ideas echoed those of reformers like Petre Andrei, who also trusted in the effectiveness of self-selection in a democratized, open system of education at the same time that he expressed concern about the quality of that education and the elites it created.

Reform Efforts after the Great Depression

The discussion of practical policies tied to this general debate on eugenic education reform was curtailed in the early 1930s by the funding problems caused by the Great Depression and Romania's general financial difficulties during this decade. Dimitrie Gusti, the Minister of Education in 1933, presided over what he considered a necessary cut (of almost two thousand jobs) in the number of teachers and professors in the public education system at all levels.[49] With a budget that represented only 60 percent of the expected allocations, the Ministry of Education needed to reconsider its priorities. Gusti considered a basic education at the primary level as one of the fundamental goals of the public education system. At the same time, he embraced the notion of a more selective distribution of revenues at the secondary and university levels as a necessity, both as a means of improving the most gifted human capital and as a means of using the reduced funds more efficiently. Overall, Gusti backed Moldovan's ideas and those of his eugenic collaborators as a useful way of reforming Romanian education. The financial problems opened the door wider for a selective implementation of existing policies in an anti-Semitic vein.[50]

The general unwillingness of the government to increase the budget for the Ministry of Education led many eugenicists to seek solutions in the sphere of private education. They continued to speak about the importance of placing greater control and more responsibilities in the area of education in the hands of the state. Yet they began to turn toward private funds in order to create the type of educational institutions they envisioned.

Astra and Eugenic Adult Education

The largest organization that helped in these efforts was Astra. From its inception Astra had aimed at educating the Romanian population in Transylvania in a nationalist spirit, with a specific focus on language, history, and cultural traditions. After 1918 these aims had been achieved by virtue of Transylvania's incorporation into the Romanian Kingdom. Fostering national consciousness became an integral part of public culture and education. When Moldovan became the president of the association in 1932, he began reconceptualizing its goals: while Astra would remain the most important source for popular education in the nationalist spirit, it would shift its focus from strictly cultural to biological issues. Astra would in time become the most important unofficial forum for educating the masses about their eugenic responsibilities.[51]

The most important efforts in educating the adult population within this institution were publications, especially calendars; conferences; and peasant schools. The calendars provided some basic notions about public and personal hygiene and, at some points, included simplified explanations of the dangers of alcoholism and venereal diseases for the next generations.[52] They were also filled with stories that praised the "good mother" and vilified the "bad mother" in terms that focused not only on the moral aspects of women's nurturing instincts but also on the biological side of women's identity.[53]

These simplistic and often vague sources of information were augmented with more complete and vivid presentations of eugenic problems through the popular conference series that the Medical and Biopolitical Section of Astra sponsored regularly during the interwar period. During its first three years (1926–28) the Biopolitical Section organized over 500 conferences.[54] Initially, these conferences were geared toward the intellectual and middle-class members of the association, as a means of familiarizing the future leaders of a wider eugenic and biopolitical program with eugenic theories. The Astra conferences focused mostly on the potential application of eugenic concepts in terms of national identity, public health measures, education, and eventually legislation.

The most impressive such series of conferences was organized by the Biopolitical Section in Cluj in 1927, focusing on the "biology of the Romanian nation." The speakers at these conferences were figures whose prominence made these events enormously significant in the intellectual debates during the interwar period. Emil Racoviță, the renowned naturalist and president of the Romanian Academy, opened the series with a paper entitled, "The Problem of the Romanian People's Evolution." He was followed by a long list of other famous individuals: the sociologist Dimitrie Gusti; Constantin Rădulescu-Motru, one of the most important Romanian philosophers during this period; the geographer Simion Mehedinți; the demographer Sabin Manuilă; Alexandru Vaida-Voevod, the prominent Peasantist politician; Alexandru Tzigara-Samurcaș, one of the most important ethnographers at that time; and other key intellectuals, all leaders in their fields of expertise and very influential in shaping public opinion at large.[55] These speakers defined notions such as "biopolitics," "biology," and even "people" (*popor*) in very different ways. Nonetheless, they were familiar with the Biopolitical Section's ideas and Moldovan's theories and engaged them within the biological-determinist paradigm set up by eugenics.

Their participation helped legitimize the intellectual authority and wider social significance of this well-publicized endeavor. According to Racoviță, these conferences aroused a lively interest among wide audiences: "so many people, . . . crowding . . . elbow to elbow, . . . young and old, civilians and soldiers, laymen and priests, boyars and ladies, teachers and students, intellectuals and merchants, high school boys and school girls, and other kinds of men and women. . . ."[56] This description indicates a broad spectrum of Romanian society was interested in the conferences.

During the following years, the Biopolitical Section organized conferences mostly in other Transylvanian cities. For instance, in 1936, 40 conferences were held in Cluj and 136 in Reghin, while in the following year 200 conferences (approximately 4 per week!) took place, mostly in Reghin.[57] The subject of these talks shifted quickly from the theoretical to the practical, focusing on basic issues of public health, such as hygiene; epidemic control; and various forms of social diseases, from syphilis to alcoholism and tuberculosis. The rhetoric of the presentations was consistent, nonetheless, with the ideas expressed by the Biopolitical Section in its initial program and by other theoretical writings by Moldovan and other Astra supporters of eugenics.[58]

The Peasant Schools: Mobilizing and Controlling Biological Capital

Aside from these occasional opportunities for educating the adult public, eugenicists tried to create more permanent programs for education within Astra. The most important efforts were the peasant schools. The first such effort was undertaken in Reghin, a region where large numbers of Hungarians lived side by side with ethnic Romanians. Its founder was Vasile Ilea, the regional leader of Astra and a regular contributor to *Buletin Eugenic și Biopolitic*. The self-avowed goal of this school was to educate groups of peasant men so that "upon their return [from the peasant school], they would *remain* peasants and become the leaders of their village and agents for cultural betterment."[59] These individuals would become role models for other peasants through the conscious cultivation of their physical and spiritual vigor.[60]

The schools selected the students presumably in accordance with their hereditary superior intelligence and aptitudes. The local teachers, priests, and doctors were responsible for nominating the students. The schools encouraged a competitive spirit, for aside from the general reward of education itself, they awarded significant prizes to those who performed well. The best students would receive various farm implements, livestock, or grains as a recognition of their efforts. These prizes were also an investment by Astra's leaders, for they viewed these awards as a means of encouraging the efforts of individuals who had proven their genetic superiority through their performance in the peasant schools.

This was not an unworthy method of encouraging education and high performance in school, but it was not standardized and clearly could be abused rather easily at the local level, where the richest peasants, rather than the most intelligent ones, probably stood the best chance of doing well in the peasant schools. The effectiveness of the schools depended on the sense of responsibility and rigor of those who ran the schools—local doctors and teachers. Another important bias of these schools was their unspoken but assumed exclusionary attitude toward ethnic non-Romanians. The schools reinforced ethnic segregation and sought to instill nationalism among their students.

In the course of their peasant school education villagers became exposed to basic notions of citizenship, with its rights and obligations; to legislation that affected their livelihood; to history; to geography; and to some forms of art. Aside from these humanist disciplines, they also received more practical training in various agricultural specializations.[61] Finally, they were immersed in a general course about hygiene. They would encounter notions about the environment—such as the public hygiene aspects of digging wells, the cleanliness of public spaces, and personal hygiene—as well as descriptions of the pathological nature and dysgenic effects of alcoholism, venereal disease, and tuberculosis. The schools emphasized the problems of alcoholism and venereal disease over all other social plagues as the most dangerous health hazards for the male population.[62] Although the local teachers played an important role in the general curriculum, doctors were in charge of teaching the most important notions of hygiene and even basic irrigation and well-digging techniques. They played a privileged role as the leading spirits of these peasant schools.

It is unclear what peasants themselves thought of these schools. The fact that they were well attended may indicate that the schools were sought after by the local population.[63] Whatever the responses of the peasants may have been, the organizers seemed to think these schools were an effective tool for educating the peasant population in general and for selecting the most promising minds from the countryside as the leaders of the coming generations. In fact, the success of the peasant schools for men prompted the Astra leadership to expand its efforts and create peasant schools for women.

The Peasant Schools for Women

Astra began to address Romanian peasant women's education in the late 1920s, when the Feminine Biopolitical Subsection of the organization was founded. Its work consisted primarily of drawing the activities of other autonomous women's organizations into Astra's framework. The most prominent of these forums was the Union of Romanian Women. It was a welfare and cultural organization for middle-class Romanian women in Transylvania, with an emphasis on Christian morality and a sense of community. Previous to its incorporation into Astra's framework, the union's activities had focused on peasant women in a haphazard fashion. It had tried to find safe employment for young peasant women who had migrated to urban areas by locating middle-class families who needed servants. It had also attempted to put together some trade schools for such women, training them as seamstresses or in other "feminine" crafts. Finally, this organization had attempted to educate peasant women about their duties as mothers and wives through occasional lectures and practical demonstrations (e.g., with regard to postpartum hygiene).[64]

All these efforts had been developed mainly at the local level, in response to specific needs or according to the particular ideas, energies, and funding of the organizers. The Union of Romanian Women acted more as an umbrella organization and a space for organizers to come together and share their specific experiences, rather than as a framework for developing a comprehensive plan for dealing with women's issues. Starting in 1927, however, when this institution merged into Astra, its activities within the Feminine Biopolitical Subsection shifted toward a more cohesive plan for action that would reflect the eugenic concerns of the Astra leadership and address short- and long-term issues connected to women's eugenic roles—"to maintain the purity and integrity of the family unit, educate the future generation, social work, protecting mother and child."[65]

The Feminine Biopolitical Subsection focused much of its attention on educating peasant women in the vein of Astra's focus on the peasantry as the natural source of the nation's biological vitality. Along with the already existing activities briefly described earlier, the Feminine Biopolitical Subsection also began organizing a peasant school for women, modeled after the schools for men. The organizers depicted their efforts as pioneering, for, they asserted, the work of feminist organizations in Romania had focused exclusively on women living in the cities. According to the Astra organizers, "the peasant woman almost does not exist" in the programs of feminist organizations.[66] Astra's feminine organization claimed to understand and represent the interests of this important segment of Romanian population better than feminist groups.

This negative rhetoric and intentional distancing from feminists betrays a sense of insecurity about the Feminine Biopolitical Subsection's sense of purpose and authority. It seems that Astra organizers viewed their relationship with feminist groups from a zero-sum game perspective: all these organizations were competing for the interest and loyalty of a small group of educated women, rather than offering a series of alternatives that might have been different, but not necessarily mutually exclusive.[67] Astra's feminine organization claimed to offer the ideal, total solution for the specific problems of peasant women, precluding any collaborative efforts with feminist groups.

The specific goals and curricula of these peasant schools fit in with the general eugenic emphasis on gearing women's education toward their roles as reproducers and as engaged educators of children in the home. The first concern of the organizers was to displace the romanticized vision of the city as a space for all possibilities with a more realistic view of what peasant women could expect if they moved there. One such critic asserted:

> We need to eliminate from the peasant woman's head the notion that true happiness is embodied by life in the city. . . . [Only] the village can offer a true life of physical and moral health.[68]

This statement also shows an important normative shift from focusing on personal happiness to focusing on *collective* health as an imperative goal for women.

According to eugenicists, the popular literature of the time, which depicted the city as a space for adventure, romance, and great opportunities, had permeated the countryside, sending alluring but dangerous messages to young women. It was more likely that those who migrated to urban areas came back with stories and artifacts that were very enticing to young women. Whatever their source, in the eyes of these reformers the appeal of the alluring images of the city caused the growing influx of young unmarried women in the cities. They also considered that this type of migration, motivated by a desire for romance, adventure, and material goods, had played an important role in the dramatic rise in prostitution since the end of World War I.[69]

This perspective betrays a class bias on the part of reformers, in spite of their scorn for middle-class feminists' own skewed view of women's issues. The previous quotation illustrates the instrumental way in which these reformers reified peasant women's concerns ("We need to eliminate from the peasant woman's head"). To begin with, urban migration was only partially motivated by the romanticized images in popular literature, since few young women in the countryside were literate and had access to such texts. Oral stories undoubtedly helped construct certain myths about life in the big city, but their impact may not have been so positive as reformers thought. In fact, those images were so removed from the universe in which most young women grew up and so remote from any aspect of their self-identity and social expectations that such images may have reinforced women's ties to the rural environment. However, because most of these reformers came in contact only with women who did end up in the city, especially as cooks or servants in bourgeois households, their perception of urban migration reflected this incomplete picture.

In its plans for a peasant women's school, the Feminine Biopolitical Subsection of Astra did not really address the issue that most likely played an important role in women's migration to urban areas—economics. For even with the land reform after World War I, many peasants were finding themselves in financial trouble by the end of the 1920s and especially in the early 1930s, during the Great Depression.[70] Some of them would send their oldest offspring to an urban area, whether a young man or a woman, with the hope of steady employment. In many cases, both men and women would try their luck in the city because of the inability of their local community to offer opportunities for making a living and to absorb all the available labor force. Women who looked for employment did not intentionally abandon their "natural" roles in search of new materialistic goals, upsetting the "traditional" social structure in the village, as eugenic reformers claimed. In fact, traditionally women had worked full-time in the countryside, not only in the home but also in the fields and in small-scale craft production. Their flight to the city was a sign of the changing structure of the economy, which no longer allowed women to perform their roles within the space of the family at the same time that family wages in the countryside were not keeping pace with the rise in the cost of living.[71]

Astra reformers failed to address this important aspect of women's economic concerns. The goals and curriculum for the peasant women's schools differed dramatically from the emphasis of the peasant schools for men on improving the economic skills of the students through special courses. This was not simply an omission, but rather an intentional construction that aimed to enforce more effectively what Astra saw as women's natural eugenic roles. Thus, instead of teaching women various skills that would help them become economically self-sufficient, these peasant schools focused on the goal of "selecting, strengthening and conserving the human biological capital."[72]

In order to live according to these eugenic goals, peasant women needed to study basic notions of heredity and learn about the significance of the family unit from a eugenic perspective. They would also have to prepare more scientifically for their role as mothers by learning how to take care of the physical and spiritual health of a child. Therefore, they would receive some basic information about social diseases (e.g., alcoholism, tuberculosis, venereal diseases, and prostitution), epidemic ailments, and individual hygiene. [73] A report from the Feminine Biopolitical Subsection describes the curriculum of one of the peasants schools as follows:

Home economics—cooking for every day of the week; sewing with a sewing machine, to sew aprons and children's cloth; . . . dying wool; . . . needle point embroidery; knitting; . . . choir; Romanian—writing and reading; literature; women's hygiene; Romanian history and geography.[74]

In other words, all the skills middle-class women might consider the minimal education for future wives and mothers. The program includes no training of any skills that would take women outside the home, save sewing. Even there, however, the report carefully lists the "appropriate" artifacts to result from this skill, aprons and children's clothes, circumscribing sewing to family- and home-related needs.

There was no thorough discussion in Romania about the connection between women's literacy and their ability to tend to the physical and spiritual well-being of their offspring. In fact, not unlike Theodore Roosevelt's depiction of race suicide two decades earlier in the United States, Romanian eugenicists blamed the decreasing birthrate among the middle classes on the abnormally high intellectual development of these women.[75] It seemed even more dangerous to these reformers to encourage the intellectual development of peasant women. Although they considered education the most important vehicle for fostering eugenic betterment, Romanian eugenicists were fully aware, especially in the case of women's education, of the double-edged nature of this tool for social change. They needed to control it very carefully and thoroughly, so that the pupils would not steal this sacred fire and turn it into their own weapon for self-empowerment. Thus, a carefully limited amount of information regarding history and literature was sufficient in the peasant schools.

Constructing a Eugenic Curriculum for Social Work Education

The same careful considerations about mobilizing and controlling women's specific "hereditary" talents lay at the foundation of another important privately established educational institution, the School for Social Work. This school was created in the late 1920s through the efforts of a number of prominent social reformers, many of whom were proponents of eugenics, and enlisted the patronage of the Royal House through Princess Ileana, who was the school's honorary directrice.[76] The aim of this institution was to create a professional core of well-educated women, trained to work in the agencies for social welfare created after World War I. Previously, various philanthropic foundations had attempted to provide short courses and some basic training for the future personnel in such welfare organizations, but all these efforts had lacked any sense of professionalism.

This school benefited from the committed leadership of Veturia Manuilă, who had a long and thorough training in social work not only in Romania but also in the United States. She had traveled there on a Rockefeller Foundation fellowship with her husband, Sabin Manuilă, the statistician student of Moldovan. She studied and wrote a doctoral thesis on social work at Johns Hopkins University and traveled from Baltimore to New York and Chicago to gain hands-on experience observing the work of various public and private welfare organizations. A great admirer of nineteenth-century reformers Jane Addams and Octavia Hill, Veturia Manuilă returned to Bucharest intent on creating a school for social work that used the latest scientific knowledge and field expertise in this profession.[77]

The school had, indeed, a very ambitious curriculum. It offered a three-year degree, which Veturia Manuilă hoped would gain academic credentials as equivalent to a university degree for men in order to offer women with professional ambitions an attractive alternative to a university degree.[78] The courses taught included a solid education in biology, psychology, public hygiene, puericulture, and nutrition, as well as special seminars on eugenics. Aside from these courses in natural science disciplines, students had to take a series of social science courses, from political science to sociology, as well as courses focusing on basic notions of civil law and economics. They would also undertake a series of courses with more practical orientations, from techniques for collective social assistance to management of welfare institutions and programs. In their six semesters at the school, students would have to take ninety-two courses to fulfill the requirements needed for obtaining a diploma.

The quality of this program was evidenced not only by the ambitious curriculum but also by the faculty who taught at the school. Many prominent names from the Romanian intellectual elite figured among the professors. They ranged from Mircea Vulcănescu (economics) and Henri Stahl (sociology) to Francisc Rainer (anatomy), Sabin Manuilă (demography), Gheorghe Banu (puericulture), and Eugeniu Botez (civil law), and some of them were very strong supporters of eugenics. Iuliu Moldovan and Dimitrie Gusti were members of the school board.[79] Some of the younger faculty had been recipients of important fellowships. For instance, Xenia Costa-Foru had obtained a Rockefeller Foundation grant to undertake some courses in sociology and social work in the United States.

The School for Social Work, which has heretofore gone unnoticed in the grand narratives of the history of public health and social work in Romania, effectively created a new profession in Romania—that of the social worker. It offered an exclusive avenue for women to enter a respectable, fulfilling, and economically viable occupation, for the students of this school were selected only from among female candidates. However, while it worked to educate and empower women, the school also aimed at restricting the avenues for professional fulfillment among its students. To begin with, the candidates came almost exclusively from the city. There was no "affirmative action" program to offer special scholarships for underprivileged peasant girls. The school, in fact, educated almost exclusively young women of the middle classes. Furthermore, Veturia Manuilă and the other faculty presented social work as the *only* type of public work suited to women, aside from training other women to become social workers. Manuilă, in particular, frowned upon feminists and considered their efforts at helping women as perversions of women's true nature.[80] Thus, while the School for Social Work became an avenue for educating and economically empowering women, it also tried to control the intellectual and professional forces it helped to nourish.

Biology in the New Curriculum

Eugenicists played an important role in the development of educational institutions not only by setting up new ways of selecting students according to inborn vocations and intellectual abilities, along class, ethnic, and gender lines, but also by seeking to change the overall structure and substance of what basic ideas education had to provide for all students in general. Eugenicists wanted nothing less than to "biologize" all education. According to one reformer, "the study of biology and hygiene should be fundamental . . . in the curricula of all schools."[81] This goal implied first and foremost the introduction of special classes that would focus on basic notions of biology from the first grade until college, something unprecedented in Romanian education. At that time, notions of biology were introduced only in high school and focused on issues of botany, zoology, and anatomy rather than on subjects such as personal hygiene, public health, and heredity in humans. This was an ambitious aim and an understandable one, since these courses would familiarize Romanian students with a scientific paradigm that represented an authoritative strand of thinking abroad, from Germany to France and the United States.

The particular angle taken in the drawing up and teaching of these courses represented, however, a clear bias toward eugenics. Reformers spoke of the need to introduce notions of biology in all education, yet they sought to present one particular vision of biology as the most authoritative one—hereditary determinism. One illustrative example is the textbook for an eighth-grade hygiene course published in 1936 by Aurel Voina, one of the more radical eugenicists, who also accepted an official position in the Antonescu-legionary coalition government in 1940. This textbook focused on long-term preventive hygiene measures rather than on curative ones, taking an intergenerational perspective on how to prevent future health problems. It also focused more on the hygiene of the community (i.e., the nation) than on the hygiene of the individual per se as a significant locus for measuring the effectiveness of hygiene measures. For instance, when speaking about the dangers of syphilis, the author asserted that it "attacks not only the organism of the individual carrier, but it can be transmitted to the offspring of the untreated patient over several generations. . . . [This is] one of the most feared illnesses, because of its long-lasting effects and its deep repercussions on the vitality of the family and the nation."[82] This view of health and illness as hereditary phenomena came through emphatically in the textbook's many discussions of specific medical conditions.

The author tied familiar problems such as alcoholism and tuberculosis to this grand view of the role played by each individual in the future health of the nation in language that both simplified the complexity of the claims about heredity (e.g., the controversy over the heredity of acquired characteristics) and dramatized the significance of individual actions. When discussing the importance of giving careful consideration to marriage and reproduction, the textbook described the issue as follows:

> The family represents only a link in a long inter-generational chain, where each generation is called forth to carry on the sacred flame of life entrusted to it by the previous generations. Today's population must be regarded as a laboratory in which the next generation of the Romanian people is being created. . . . The quality of a nation

is measured in the number and quality of its sons. . . . Thus, the duty of each citizen is to create a family.[83]

In this description eighth graders learned that their individual actions acquired significance only when placed in the larger context of the nation's biological interests and that citizenship included genetic responsibilities.

This particular way of inserting eugenic notions into the teaching of biology at the level of primary and secondary education did not represent a radical departure by Romanians from the practice of other eugenicists abroad. Textbooks similar to Voina's were already in use in Germany and the United States. In these countries, however, such texts provided but one of several versions of teaching biology. They were offered to a public that was already familiar with other, noneugenic notions of hygiene and biology. Consequently, the arguments made by eugenic textbooks abroad were more sophisticated, and their overall impact more questionable. In Romania, on the other hand, these notions were being taught for the first time in primary and pre–high school classes. Parents and teachers often knew as little about the scientific basis of the eugenic view of biology as the students did. Therefore, the hereditary determinism in the eugenic discussions of health went largely unquestioned by those who were teaching these notions and even more so by their students.

By the mid-1930s, the directives of the Ministry of Education with regard to teaching notions of biology and hygiene reinforced the significance of these disciplines as "a chief preoccupation for teachers and students. Preserving one's health [and] the strengthening of the body have very close ties to the future of the Fatherland, which will require robust and healthy ploughmen and workers, healthy intellectuals, strong and swift soldiers."[84] The implications and specific means for addressing this goal remained unstated. Ştefan Bârsănescu, another important figure in the movement for education reform along eugenic lines, did put these ideas into more direct language. While "education cannot create dispositions, but only influence inborn characteristics," the author claimed that the role of teachers was to mold each student according to the laws of the human species, community interests, and finally individual characteristics.[85]

Eugenicists focused their most thorough efforts on biologizing higher education. Advanced notions of biology, especially with regard to the social aspects of heredity, would thus become a compulsory part of a university education.

During this period Dimitrie Gusti, at that point Minister of Education, embarked on another project that focused on the importance of social action in the educational process—his by-now-famous monographic school for social research.[86] A supporter of Moldovan's biopolitics, Gusti included notions of hereditary biology in both his seminars on sociology and his fieldwork. One of the first specialists to introduce these notions in the seminars overseen by Gusti was Iordache Făcăoaru.[87] In their analyses of various problems in the village, students had to investigate the extent of social illnesses, such as alcoholism, and account for these problems as potential threats to the biological well-being of the villagers—not only in the present but also in the long-term future.[88] In addition, in their fieldwork, the teams set up genealogical-biological files for each inhabitant, which recorded not only the vital statistics of the individual subjects but also a series of data about that person's genealogy, focusing on any hereditary pathologies of past generations, from syphilis to alcoholism and criminal behavior. These databases set the stage for future eugenic research and modern technologies for controlling individual citizens' bodies and behavior.

This strategy of combining field experience with a decidedly biological perspective on sociology became even more central in higher education in the late 1930s. During this period Gusti, as the Minister of Education, launched a program that would encompass all university students—the Social Service.[89] In order to receive their degrees, all university students had to spend one summer in the countryside doing the type of sociological fieldwork with which Gusti had been experimenting since the late 1920s. This experience would have an important formative impact on the participating students at many levels. For our purposes here, it is important to stress the students' familiarization with the notions of hereditary illnesses and eugenics that were included in the curricula of these summer programs. This was especially the case in Transylvania, where Astra's leadership was in charge of implementing the specific provisions and programs of the Social Service.[90]

The eugenicists' aims at biologizing education went beyond introducing specific courses on biology at all levels of education. They hoped to revise the curricula of all other disciplines and imbue the specific notions taught in each course with the spirit of eugenic responsibility. For instance, when teaching arithmetic, they proposed introducing problems that would solve practical eugenic problems instead of measuring apples and pears or distances between two points. Students would start to learn about recessive genes from math problems that asked for the percentages of offspring with recessive characteristics in a given set of data.

Similarly, literary selections for teaching reading and grammar would be taken from texts that not only described the glorious past of the Romanian people but also focused specifically on the national characteristics of this people in biological terms. Other texts would emphasize gender roles, praising motherhood as the fulfillment of every girl's natural instincts and offering examples of the brave conduct of men on the front and as breadwinners. These selections would also present stories about feminists and drunkards, vilifying the behavior of these literary characters as inappropriate and dysgenic. Thus, students would learn small lessons about eugenics in each discipline, and these notions would be reinforced many times during their years in school.

It is difficult to assess how much impact these ideas had in the classroom. To begin with, these reforms were first suggested in the mid-1930s and only slowly incorporated into the general curricula. The Ministry of Education and various reformers, such as Bârsănescu, made special efforts to train teachers in this direction. However, aside from Bârsănescu's work, other important texts that could have served as guidelines for teachers in the classroom are difficult to locate. Rewriting the textbooks for the traditional disciplines according to eugenic ideas proved difficult. The Ministry of Education favored such changes in principle. However, with a reduced budget since the mid-1930s, such an endeavor seemed unfeasible. Therefore, exposure to eugenic ideas remained limited in most cases to the special courses on hygiene and biology introduced during this period. Furthermore, most of these reforms were put aside during the war. After 1944, their supporters gradually fell from grace.

Medical Education and the Future Eugenic Leadership

Reforming medical education remained an ongoing preoccupation for eugenicists throughout the interwar period. This was a top priority, for eugenicists' notion of controlled social reform meant that the future leadership of the eugenic state, doctors in particular, had to receive a very thorough and constantly updated education that would enable them to play their elite role responsibly. The main issues on which eugenicists focused their efforts of reform were: (1) introducing hygiene and preventive medicine as fundamental courses in the curriculum, along with anatomy and pathology; (2) introducing a more advanced level of specialization in the upper-division courses; and (3) imbuing doctors with a sense of their social responsibility. Discussions about these issues took place throughout the 1920s, and several institutions, such as Moldovan's Institute of Hygiene in Cluj, introduced courses for specialization in preventive medicine and experimental programs to encourage more research and expanded medical practice in the countryside.

In 1929, Moldovan's appointment as General Secretary of the Ministry of Health offered proponents of eugenics the opportunity to address medical education reform through a project for comprehensive public health reform, written and successfully promoted by Moldovan himself. The Moldovan Law (1930) defines the category of "hygiene doctor" as one of the five fundamental categories for organizing medical education and practice.[91] These doctors would receive a specific education and would focus on forms of preventive medicine and social work that reflected eugenic interests. Some of their responsibilities included:

> to study and recommend necessary measures for water supply; to control industrial establishments; to oversee food hygiene in the food industry and public market places; to inspect public places where food and drinks are served and enforce hygiene standards; to oversee the fight against venereal diseases . . . ; to take measures regarding any problems of hygiene and public health; to control and oversee school hygiene.[92]

The language of the law does not make explicit reference to eugenics, but the "fight against venereal diseases" and the "problems of public health" are in fact ambiguous enough to encompass eugenic measures.[93] The law also describes in great detail the types of courses such doctors would need to complete in order to qualify for their specialization.[94]

Finally, this law created special programs—such as the Gilău "health station" (*plasa sanitară*)—and financial incentives for young doctors to opt for practicing medicine in the countryside, where medical help was needed most urgently.[95] The 1930 law became one of the fundamental pieces of legislation for organizing medical education and practice throughout the interwar period. In fact, its provisions with regard to medical education remained largely unchanged u..til 1948, when the institutional structure of medical education and practice were thoroughly revised under the communist regime.

Physical Education and Eugenic Vigor

Another educational reform that ranked high among eugenic programs was the introduction of more physical education in schools. This measure was complemented with extracurricular organizations modeled on scouts' groups abroad. This interest in body culture was an integral part of the eugenicists' vision of reshaping Romanian society, for they favored the *mens sana in corpore sano* approach to education, very much in vogue during the interwar period everywhere in Europe.[96] As early as 1927 Astra created a Subsection for Physical and Moral Education within its Biopolitical Section. This organization predated by five years the creation of a better-known boy scouts group, the Cercetași, under the patronage of Carol II.[97] The Astra group, the Carpathian Falcons, set out to educate young boys in matters of morality and courage as much as in matters of personal and public hygiene and future eugenic responsibilities (e.g., with regard to marriage choices).[98]

The language used in the statutes of this organization, published for the first time in the *Buletin Eugenic și Biopolitic,* marks the essential differences that set it apart from other contemporary scouts' organizations in its overall eugenic orientation. The Falcons' credo read as follows: "I will keep untainted the hearth of my family, will keep watch over all that could jeopardize the physical and spiritual vigor of future generations . . . [and] I will guard against any dangers to the health of others."[99] In this statute valor and virtue were redefined from moral and ethical issues to medical ones. In fact, the Carpathian Falcons would help reconstruct a sense of moral obligation in accordance with a hereditary concept of health. Fostering one's biological consciousness and responsibility as active factors in the health of present and future generations featured prominently among the goals of the Carpathian Falcons.

The organization was open to all except "the drunkard, the criminal, the traitor, those who consciously infect another and those who disdain the notion of Romania."[100] Membership was defined in keeping with eugenic concepts of normalcy and health. Since drunkards were usually branded as carriers of dysgenic characteristics, as were criminals in many instances, these individuals were denied the right to membership in an organization that stood for biological cleansing. However, the statutes blended nationalist political with biological concerns. Traitors and "those who disdain the notion of Romania" could not be defined in genetic terms, but they were still presented as dysgenic elements.

This provision opened up the possibility for denying membership along ethnic lines, for one could easily lump Hungarians into one of these categories, especially given the fear of Hungarian revisionism among many Romanians. The text, however, made no clear-cut mention of Hungarians or other minorities, allowing in principle the right for anyone to apply, if not to be admitted to, the ranks of the Carpathian Falcons. This organization grew rapidly and reached a membership of twenty thousand by 1934, presumably mostly from Transylvania.[101] Aside from constantly educating the young Falcons according to eugenic principles through contests, outdoor activities, and community involvement, the organization built a sports park in Cluj. It was completed in 1928 and is still enjoyed by many today under the name of the Falcons' president, Iuliu Hațiegan. Only a handful of Romanians today are aware, however, of the eugenic overtones of this organization's initial goals.

Eugenic Education under the Antonescu Regime

From 1940 until 1944, some of the more comprehensive education reforms envisioned by eugenicists had to be put on hold. For instance, revising the entire curriculum for the secondary schools, biologizing every textbook and discipline, and implementing the programs of the Social Service proved unrealistic, especially with regard to finances and personnel. However, the short-lived legionary government and then Antonescu's regime preserved many of the changes already undertaken in the previous decade.[102] The same strict norms for medical training and emphasis on preventive medicine remained on the books. Doctors and teachers were still entrusted with the responsibility for educating the rural masses about basic notions of hygiene and heredity.

Some important changes intervened, however, in the discourse about health, heredity, and eugenic betterment in the various educational forums. The fundamental parameters for organizing education went from focusing on selecting students according to hereditary talents, aptitudes, and intellectual abilities in a comprehensive, complex fashion to simply excluding Jews from the student body. In 1940, paraphrasing the newly appointed legionary Minister of Education, Traian Brăileanu, one author stated simply that "the Romanian school, purified of Jews . . . will be able to follow its normal course. . . ."[103] This represented a radical departure from the initial eugenic attempt to foster the selection and education of all students according to their various intellectual abilities and aptitudes.

The wartime regime did not follow up on the attempts to modernize all educational institutions and pedagogical practices according to the latest scientific developments and Romania's needs in the increasingly competitive international situation. The government did not encourage a comprehensive effort to include all students in educational reform and change the education structures. Rather, it replaced this view with a simpler, quicker "solution"—excluding the "dysgenic" Jewish students. In this extremist view, Romanians were unambiguously assumed to be superior on the basis of their biological makeup.

This was a point of view to which Moldovan and many other eugenicists did not subscribe. In a brief but significant note that appeared below an overtly anti-Semitic article published by Iordache Făcăoaru in the *Buletin Eugenic și Biopolitic* in 1943, the editorial board of the journal mentioned that "out of a wish to present our readership with various points of view on the general themes that preoccupy our publications, we have published this article, although we do not agree with the author's conclusions regarding 'the hierarchy of ethnic groups.'"[104] Unfortunately, the very institutional reforms and curriculum changes advocated by eugenicists lent themselves to anti-Semitic interpretations, pursued with vigor by individuals like Brăileanu, Făcăoaru, and Voina while in power.

■ ■ ■

T H E legacy of eugenic education reforms was ambiguous: they professed to embrace diversity and modernization but often lent themselves to limiting, exclusionary interpretations. During World War II the concern with modernizing educational technologies—structures and methods—for social mobilization and control was gradually replaced by a more radicalized rhetoric and policy of exclusion. Policy makers tried to build a sense of identity and community by distancing certain populations from the "other" in terms of biological hereditary differences rather than by exploring the positive potential in the ambiguities of these divisions, as eugenicists often had.

Yet while it is important to make this distinction between eugenic intentions and their reinterpretation by the policy makers of the wartime regime, one cannot deny the impact of eugenics on the rhetoric and programs of right-wing radicals. This study, however, does not seek to identify the guilty in this process, for the insights to be gained by finding any one individual who could be held responsible for biologizing right-wing extremism during this period seem rather limited. More significant is the fact that eugenic ideas about biological heredity had gained greater currency by the late 1930s and were increasingly reconstructed in a negative exclusionary rhetoric that spelled out the need for the state to assume coercive control over the education of its citizens more clearly than eugenicists themselves may have intended.

CHAPTER 6

FOR THE HEALTH

OF THE NATION

Measures in Public Health and Reproductive Control

> Instead of natural selection, man should practice rational selection.
>
> Eugen Relgis, *Umanitarism şi eugenism*

> [Iuliu Moldovan] appears to have a sincere desire to reorganize the sanitary service of the country on a modern and constructive basis and a belief in his ability to do so.
>
> Rockefeller Foundation Report, 1929

IN ADDITION to eugenicists' important contributions to changing education, their discourse about reform translated into a series of laws and programs regarding public health. What drove these efforts was the same fundamental concern shared by eugenicists elsewhere for improving the healthy "stock" and limiting the growth of dysgenics. Thus, concern with reproduction was behind all specific measures, as unrelated as they may seem at first glance. The specific measures eugenicists focused on revolved around a few central issues: infant mortality, venereal disease, alcoholism, tuberculosis, and immunization against epidemic diseases. Their goal was to convert these somewhat marginal issues into central concerns for the state. While they did not succeed in increasing significantly government spending on public health, they helped expand the responsibilities of the state toward its members and create important, pioneering institutions, legislation, and programs for public health. These efforts bore unexpected and *unintended* fruit after 1944, when the communist regime took over these institutions, expanding and gradually modifying their functions.

This chapter follows eugenicists' attempts to reform public health from 1918 until 1948 and shows their close links with the NPP's health-reform programs. Relations between the Antonescu regime and the eugenics movement are less clear. The wartime regime retreated from preventive programs set up to help the "eugenically sound" populations. At the same time, the policies of this regime vis-à-vis the Jews and nonethnic Romanians in general suggest some links with the aggressively restrictive positions of some Romanian eugenicists, such as Făcăoaru, Herseni, and even Sabin Manuilă. Eugenicists never criticized the racist policies of the wartime regime for obvious reasons—censorship was enforced, and it is likely that they stood by Antonescu as a matter of wartime loyalty as well as because of fear of defeat by the Soviet Union. Some, however, like Făcăoaru and Herseni, were full-fledged supporters of the wartime regime, especially with regard to its fascist orientation. Yet even before the war ended, some eugenicists, such as Moldovan, began to criticize the wartime regime's neglect of public health issues. As this discussion shows, these eugenicists then started anew, rebuilding programs cut short by the war and reinstating oncesuspended public health laws. These attempts were cut short again by the communist takeover in 1948 but nonetheless left a lasting legacy.

Background to the Development of Public Health after 1918

Governmental concern with public health in Romania stretched back to the 1830s, when the Organic Statutes created the first comprehensive network of laws and institutions to regulate health care and hygiene. The first period of real growth in this area came from the 1850s to the mid-1860s. Under the leadership of Nicolae Krețulescu, Iacob Felix, and especially Carol Davilla, education, legislation, and the general state of public health saw remarkable growth. The measures passed and partly implemented during this period represented the first concerted attempt to link health care to state responsibilities. Standards of pharmaceutical production and distribution were passed, and attributes of precepts regarding public health concerns were set in law.[1]

During the War of Independence, the Ministry of War created a special health service for the first time, intended to provide efficient assistance from a well-trained medical corps for the various health problems produced by the new type of trench warfare. Medical help beyond caring for the wounded was vital for securing the physical integrity of the troops, because of a host of hygienic and epidemic problems at the front. Thus, the War of Independence became a pivotal moment in early state-initiated public health.

Over the next few decades, efforts by the next generation of medical leaders, such as Victor Babeş and Ioan Cantacuzino, led to some improvement in legislation regarding government spending on and regulation of public health. During the same period Iacob Felix wrote influential studies that focused on the long-term losses incurred by the Romanian economy and society at large as a result of the nutritive and toxic problems rampant among the rural population, as well as the lack of adequate vaccination programs against epidemics that were still ravaging the countryside, while they had been successfully contained, if not eradicated, elsewhere.[2] Felix depicted the public health deficiencies in Romania as an important cause of economic backwardness and urged authorities to look into these issues as a matter of securing the future labor force.

After the peasant revolt of 1907 exposed some of worst aspects of malnutrition and rural poor health, many more intellectuals and politicians began to include items relating to hygiene and nutrition in their programs for social reform.[3] Yet they had relatively little impact on policy. Government involvement with public health remained limited to the poorly funded service within the Ministry of War. The fortunes of this ministry soared again during the Balkan War of 1913 and especially during World War I, but these conflicts also brought unprecedented public health problems. In addition to the high death toll, several epidemics spread quickly, and a series of new problems began to appear. Syphilis, for instance, had not been a significant problem in Romania before 1914. By the end of the war, however, it had turned into a veritable epidemic, along with a number of other venereal diseases.

One important step toward more comprehensive institutional support of public health by the state was a law passed in 1910, named after its main promoter, Ioan Cantacuzino. The law provided the first elaborate definition of the responsibilities and powers of doctors in public health matters.[4] It also attempted to delineate what constituted public health and fell under the responsibility of the state. However, the law had an image of health care that emphasized more the curative, reactive aspect of medicine, rather than the preventive one, which would become the hallmark of the reform efforts during the interwar period.

Debates over Public Health between Liberals and Eugenicists (1918–28)

By 1918, many doctors had been mobilized during the war and had seen some of the more gruesome problems both in the trenches and on the home front. They became convinced that the health of the Romanian population was in a period of crisis, which, if uncontained, could lead to the demise of this people, in spite of the victorious peace after World War I. In response, doctors with various political loyalties called for a separate Ministry of Health with the political and financial power to address all issues relating to the health of the nation. In 1921 Victor Babeş asserted that state institutions had been uncaring vis-à-vis the health of the Romanian people. He pointed an angry finger at the politicians who had not upheld their responsibilities toward the masses and called for the creation of a Ministry of Health based on the principle of equal access to health care for all:

> Just as death is equally fatal for everyone, all [living] individuals are also equal and must be treated equally, and the state has an obligation toward its members to spend no less and no more than the strictly necessary amount to ensure the health of all citizens and cure their ailments.[5]

What is significant about Babeş's critique is the inclusiveness of his remarks and his sense of responsibility toward all citizens of Romania, regardless of ethnicity. At the same time, as eugenic ideas began to display various degrees of ethnocentrism and exclusivism, Babeş never criticized these tendencies. Rather, he remained a faithful supporter of Moldovan's ideas and public health projects.

Scathing critiques such as Babeş's were not uncommon in the early postwar years. Similar proposals for creating a more comprehensive state infrastructure came from other corners of the country as well, most prominently from Cluj. Here Iuliu Moldovan helped reorganize public health institutions after the union of Transylvania with the Romanian Kingdom on 1 December, 1918.[6] In his two years at the helm of the Service for Public Health and Social Assistance within the Directing Council, Moldovan had promoted the creation of a state infrastructure that would address not only present problems, such as controlling current epidemics, but also long-term goals. Concerned with preventive medicine, he sent numerous teams of doctors into the countryside to control some of the ongoing epidemics by immunizing and educating the rural population.[7]

Moldovan's policies were already shaped by his eugenic vision of public health. In 1921 he called for creating a Ministry of Health whose main focus would be the "qualitative development of the entire population."[8] It is important to stress that at this early stage, Moldovan's concerns for the health of the nation were much more inclusive than in his later writings. He was less willing to single out any particular groups that threatened the health of the nation, perhaps because the Directing Council was only a junior partner in the newly created Greater Romania. Whatever his reasons, these early efforts encompassed the whole population of Transylvania, echoing Babeş's own vision of equal access to public health for all citizens.

Another early proponent of eugenic public health programs was Alexandru Vaida-Voevod, the prominent Peasantist politician who later gravitated toward the extreme right. At a conference held in April 1921, he accused the liberal government of Social Darwinist thinking about public health and of irresponsible behavior, for it claimed to be dealing with critical public health issues by letting them work themselves out as a means of "race selection." Vaida-Voevod branded such thinking as tyrannical and politically corrupt and lent his support to creating a Ministry of Health that would address problems of national health in a more responsible and effective manner.[9] From early on the National-Peasant Party was more interested than the National Liberal Party in expanding the state's responsibilities for public health. Not only Vaida-Voevod but also Iuliu Maniu expressed his support for Moldovan's ideas.[10] Later, when the NPP briefly came to power in 1928, Maniu appointed Moldovan as General Secretary at the Ministry of Health and gave him a free hand in writing a comprehensive public health law.

In the early 1920s, however, the National Party in Transylvania was still an opposition force, while Brătianu's National Liberal Party presided over the founding of a Ministry of Health in 1923. Moldovan and other supporters of a reformed Ministry of Health found it impossible to work with the liberal regime from the very beginning. After all, Brătianu's party had abolished the Directing Council and swallowed up the regional institutions developed by Moldovan between 1918 and 1920 into a centralized infrastructure. Both Moldovan's concern with regional problems and his innovations in public health programs fell on deaf ears in Bucharest. This embittered the Transylvanian doctor, who was demoted to the position of General Hygiene Inspector for this region, in charge of overseeing legislation generated directly in Bucharest.[11] Thus, Moldovan and other Cluj doctors interested in eugenic public health reform turned toward the newly created NPP as a potential ally in supporting their interests.

During the 1923–28 period the liberal regime oversaw a rapid expansion of the institutions, budget, and programs of the Ministry of Health. In 1926 Prime Minister Brătianu reported that the budget of this ministry had jumped almost twofold, from 158.5 million lei in 1923, its founding year, to 353.5 million in 1925. This budget was divided among categories such as "food and utilities," "medicine," "surgical instruments and other tools," "schools for secondary personnel," "linens," "campaigns against social diseases," and "tuberculosis."[12]

This list of spending categories illustrates the haphazard way in which the Ministry of Health developed. It seems that each spending category developed as a response to a particular need for expanding an already existing institution. For instance, the schools for secondary medical personnel are listed under the budget of the Ministry of Health, while higher medical education fell under the responsibilities of the Ministry of Education. This inconsistency developed because medical education had previously been part of the Ministry of Education's budget. In the mid-1920s, when the authorities finally recognized the need for certified nurses, sanitary agents, and midwives, they turned the responsibility for organizing the training of such secondary personnel over to medical specialists in the Ministry of Health.[13]

The largest part of the budget went toward hospital care. The same report mentioned earlier justifies this spending by depicting the institutions for curative medicine, especially hospitals, as being in complete disarray as a result of the war.[14] Brătianu took pride in the work undertaken to rebuild these institutions as a form of national reconstruction. By contrast, the preoccupation of the ministry with preventive medicine, immunization, and hygiene seemed marginal. Only 10 million lei were spent on such issues in 1923, a sum that grew to 33.5 million by 1925, still a negligible amount (less than 10 percent of the total budget).[15]

More importantly, however, all policies to improve public health were undertaken in a piecemeal fashion, rather than as part of a more comprehensive reform. For instance, the ministry gave generous subventions to various private foundations that worked to treat and help prevent tuberculosis. However, it did not make any attempt to study the causes and the spread of tuberculosis in the country in general. The same could be said of the antimalaria campaign. Many doctors, especially those whose interests favored greater emphasis on preventive medicine, were frustrated by this type of change.

Doctors in Transylvania felt especially shortchanged by these developments. The Brătianu report, for instance, gave little credit to public health institutions in Transylvania, describing their achievements as a result of efforts originating in Bucharest. In his discussion of improvements in secondary health education, Brătianu conceded that "we must mention . . . that in Transylvania, where sanitary agents have been introduced just recently, their role in improving health in the rural areas has been unanimously recognized."[16] One can only imagine that Moldovan and other doctors who had been part of the Directing Council found this remark inaccurate and insulting, for they had worked hard and with great results to improve health care in the countryside long before the Ministry of Health introduced sanitary agents in Transylvania.

Instead of battling with these Bucharest windmills, Moldovan focused his efforts for public health reform at the regional level, first as General Hygiene Inspector and director of the Institute of Hygiene in Cluj and later as president of Astra. The Institute of Hygiene in Cluj, founded by Moldovan in 1919, served as a powerhouse for the development of research on public health programs for the region.[17] Here future specialists in preventive medicine received their training, the broad and specific goals of the major public health institutions in the region were outlined and monitored, research in epidemiology was undertaken, and new programs for preventive medicine were experimented with. Along with the institute, Moldovan helped found other related institutions, from a school for nurses and secondary medical personnel to a hospital for cancer patients, which was also a laboratory for research on cancer, and a hospital for women, which focused not only on obstetrics and gynecology but also on puericulture. Combining research with praxis was one of the lasting effects Moldovan's education in Western Europe had on his vision of public health. He strove to imbue this spirit in all his activities at the Institute of Hygiene and at the medical school in Cluj.

One of the most important measures undertaken by Moldovan in 1919 was the creation of nineteen mobile dispensaries. They monitored the general level of health of the rural population by periodically gathering information from various regions and were equipped with the medical supplies to deal with any epidemic outbreaks. The mobile dispensaries also worked as centers of immunization against malaria and scarlet fever, as well as centers for the treatment of social diseases, especially syphilis, deemed one of the most crucial health problems in the countryside because of its potential degenerative effect on reproduction. Finally, the mobile dispensaries offered prenatal advice to pregnant women and helped educate them about safe methods of giving birth and caring for infants. Occasionally, they offered help with difficult births and various health problems during the immediate postpartum period. All of these measures were unprecedented in the countryside, and their effects were far-reaching. In a report about the state of public health in Transylvania in the first postunion decade, Aurel Voina spoke proudly of the activities undertaken by the mobile dispensaries: "The total number of consultations given over the last ten years has risen to impressive figures. The results of these actions have been wonderful, especially if we take into account the modest material means employed in their mission."[18]

These institutions functioned through the continued efforts of Moldovan and other prominent doctors in Cluj, such as Iuliu Hațiegan.[19] At the same time, friction with the Bucharest authorities grew until 1922, when Moldovan was accused of embezzling state funds by the civil authorities appointed from Bucharest.[20] Moldovan was eventually acquitted, but this investigation served to embitter him even further toward the political powers in Bucharest. In 1924 he resigned from his official position as General Hygiene Inspector and turned to local resources to continue some of the programs he had helped start in his previous official capacity.

The Ministry of Health did sustain some of the reforms started under Moldovan's patronage, from the Institute of Hygiene to the School for Nursing and from the hospital for women to the mobile sanitary program. However, the Bucharest officials did not increase the subsidies for the mobile dispensaries, for instance, which remained at the insufficient number of nineteen throughout the 1920s. Although the cost-effectiveness of the mobile dispensaries had been thoroughly documented by Moldovan's followers, the Ministry of Health did not spare any funds to increase this program.

Eugenicists sought to augment these efforts with the funds and programs they created through Astra. However, the financial situation of this organization was itself insecure during the mid-twenties. The greatest contribution made by Astra to promoting the public health goals envisioned by Moldovan and other eugenicists was to publish a series of inexpensive brochures and articles in the annual *Calendar,* describing in a simplified manner the causes of various illnesses, such as tuberculosis, and the most effective measures to prevent their occurrence and spread. At the same time, the Medical and Biopolitical Section of Astra called upon doctors who were active members in the organization to promote this type of literature, not only at conferences open to the public but also by increasing the number of their consultations with the underprivileged rural masses.

Searching for Alternatives: The Role of the Rockefeller Foundation

Eugenicists' efforts to spread public health measures were helped by the arrival on the scene of another important source of financial assistance—the Rockefeller Foundation. This organization had been sending representatives to examine the situation in Romania since 1923. By the late 1920s they decided that the Cluj medical center, rather than the one in Bucharest, would become their main focus of philanthropic activities in Romania, for they considered the institutions and programs developed in Cluj as more modern and more progressive than similar programs in Bucharest.[21] Yet the financial assistance of the Rockefeller Foundation remained rather limited until 1928, when the NPP came to power and helped the fortunes of Moldovan's eugenics.

In 1929, the Rockefeller Foundation decided to allocate the generous sum of 150,000 dollars for the construction of an Institute of Hygiene in Bucharest, because of their increased faith in the reliability of the Romanian officials to pursue comprehensive reform in public health:

> With the formation of the new National Peasant Party government ... the prospects of carrying out a broader program are much improved. These men appear to have a sincere desire to reorganize the sanitary service on a *modern and constructive* basis.... A small group, including Professor Moldovan, who is the technical chief of the ministry, have had either good foreign training or valuable experience in Rumania.[22]

In addition to their support for this project, the Rockefeller Foundation allocated funds to the local health stations in Gilău and Iaşi, the Schools for Nursing in Cluj and Bucharest, and the bureau of vital statistics of the Ministry of Health. It is unclear how much money was funneled into these projects by 1940, but the total sum exceeded 80,000 dollars, in addition to the 150,000 dollars allocated for the Bucharest Institute of Hygiene.[23] When translated into lei, these sums constituted a very important source of revenue and a sizable portion of the Ministry of Health's total budget.[24] The Rockefeller Foundation's contributions were predicated, however, on the promise that the Ministry of Health in Bucharest would match these funds. During the 1930s, the most time-consuming work undertaken by the Rockefeller Foundation in Romania was the effort to secure matching funds, which were denied at every step by the liberal authorities after the NPP lost control over the government.[25]

The Moldovan Law (1930)

Under the short-lived Peasantist regime, eugenicists were finally able to lay the foundations for comprehensive public health reform. In 1930, after prolonged debates with other doctors and policy makers in the Ministry of Health over the nature and extent of the reform, Moldovan was able to push through the Public Health and Welfare Law that bears his name.[26] This legislation addressed the global problems of Romanian health care with a long-term eugenic vision and at the same time included very specific measures about every aspect of health care, from education to medical practice and administration.[27] Aside from a very thorough description of the education standards, powers, and responsibilities of all employees under the jurisdiction of the ministry, the Moldovan Law also constructed new responsibilities and powers for the ministry.

In particular, this law described in great detail new methods for combating venereal disease, especially syphilis.[28] The law stipulated that medical rather than police personnel should oversee the containment of venereal disease by making treatment obligatory and free for those who could not afford it. Moldovan and the other doctors who played a role in writing these provisions hoped to increase the willingness of the population to cooperate by eliminating the ominous presence of police authorities. The law held both patients and doctors responsible in this process, an important change in conceptualizing public health legislation. However, no parallel legislative reform in the Penal Code was passed until the 1938, a failure that lessened the incentive of both parties to cooperate with the law, since there was no effective threat of retribution.

Some of the most important provisions of the Moldovan Law had to do with hygiene. It included a chapter outlining guidelines for hygiene in public places and assigning important powers to hygiene doctors in overseeing the enforcement of these standards:

The hygiene doctor has the authority to visit . . . all public establishments in order to examine their cleanliness and take measures against insalubrious situations that are dangerous to public hygiene. He must uphold an objective attitude. . . . He must examine any complaint and has the right to order any changes deemed necessary. Those not abiding by these orders will have to pay a fine of 100 to 10,000 lei. . . . The fines will be paid into the county or municipal public health fund.[29]

The thoroughness of these regulations and the strict standards they sought to enforce made the Moldovan Law an unprecedented effort at creating norms for cleanliness in public spaces, on a par with legislation in Western Europe and the United States, which far surpassed past concern with public hygiene in Romania. The law set down strict specifications for the most varied cases, from architectural, structural, and hygiene standards for operating a public service establishment to regulations over sewage and water service and even restrictions on the size and location of private residences.

These new regulations also opened up a potential source of revenue for public health programs, because they required public establishments, like beauty salons and restaurants, to pay fees to hygiene inspectors in order to operate. A series of fines for violating public hygiene norms were also listed, giving the hygiene officials full authority over enforcing the law. Doctors now had greater power in acquiring and autonomously administering public funds. For instance, fines for violations of the hygiene standards would be paid directly into the municipal or regional public health revenue fund and administered for local expenses by the public health officials at this level.[30] This decentralization of the budget into the hands of local medical authorities was also an unprecedented move.

At the same time, the law included provisions that would *punish* doctors who did not responsibly and conscientiously oversee the implementation of these norms and did not address hygiene problems through retribution against the culprits.[31] These were also unprecedented measures, for they gave doctors significant power in public policy making and implementation, matched by legal responsibilities.

Until 1930, such powers and responsibilities had rested only in the hands of public authorities such as local mayors and other members of the administrative bureaucracy—the police and the courts of law. These individuals came to resent the newcomer doctors, whose newly acquired official position threatened to reduce the authority of other government officials, especially over the administration of public funds. The power of hygiene officials was unsettling to the arrangements reached at the local level between some of the corrupt bureaucrats and the well-to-do potential culprits. This friction would become more apparent over time, when memoranda and letters of protest began to pour into the Ministry of Health in large numbers, protesting doctors' allegedly arbitrary and harsh policies toward local industrial and commercial establishments.[32] In 1933, for instance, the Commission for Industrial Hygiene at the Ministry of Health made over thirteen hundred decisions based on such complaints and memoranda from local hygiene officials.[33] Although a great deal of frustrating negotiation and paperwork were generated by this policy of stricter control over public hygiene, the provisions of the Moldovan Law also enabled the ministry to acquire more revenue and expand its other programs of preventive health care and immunization.

Another essential aspect of the Moldovan Law was its emphasis on decentralizing the authority of public health administration. Before this law, local institutions and organizations had two options for acquiring funding: (1) if they wanted the official sanction of the government they had to depend entirely on Bucharest for their revenues and were thus vulnerable to the political vagaries of the central government; (2) if they sought to remain autonomous, they would not be able to benefit from privileges and protection from Bucharest. Astra's highly unsuccessful effort to secure official status while keeping its local autonomy was a good case study for Moldovan.[34] In his capacity as president of Astra and even before that, as a member of the Directing Council, he had already tasted the fruits of frustration in his negotiations with Bucharest over issues of regional autonomy and official recognition.

The 1930 law finally enabled Moldovan to bring to life what had become one of his strongest convictions: that comprehensive public health reform could not succeed unless the authorities combined a system of centralized decision making by a group of elite technocrats—doctors—with a decentralized system of implementing these policies, so that they might respond to specific local needs. Moldovan wanted to allow local public health officials to tailor their actions to the issues of greatest concern in each community. His vision went so far as to offer a large degree of autonomy at this level over spending and raising money. However, along with increasing the degree of local autonomy regarding public health matters, the Moldovan Law also stipulated that public health institutions needed to become more self-reliant and begin to draw their funds from the local administration, through either local, regional, or municipal taxes or lottery funds.[35] Moldovan integrated into his plan for decentraliz-ing public health administration the notion of responsibility as a corollary to the increased power of government officials.

However, this decentralizing policy did not fit with other laws that governed the use of public funds at the local level and established jurisdiction in regulat-ing public actions. As a result, the effects of the Moldovan Law were not quite as dramatic as Moldovan and other policy makers had hoped. Local public health officials had to negotiate continuously with other appointed officials over access to the funds allocated to them by the Moldovan Law but not sanc-tioned by other administrative laws. The constant flow of complaints about the doctors' alleged abusive use of fines vis-à-vis local entrepreneurs vividly illus-trates this tension. Most complaints came from entrepreneurs whose businesses had been fined by the hygiene inspectors and who sought to appeal these deci-sions directly to the ministry rather than to any regional authorities. In 1932 alone there were over fifteen hundred such complaints.[36]

Moreover, the fact that the central authorities at the Ministry of Health had to resolve many of the debates between local public health officials and other government employees shows that effective decentralization was more of a hope than a reality. In effect, many of the decisions that should have been made at the local level in a speedy manner turned into long, drawn-out arguments between local and Bucharest officials, which paralyzed local programs because of a lack of funds while decisions pertaining to local questions reverted back to the central government. Even with these important shortcomings, the Moldovan Law did introduce a new way of conceptualizing the relationship between cen-tral and local administration, which redistributed government authority. The law empowered local technical officials at the expense of the central adminis-trative bureaucracy, while allowing the technocratic elite at the top of the min-isterial hierarchy to retain control over long-term policies. This remained one of the important reforms enacted by Romanian eugenicists in their efforts to place a technocratic elite of specialists in positions of greater control over the public's well-being and the future health of the nation.

The Impact of the 1930 Law

After Moldovan lost his position at the Ministry of Health due to the change back to a liberal majority, the 1930 Moldovan Law was criticized as unattainable. Initially, Gheorghe Banu was appointed as Moldovan's successor and tried to make the reforms envisioned by his predecessor more feasible. Banu was himself a wholehearted promoter of eugenics, yet he found the Moldovan Law problematic:

> Unfortunately, the 1930 law demonstrated a great degree of eclecticism in acquiring theoretical concepts from several European countries and the United States, disregarding entirely the slow evolution of the culture and hygiene of our population at all levels, as well as our rather limited possibilities for implementing these ambitious programs on the ground. . . . It was clear from the start that it would be impossible to implement effectively the largest part of the provisions in this law. This issue was signaled early on by the protests of the medical corps, [who noted] the difficulties of implementing this law in an integral fashion.[37]

However, Banu rejected only the unrealistic expectations, not the principles, of the Moldovan Law. He lent his support to programs for preventive medicine and especially pre- and postnatal care, for he regarded the high infant mortality rate as the most important eugenic problem in Romania.

In the early 1930s, Moldovan was forced into the position of critic rather than policy maker with regard to public health. He saw his important achievements criticized by his successors and soon openly challenged by various modifications in the original provisions. Thus, by 1934 Moldovan was reduced to writing a series of harsh articles that castigated these changes as antimodernizing. He considered these challenges a premeditated attack against his law, "prepared by the defenders of the *traditional* organizations from the first moment when the [1930] law was promulgated, which was presented as hyper-modern, inapplicable and a fantasy."[38] Although some of the provisions in the law were modified, most prominently the attempts to decentralize public health administration, many of the programs that encouraged greater responsibility vis-à-vis venereal disease and welfare measures for poor mothers remained on the books.

Even those who did not openly acknowledge Moldovan's important contribution in framing certain general principles for public health policies ended up using the very channels set up by the Moldovan Law. For instance, *Enciclopedia Romậniei* (1938) contained an article that took stock of public health in Romania without any direct reference to Moldovan, although it did mention the 1930 law. The authors praised the turn toward preventive medicine during the previous decade and the focus of public health programs on venereal disease and infant care. Their recommendations focused on the need for sending a greater number of doctors into the countryside and creating a specialized corps of hygiene specialists to oversee the successful implementation of more preventive programs.[39] Although the authors did not make any reference to Moldovan's own work in public health legislation and programs, these recommendations echoed very closely the concerns and solutions proposed by the Transylvanian doctor for over a decade.

Controlling Reproduction: Marital Choice

Eugenic measures of comprehensive public health control went beyond programs that would help prevent the recurrence of epidemics, the spread of venereal disease, and the growth of social maladies such as tuberculosis and alcoholism. Another important concern was population growth. Eugenicists looked at various aspects of this issue, from birth to infant mortality rates, and attacked the decreasing population growth on both fronts. The impact of eugenic measures reached beyond demography and medicine into the political arena, reshaping the very notion of citizenship. Legislation that sought to improve the quantity and quality of reproduction redefined the rights and obligations of individuals with regard to marital choice and birth control, enlarging the prerogatives of the state in imposing greater control over individual behavior. Some of these measures of increased social control by the state would later find a continuation in the restructuring of state powers vis-à-vis individual rights when the communist regime came to power after 1945.

One of the earliest debates on the issue of population control focused on the need to organize and even require prenuptial certificates for all young couples. In 1923, several articles appeared in two important newspapers, *Universul* and *Adevărul*, in which the authors debated the importance of prenuptial certificates and the legalization of abortion.[40] The Jewish doctor "Ygrec," who had a regular medical advice column in *Adevărul*, praised the German policy of prenuptial certificates and urged doctors to propose similar legislation before the Romanian parliament as a means for "improving the human race."[41] In these articles he also attacked directly another regular writer for *Universul*, starting a polemical exchange that continued for an entire month on the front page of the two newspapers, rendering this issue a prominent topic of interest for the general public. While his opponents spoke about moral and social questions (would the control over marriage and reproduction be different for the upper classes versus the rest of the population?), "Ygrec" returned to his initial support for prenuptial certificates and the legalization of abortion "from the point of view of race [plural] hygiene."[42]

The issue of prenuptial counseling persisted in public debates into the 1930s, especially through the efforts of several eugenicists who published numerous articles on the "imperative need" to pass legislation that would limit the ability of individuals to make their own marital choices.[43] While in the past this had been an issue subject to minimal public control, eugenicists considered this freedom of choice a potentially abusive use of individual liberty, for it allowed those with hereditary illnesses to affect the health of other human beings and of future generations, or so they argued. They believed that the state needed to act as a protective agent of future generations and control individual behavior in these matters. Eugenic arguments forced the discussion of marriage into the realm of biology and unhesitatingly identified eugenics as a normative answer to this problem: "We must start from the principle that absolute freedom of reproduction cannot be allowed today."[44]

One of the aspects of marital choice over which eugenicists attempted to impose stricter control was ethnic purity, especially with regard to the urban population in Transylvania. Before 1918, the cities in this region had been overwhelmingly Hungarian and German. Eugenicists believed that the Romanian population needed to catch up in order to assure the future of their ethnic community, and therefore they used a negative rhetoric of crisis to discourage Romanians from marrying non-Romanians, especially Hungarians.[45] In the arguments about the dysgenic effects of such marriages, eugenicists depicted women as either weak, if they married non-Romanians, or as devious, if as Hungarians they married Romanians. In both cases, they advocated greater control by the male head of the household over women's marital choices.[46] The earlier trust in women's ability to act as responsible autonomous individuals had disappeared.

By singling out women as dysgenic agents, eugenicists hoped to restore faith in men's abilities to exercise their individual liberties responsibly. Their notion of legitimate individual freedom was as much defined along gender lines as it was along ethnic lines. Ironically, however, it was a man's ability to choose a wife that came under closer legal restriction. By 1938, the Penal Code included a law that forbade Romanian officers from marrying non-Romanian women, as a guarantee of the reproduction of "healthy stock."

Another article of the 1936 Penal Code (no. 377) criminalized the marriage of a healthy person to someone suffering from a venereal or other epidemic disease. This act was punishable by a prison sentence of one to three years and a fine of 2,000 to 5,000 lei (a considerable sum at that time).[47] The crime in this case consisted of endangering the health of another human being and the nation's future. Anyone who was suffering from a venereal disease and knowingly transmitted this illness to someone else would suffer a similar punishment. It is interesting to note, however, that the punishment was less severe in this case, presumably because the guilty party did not attempt to engage in a lifelong relationship with the victim.[48] In other words, the sick person would more likely affect the health of the community and its biological "capital" through marriage than through casual sex. Both of these actions fell under the rubric of crimes against public health, punishable because of their impact on the present and especially future health of the national body.

The deterrent effect of the punishments was weakened, however, by the stipulation that the state could punish such individuals only at the direct request of victims. This meant that certain individuals were more likely to assert this right than others, on the basis of their status in society and their power within the marital relationship. In other words, a poor, seduced woman would not very likely bring a rich man to court on charges of infecting her with syphilis or another venereal disease in the course of a chance sexual encounter. She stood a greater chance of being compromised by such a suit than the man did, for she would likely be accused of prostitution and even prosecuted for that. Similarly, in the case of a marriage between a healthy person and someone suffering from a venereal disease, if the victim was a woman, she stood to gain very little from suing her husband, for in the case of divorce she had little chance of getting remarried, and as a young divorcée with a tainted past she would have a difficult time even finding employment in a respectable establishment.[49]

The male victim of such a "criminal" act stood a better chance of emerging victorious. The courts and public opinion tended to be lenient toward men's sexual trespasses, while remaining unforgiving toward such behavior on the part of women. Therefore, a woman who married a man knowing she suffered from a venereal disease would likely not only be divorced without any settlement in her favor but would also end up with a large fine and even a jail sentence. Thus, this legislation provided a greater disincentive for women than for men to enter a marriage while suffering from a venereal disease. Women's public behavior and individual freedoms thus came under closer scrutiny than men's in this regard.

In addition to legislation that sought to control marital choice, eugenicists initiated a series of local programs for prenuptial exams. Through the publications and congresses of Astra and through Moldovan's personal encouragement, a number of local village doctors began their own programs of educating young peasant couples about the need to consider hereditary health problems when considering marriage. One such doctor, Aurel Tiniş, published a report in the prestigious journal *Ardealul Medical*, in which he described his introduction of obligatory medical prenuptial exams in his area of practice, focusing initially on the control of venereal diseases and expanding gradually to other "dysgenic" illnesses. He believed that most individuals had been eager to abide by his advice and had begun to act with greater eugenic responsibility since the introduction of his prenuptial exam program.[50]

In the 1930s Gheorghe Cosma, an official hygiene doctor for the Haţeg region, initiated a similar program. He continued his efforts throughout the war. In 1944 alone, the doctor examined 102 couples and forbade marriage in thirteen cases he hinted were dysgenic.[51] Therefore, the impact of the well-published eugenic ideas about the necessity of prenuptial exams extended well beyond national legislation, being taken over by local doctors eager to play a significant role in "correcting" the hereditary "capital" of the nation.

Eugenics and Reproductive Choice: Regulating Abortion

A corollary problem regarding population control, which came under fiery debate from the mid-1920s until the late 1930s, was the criminalization and later legalization of abortion in certain cases where it was considered eugenically sound. The same doctor "Ygrec" who advocated prenuptial certificates in the pages of *Adevărul* also wrote a series of articles on abortion. He spoke on behalf of legalizing abortion, since this form of birth control was already widely used and unnecessarily claimed the lives of many young women.[52] "Ygrec" believed that the state could not hope to improve the population growth rate quantitatively and qualitatively by criminalizing abortion but needed instead to focus on measures of decreasing the infant mortality rate by protecting the health of mothers and infants in the critical first year after birth. His argument on behalf of decriminalizing but regulating abortion focused first and foremost on the impact of such actions on the future health of the nation. Yet "Ygrec" also thought it important to stress the ways in which the criminalization of abortion affected women, not only as carriers of another life but also as *individuals* with both rights and obligations within the state. His discussion of the effects of criminalizing abortion drew the following picture: "Because of this absurdity of our legislation, we see cemeteries filled with the corpses of young women as a result of clandestine abortions."[53] This image was designed to elicit sympathy for women themselves as the victims, rather than for the nation as a whole.

Other interlocutors in this heated debate over the criminalization of abortion, even among dedicated proponents of eugenics, echoed "Ygrec's" concern for the rights of women. For instance, Sabin Manuilă published a lengthy article in 1936 in which he emphatically stressed the need to negotiate a modus vivendi between the state's concern for the growth of the birthrate and its responsibilities in protecting the health and rights of individual citizens:

> These two opposite interests must be reconciled. We must find a means that would protect women's entire freedom and doctors' entire freedom of practice in performing an abortion, without turning these rights into an obstacle to the normal growth of the country's population.[54]

Manuilă's outlook on abortion was very pragmatic. He believed this form of birth control would continue regardless of its criminalization, for it would be difficult to control it completely.

Legalizing and regulating abortion, Manuilă believed, would enable the authorities and especially doctors who specialized in issues of public health and eugenics to understand the reasons behind these practices and to start educating women about the negative effects of abortion on their health and that of the community in general. Such an approach to regulating abortion would also induce individuals to be tested more often for hereditary illnesses and to subject themselves willingly to various preventive measures of birth control as means of preventing the reproduction of dysgenic hereditary baggage. Manuilă's main premise in taking this approach toward abortion as a form of birth control was that in this process doctors would be guided by a sense of responsibility toward the health of their patients and, more importantly, the nation's future. He did not express any concern about doctors' abusing their role in regulating abortion under the incentive of material profit.

Other supporters of eugenics unambiguously attacked abortion as a danger-ous, destructive force in society, since it encouraged a disregard for common health priorities and placed the egotistical interests of the individual above those of the nation.[55] Ioan Manliu believed that the selection of who should or should not reproduce in accordance with eugenic priorities would have to take place before conception. Couples needed to consult a doctor about their heredi-tary baggage and any potential problems with their offspring before deciding to reproduce. More radically, he advocated the sterilization of those individu-als whose hereditary pathologies rendered them a liability to the health of the nation.[56]

Many other proponents of eugenics focused on the issue of whether doctors should use coercive measures such as sterilization or corrective measures such as abortion (not forced, but simply as a legal option) to ensure the quality of the offspring. However, most Romanian eugenicists were sensitive to the intrusive implications of sterilization and the extent to which this procedure represented the complete loss of individual autonomy. Although Banu tried to deemphasize these implications by depicting sterilization as "an inoffensive surgical opera-tion," he was unwilling to promote its forced implementation. Rather, he sug-gested that "ideally, sterilization would be voluntary, freely agreed to by those interested."[57]

According to Romanian eugenicists, education and preventive propaganda through prenuptial counseling offices and certificates remained more effective, fitting policies than coercive sterilization. By promoting this seemingly moder-ate solution to curb individual freedom over marital and reproductive choice, Romanian eugenicists attempted to walk the tightrope between social control and mobilization, as they sought to engage members of the state in creating a eugenic order. They wanted to appeal to the conscience and sense of responsi-bility of individual citizens in this process, as they attempted to increase the power of the state over its members.

After more than a decade of debate over the issue of abortion, the parlia-ment finally endorsed a law that criminalized abortion in all instances other than the pregnancy of a couple in which one of the parents suffered from a se-vere mental illness or when it was "certain" that the child would suffer from a mental deficiency.[58] The law did not define clearly what "severe mental illness" represented. Many eugenicists and other reformers, especially lawyers, were still fearful about the ways in which this legislation empowered women to control their bodies. They suggested that the provisions of the law made it relatively easy for women to claim an imaginary hereditary illness in order to have an abortion. Therefore, the law also stipulated that a doctor who specialized in such hereditary illnesses would have the final word in approving an abortion. Thus, the control over individual behavior and reproduction reverted back to technical specialists empowered by the state—doctors.

The incomplete and inconsistent statistics on the birthrate make it hard to evaluate the effectiveness of these policies in improving the quantity and quality of population growth during the 1930s. The unavailability of statistics for the duration of the war, compounded by specific problems such as the mobilization of most men of childbearing age and the increased mortality rate as a direct result of the war, makes it impossible to evaluate the effectiveness of any public health and birth-control policies during this period.

For the interwar period it is possible, however, to measure at least in part the evolution of the birth and mortality rates. According to one source, in the early 1920s Romania had a birthrate of 32/1000 in the urban areas and 44/1000 in the rural areas, which greatly surpassed the European average of 19.5–38/1000.[59] In the early 1930s the birthrate figures still remained the highest in Europe at 35.9/1000. However, the same study noted that if one broke down the birthrate between the rural and the urban population, the growth of the birthrate in the countryside accounted for 93.8 percent of the "natural surplus."[60]

These statistics concerned eugenicists, for they saw in this differential birthrate proof of their fears of "race suicide" by the social elites.[61] Much like eugenicists in the United States and Western Europe at that time, they viewed the small urban birthrate as a result of middle-class women's abusive use of abortion as a form of birth control. Thus, the arguments about the criminalization of abortion did, in fact, focus in large part on the educated urban population and especially on well-to-do women.

With regard to infant mortality, the figures for Romania remained very high in comparison to the European average, placing this country as second highest after Hungary in 1932, with 18.5 infant deaths per 100 births.[62] However, statistics also indicate that mortality figures had gone down significantly, from 20.2 percent in 1901. The numbers continued to go down, to 17.4 percent in 1933 and 13.9 percent in 1940.[63]

The overall population growth rate placed Romania in a favorable position in Europe. In 1932 it was second highest on the continent after Bulgaria, with

13.3/1000 inhabitants.[64] This net growth went down to 12.9/1000 in 1934 and to 10.3/1000 in 1940. While these figures still placed Romania in a leading position in Europe with regard to population growth, the gradual decrease suggests that a growing number of individuals practiced various methods of birth control, for during the same period the infant mortality rate was decreasing very quickly. Therefore, it seems that eugenicists' attempts to regulate abortion were frustrated by the inability or unwillingness of the authorities in charge (the police and practicing doctors) to enforce the anti-abortion legislation. Between the rampant corruption in public office and the lack of communication between the central and local levels of administration, many laws simply remained stillborn.

Searching for Public Health Reform Models in the 1930s

During the 1930s, another important shift began to occur in eugenicists' vision of public health. With the growing interest in eugenically oriented public health legislation abroad, Romanian eugenicists began to examine the effectiveness of various measures by observing their implementation in other countries. For instance, Făcăoaru looked constantly toward the accomplishments of the Third Reich as the most useful example for the Romanian state. He had only praise for the Nazi programs that implemented coercive negative measures, contrasting them with the ineffectual voluntary measures enacted elsewhere, such as in Norway. In fact, Făcăoaru criticized even early German legislation for failing to regulate certain groups, such as "moral degenerates, seducers, perverts, inmates in correctional institutions, drug users, prostitutes and professional vagabonds."[65] Făcăoaru's unabashed support for the eugenic public health policies of the Third Reich later won him the recognition of the Iron Guard.

Other eugenicists cast their nets more widely, comparing the accomplishments of the comprehensive German legislation with similar measures in the United States, France, Italy, Belgium, Hungary, Austria, Yugoslavia, Greece, and the Soviet Union. Although Germany appeared to be an avant-garde country because of the Nazi regime's sweeping institutional reform and its ability to control all aspects of public and private life, many Romanian eugenicists also looked elsewhere for worthy models.

Banu recognized the effectiveness of German policies but stressed the fact that the German government's ability to implement coercive measures successfully was due precisely to the totalitarian nature of the regime.[66] His remark implies that this was a very high price to pay, for the Romanian state did not even come close to resembling a totalitarian structure, and in fact the general political and social atmosphere did not favor the rise of such a regime. Banu was confident that positive eugenic policies and a greater emphasis on measures that would protect the health of mothers and infants, in particular, were more suited to Romania.[67] He singled out France as a positive example of such policies, along with Yugoslavia, a country whose problems in political, social, and economic life greatly resembled those of Romania. Banu had only praise for the comprehensive measures undertaken by the Belgrade government since 1918, holding them up as an example of what could be achieved in Romania, since the two countries had similar resources.[68]

Moldovan also regarded the public health policies in Yugoslavia as a worthy example. In fact, in 1928 Queen Marie herself promised him an official position as part of her entourage on her next visit to Yugoslavia in order to enable Moldovan to make contacts with the public health reformers there.[69] His interests turned, however, more consistently toward the United States and Germany. He cultivated a close working relationship with the Rockefeller Foundation until 1947 and looked toward the volunteerist spirit and decentralized framework of public health programs in the United States as effective models for similar measures in Romania.[70] At the same time, he felt a closer kinship with the German policies than Banu, as he was far more impressed with the efficiency of Germany's public health infrastructure than wary about the political price paid by the Germans in order to achieve this goal. After all, Moldovan's own biopolitical total state partly resembled the Third Reich.

Toward More Aggressive Restrictive Measures (1938–44)

Eugenicists' fortunes in contributing to public health measures took a turn for the better when Carol II's Front for National Renaissance assumed power in 1938. Iuliu Moldovan, along with a few other eugenicists, was appointed as a member of the Superior Council, the front's permanent consulting body.[71] Iuliu Hațiegan, his close collaborator, became a member of the new government, the "Directorate," in charge of public health and welfare issues.

Though this was a puppet government in many areas, such as public administration, finance, and foreign policy, its members did have an important say with regard to public health policy. Carol himself expressed his regime's increased concern with protecting the health of the nation: "After the primacy of national defense, our next priority must be public health."[72] The Front for National Renaissance oversaw a new reform that reorganized the Ministry of Health, explicitly framing its attributes in terms of protecting the health of the family and the national biological patrimony.[73] This new law sought to revive the spirit of the 1930 law, but with more modest aspirations concerning the ability of the ministry to bring about sweeping rapid change.

A more important reform of the short-lived Carol dictatorship was the creation of the Social Service program, whose architect was Dimitrie Gusti. As mentioned in the earlier discussion of education reforms, this program served as an important tool for educating college students, its main participants, about the important public health problems that plagued the countryside.[74] The Social Service had a significant impact on those receiving aid as well, for it helped create new local institutions that would address some of these problems—the Cultural Hearths.[75]

In 1939 approximately three thousand such institutions were founded.[76] The Hearths were built with local funds, another illustration of the renewed emphasis on decentralization and greater self-reliance at the local level. Some of them were very small, but they all had to include among their leaders a doctor, who not only oversaw various programs for educating the public about hygiene and general health matters but also offered medical assistance in these new spaces. The provisions regarding the Cultural Hearths stipulated that the role of doctors in these public service institutions was to expand over time. This measure was extended not only to doctors who occupied official functions, such as hygiene inspectors, but also to those engaged solely in private practice in a given area.[77] In other words, the state wanted to extend the official responsibilities and powers of all medical personnel, even when these individuals were not formally working for the state. Unfortunately for doctors, the program's effectiveness was cut short by Antonescu's assumption of power in September 1940.

Among the most radical legacies of Carol II's dictatorship in terms of reframing the power of the state were the anti-Jewish laws passed on 8 August, 1940.[78] The most prominent was a law interdicting mixed marriages between Jews and Romanians, defining ethnicity in terms of biology (blood), rather than religion, language, or other cultural elements:

We have considered the Romanian blood as a fundamental element for the founding of the Nation; but beyond the physical structure of the blood and possibilities to
determine it mathematically, we have arrived at a Romanian formula of considering
Romanian blood as an ethnic and moral element, whose determination can only be
accomplished through discrimination . . . of the notion of "Jew."[79]

Direct links between the work and writings of most Romanian eugenicists
(save Făcăoaru, Ioan Vasilescu-Buciumi, and Herseni) and the framing of this
legislation, which clearly rendered anti-Semitism a central element for defining Romanianness, cannot be clearly made. The inspiration behind this legislation was, rather, the Nuremberg Laws.[80] However, it can be safely said that
the eugenic discourse about the need to control the health of the nation and
cleanse it of potential dysgenic threats from other ethnicities did prepare the
ground for such radical legislation.

Another important law passed at the same time expelled all Jewish doctors,
pharmacists, and other auxiliary personnel from membership in officially sanc-
tioned organizations and institutions. Their practices and positions would be
allocated to ethnic Romanians. Jewish doctors could presumably continue to
practice their profession, but their clientele was limited to the Jewish population, and they were stripped of a large portion of their operating capital.[81] Such
aggressively anti-Semitic policy had not been part of earlier eugenic discourse
and public health legislation. In fact, this measure promised to compound a
problem that eugenicists had focused on—the insufficient number of well-
trained doctors and especially hygiene specialists. Yet Romanian eugenicists did
not protest this policy in any way. Whether tacit supporters or indifferent observers, eugenicists, along with all other Romanian doctors, were certainly implicit partners in the implementation of this policy.

The short-lived partnership between Antonescu and the Iron Guard insti-
tuted other sweeping changes in public health. The government decreed the
need to base all programs for public health on the idea that "the nation was a
biological unit."[82] The discourse about reform that went along with what legionaries identified as a new vision of public health in fact replicated many of
the arguments and specific measures advocated by eugenicists for over a decade.
However, Moldovan and other prominent eugenicists (e.g., Banu, Marinescu,
Iuliu Hațiegan) were conspicuously absent from this discussion. Instead, the
spokesmen for the legionary movement went directly to "the source," identify-

ing their aims with similar programs enacted under the Mussolini regime since the mid-1920s and under the Third Reich since 1933.[83] Two prominent proponents of eugenics from Moldovan's circle, Făcăoaru and Voina, did provide a direct link between the public health policies promoted by Romanian eugenicists and the aims of the legionary government. However, most other proponents of eugenics—most prominently Moldovan, Banu, and Hațiegan—did not identify themselves with the aims of the new regime.

In fact, the 1940–44 Antonescu regime enacted legislation that changed many aspects of the way in which Romanian eugenicists had envisioned public health policies. To begin with, the regime predicated the new reforms on "cleansing" the medical profession of Jews, continuing in the footsteps of the legislation passed by Carol II in August 1940. These policies offered no solution that would increase the number of Romanian doctors to replace their Jewish colleagues, but simply decreed that this switch had to take place. Thus, this policy in effect empowered individuals without great training, a good academic record, or practical experience to occupy positions of responsibility and determine the present and future health of the nation. This was a change that ran counter to the reforms advocated by eugenicists in medical education and practice.

Furthermore, the Antonescu-legionary government also wished to centralize the administration of public health programs. It wanted to keep local institutions such as the Communal Hearth (rebaptized now as the Legionary Communal House) but tie their responsibilities much more closely to the ideology and interests of the national government, rather than to those of the local community.[84] These centers would provide a way for the government in Bucharest to oversee the implementation of legionary doctrines and prerogatives in every city and village. Again, this spirit of centralization was diametrically opposed to eugenicists' focus on responsibility and self-reliance at the local level.

After Antonescu parted ways with the Iron Guard in January 1941, some eugenicists began to play more important roles in public health policy making. Iuliu Moldovan and Ovidiu Comșia were appointed to the Commission for Social Hygiene set up by the Antonescu regime.[85] The new government also created other important institutions of public health: In 1940 it founded the Institute for the Study and Prophilaxy of Hereditary and Tumoral Diseases and the Patronage Council, which would become the most important welfare government institution during the war.[86] Even so, with the beginning of the war the government shifted its emphasis from preventive medicine and issues of prophilaxy and hygiene at the local level to curative medicine that catered directly to the health of the troops at the front. A great number of doctors were mobilized for duty at the front, leaving many areas devoid of any medical personnel, while those who remained in the country had to perform public service in hospitals.[87]

The Antonescu regime continued its rhetorical support of preventive public health measures without taking vigorous action. Moldovan's eugenic group retreated to its regional concerns in Transylvania through the work at the Institute of Hygiene and Astra, both located in Sibiu for the duration of the war. At the same time, Banu and other proponents of eugenics in Bucharest continued their limited efforts within the Institute of Hygiene and the Health Center in Bucharest.

Finally, in 1943 a new public health reform was passed that revived many of the measures that had been at the heart of the Moldovan Law.[88] It is unclear who formulated this new law, for the Ministry of Health's archives for the years 1940–44 have not yet been opened to the public. However, both Banu and Moldovan published several important articles in 1943 on the need to reorganize public health and assure the future health of the nation through a focus on preventive medicine. The disastrous results of the war had become a weapon for eugenicists, as an illustration of the terrible results of neglecting public health:

> This negative attitude [toward the future health of the nation] cannot and will not last much longer, because this war, with the monstrous sacrifices it has demanded, will prompt us to come together in our concern for the future of our nation [*neam*] and will force us to move without any delay towards a systematic preventive program. . . . The fulfillment of our ethno-biological patrimony will become the center of all preoccupations in public life.[89]

The 1943 legislation linked the powers of the Ministry of Health—and hence of the state—to its responsibilities for "conserving and propagating the national biological patrimony" more emphatically than any previous legislation.[90] This law also contained an entire chapter on measures for improving the health of mothers and infants, a significant change from the emphasis on the health of military personnel during the previous three years. This renewed interest in puericulture reflected Banu's suggestions.[91]

Increased concern with venereal disease generated yet another comprehensive piece of legislation, the October 1943 "Regulation no. 24 for combating venereal diseases." Its source was probably the growing problems at the front and the high incidence of venereal disease among the troops. All states fighting in World War II were confronted with this issue. This new law went beyond any previous legislation in emphatically identifying health with civic duty, making participation in programs for combating venereal diseases mandatory not only for private individuals but also for businesses in service industries.[92] In addition to its general concern for the effects of venereal disease, the law forbade marriage for the infected.[93]

The role of civilians such as doctors and public health officials in the Holocaust in Romania has only been recently explored by two important studies.[94] Though both offer important information, they also leave many questions unanswered, in part because of the ways in which pertinent archival sources were organized then and have been reorganized, hidden, and only partially revealed since. This is particularly true with regard to the Transnistrian Holocaust, about which documents are located in Odessa, Jerusalem, Bucharest, and Washington. Although some of these documents are still unavailable (particularly those of the Romanian Ministry of Health between 1940 and 1944), the existing historiography suggests possible links between two aspects of the Romanian Holocaust and the eugenics movement. The first is the role of Romanian doctors in the horrendous typhoid fever epidemic that claimed the lives of tens of thousands of Jewish deportees in Transnistria after September 1941 and until 1943.[95] It is clear that the Romanian military authorities did nothing to help the Jews and simply treated those infected as a health threat to the rest of the population in Transnistria. Isolation, not treatment, was the general policy, without much effort to encourage the purification of water sources or to effect various other environmental changes that could have reduced the incidence of typhoid fever in the Jewish camps or possibly have brought down the number of fatalities.[96]

Because of the choices made by the Romanian administration, historian Jean Ancel views this outbreak of typhoid fever as a genocidal weapon, an integral part of the policy of eliminating Jews, rather than as a badly mishandled health problem. He also links the policies of the Romanian military administration to the role played by doctors in this process. After all, military doctors filed reports on a regular basis with both the military local administration and back in Bucharest. He considers these doctors as important agents in the unfolding tragedy of the typhoid fever epidemic; they acted as intermediaries in implementing the appalling measures (or lack thereof) taken by the Romanian administration:

> The responsibility for liquidating the Jews of Odessa falls also on the shoulders of the Romanian doctors, who continued to see the weak Jewish presence in the Berezovca county as a source of irritation. . . . [They] participated without any reservations to the great experiment of cleansing Bessarabia, Bukovina, and Transnistria of any Jewish trace. As a part of this policy, they initiated measures and made decisions that contradicted the Hippocratic oath, their profession, and human values. In brief, they helped and amplified the genocide.[97]

This is a strong indictment, especially when little is known about the actual power relation between these military doctors, on the one hand, and military administrators and the Bucharest administration, on the other hand.

Radu Ioanid is more reserved in his view of the typhoid epidemic, which he discusses in the larger context of the Romanian army's inefficiency in carrying out many of its policies.[98] He also reaches an opposite conclusion from Ancel in his evaluation of Romanian doctors' role in the epidemic: "Romanian military doctors struggled selflessly against the typhus epidemic in Moghilev."[99] Neither author focuses sufficiently on this topic to elucidate the question of doctors' responsibility, though Ancel does provide more documentary evidence to support his claims. Therefore, this remains an open question.

A few remarks about links between the Holocaust and eugenics can still be made, however. Though no names of supporters of eugenics among the military doctors in Transnistria surface in either Ancel or Ioanid's accounts, it is safe to assume that people like Sabin Manuilă, Făcăoaru, and Moldovan knew about the epidemic.[100] Făcăoaru was working on an anthropometric study in Transnistria at that time and later reported his findings directly to Manuilă. Both were in touch with Moldovan during this period. For the entire duration of the war, the only article published by the *Buletin Eugenic şi Biopolitic* that made any reference to Transnistria was Făcăoaru's study of the bioanthropometric measurements of ethnic Romanians in Transnistria.[101] The silence of the most important eugenic publication in Romania regarding a public health problem of such great proportions suggests that even those who were not supporters of the policies in Transnistria did have an ethnically, or maybe even racially, hierarchical view of the important health problems in Romania. This, however, does not mean they were partners of the state in the Holocaust in any way comparable to the role of German doctors who worked actively to support the Final Solution.

Another aspect of the Romanian Holocaust also suggests some possible links with eugenics. The Antonescu regime set up the Patronage Council—an institution headed by Antonescu's wife, Maria Antonescu—as the most important organization in overseeing social-help works, from childcare and public health for the poor to soup kitchens and various forms of public support for the war effort. The *Buletin Eugenic și Biopolitic* praised the work of the Patronage Council as both efficient and forward looking.[102] Yet the Patronage Council was funded in great part by money that came from the Jewish population, money that was legally or illegally, but certainly coercively, obtained through the Central Office of Romanian Jews.[103] At the same time, the Patronage Council limited its activities to ethnic Romanians, even when members of the Red Cross made desperate appeals to its rich coffers during the typhoid fever epidemic in Transnistria.[104] The silence of Romanian eugenicists over this important aspect of the Patronage Council's activities suggests that at least some among them found its discriminatory, exploitative, and racist policies at least unproblematic, if not outright acceptable. Still, as with the questions regarding policies in Transnistria, the works of the Patronage Council need to be further investigated before a clearer picture of the links that may have existed with Romanian eugenics can be established.

Postwar Attempts to Revive Eugenic Public Health

The dramatic events of the German defeat and Soviet occupation in the summer of 1944 did not intimidate Romanian eugenicists. On the contrary, they used the results of the war and even the presence of Soviet troops on Romanian soil for their legislative agenda. For example, Iosif Stoichiția, a Moldovan student who after 1944 was appointed General Hygiene Inspector for the Cluj region, argued:

> We had to be tested by the horrors of a new world war, with all of its disastrous consequences for the biological evolution of our nation, in order finally to initiate an effective program of action in this essential sector [health care] of public life.[105]

Stoichiția and other eugenicists had faith in the new regime, hoping it would mobilize behind their proposals for a sweeping reform in health care and public life in general.

This optimism was justified, for Moldovan and most of his collaborators were appointed to regional positions of responsibility after the liberation of Northern Transylvania, and some even gained important governmental positions in Bucharest. In 1944, for instance, Moldovan was reinstated as director of the Institute of Hygiene in Cluj and Mihai Kernbach, one of Moldovan's students, became dean of the medical school in Cluj. A new academic position was created for Râmneanțu in his home region, as professor of hygiene studies at the Polytechnic Institute in Timişoara. Among the many individuals who occupied the position of Minister of Health during the 1944–47 transitional period, several were doctors familiar with the eugenics movement in Romania, and one minister, Salvator Cupcea, was a strong supporter.

Indeed, this was a period of great fluidity in public health policies and for the proponents of eugenics. Many institutions from the pre-1944 period were under increasing attack, prefiguring the more sweeping "cleansing" measures that would follow in the late 1940s and especially the early 1950s. Already in mid-1944 Kernbach, who in the previous decades had advocated stricter governmental control over the masses because of their hereditary criminal instincts, began to depict the working classes as the group with the greatest eugenic potential.[106] Stoichiția was also beginning to march to the beat of a different drummer, for in December 1944 he published an essay praising public health measures in the Soviet Union. He had toned down his emphasis on the eugenic perils of the lack of concern for preventive medicine, but he still retained the essence of his eugenic convictions. For instance, in describing Soviet policies regarding maternal care, he referred to motherhood as "the most important social role for a woman and an infant, who represents the *most valuable capital for the nation.*"[107]

While these proponents of eugenics had sensed a definite change in the political orientation of the postwar state, others felt confident enough in the measure of goodwill shown by the new government to continue their crusade for eugenics without any apologies to the Soviet presence in Romania. Moldovan and Râmneanțu continued to publish works that advocated reform in public health in accordance with their eugenic ideas, without reference to notions of class. Together with some of their eugenic collaborators, they published a *Tratat de medicină socială* (1947), which sought to lay the foundations for a definitive reform in public health. It was an impressive work that tackled every aspect of health care and proposed very detailed measures for comprehensive reform within the new political framework. Its positive reception is evident in the fact that it went through three printings in one year.

Indeed, the actions of the Ministry of Health during this period reflect a continued interest in eugenic concepts of public health, as many of the measures first outlined in 1930 were embraced. Several new pieces of legislation went even further in enforcing a eugenic vision of public health. For instance, the programs for monitoring social diseases and especially venereal diseases continued during this period. The ministry even made use of forms printed in 1939 that contained categories devised by proponents of eugenics, such as "alienated individuals," a rubric that registered hereditary physical and mental handicaps.[108] Other requirements, such as prenuptial health certificates for potential couples, remained in effect as means of monitoring and containing the spread of venereal diseases.[109]

The ministry also modified some of the earlier legislation in order to increase its effectiveness. For instance, beginning in 1945, all prostitutes were required to carry a health passport that would be updated periodically. The arguments for this policy echoed eugenic concerns, for they depicted violators of the new legislation as persons dangerous to the health of innocent families and especially their offspring.[110] It comes as little surprise then that proponents of eugenics looked with hope at official policies until 1948.

The radical shift in the regime after King Michael's forced abdication in December 1947 brought about a demise in most eugenicists' fortunes. Moldovan was forcibly retired and soon thereafter sent to prison at Sighet, where he spent six years as an ex-member of a "bourgeois" government cabinet.[111] Only those of his collaborators who had already begun to shift their discourse toward a Soviet version of eugenics made the transition into the new regime successfully. The communist government presided over a sweeping reorganization of public health institutions, making extensive personnel changes that replaced "bourgeois" technocrats with faithful apparatchiks. Even so, some of the policies of the new regime, with its increased funding for preventive health care and forceful introduction of doctors to all rural areas, in fact continued some of the eugenicists' dreams, albeit to a different end. During the next half century public health policies in Romania focused more on the quantity of services provided than on their efficiency, a legacy that persists today.

■ ■ ■

EUGENICISTS played an important role in the process of creating public health institutions and programs in interwar Romania. Although their discourse focused on qualitative, not quantitative, health care change, their actions affected both. First and foremost, eugenicists contributed to the expansion of the medical profession, especially regarding auxiliary medical personnel, and they helped increase the involvement of the state in public health issues. Eugenicists also helped to reshape various specializations in the medical profession and to shift the emphasis of medical practice from curative to preventive medicine. Furthermore, they helped to expand doctors' responsibilities toward the community at large and future generations. The various laws passed to protect these interests gave doctors a great deal of authority and responsibility. Finally, eugenic public health measures helped usher in the notion that the state had to control not only public behavior but also private decisions, such as entering into a marriage. By introducing legislation that would control such choices, eugenicists helped politicize the private sphere, a process that would accelerate after 1948.

However, the legacy of eugenicists' discursive practices vis-à-vis public health and the continuation of these institutional developments after the communist takeover were largely unintended. The language eugenicists sought to set up, the categories they used to argue on behalf of increasing state involvement in public health in controlling the population and devoting larger funds to preventive medicine, became language that public health administrators and party apparatchiks reinterpreted in a different register for the next half century.

CONCLUSION

E U G E N I C S played an important role in interwar Romania. Proponents of eugenics used their positions of authority in public life to popularize theories of hereditary determinism, bringing them into the realms of intellectual discourse and social reform. Eugenic discourse gained significant support among a variety of professionals, from doctors to lawyers and from anthropologists to biologists, who adopted the language and arguments of hereditary determinism without necessarily identifying themselves as proponents of eugenics. Nonetheless, many educated professionals used these ideas in their own discussions of developing various academic disciplines, modernizing Romania, or reforming the relationship between individuals and the state within the body politic. In doing so, they helped reconceptualize both the problems experienced by Romanians after World War I, casting them in a biologizing discourse, and the solutions to these problems, constructing them around the body and the laws of heredity rather than fashioning them out of sociocultural traditions.

Thus, eugenics served as a vehicle for implanting biology in the mainstream of intellectual debates and especially in academia. Eugenicists played an important role in introducing a biologizing scientific paradigm, especially in various social sciences. From geographers such as Simion Mehedinți to sociologists such as Dimitrie Gusti and Petre Andrei, and from lawyers such as Ioan Vasilescu-Buciumi to anthropologists such as Constantin Velluda and Francisc Rainer,

Romanian social scientists embraced biological determinism and the importance of heredity as fundamental truths that shaped their disciplines. Consequently, they made a conscious effort to address the ways in which these truths
redefined not only the variables with which sociologists and historians worked
but also the aims of their disciplines. In the eyes of many of these intellectuals,
their professions would have to go beyond analyzing all the facts dispassionately to becoming involved in policy making. For if heredity linked one generation to the next, one could not stop at the present in analyzing various data
but in fact needed to project such analysis into the future.

As a corollary to their popularization of the language and arguments of science, eugenicists also challenged established fundamental traditions in Romanian society, the most significant being the authority of the Orthodox and Uniate
Churches. In strong, sometimes apocalyptic language, eugenicists depicted eugenics as a vehicle for healing, progress, and even salvation (i.e., saving the community's future) by placing the health of the ethnically circumscribed nation at
the center of individual preoccupations. At the same time, they often criticized
the church for disregarding the biological aspects of life. By successfully enlisting the assistance of the clergy in their work of eugenic education, Romanian
eugenicists were able to effectively overcome the potential opposition of this
institution. They ultimately helped displace the church from its central role in
the community, particularly in Transylvania, where they were most active. Eugenicists offered alternative institutions and the image of the doctor as a healer
of the nation—as forces whose significance surpassed the role played by the
priest or the church in the community.

Eugenicists played a significant role in the political arena as well. In their alliances for power within the body politic they most often split between two
groups. The most significant political faction to support eugenic programs was
the National-Peasant Party, during whose short-lived regime eugenicists passed
the most comprehensive piece of public health legislation in interwar Romania.
In the late 1930s, many eugenicists gravitated toward Carol II, but his personal
rule gave way quickly to a wartime regime with much more radical right-wing
leanings. During World War II, several eugenicists became active supporters of
the Iron Guard and subsequently the Antonescu regime, while others retreated
to less political positions of authority within academia—either as professors or
as members of research centers.

Whatever their political alliances (sometimes prompted by sheer pragmatism rather than ideology), eugenicists played an important, if unrecognized, role in delegitimizing liberal parliamentary ideas, especially among the educated public and students in higher education institutions. Eugenicists used the language of science and objectivity to delegitimize the principles of liberty and democracy by portraying these concepts as antirational, since they allegedly ran against the universal laws of heredity, differentiation, and evolution. According to eugenicists, to claim individual autonomy over one's actions meant acting irresponsibly, showing disregard for the hereditary factors that conditioned individual development and behavior. Furthermore, democracy seemed a dangerous practice, for it allowed for what Alexis de Tocqueville had described as the "tyranny of the masses." In the eyes of eugenicists, democratic rule allowed the mediocre to impose their will over the superior and thus ran counter to the principle of evolution through controlled selection. In its place eugenicists advocated responsible action by a leadership selected from the hereditary elite. This leadership would consist of technocrats who understood and believed in applying the principles of hereditary biology to social and political action.

Critiques of parliamentary democracy and liberal politics were woven into the very language eugenicists used to explain their theories. Proponents of eugenics implicitly and often explicitly framed their ideas as challenges to the apparently disastrous effects (e.g., materialism, the decline of the moral fiber of society, health problems, the increase in criminality) of liberalism during the nineteenth century. They included these critiques not only in scholarly debates but also in their teaching, whether of biology, anthropology, or other social sciences. This phenomenon helps explain in part the attraction of many youths in the early 1930s to antiliberal politics. Such students were persuaded not only by right-wing ideologies but also by professors who identified scientific objectivism and progress with the rejection of liberal democracy.

The impact of eugenics in interwar Romania went beyond intellectual discourse and political ideas. Eugenicists in positions of authority in public life presided over important reforms in education, public health, and even civil rights. Their vision of refashioning the education process with eugenic considerations in mind implied a continuous selection process of students according to their inborn aptitudes and a structuring of the education system in keeping with the variety of students' genetic endowments. These reforms sought to reinforce what eugenicists saw as a natural hierarchy among classes and innate biological differences between men and women and among ethnic groups.

In addition to changing pedagogy so that it might nurture different talents and the genetic intellectual hierarchy among students, eugenicists sought to introduce biology as a fundamental academic discipline, from primary to higher education. Furthermore, Moldovan and other eugenicists worked actively to restructure medical education, reorienting it from a focus on curative specializations to preventive ones. Eugenicists played an important role in increasing the number of educational institutions for auxiliary medical personnel, particularly nurses and midwives. The Moldovan Law and its subsequent amendments were intended to produce stricter standards for the training of medical personnel and more emphasis on hygiene in medical education.

Eugenicists also contributed to expanding the availability of basic medical services in the countryside among ethnic Romanians and educating rural and urban populations about the importance of personal hygiene and eugenic responsibilities when deciding to marry and reproduce. Eugenic public health reforms also introduced private businesses, especially in the service industries, to the issue of responsibility toward the public and especially the health of the nation. By giving doctors authority over the ability of such businesses to operate, eugenicists reaffirmed their belief that it was this group of technocrats, with their expertise in public health and their sense of responsibility, who needed to preside over the modernization of the Romanian state and society.

Legislative reforms initiated by eugenicists sought to reconceptualize not only the rights and limitations of corporate bodies and businesses but especially those of individual bodies. In as much as they asserted that the state needed to become more responsible for the health of its citizens, eugenicists also wanted to limit individual choices within the framework of the modernized eugenic state in accordance with the interests of the present and future communities.

Individuals' choices came to be controlled strictly not only with regard to access to education and a career but also with regard to what had previously been regarded as private actions—marriage and reproduction. Communities had always exerted influence over such choices, but the pressure had been informal and always negotiable. Through the measures enacted by eugenicists, the state gained the power to control individual decisions and implement its will over that of its members, if need be. To most Romanians' benefit, these measures were not thoroughly implemented, for in fact the efforts at radically reforming state structures in accordance with eugenic priorities were not successful. Therefore, the various legislative reforms proposed by eugenicists were left in the hands of an administration that was not very effective in exercising state power at its fullest over individual citizens.

World War II

The relationship between Romanian eugenics and the policies of the Antonescu regime, especially with regard to its treatment of "undesirable" minorities—the Jews and Roma—remains unclear. That the anti-Semitic laws enacted during the war had a biologically determinist view of Jewish identity and this population's deleterious impact on the Romanian nation is evident from the language of both legislation and the press.[1] It is less apparent, however, to what extent this vision was directly linked to the work of Romanian eugenicists. Eugenicists Iordache Făcăoaru, Traian Herseni, and a few other Iron Guard members who held official positions in Antonescu's government were influential in these policies at least at some level. Făcăoaru was active, for instance, in doing anthropometric measurements on the Transnistrian Romanian population in 1942. He hoped at that time to demonstrate the "authenticity" of that population as true Romanians and establish some "scientific" criteria for weeding out undesirable "others."[2]

Moldovan and his collaborators from Cluj moved to Sibiu in 1940, where they continued some of their activities on a reduced scale, focusing especially on education (conferences and courses on "social hygiene"). In 1942, at Moldovan's initiative, Astra founded its Biopolitical Section as an entity separate from the Medical Section.[3] The minutes of the founding meeting restate Moldovan's biopolitical ideas briefly but strongly: "The laws of life, biopolitics, represent the foundation of [the state]. . . . Biopolitics is not racist as a concept, and race [purity] is not our goal, especially as there are no such things as uniracial people [*neamuri*]."[4] This statement was ambiguous at best in terms of this organization's take on the situation of minorities in Romania at that time. Still, it did not have the aggressive and self-assured anti-Semitic and xenophobic tone of the press or of many official government statements.

Available archival resources reveal only limited activities of this organization. They included conferences, public health measures such as routine checkups for the rural Romanian population, and some forms of social welfare for poor mothers. There was certainly no overt or concerted effort on their part to eliminate Jews or Roma from Romanian society. Yet further work on the Holocaust may reveal a very different picture. Recent works by Jean Ancel and Radu Ioanid have opened up questions regarding the role of doctors in the typhoid fever epidemic in Transnistria during the war, especially among Jewish deportees.[5] They have also tangentially touched on the role of the Patronage Council in social welfare and public health measures with which eugenicists may have been affiliated. Though some links between eugenics and these developments can be inferred, further research needs to be done before the questions raised by Ancel, Ioanid, and this analysis can be addressed with greater clarity.

One recent study of the history of the Roma in Romania also asserts that although some of the eugenicists identified with the extreme right (e.g., Iordache Făcăoaru) wrote in the 1930s about the need to eliminate the Roma, there was no transformation of these ideas into policy making after 1940.[6] The author claims the government undertook deportations of Roma populations based on economic and cultural criteria. It selected nomadic populations and allowed the Roma who were "useful" to their communities as skilled and semiskilled workers to remain in place. Writing about the same subject, Ioanid reaches a different conclusion—that the treatment of the Roma represents an element in the continuum of racist attitudes shared by many government authorities, both central and local.[7] It is important to note that neither of these studies connects these atrocities directly to Romanian eugenics. This conclusion may change, however, when the archives of the Ministry of Health for the wartime period are opened and when the Astra archives in Sibiu are finally catalogued.

Developments after World War II

After 1944, the degree to which eugenic theories played an important role in the scientific community fluctuated with political changes. Initially, during the process of transition to a communist, Soviet-controlled regime, intellectuals were still unaware of the powerful impact the political changes at hand would have over their lives. Antonescu's wartime dictatorship had allowed the ethnically Romanian scientific and academic communities some autonomy. Intellectuals assumed that the ongoing changes would affect them in a similar fashion. Thus, Moldovan returned to Cluj, Banu to his position as professor of social medicine in Bucharest, and a series of works that dealt with social medicine in a eugenic vein continued to be published. For instance, the *Buletin Eugenic și Biopolitic* continued to appear until December 1947.

By 1948, however, an irrevocable shift had occurred, and the leaders of the eugenics schools in Romania had been forcibly retired.[8] Their students, however, continued to occupy positions of authority in the medical profession and education. For instance, Stoichiția stayed on as a General Hygiene Inspector at the regional level and Râmneanțu went on to teach and do research at the Polytechnical Institute in Timișoara.[9] Their ability to make a successful transition into the communist period had much to do with their willingness to reconstruct scientific arguments and research in the service of communist ideology.

Furthermore, the academic curricula eugenicists helped set up remained partially in place. Medical students still had to learn about hereditary determinism and evolution and their ties to preventive medicine.[10] The scientific arguments and language of hereditary determinism that eugenicists had helped to introduce a few decades earlier were becoming widely accepted, although the new academic elites were slowly shifting their ideological outlook, giving less and less credit to people like Moldovan, Râmneanțu, and Banu for ideas about the impact of heredity on the medical profession's shape and goals and emphasizing more the Soviet model.[11]

The eugenic dream of an effective state apparatus that could implement eugenic ideas thoroughly came about only with the demise of the eugenics movement after 1948. As Banu had pointed out in 1937, only a totalitarian regime could realize a comprehensive reform program. However, the communists had their own vision of reform, and while they tolerated the continuing presence in public life of many supporters of eugenics, they identified eugenics with the bourgeois and Nazi regimes. Eugenics became a taboo word until the 1960s. The names of various proponents of eugenics, most significantly Moldovan and Banu, were slowly rehabilitated only in the 1970s.

During the 1950–70 period, the influence of the Bucharest and Cluj eugenics schools on the development of life sciences and medicine was suppressed by the Communist Party.[12] At the beginning of the Stalinist period, a number of intellectuals and members of academia who had been students and proponents of eugenic theories had to "repent" publicly for such past connections and promise to disassociate themselves from all notions of hereditary determinism in their future work in order to survive the purges.[13]

Nonetheless, some works still made reference to hereditary determinism. It seems that these ideas had become so accepted that this "bourgeois legacy" needed to be exorcised over and over again. Victor Preda's repeated repudiation of any ties to hereditary determinism is a case in point. While in the inter-war period he had expressed interest in applying eugenics to his practice of anthropology, in the 1950s and 1960s he published several works in which he condemned this "bourgeois" theory. In a sense, his relentless critique gave hereditary-determinist theories a renewed lease on life, for his works rehearsed the arguments for his audience, familiarizing even ignorant readers with the basics of eugenics.[14]

Eugenic ideas resurfaced with the debate over birth control and abortion in the 1960s, as a resurgence of the discourse generated by eugenicists in the 1920s about the relationship between the state and individuals.[15] During the early periods of the communist regime, control over abortion was not very thorough. This procedure was even decriminalized completely in the late 1950s, when the regime legalized abortion on demand through Decree no. 463 of 30 September, 1957.[16] However, by the mid-1960s the communist leadership had become concerned about the declining birthrate, which threatened to affect the availability of the labor force within a generation. At a time when rapid industrialization was one of the central goals of the party leadership and especially of its newly appointed General Secretary, Nicolae Ceaușescu, this trend represented alarming news.

While Ceaușescu and other leaders began to raise such issues publicly, Râmneanțu, Moldovan's old disciple, also began to send various memoranda about the same issues, seeking audiences at the Ministry of Health and the Central Committee. He depicted the birthrate decline in Romania as a degenerative phenomenon and suggested a series of reforms to address this problem, which directly affected "the vital interests of the nation's future."[17] Râmneanțu's language and measures closely resemble his interwar ideas about controlling women's access to birth control and fostering more "responsible" (i.e., eugenically minded) behavior among couples of childbearing age. In one memorandum, he focused on educating women more effectively about their duties as mothers and on introducing "genetic" awareness at all levels of education. Most importantly, Râmneanțu called for the criminalization of abortion and the control of all forms of birth control by the state.[18] He recommended severe punishment of both mothers and medical personnel who assisted in abortions. Finally, Râmneanțu recommended positive incentives for reproduction, by increasing child allocations as the number of children increased.[19]

He sent this detailed memorandum to the Ministry of Health and to

Ceauşescu in the summer of 1965. It is unclear whether his analysis elicited any direct response from either the ministry or Ceauşescu. However, Râmneanţu was certainly not reprimanded for his proposals or the strong language of hereditary determinism he used.[20] In fact, on 1 October, 1966, the parliament passed the infamous Decree no. 770, which recriminalized abortion. Over time, this law became one of the most intrusive forms of government control over individual privacy under the communist regime. Widespread hatred for its abusiveness is vividly illustrated by the fact that the abrogation of the anti-abortion decree was one of the first measures passed by the National Salvation Front after the December 1989 revolution.[21]

For our purposes here it is important to call attention to the language of this law, for it echoes that of the Carol II Penal Code, which had been passed with eugenic concerns in mind:

> Interrupting pregnancy represents an act with grave consequences for the health of the nation and brings serious prejudices to the nation's population growth. [This action] is illegal unless: (1) the woman's life is in danger; . . . (2) one of the parents suffers from a *hereditary* disease; (3) the mother has serious physical, psychological or sensory handicaps; (4) the mother is over 45 years old; (5) the mother is already taking care of four children; (6) the pregnancy is the result of rape or incest.[22]

All but one item (the age-related issue) comes close to the exceptions stipulated by the eugenic anti-abortion legislation of 1938, to the point of using the same language. There was no stated eugenic aim in either the decree or in the additional literature that discussed it, but this law represented, in fact, a reassertion of eugenic ideas.

Moldovan and his collaborators would have been pleased to see that this time the anti-abortion legislation was implemented with greater "effectiveness" by the responsible state institutions, to the point that it terrorized most young couples and especially women. From 1966 until 1989, this legislation and a few corollary laws helped bring the bodies of all women of childbearing age under direct and continuous state scrutiny, from routine checkups to monthly checks at ovulation time.[23]

Although eugenicists had allowed women a certain degree of privacy and individual autonomy, the post-1966 communist regime imposed direct control over their bodies, turning women into reproductive machines more thoroughly than eugenicists had even dreamed. The issue of parenting, of offering children an environment that would nurture them, came second to that of reproducing. For instance, even teenage single mothers were ordered to carry their pregnancies to term, even though the state would often throw such children into appallingly managed orphanages.[24]

It is less clear, however, whether these policies were implemented preferentially along ethnic lines. Gail Kligman writes that the anti-abortion policies were ethnocentric, attempting to prevent the decline of ethnic Romanians in relation to other groups: "Population decline was viewed as synonymous with national decline and was intolerable for the national ideology of Ceauşescu's socialism."[25] Yet Romanians never went so far as to attempt to sterilize the Roma population, as the Czechoslovak regime did for over a decade.[26] Viorel Achim's analysis implies that Roma did continue to have higher birthrates than the Romanian population, either because there was no differential implementation of the anti-abortion legislation or because they chose to have more children. (Achim leans toward the latter, citing child allocations as one of the incentives.) The Romanian government did react in an alarmed manner to this rapid growth rate, but not with violent, aggressive measures. Instead, it made allocations conditional upon the employment of one of the parents and school attendance by the children.[27] Whether women suffered differently along ethnic lines under these anti-abortion policies remains to be further researched.

During the period of ideological thaw that followed the Prague Spring of 1968, interest in the contributions of eugenics to the development of Romanian science and medicine reemerged among many doctors and scientists. Most notably, a commemorative collection of essays, documenting the life and contributions of the most influential figures at the Medical School in Cluj. It included Moldovan and a number of other individuals from Iuliu Haţiegan to Victor Papilian and Constantin Velluda who, at one time or another, had stated explicitly their support for eugenic theories.[28] This recognition was not uncritical, for the authors contrasted what they believed to be the positive legacies of these individuals—Moldovan's vision of preventive social medicine, for instance —with the negative aspects of their lives and careers. Hugo Strauss, a historian of medicine from Cluj, criticized Moldovan on the basis of his "inability to understand that the bourgeois state could not realize his ideals and that only a socialist state could help bring about a public health system closely connected to the realities and needs of the nation."[29]

In other words, the scientific community under the communist regime did not contest the eugenicists' claims that their theories were scientific and based on objective truths. Rather, they identified the greatest shortcoming of these ideas with their ties to a political system rejected by the communists. This was an ironic critique, for eugenicists themselves had actively questioned the politics of the bourgeois liberal regime in Romania, with which their communist critics now identified them. It is significant that Strauss did not associate Moldovan's name with interwar right-wing politics, an accusation made earlier by one of his colleagues from Cluj.[30] By passing over in silence such damning criticisms, this evaluation lent greater legitimacy to eugenic legacies because it created a less politically problematic link between interwar eugenic ideas and medical education and scientific thinking in Romania after 1945.

Indeed, by 1979 Victor Săhleanu stated with great confidence that "the evolution of science has done justice to the proponents of heredo-biology such as Gheorghe Marinescu, Banu and Moldovan, and not to its denigrators, such as Lysenko and those who wrote and spoke against Banu and Moldovan."[31] Săhleanu placed these Romanian proponents of hereditary determinism within the most reputable traditions of twentieth-century scientific thought, identifying them as precursors of the post-1945 development of genetics.[32]

Developments after 1989

Since 1989, this legacy has been even more widely recognized within scientific circles in Romania. In my recent interviews, several current or retired doctors and members of the Medical School in Cluj expressed deep respect for Moldovan as a man of integrity and for his ideas. In a symbolic gesture, the amphitheater at the Institute of Hygiene that he helped to found was renamed for Iuliu Moldovan; for a short period in the early nineties, the whole institution carried his name. In addition, a commemorative plaque was unveiled in October 1994 in Cluj on the facade of his house. It is dedicated to Iuliu Moldovan, "man of science." Several members of the medical faculty also lobbied to have a street in Cluj renamed for him.

A recent publication of Moldovan's memoirs (1996) attempts to provide a more complex view of his work but ends up as an apology focusing on his important scientific contributions and his supposed humanism. The book contains a number of essays on Moldovan's work and life, one of them by the noted historian of medicine, Gheorghe Brătescu. In his critical evaluation of

Moldovan's complex legacy as evidenced by his memoirs, Brătescu asserts that "insofar as nationalism (not chauvinism) represents a special link with the interests of one's people (without any unfairness towards other nations), we can consider Iuliu Moldovan a nationalist, but also a democrat."[33] The meaning of this apology becomes clearer in the next sentence, where Brătescu compares Moldovan's democratic nationalism with that of Nicolae Iorga. This is, of course, an ironic comparison, for while it tries to depict Moldovan in a very positive light, it succeeds in reminding a critical reader of the dark, exclusionary undercurrents in his work.[34]

Thus far, however, the rehabilitation of Romanian eugenicists has not reached beyond a small academic circle. Since 1989, the mainstream discourse about reform, transition, and catching up with the West has revolved around economic, social, and cultural issues. At the same time, there is a resurgence of extremist nationalism on the Romanian political scene, especially among formations such as Vatra and România Mare. However, more mainstream politicians share some of their xenophobic and anti-Semitic fears, if in a milder version. In fact, political analyst Michael Shafir has written recently that radicalization and ethnocentrism of several exclusionary varieties (anti-Semitism, most prominently) have been essential components of Eastern European politics since 1989.[35] Vladimir Tismăneanu has identified this phenomenon as a form of mythmaking that combines victimization and collective narcissism by focusing on the Jew as the "other."[36]

The Roma, who many Romanians define along biological lines and wish to isolate, have become favorite scapegoats for the new radical parties. Many blame the Roma population for the economic and social problems in Romania today. This attitude has not grown to the level of open official discussion, but many individuals in positions of authority have it, while even more individual citizens act in accordance with such prejudices.

These tendencies are threatening the development of a stable political system and pluralist civil society. It is less clear, however, how much appeal ideas of biological determinism could have for this type of radical politics. România Mare, through its namesake publication, has been known to use biologizing language in attempting to denigrate real and imagined Jews and Roma as inferior species. The presidential campaign in 2000 demonstrated, however, that this type of discourse is spreading to other publications of a less sensationalist and radical nature.[37] In the first round, the România Mare candidate, Corneliu Vadim

Tudor, won 25 percent of the vote, placing second in the runoff after the neo-communist candidate, Ion Iliescu.

Another site where biological determinism may again reemerge as a strong force is the body, especially with regard to women's reproductive choices (abortion in particular), AIDS, and sexuality (especially as it affects homosexuals). In a recent article on gender and postsocialism, Gail Kligman and Susan Gal examine the central role of reproduction in the development of politics in Eastern Europe since 1989. They describe the political discourse as nationalist and as essentializing of gender roles. If the current nationalists "focus on motherhood and women as 'vessels of the nation,'" one can see a link between this normative view of gender roles and the ideas espoused by eugenicists in the interwar period.[38]

Eugenicists believed education was the best tool for raising the level of biological responsibility. I also believe that it is only through a conscious public educational effort that Romanians can learn to distance major political, economic, and social problems during this period of transition from a short-sighted biologizing identification of these issues with the "other"—be they Roma, Jews, Hungarians, gays, or women wanting to control their bodies. Some politicians have found a biologizing strategy expedient and have exploited it, for these biologizing arguments seem to offer solutions that would not require self-criticism but would, instead, assure progress by simply eliminating those viewed as "degenerate."

Until recently, these ideas remained marginal in the current political and intellectual discourse. Yet the surprisingly high popularity of România Mare in the 2000 elections signals a potential resurgence of this exclusionary biologizing discourse. The important players in public life—politicians, journalists, nongovernmental organizations, educators—need to assert a more responsible role, however, in order to educate the public about what is at stake in these criticisms and in their far-reaching implications, not only for Roma and Hungarians but also for the individual lives of ethnic Romanians. I hope my study will prompt a critical reexamination of these arguments both by their proponents and especially by other educated Romanians who hold positions of responsibility in the public sphere, from educators to politicians.

NOTES

INTRODUCTION

1. Simion Mehedinți, *Trilogii: Știința—școala—viața: Cu aplicări la poporul român* (Bucharest, [1940?]), 417. This and all subsequent translations belong to the author, unless otherwise noted.

2. Some of the more recent titles in this rapidly growing field are Paul Weindling, *Health, Race and German Politics Between National Unification and Nazism, 1870–1945* (Cambridge: Cambridge University Press, 1989); William Schneider, *Quality and Quantity: The Quest for Biological Regeneration in Twentieth-Century France* (Cambridge: Cambridge University Press, 1991); Pauline M. H. Mazdumar, *Eugenics, Human Genetics and Human Failings: The Eugenics Society, Its Sources and Its Critics in Britain* (New York: Routledge, 1992); Cathrine Clay and Michael Leapman, *Master Race: The Lebensborn Experiment in Nazi Germany* (London: Hodder and Stoughton, 1995); Aly Gotz, Peter Chroust, and Christian Pross, *Cleansing the Fatherland: Nazi Medicine and Racial Hygiene* (Baltimore: Johns Hopkins University Press, 1994); Martin S. Pernick, *The Black Stork: Eugenics and the Death of "Defective" Babies in American Medicine and Motion Pictures Since 1915* (New York: Oxford University Press, 1996); Mark B. Adams, ed., *The Wellborn Science: Eugenics in Germany, France, Brazil, and Russia* (New York: Oxford University Press, 1989); Gunnar Broberg and Nils Roll-Hansen, eds., *Eugenics and the Welfare State: Sterilization Policy in Denmark, Sweden, Norway, and Finland* (East Lansing: Michigan State University Press, 1996); Edward Larson, *Sex, Race, and Science: Eugenics in the Deep South* (Baltimore: Johns Hopkins University Press, 1995); and Anne Carol, *Histoire de l'eugénisme en France: Les medecins et la procreation, XIX-e–XXe siècle* (Paris: Seuil, 1995).

3. The one significant discussion of eugenics in Eastern Europe outside of Russia is Maria Kovacs, *Liberal Professions and Illiberal Politics: Hungary from the Habsburgs to the Holocaust* (Washington, D.C.: Wilson Center Press and Oxford University Press, 1994). An analysis of the rise of the liberal professions in Hungary before World War II,

it focuses in part on the development of the medical profession and the preoccupation of many Hungarian doctors with eugenics in connection to a wider anti-Semitic political agenda.

4. The archives of the Ministry of Health were available to me for research only up to 1940 and after 1945. The National Archives explained the gap as a result of the difficulty of inventorying the wartime years. They did not provide any information about when any of the material from the wartime years would become available for research. I also suspect that the National Archives purged some of the files from 1940 of potentially compromising materials. One file inventoried under the description "anti-Semitic policies against doctors" was given to me after some delay (the archivists justifying the delay by claiming the file was brittle and needed to be restored), at which point only one page in the whole file had any connection to anti-Semitic policies—a bureaucratic, brief, and uninteresting letter.

5. Jean Ancel, *Transnistria*, 3 vols. (Bucharest: DU Style, 1998); and Radu Ioanid, *The Holocaust in Romania: The Destruction of Jews and Gypsies Under the Antonescu Regime, 1940–1944* (Chicago: Ivan R. Dee, 2000). See chapter 6 for further discussion of this issue.

6. *Eugenical News* 21 (July–Aug. 1936), 84–85, puts the total number of members at seventy, but numbers were certainly higher then and continued to grow throughout the 1930s. For instance, not only people who were nominally members of the Biopolitical Section of Astra were active in eugenics. Activities of many of its other sections (e.g., the Feminine Subsection, the Physical Education Subsection) had a eugenic character.

7. Frank Dikötter, "Race Culture: Recent Perspectives on the History of Eugenics," *American Historical Review* 103, no. 2 (Apr. 1998): 467. See also Frank Dikötter, *Imperfect Conceptions: Medical Knowledge, Birth Defects, and Eugenics in China* (New York: Columbia University Press, 1998).

8. Philip J. Pauly, "Essay Review: The Eugenics Industry—Growth or Restructuring?" *Journal of the History of Biology* 26, no. 1 (spring 1993): 131–45; Dikötter, "Race Culture."

9. Richard J. Hernstein and Charles Murray, *The Bell Curve: Intelligence and Class Structure in American Life* (New York: Free Press, 1994). The number of articles that appeared after the publication of *The Bell Curve* is staggering. For a sample of the various reactions to it, see Richard Lacayo, "For Whom the Bell Curves," *Time* (24 Oct. 1994): 66–67; Adam Miller, "Professors of Hate," *Rolling Stone* (20 Oct. 1994): 106–14; Alan Ryan, "Apocalypse Now?" *New York Review of Books* (17 Nov. 1994): 7–11.

10. William B. Provine, *The Origins of Theoretical Population Genetics* (Chicago: University of Chicago Press, 1971); Mark H. Haller, *Eugenics: Hereditarian Attitudes in American Thought* (New Brunswick, N.J.: Rutgers University Press, 1963); Loren R. Graham, "Science and Values: The Eugenics Movement in Germany and Russia in the 1920s," *American Historical Review* 82, no. 5 (Dec. 1977): 1133–64; Diane Paul, "Eugenics and the Left," *Journal of the History of Ideas* 45, no. 4 (Oct.–Dec. 1984): 567–90.

11. Adams, *Wellborn Science;* Diane Paul, *Controlling Human Heredity, 1865 to the Present* (Atlantic Highlands, N.J.: Humanities Press, 1995); Dikötter, *Imperfect Conceptions.*

12. Paul, *Controlling Human Heredity;* Larson, *Sex, Race, and Science.*

13. Schneider, *Quality and Quantity,* 4.

14. Nancy Leys Stepan, *"The Hour of Eugenics": Race, Gender and Nation in Latin America* (Ithaca: Cornell University Press, 1991), 67–76. See also Dikötter, "Race Culture," 472–73.

15. Paul Weindling makes a clear departure from this approach, however, when he states that "eugenics was authoritarian in that it offered the state and professions unlimited powers to eradicate disease and improve the health of future generations. But it was neither a product of the theory of a superior Aryan race, nor was it inherently Nazi." Weindling, *Health, Race and German Politics,* 7.

16. Weindling, *Health, Race and German Politics;* Haller, *Eugenics.*

17. Stepan, *"Hour of Eugenics,"* 6. Dikötter makes a similar argument in *Imperfect Conceptions.*

18. Atina Grossmann, *Reforming Sex: The German Movement for Birth Control and Abortion Reform, 1920–1950* (New York: Oxford University Press, 1995).

19. Gisela Bock makes a similar argument in "Racism and Sexism in Nazi Germany: Motherhood, Compulsory Sterilization, and the State," in *When Biology Became Destiny: Women in Weimar and Nazi Germany,* ed. Renate Bridenthal, Atina Grossmann, and Marion Kaplan (New York: Monthly Review Press, 1984), 271–96.

20. Frank Dikötter draws attention to this problem as well: "Eugenics outside Europe is sometimes dismissed as a derivative manifestation of a more authentic discourse, a misleading interpretation that can only impoverish our understanding of the complexities of cultural history." See "Race Culture," 472. I would modify this statement, however, to include specifically Western Europe and the United States.

21. See Weindling, *Health, Race and German Politics,* chapter 5.

22. Loren R. Graham, *Science in Russia and the Soviet Union: A Short History* (New York: Cambridge University Press, 1993); Mark B. Adams, "Eugenics in Russia, 1900–1940," in Adams, *Wellborn Science.*

23. Schneider, *Quality and Quantity,* 11.

24. On the involvement of volunteer-based eugenic efforts and the limits of the impact on state policies by nongovernmental organizations, see Daniel Kevles, *In the Name of Eugenics: Genetics and the Uses of Human Heredity* (New York: Knopf, 1985); Edward Larson, "The Rhetoric of Eugenics: Expert Authority and the Mental Deficiency Bill," *British Journal of the History of Science* 24, part 1, no. 80 (Mar. 1991); Mazdumar, *Eugenics and Human Failings;* and Schneider, *Quality and Quantity.*

25. See Daniel Chirot, "Ideology, Reality and Competing Models of Development in Eastern Europe Between the Two World Wars," *East European Politics and Societies* 3, no. 3 (fall 1989): 396, for a discussion of Andrzej Walicki, "The Controversies Over Development and Modernization in Partitioned Poland" (paper presented at the Conference

on Models of Development and Theories of Modernization in Eastern Europe Between the Two World Wars, Budapest, 10–15 Sept. 1988). See also Kovacs, *Liberal Professions;* Ivo Banac and Katherine Verdery, eds., *National Character and National Ideology in Interwar Eastern Europe* (New Haven, Conn.: Yale Center for International and Area Studies, 1995); and Kenneth Jowitt, ed., *Social Change in Romania, 1860–1940: A Debate on Development in a European Nation* (Berkeley: University of California Press, 1978).

26. Chirot, "Ideology," 378–411.

27. Chirot, "Ideology," 392.

28. See, for instance, Jowitt, *Social Change.*

29. Marshall Berman, *All That Is Solid Melts Into Air* (New York: Penguin, 1988), 16.

30. Virgil Nemoianu, "Variable Sociopolitical Functions of Aesthetic Doctrine: Lovinescu vs. Western Aestheticism," in Jowitt, *Social Change;* Dumitru Micu, *"Gîndirea" și gîndirismul* (Bucharest: Ed. Minerva, 1975).

31. Leon Volovici, *Nationalist Ideology and Antisemitism: The Case of Romanian Intellectuals in the 1930s* (Oxford: Pergamon Press, 1991); Z. Ornea, *Anii treizeci: Extrema dreaptă românească* (Bucharest: Ed. Fundației Culturale Române, 1995).

32. See chapter 3 for an in-depth discussion of this issue.

33. Judith Walkowitz, *City of Dreadful Delight: Narratives of Sexual Danger in Late-Victorian London* (Chicago: University of Chicago Press, 1992); Paul Rabinow, *French Modern* (Cambridge: MIT Press, 1989).

34. See Michel Foucault, *Discipline and Punish: The Birth of the Prison* (New York: Vintage Books, 1979); and Michel Foucault, *The Archaeology of Knowledge* (London: Tavistock Publications, 1972).

35. Dominique LaCapra, *Rethinking Intellectual History: Texts, Contexts, Language* (Ithaca: Cornell University Press, 1983).

36. Eugen Lovinescu, *Istoria civilizației române moderne,* vol. 1 (Bucharest: Ed. Minerva, 1992), 17. Although his usage of the term "race" cannot be equated with its meaning today, it still illustrates the fact that he was familiar and comfortable with notions of biological determinism.

37. Kathleen Canning, *Languages of Labor and Gender: Female Factory Work in Germany, 1850–1914* (Ithaca: Cornell University Press, 1996); Marion A. Kaplan, *The Making of the Jewish Middle Class: Women, Family, and Identity in Imperial Germany* (New York: Oxford University Press, 1991).

CHAPTER 1

1. Gheorghe Brătescu, *Biological and Medical Sciences in Romania* (Bucharest: Ed. Stiințifică și Enciclopedică, 1989), 30.

2. C. Popazolu, *Ereditatea* (Bucharest: Tipografia ziarului "Universul," 1915). Some of these publications, such as Popazolu's, were written by veterinarians. Although these doctors did contribute to publicizing some of the biological determinist ideas and language central to eugenics discourse, I chose not to focus on their works. This is because

eugenicists themselves made moral and intellectual distinctions between controlling animal and human reproduction.

3. Iacob Felix, *Despre progresele igienei din cei din urmă ani* (Bucharest, 1885); Petrini (de Galatz), *Filosofia medicală: Despre ameliorarea rasei umane* (Bucharest: Tipografia D. A. Laurian, 1876). One important critic of social darwinism and advocate of more comprehensive social-welfare policies from a biological perspective was Ştefan Stîncă, an active socialist. See his *Mediul social ca factor patologic* (Iaşi: Tip. H. Goldner, 1897).

4. See Schneider, *Quality and Quantity,* chapter 3.

5. Maria Bucur, "Philanthropy, Nationalism, and the Growth of Civil Society in Romania," Working Papers of the Johns Hopkins Comparative Nonprofit Sector Project, no. 31, ed. Lester M. Salamon and Helmut K. Anheier (Baltimore: The Johns Hopkins Institute for Policy Studies, 1998).

6. Phillip G. Eidelberg, *The Great Rumanian Peasant Revolt of 1907* (Leiden: Brill, 1974).

7. Constantin Dobrogeanu-Gherea, "Neoiobăgia," in *Opere complete,* vol. 4 (1910; reprint, Bucharest: Ed. Academiei R.S.R., 1977); David Mitrany, *The Land and the Peasant in Rumania* (London: H. Millford, Oxford University Press, 1930); Joseph Love, *Crafting the Third World: Theorizing Underdevelopment in Romania and Brazil* (Stanford: Stanford University Press, 1996).

8. Gheorghe Banu, *Sănătatea poporului român* (Bucharest: Fundaţia pentru literatură şi artă "Regele Carol II," 1935), 46–48.

9. Harald Heppner, "Die Universtät Graz und die rumänischen Länder," *Révue Roumaine d'Histoire,* nos. 3–4 (1996): 213–17; Mihai Sorin Rădulescu, "Rumänische Studenten an den universitaten in Tubingen und halle zwischen 1848–1918," *Révue Roumaine d'Histoire,* nos. 1–2 (1997): 27–49; Uwe Dathe, "Studenten aus Rumänien an der Universtät Jena in den Jahren 1801 bis 1918," *Révue Roumaine d'Histoire,* nos. 1–2 (1997): 50–56; Elena Siupiur, "The Formation of Romanian Intellectuals in the Nineteenth Century" (paper presented at Culture and the Politics of Identity in Modern Romania, Bucharest, May 1998); Liviu Rotman, "Romanian Jewish Students at European Universities" (paper presented at the Romanian Cultural Foundation International Conference, Braşov, June 1998). I'd like to thank Liviu Rotman for bringing to my attention the articles in *Révue Roumaine d'Histoire.*

10. Weindling, *Health, Race and German Politics;* Schneider, *Quality and Quantity;* Mazdumar, *Eugenics and Human Failings.*

11. V. L. Bologa et al., *Istoria medicinei româneşti* (Bucharest: Ed. medicală, 1972); Gheorghe Brătescu, ed., *Din tradiţiile medicinii şi ale educaţiei sanitare: Studii şi note* (Bucharest: Ed. medicală, 1978); Gheorghe Brătescu, ed., *Trecut şi viitor în medicină: Studii şi note* (Bucharest: Ed. medicală, 1981).

12. See chapter 6.

13. Banu, *Sănătatea,* 48–53; Bologa et al., *Istoria,* 229–30.

14. Cantacuzino remained a supporter of Moldovan personally and supported his ideas during the interwar period.

15. Bologa et al., *Istoria*, 275–80.

16. Iuliu Moldovan, *Amnitiri şi reflexiuni* (Bucharest: Ed. Universitară Carol Davilla, 1996); Petre Râmneanţu, "Iuliu Moldovan: Viaţa, realizările şi epoca sa" (Bucharest, 1977).

17. The Directing Council came into being on 15 December 1918, and gradually tapered off its activities as a legislative and administrative body until April 1920, when Transylvania was effectively incorporated into the governmental administrative and legislative institutions of the Romanian Kingdom. For a detailed discussion of this issue, see Gheorghe Iancu, *Contribuţia consiliului dirigent la consolidarea statului naţional unitar român (1918–1920)* (Cluj-Napoca: Ed. Dacia, 1985).

18. Iancu, *Contribuţia*, 284–91; Râmneanţu, "Iuliu Moldovan," 14–18.

19. He continued to be the head of the Institute of Hygiene after its move to Sibiu for the duration of the war.

20. See chapter 6.

21. Iuliu Moldovan, "Motive pentru înfiinţarea Ministerului Sănătăţii Publice," *Sănătatea Publică* 1, no. 1 (Jan. 1921): 10–11.

22. Iuliu Moldovan, "Un program biopolitic," *Societatea de Mâine* 1, no. 3 (27 Apr. 1924): 69–70.

23. Iuliu Moldovan, "Raport că Ministerul Justiţiei/Suguranţa Internă, 22 iunie, 1992," Iuliu Moldovan, fond personal, dos. 1, Arhivele Naţionale, Filiala Cluj, 3.

24. Moldovan, fond personal, dos. 1, docs. 1–4.

25. Irina Livezeanu, *Cultural Politics in Greater Romania: Regionalism, Nation Building and Ethnic Struggle, 1918–1930* (Ithaca: Cornell University Press, 1995). See esp. chapter 1.

26. "Programul Partidului Naţional-Ţărănesc," *Aurora* 6, no. 1481 (13 Oct. 1926): 4. My italics.

27. "Numirea membrilor directoratului Frontului Renaşterii Naţionale," *Lumea Românească* 3, no. 591 (22 Jan. 1939): 3.

28. Ovidiu Bădina, *Cercetarea sociologică concretă: Tradiţii româneşti* (Bucharest: Ed. politică, 1966).

29. *"Astra" în anii de după răsboiu (1918–1928)* (Sibiu, [1928?]), 24.

30. *"Astra" în anii*, 20.

31. *"Astra" în anii*, 20. My italics.

32. For an analysis of this process, which was defined more often by conflict than by cooperation, see Pamfil Matei, *"Asociaţiunea transilvană pentru literatură şi cultura poporului român" (Astra) şi rolul ei în cultura naţională (1861–1950)* (Cluj-Napoca: Ed. Dacia, 1986), 65–66.

33. *Eugenical News* 21 (July–Aug. 1936): 84–85.

34. *Buletin Eugenic şi Biopolitic* 1, no. 1 (Jan. 1927): 28.

35. Emil G. Racoviţă, *Evoluţia şi problemele ei* (Cluj: Ed. Asociaţiunii, 1929), 7–8.

36. Some of these lectures were later published and showed that their authors were both familiar with and supportive of eugenics. See, for instance, Alexandru Vaida-Voevod, "Politică naţională şi capitalul biologic naţional," *Buletin Eugenic şi Biopolitic* 1, nos. 7–8 (July–Aug. 1927): 199–211.

37. Gheorghe Preda, *Activitatea "Astrei" în 25 ani dela Unire (1918–1943)* (Sibiu, 1944), 28.

38. Although many historians have written at length about Astra as an institution that was important in the nationalist movement and for Romanian culture in general, only one has focused on this particular aspect during the interwar period. However, this historian has chosen to identify eugenics as an ideology forcibly imposed by Moldovan rather than willingly sanctioned by Astra's members at large. There is no evidence, however, that the membership found Moldovan authoritarian and disapproved of his choice to focus Astra's spending on eugenic publications and programs. See Matei, *Asociațiunea transilvană*, 101–6.

39. There is no direct evidence of this, but it would have taken such a promise for Moldovan to go back into a governmental position that he had grown very distrustful of by 1925, especially when his academic position and his involvement in Astra already afforded him outlets for his ideas and programs of action. There is one source that further indicates Maniu's commitment to help Moldovan. In an interview with W. Leland Mitchell, a representative of the Rockefeller Foundation visiting Romania in December 1928, Iuliu Maniu asserted that he liked Moldovan's work very much. With regard to Moldovan's ideas about public health reform, Maniu stated that he "would do everything to further its development along modern lines, [since] . . . the human capital of the country comes before all else and its health must be guarded." W. Leland Mitchell, "Roumania: Observations regarding public health work on visits to in 1927 and 1928," folder 8, box 2, record group 1.1, series 783, Rockefeller Foundation Archives, Rockefeller Archive Center (RAC), North Tarrytown, N.Y., 18. Translation in the original.

40. The debates were recorded and can be found in Cluj. See Moldovan, fond personal, dos. 10d, 1–3. For a discussion of the implementation and impact of the 1930 Moldovan Law, see Gheorghe Brătescu, *Istoria sănătății publice în România: Sinteză* (Bucharest, 1981), 39–40.

41. The right-wing legionary movement, led by Horia Sima, was Marshal Ion Antonescu's main ally when Antonescu took over in September 1940. Historians still debate the closeness of the relationship between Antonescu and the Iron Guard. It is certain, however, that by the beginning of 1941 their relationship was strained beyond repair. The legionaries attempted a coup in January 1941, which Antonescu suppressed. Until 1944, he ruled with the help of the army. For a balanced account see Keith Hitchins, *Rumania 1866–1947* (Oxford: Clarendon Press, 1994), 457–71.

42. See introduction, note 4.

43. Weindling, *Health, Race and German Politics*, chapter 8.

44. See chapter 3.

45. Moldovan, *Amintiri*, 108. The sentence was not directly related to his work in eugenics but rather to his having served as General Secretary at the Ministry of Health in 1929–30.

46. Petre Râmneanțu, "Origine ethnique des Szeklers de Transylvanie," *Révue de Transylvanie* 2, no. 1 (Aug.–Sept. 1935): 45–59.

47. The Szeklers were a Hungarian-speaking group that had been brought into Tran-

sylvania during the Middle Ages as a "frontier" population to protect the borders between Transylvania (then part of Hungary) and its southeastern neighbors. They were
then and continue to be considered ethnically distinct from the rest of the Hungarian-
speaking population of Transylvania.

48. Personal communication with Romeo Lăzărescu, Bucharest, Apr. 1995.

49. Petre Râmneanțu, letter to Nicolae Ceaușescu, President of the State Council of
the Socialist Republic of Romania, 17 Mar. 1978. Courtesy of the Romeo Lăzărescu personal archive, Bucharest.

50. Personal communication with Victor Săhleanu, Bucharest, July 1993. Ironically,
the Făcăoaru couple did not have any children.

51. Dimitrie Gusti, *Opere alese*, vol. 1, ed. Ovidiu Bădina and Octavian Neamțu
(Bucharest: Ed. Academiei R.S.R., 1968), 424–26.

52. Iordache Făcăoaru, letter to Petre Râmneanțu, 1 Jan. 1978, 5. Courtesy of the
Romeo Lăzărescu personal archive, Bucharest.

53. Gusti, *Opere alese*, vol. 1, 424–26.

54. Weindling, *Health, Race and German Politics*, 471–78.

55. Iordache Făcăoaru, "Înmulțirea disgenicilor și costul lor pentru societate și stat,"
Buletin Eugenic și Biopolitic 6, nos. 4–5 (Apr.–June 1935): 169–83.

56. Ancel, *Transnistria*, vol. 3, 196–99.

57. Iordache Făcăoaru, "Cercetări antropologice în patru sate din Transnistria," unpublished ms., 1943, United States Holocaust Memorial Museum Institute, RG-31
(Ukraine) / 004 m, Reel 2. I would like to thank Radu Ioanid for bringing this document
to my attention.

58. The latest source I could trace to Făcăoaru's authorship is dated 1 Jan. 1978.
Făcăoaru, letter to Petre Râmneanțu, 1 Jan. 1978, 5.

59. Iuliu Moldovan, *Statul etnic* (Cluj, 1943), 16.

60. Moldovan, *Statul etnic*, 17.

61. See chapter 6.

62. Făcăoaru, letter to Petre Râmneanțu, 1 Jan. 1978, 3–4.

63. Overall, Bucharest led the way in this regard. Some doctors and scholars in social
sciences from Iași showed interest in eugenics but did not pursue the study of this theory, its popularization, and discussions of policy making as actively as some of their colleagues in Bucharest and Cluj. One exception was interest expressed by several doctors
in puericulture. For a discussion of the Iași medical school and local specializations, see
Constantin Romanescu and Cristina Ionescu, eds., *Pagini medico-istorice* (Iași: Institutul de medicină și farmacie Iași, 1973); and Bologa et al., *Istoria*.

64. Mircea Vulcănescu et al., eds., *Dimitrie Gusti și Școala Sociologică dela București*
(Bucharest, 1937); Henri H. Stahl, *Amintiri și gînduri din vechea școala "monografiilor sociologice"* (Bucharest: Ed. Minerva, 1981); Chirot, "Ideology."

65. D. C. Georgescu, "Secția de demografie, antropologie și eugenie a Institutului Social Român," *Sociologie Românească* 1, no. 1 (Jan. 1936): 56–57.

66. See chapter 5.

67. Dimitrie Gusti, *Opere alese,* vol. 3, ed. Ovidiu Bădina and Octavian Neamțu (Bucharest: Ed. Academiei R.S.R., 1968), 248.

68. Stahl, *Amintiri,* 396.

69. See, for instance, Iordache Făcăoaru, "Reviste în schimb cu Buletinul," *Buletin Eugenic și Biopolitic* 7, no. 12 (Dec. 1936): 381–82.

70. Some of Banu's most important works include *L'Hygiène de la race: Étude de biologie héréditaire et de normalisation de la race* (Bucharest and Paris, 1939); *Tratat de medicină socială* (Bucharest: Casa școalelor, 1944); and the numerous articles he published in *Revista de Igienă Socială.* Among these articles are "Principes d'un programme d'hygiène de la race," *Revista de Igienă Socială* 6, no. 10 (1936): 565–94; and "Eugenia poporului românesc," *Revista de Igienă Socială* 11, nos. 11–12 (Nov.–Dec. 1941): 341–97.

71. Banu, "Principes," 575.

72. See Victor Săhleanu, *Începuturile medicinii sociale în România: George Banu* (Bucharest, 1979), chapter 4.

73. See chapter 3.

74. In 1933 almost 40 million lei were allocated to treating social illnesses, tuberculosis, and syphilis and to running the rural nets (*plăşi rurale*) that focused on basic preventive medical services in the countryside. The budget for that year was 818,003,100 lei. The amount spent on prophylactic medicine represented a significant increase from the 25 million lei allocated in 1928. "Buget," Arhivele Ministerului Sănătății, 1933, dos. 355, 1928, dos. 137, Arhivele Naționale, Filiala București.

75. The organization of the bureau was modified, as it became the Section for Human Biology and Anthropology, part of the Institute for Demography and Census, under the leadership of Sabin Manuilă, along with the Section for Minorities Studies.

76. Though his biographer does not mention this fact, it is likely that Banu, as a member of several "bourgeois" governments, also spent time in prison during the Stalinist period.

77. George Marinescu, *Despre hereditatea normală şi patologică şi raporturile ei cu eugenia,* Academia Română, Memoriile secțiunii științifice, seria III, tom XI, mem. 7 (Bucharest, 1936).

78. See Sabin Manuilă, "Societatea regală română de eugenie şi studiul eredității," *Sociologie Românească* 1, no. 5 (May 1936): 31–32.

79. Dinu C. Daniel, *Les Elites psychobiologiques et leurs rapport avec l'ethographie* (Bucharest, [1940]).

80. I would like to thank one of the anonymous readers of the manuscript for bringing some of these issues to my attention.

81. Francisc Rainer, *Enquêtes anthropologiques dans trois villages roumains des Carpathes* (Bucharest: Monitorul Oficial, 1937).

82. Francisc Rainer, "Amendamentul unui om de știință: Scrisoare deschisă d-lui Ion Mihalache, Ministru al Agriculturii," *Adevărul* 42, no. 13954 (21 June 1929): 1–2.

83. For a very positive assessment of Rainer's work that makes no mention of eugenics see Th. Enăchescu, "Contribuțiile profesorului Francisc J. Rainer la dezvoltarea antropologiei românești," *Studii și Cercetări Antropologice* 7, no. 2 (1970): 165–79.

84. Ioan Vasilescu-Buciumi, "Criminologia și eugenia," *Revista de Medicină Legală* 1, no. 1 (1936): 84–90.

CHAPTER 2

1. These two works will be the main focus of my discussion in the next chapter.

2. This differentiation is not as significant in the case of Romania, where interest in hereditary determinism in the realm of botany and zoology was not as prominent as in the realm of human biology. By contrast, in Russia biologists with an interest in hereditary determinism helped shape the development of eugenics in significant ways. See Adams, "Eugenics in Russia."

3. William Coleman, *Biology in the Nineteenth Century: Problems of Form, Function, and Transformation* (New York: Wiley, 1971); Adrian Desmond, *The Politics of Evolution: Morphology, Medicine, and Reform in Radical London* (Chicago: University of Chicago Press, 1989); Charles Rosenberg, *No Other Gods: On Science ad American Social Thought* (Baltimore: Johns Hopkins University Press, 1976); Carl N. Degler, *In Search of Human Nature: The Decline and Revival of Darwinism in American Social Thought* (New York: Oxford University Press, 1991).

4. Adams, *Wellborn Science.*

5. This was not so much the case in the Scandinavian countries, where eugenics developed more as a strategy of modernization during the twentieth century. See Broberg and Roll-Hansen, *Eugenics and the Welfare State.*

6. In Transylvania, the Catholic Church, as the main and court-supported religion, had similar control over education and science. A portion of the Romanian population, the Uniates, fell formally under the control of the Catholic Church, although they were less strictly supervised than Romano-Catholic subjects of the church. Moldovan was himself a Uniate.

7. Keith Hitchins, *L'Idée de nation chez les Roumains de Transylvanie, 1691–1848* (Bucharest: Ed. științifică și enciclopedică, 1987).

8. Hitchins, *L'Idée de nation.*

9. See Mazdumar, *Eugenics and Human Failings*, esp. chapter 1, on England. See Weindling, *Health, Race and German Politics*, on Germany.

10. Petrini, *Filosofia medicală.*

11. Vasile Conta, *Teoria ondulațiunii universale* (Iași, [1876–78]), 26–30.

12. Al. Suțu, "Eugenica și hereditatea," *Gazeta de Medicină Chirurgicală a Spitalelor* 5, no. 12 (15 Sept. 1874): 186; Stîncă, *Mediul social;* Panaite Zosin, *Determinismul* ([Bucharest]: Lito-Tipografia Motatzeanu and Lambru, 1895); A. Aronovici, *Omul și sociologia dupe Darvin, Lamark, Herbert Spencer, Letourneau, Buchner, etc.* (Galați: Lib. G. D. Nebuneli și Fii, n.d.); N. Leon, "Generațiunea spontanee și darvinismul," *Convorbiri Literare* 37, no. 4 (1903).

13. Graham, "Science and Values," 1142–43; Paul, *Controlling Human Heredity*.

14. Larson, "Rhetoric of Eugenics," 49–50.

15. Schneider, *Quality and Quantity*, 283.

16. See chapter 3.

17. Weindling, *Health, Race and German Politics*, chapter 2.

18. Sheila Faith Weiss, *Race Hygiene and National Efficiency: The Eugenics of Wilhelm Schallmayer* (Berkeley: University of California Press, 1987), 103.

19. Weindling, *Health, Race and German Politics*, 48–59.

20. Sheila Faith Weiss, "The Race Hygiene Movement in Germany, 1904–1945," in Adams, *Wellborn Science*.

21. I. Manliu, *Crâmpeie de eugenie și igienă socială* (Bucharest: Tip. Jockey Club, 1921), 29.

22. Kevles, *In the Name*, 97–104.

23. Manliu, *Crâmpeie*, 29.

24. Frank Dikötter makes a similar claim regarding Chinese eugenics. See *Imperfect Conceptions*, chapter 1.

25. See Ștefan Bârsănescu, *Politică culturală în România contemporană: Studiu de pedagogie* (Iași, 1937), 50.

26. Hitchins, *Rumania*, 157.

27. Hitchins, *Rumania*, 298–300, 295–96.

28. Supporters of religious authority included Nichifor Crainic, who would become a strong supporter of the extreme right and founder of the "Gândirist" movement, loosely based on fundamental tenets of Orthodox theology. See Keith Hitchins, "*Gândirea*: Nationalism in Spiritual Guise," in Jowitt, *Social Change*, 140–73, for a critical analysis of the movement. One prominent name among the supporters of secularization was the sociologist Petre Andrei, whose work was influenced by Durkheim and Weber and who was later favorably impressed by Romanian eugenics. See chapter 3.

29. Suțu, "Eugenica și hereditatea"; Brătescu, *Biological and Medical Sciences*.

30. A. C. Cuza, *Meseriașul român* (Bucharest, 1893).

31. Ornea, *Anii treizeci*; Cristian Sandache, *Doctrina național-creștină în România* (Bucharest: Paideia, 1997); Volovici, *Nationalist Ideology*.

32. See I. Ludo, *În jurul unei obsesii* (Bucharest, 1936), as quoted in Volovici, *Nationalist Ideology*.

33. Volovici, *Nationalist Ideology*; William Oldson, *A Providential Antisemitism: Nationalism and Polity in Nineteenth Century Romania* (Philadelphia: American Philosophical Society, 1991).

34. Vasile Pârvan, *Idei și forme istorice: Patru lecții inaugurale* (Bucharest: Ed. Cartea românească, 1920).

35. Hitchins, *Rumania*; Jowitt, *Social Change*; Z. Ornea, *Tradiționalism și modernitate în deceniul al treilea* (Bucharest: Ed. Eminescu, 1980).

36. Keith Hitchins, *Mit și realitate în istoriografia României* (Bucharest: Ed. enciclopedică, 1997), 286–94; Gusti, *Opere alese*, vol. 3, 10–11.

37. Iuliu Moldovan, *Introducere în etnobiologie și biopolitică* (Sibiu, 1944), 23–49.

38. Graham, "Science and Values," 1142–43.

39. Graham, "Science and Values," 1142–43.

40. Stepan, *"Hour of Eugenics."*

41. Kevles, *In the Name,* 43–44.

42. Mazdumar, *Eugenics and Human Failings,* chapter 2.

43. Paul, *Controlling Human Heredity.*

44. Paul, *Controlling Human Heredity;* Dikötter, *Imperfect Conceptions.*

45. Graham, "Science and Values," 1142–43.

46. Kevles, *In the Name,* 44.

47. A similar ambivalence—with, however, a distinctive neo-Lamarckian outlook—characterized Chinese eugenics. See Dikötter, *Imperfect Conceptions,* 117–18.

48. Weindling, *Health, Race and German Politics,* 298–304.

49. V. Puşcariu, "Teoriile evoluţiei: Lamarck şi Lamarckismul: Geoffroy Saint-Hilaire," *Buletin Eugenic şi Biopolitic* 1, no. 2 (Feb. 1927): 35–37.

50. V. Puşcariu, "Mendelismul la om: Ereditatea caracterelor fiziologice," *Buletin Eugenic şi Biopolitic* 1, no. 3 (Mar. 1927): 66–71.

51. Marinescu, *Despre hereditatea.*

52. Iordache Făcăoaru, *Curs de eugenie* (Cluj, 1935), 32. Original emphasis.

53. Făcăoaru, *Curs de eugenie,* 32.

54. Maria Bucur, "From Private Philanthropy to Public Institutions: The Rockefeller Foundation and Public Health in Interwar Romania," *Romanian Civilization* 4, no. 2 (summer 1995): 47–60.

55. Bucur, "Private Philanthropy," 53–54.

56. Iuliu Moldovan, letter to C. K. Strode, 2 Jan. 1941, folder 1, box 1, record group 1.1, series 783, Rockefeller Foundation Archives, RAC. This letter mentions the subscriptions funded by the Rockefeller Foundation and asks for their renewal. Among the listed journals are the *Eugenics Review* and the *Journal of Heredity.*

57. Bucur, "Private Philanthropy," 52.

58. Iuliu Moldovan, "Jurnal de călătorie în America," 22 Apr., Moldovan, fond personal dos. 2a.

59. Iordache Făcăoaru, "Legea pentru apărarea sănătăţii ereditare a populaţiei Germane," *Buletin Eugenic şi Biopolitic* 7, nos. 1–2 (Jan.–Feb. 1936): 49–53.

60. Iordache Făcăoaru, "Privire critică asupra legii finlandeze de sterilizare în comparaţie cu legea germană," *Buletin Eugenic şi Biopolitic* 8, nos. 10–12 (Oct.–Dec. 1937): 33–54.

61. Sorin Soma, "Politică demografică în Italia," *Preocupări Universitare* 1, no. 1 (Dec. 1943): 106–7.

62. Mehedinţi, *Trilogii.*

63. Banu, *Tratat,* contains a rich bibliography that includes names such as M. Nisot, A. Lumière, and the Belgian writer and reformer René Sand.

64. Săhleanu, *Începuturile medicinii sociale,* 12.

65. Henry Eversole, "Medical Education in Roumania," folder 17, box 3, record group 1.1, series 783, Rockefeller Foundation Archives, RAC, 18.

66. C. C. Gheorghiu, "Demofilia și eugenia ca principii divergente în doctrina populației," *Revista de Igienă Socială* 3, no. 4 (1937): 211–17.

67. V. Noveanu, "Mișcarea eugenică în Franța," *Buletin Eugenic și Biopolitic* 3, nos. 1–2 (Jan.–Feb. 1929): 26–31.

68. Moldovan, *Introducere*, 33.

69. Moldovan, *Introducere*, 33.

70. Weindling, *Health, Race and German Politics*, 19.

71. Hitchins, *Rumania*, 295–97.

72. Hitchins, *Rumania*, 300–304.

73. Moldovan, *Introducere*, 23.

74. Moldovan, *Introducere*, 28.

75. Moldovan, *Introducere*, 33.

76. Foucault, *Discipline and Punish;* Thomas Laqueur, *Making Sex: Body and Gender from the Greeks to Freud* (Cambridge: Harvard University Press, 1990).

77. Foucault, *Discipline and Punish*, 79–103.

78. See Dumitru Ghișe and Pompiliu Teodor, *Fragmentarium Iluminist* (Cluj: Ed. Dacia, 1972).

79. Moldovan, *Introducere*, 33.

80. Ovidiu Comșia, "Politică și biopolitică. Pagina biopolitică," *Transilvania* 68, no. 2 (Mar.–Apr. 1937): 113.

81. Iuliu Moldovan, *Biopolitica* (Cluj: Ed. Asociațiunii, 1926), 80.

82. Ornea, *Anii treizeci.*

83. Ornea, *Anii treizeci*, esp. 60–61.

84. Moldovan, *Introducere*, 33.

85. Salvator Cupcea, *Probleme de eredobiologie* (Sibiu, 1944), 35.

86. Traian Herseni, "Anchetă bio-socială," *Buletin Eugenic și Biopolitic* 18, nos. 9–12 (Sept.–Dec. 1947): 184–96.

87. Hitchins, *L'Idée de nation*, 148–79.

88. Hitchins, *L'Idée de nation.*

89. Gábor Barta et al., eds., *Erdély rövid története* (Budapest: Akadémiai Kiádo, 1989).

90. Ovidiu Comșia, "Biologie și istorie," *Buletin Eugenic și Biopolitic* 9, nos. 5–6 (May–June 1935): 164–80.

91. Petre Râmneanțu and P. David, "Cercetări asupra originii etnice a populației din Sud-Estul Transilvaniei pe baza compoziției serologice a sângelui," *Buletin Eugenic și Biopolitic* 6, nos. 1–3 (Jan.–Mar. 1935): 36–66.

92. Moldovan, *Introducere*, 36–37.

93. Moldovan, *Introducere*, 36–37.

94. Marinescu, *Despre hereditatea.*

95. Racoviță, *Evoluția.*

96. See, for instance, Francisc Rainer, "Rasele umane: Conferință," *România Medicală* 12, no. 10 (15 Mar. 1934): 142.

97. Hitchins, *Rumania*, 293–94.

98. Petre Andrei, *Sociologie generală* (Craiova: Ed. Scrisul românesc, 1936), 25–30.

99. Andrei, *Sociologie generală*, 470.

100. Andrei, *Sociologie generală*, 470.

101. George Călinescu, *Istoria literaturii române de la origini pînă în prezent*, 2d rev. ed. (Bucharest: Ed. Minerva, 1982).

102. Călinescu, *Istoria;* Lovinescu, *Istoria civilizației române moderne,* vol. 3 (Bucharest: Ed. Minerva, 1992), 111–43.

103. For a critical evaluation of this group's ideas and contribution to the intellectual and political debates in interwar Romania see Ornea, *Anii treizeci;* Micu, *"Gîndirea";* and Hitchins, *Rumania,* 298–319.

104. See chapter 3 for a discussion of Crainic's related concept of ethnocracy.

105. Ioan Agârbiceanu, *Preotul și familia preoțească: Rostul lor etnic în satul românesc* (Sibiu: Editura subsecției eugenice și biopolitice a Astrei, 1942).

106. See chapter 3. Although some of the important writings on this matter do not identify any denominations in particular, authors more often than not refer to the Orthodox and Uniate Churches, whose membership encompassed almost all ethnic Romanians.

107. V. Gomoiu, "Preoțimea în slujba operelor de ocrotire și medicină socială," *Analele Ministerului Sănătății și Ocrotirilor Sociale* 4 (40), nos. 4–9 (Apr.–Sept. 1927): 82–101.

108. One of the Rockefeller Foundation officers who traveled to Romania, Elisabeth F. Crowell, gave a dismal description of these institutions in 1923. See Elisabeth F. Crowell, "Memorandum Regarding the Study of Sick Nursing and Health Visiting in Roumania," folder 22, box 3, group record 1.1, series 783c, Rockefeller Foundation Archives, RAC, 25.

109. Veturia Manuilă, "Asistența socială," *Buletin Eugenic și Biopolitic* 1, no. 1 (Jan. 1927): 22–24.

110. Veturia Manuilă, "Asistența socială," 22–24.

111. Gheorghe Preda, *O încercare de apropriere a raporturilor între știință și religie* (Sibiu, 1925).

112. Gheorghe Preda, *O încercare,* 12.

113. Initially eugenicists had proposed a number of cultural and health homes, to be developed at the grassroots level. See Iosif Stoichiția, "Casa culturală și de sănătate," *Transilvania* 68, no. 2 (Mar.–Apr. 1937): 108–11. By 1939, after Carol II's coup, proposals for such institutions had grown to the national level. Dimitrie Gusti, the sociologist, was the architect of the Law for Social Service, which called for creating a Cultural Hearth in each village, under centralized supervision. Moldovan was to be one of the permanent members of the three-member committee that would oversee the growth and implementation of this program. See "Legea Serviciului Social," *Buletinul Serviciului Social* 1, no. 1 (Mar. 1939): 3–10; also see chapter 5.

114. "Legea Serviciului," 8.

115. "Legea Serviciului," 6–8.

116. "Legea Serviciului," 6.

117. Iuliu Hațiegan, "Ce este secția medicală și biopolitică a Astrei?" in *Calendarul*

Asociațiunii pe anul comun 1927, comp. Horia Petra-Petrescu (Sibiu: Ed. Asociațiunii, 1926), 36–38.

118. Vasile Ilea, *Școala superioară țărănească* (Sighet, 1933).

119. In 1932, when Banu was Minister of Health, doctors appointed by the ministry and working in the countryside received between 9,000 and 16,000 lei per year, depending on experience and responsibilities. After Banu lost his position in 1933, the salaries went down to 6,650–9,450 lei per year. It took another four years for these salaries to reach their 1932 levels. See fond Ministerul Sănătății și Ocrotrii Sociale, 1933, dos. 355, 1937, dos. 778, Arhivele Naționale.

120. The effectiveness of these programs impressed foreign observers. A 1940 Rockefeller Foundation report praised the experimental health station in the village of Gilău in glowing terms. See folder 30, box 3, record group 1.1, series 783j, Rockefeller Foundation Archives, RAC.

121. Tiberiu Ionescu, "Dr. Casian Topa: Monografia sanitară a circumscripției Văscăuți (Storojineț), pe anii: 1931–35," *Sociologie Românească* 3, nos. 4–6 (Apr.–June 1938): 272–74.

122. The first two publications were edited by Iuliu Moldovan, a fact that points clearly to the impact of eugenics in stimulating rural medical practice. The other two journals had a few proponents of eugenics on their editorial staffs; they looked to Moldovan as a visionary figure and probably followed in his footsteps by trying to encourage a positive image of rural medical practice.

CHAPTER 3

1. Brief analyses of these debates can be found in Hitchins, *Rumania,* chapters 7–9; and Vlad Georgescu, *The Romanians, a History* (Columbus: Ohio University Press, 1991). See also Jowitt, *Social Change.* For an excellent analysis of the agrarian problems in Romania see Henry Roberts, *Rumania: Political Problems of an Agrarian State* (Hamden, Conn.: Archon Books, 1969).

2. I use the term "totalitarian" as defined by Hannah Arendt in her classic work *The Origins of Totalitarianism* (New York: Harcourt Brace Jovanovich, 1973). Though much criticized and somewhat flawed with regard to the fulfillment of totalitarian projects, her analysis has remained a valuable tool for examining the development and specific elements of ideology in the twentieth century.

3. Eugenics has often been labeled as a pseudoscience. Though few dispute this today, in the early part of the century eugenicists operated within a scientific discourse, using arguments and a language that were grounded within scientific paradigms.

4. Volovici, *Nationalist Ideology;* Hitchins, *Mit și realitate;* Ornea, *Tradiționalism;* Micu, "*Gîndirea.*"

5. Irina Livezeanu has analyzed this issue from the prism of education policies in the newly acquired territories of Transylvania, Bukovina, and Bessarabia. See *Cultural Politics.*

6. Iuliu Moldovan, *Igienă națiunii* (Cluj: Ed. Asociațiunii, 1925), 62–63.

7. Moldovan, *Igiena*, 53.

8. Moldovan, *Biopolitica*, 71.

9. The legionaries were members of a group founded in 1927, the Legion of the Archangel Michael, led by its "Căpitan" (i.e., supreme leader), Corneliu Zelea-Codreanu. Though their founding followed the publication of *Biopolitica*, the influence of this book began to spread in 1927. The ideology and organization of this group bore some important similarities to fascist movements elsewhere but also displayed certain characteristics specific to the Romanian context alone, such as their mystical Orthodoxism. For a brief, basic description of the Legion's particularities in comparison with other fascist contemporary movements, see Eugen Weber, *Varieties of Fascism* (New York: Vintage Books, 1964). Several monographs provide more in-depth analyses: Radu Ioanid, *The Sword of the Archangel* (Boulder, Colo: Columbia University Press, East European Monographs, 1989); Armin Heinen, *Die Legion "Erzengel Michael" in Rumanien* (Munich: Oldenbourg, 1986); and Nicholas Nagy-Talavera, *The Green Shirts and Others: A History of Fascism in Hungary and Rumania* (Stanford, Calif.: Hoover Institution Press, 1970).

10. See chapter 2 for my comments regarding such claims in Ornea's *Anii treizeci*. Other recent works that critique the view of illiberalism as a fringe position in Romanian politics include Ioanid, *Holocaust in Romania*, and Livezeanu, *Cultural Politics*.

11. Some recent publications on Moldovan by historians of medicine provide an equally glowing picture of his supposedly impeccable record. See George Brătescu, "Viziunea biosociomedicală a lui Iuliu Moldovan," in Moldovan, *Amintiri*.

12. Moldovan, *Biopolitica*, 19.

13. Moldovan, *Biopolitica*, 25.

14. The same can be said for the development of political discourse in other Eastern European countries. Poland, for instance, saw the rise of parties that were nationalist and socialist, some with anti-Semitic elements and others with great emphasis on tolerance regarding minorities. See Antony Polonsky, *Politics in Independent Poland 1921–1939: The Crisis of Constitutional Government* (Oxford: Clarendon Press, 1972).

15. Hans Kohn, *The Idea of Nationalism: Its Origins and Background*, 2d ed. (New York: Macmillan, 1961).

16. Lovinescu, *Istoria*, vol. 1, 11. "Junimea" was a literary society founded by Titu Maiorescu, a prominent Moldavian politician during the second half of the nineteenth century. This group criticized the attempts to liberalize Romanian political and social institutions as "form without substance," claiming that they ran against the particularities of Romanian cultural and social traditions. Hitchins, *Rumania*, 56–59.

17. E. J. Hobsbawm, *Nations and Nationalism since 1780* (Cambridge: Cambridge University Press, 1990).

18. Anthony D. Smith, *Theories of Nationalism*, rev. ed. (New York: Holmes and Meier, 1983), xxxi.

19. John Hutchinson, *The Dynamics of Cultural Nationalism* (London: Allen and Unwin, 1987), 30–36. My own view of Romanian eugenicists' nationalism comes close to Hutchinson's.

20. Moldovan, *Biopolitica*, 5.

21. John Breuilly, *Nationalism and the State* (Manchester: Manchester University Press, 1982), 348–51.

22. Iuliu Moldovan et al., eds., *Tratat de medicină socială*, 2d ed., vol. 1 (Cluj, 1947), 3.

23. Hitchins, *Rumania*, 338.

24. Iuliu Moldovan, "Circulara no. 2, nos. 1667/1939: Instrucţiuni, privind aplicarea prin Astra a Legii Serviciului Social în Ţinuturile Someş, Mureş şi Timiş," *Transilvania* 70, no. 2 (Mar.–Apr. 1939): 3.

25. Hitchins, *Rumania*, 403.

26. See Volovici, *Nationalist Ideology*, esp. chapter 1; Ezra Mendelsohn, *The Jews of East Central Europe between the World Wars* (Bloomington: Indiana University Press, 1987); and Ioanid, *Holocaust in Romania*.

27. Moldovan, *Biopolitica*, 75–76.

28. Grossmann, *Reforming Sex;* Paul, *Controlling Human Heredity*.

29. Calypso Botez, "Drepturile femeii în constituţia viitoare," in *Constituţia din 1923 în dezbaterile contemporanilor*, comp. Institutul Social Român (Bucharest: Humanitas, 1990); Paraschiva Câncea, *Mişcarea pentru emanciparea femeii în România* (Bucharest: Ed. politică, 1976).

30. Iuliu Moldovan, "Familia ca unitate biologică," *Sora de Ocrotire* 2, nos. 3–4 (1944): 25–31.

31. Moldovan, *Biopolitica*, 52.

32. Eleonore Davidoff and Catherine Hall, *Family Fortunes: Men and Women of the English Middle Class, 1780–1850* (Chicago: Chicago University Press, 1987); Robert Shoemaker, *Gender and English Society, 1650–1850: The Emergence of Separate Spheres* (New York: Longman, 1998).

33. Iuliu Moldovan, "Familia ţărănească şi familia burgheză: Biologia lor," *Transilvania* 73, no. 10 (Oct. 1942): 735–41.

34. Maria Bucur, "In Praise of Wellborn Mothers: On Eugenicist Gender Roles in Interwar Romania," *East European Politics and Societies* 9, no. 1 (winter 1995): 123–42. Similar trends were occurring at that time in France, Germany, and the Soviet Union, driven by a defense-oriented pronatalist agenda.

35. Ovidiu Comşia, "Biologia familiei. VI. Din biotipologia femeii," *Buletin Eugenic şi Biopolitic* 7, nos. 1–2 (Jan.–Feb. 1936): 32–37.

36. Moldovan, *Biopolitica*, 19.

37. Moldovan, *Biopolitica*, 54.

38. Moldovan, *Biopolitica*, 53.

39. Bock, "Racism and Sexism," makes a similar point with regard to the effect of Nazi policies on women's role in society.

40. The views espoused by Moldovan regarding the privileged position of doctors under the biopolitical order are not unusual when compared with the views expressed by some of his counterparts abroad, in Great Britain and Germany, for instance. In fact, this type of position helps explain the appeal of eugenics for doctors in comparison with its appeal for other professional groups (e.g., lawyers). For comparisons with other

countries see Weindling, *Health, Race and German Politics;* Mazdumar, *Eugenics and Human Failings;* or Kovacs, *Liberal Professions.*

41. Moldovan, *Biopolitica,* 24.

42. The term *"mahala"* entered Romanian from Turkish. It originally referred to any neighborhood, in a sense parallel to the French *"quartier."* However, *"mahala"* came to connote a shantytown, the slumlike appearance of a neighborhood that grew incrementally by ad hoc additions rather than according to any city planning or regulations.

43. Rabinow, *French Modern,* 234–40.

44. For other discussions of Taylorist principles see Grigore Cristescu, "Cultul competenței și organizarea elitelor sociale," *Transilvania* 59, no. 4 (Apr. 1928): 302–13; and Ioan Saizu, "Dezbateri interbelice privind 'raționalizarea' culturii românești," in *Dezvoltare și modernizare în România interbelică: 1919–1939,* ed. Vasile Pușcaș and Vasile Vesa (Bucharest: Ed. politică, 1988).

45. Moldovan, *Biopolitica,* 50.

46. For a good historical analysis of the debates surrounding the 1921 land reform and the actual results of this law, see Mitrany, *Land and the Peasant,* and Roberts, *Rumania.*

47. Moldovan, *Biopolitica,* 51.

48. Rainer, "Amendamentul," 1–2.

49. Moldovan, *Biopolitica,* 48.

50. For some of the features of the system of tariffs and taxation in Romania during this period, see Roberts, *Rumania.*

51. See Ancel, *Transnistria;* Ioanid, *Holocaust in Romania.*

52. Moldovan, *Biopolitica,* 48.

53. He used the term "church" generically, without specific reference to Orthodoxy as the most important religious denomination in Romania.

54. Agârbiceanu, *Preotul.* Agârbiceanu, himself a priest, was a proponent of eugenics and a frequent contributor to *Transilvania,* whose editor in chief during the 1930s was Iuliu Moldovan. Agârbiceanu published many articles in this journal, in which he called on priests to become the voices of eugenic education in their parishes.

55. Moldovan, *Biopolitica,* 55.

56. Moldovan, *Biopolitica,* 58.

57. Livezeanu's *Cultural Politics* focuses in part on this issue. See 161–66.

58. Moldovan, *Biopolitica,* 62.

59. Moldovan, *Biopolitica,* 64.

60. Moldovan, *Biopolitica,* 66–67.

61. Iuliu Moldovan, *Statul etnic,* 6.

62. Abbott Gleason, *Totalitarianism: An Inner History of the Cold War* (Oxford: Oxford University Press, 1995), 28–29.

63. This issue will be explored later in this chapter. See also chapter 1.

64. Gleason, *Totalitarianism,* 21.

65. The view of Schmitt as revolutionary rather than static is shared by Jerry Muller in his discussion of Schmitt's commentary on the total state in the period immediately

preceding the Nazi takeover (1929–33). See Jerry Muller, *The Other God that Failed: Hans Freyer and the Deradicalization of German Conservatism* (Princeton: Princeton University Press, 1987).

66. John P. McCormick, *Carl Schmitt's Critique of Liberalism: Against Politics as Technology* (Cambridge: Cambridge University Press, 1997). See also William Scheuerman, *Carl Schmitt: The End of Law* (Lanham, Md.,: Rowman and Littlefield, 1999); David Dyzenhaus, ed., *Law as Politics: Carl Schmitt's Critique of Liberalism* (Durham, N.C.: Duke University Press, 1998); and Chantal Mouffe, *The Challenge of Carl Schmitt* (London: Verso, 1999).

67. The first in-depth public debate on the issue took place in 1923 in the context of a series of public talks sponsored by the Romanian Social Institute, entitled "The Political Doctrines." Aside from liberalism, conservatism, peasantism, and nationalism, a number of speakers focused on "solidarism" and "corporatism." See Institutul Social Român, comp., *Doctrinele partidelor politice* (Bucharest, [1923]). One of the speakers in this series, Mihail Manoilescu, the most prominent spokesperson on corporatism in Romania, later became famous worldwide for his analysis of economic underdevelopment in peripheral areas. See Love, *Crafting the Third World.*

68. M[ihail] M[anoilescu], "Date rasiale româneşti," *Lumea Nouă* 10, nos. 5–8 (May–Aug. 1941): 282–83.

69. Crainic's own writings do not point to any such influences explicitly. Crainic does mention by name other people who had influenced him, but this group does not include any of the Romanian eugenicists. Nichifor Crainic, *Ortodoxie şi etnocraţie* (Bucharest: Ed. Albatros, 1997).

70. Crainic, *Ortodoxie*, 251–52. See also his *Puncte cardinale în haos* (Iaşi: Ed. Timpul, 1996).

71. See chapter 1.

72. Iuliu Moldovan, "Cuvântul Preşedintelui 'Astrei,'" *Transilvania* 67, no. 5 (Sept.–Oct. 1936): 489.

73. Hitchins, *Rumania*, 416–25.

74. Moldovan, *Statul etnic*, 7.

75. Paul, *Controlling Human Heredity.*

76. Iuliu Moldovan, "Cuvânt la deschiderea Adunării generale din Tîrgu-Mureşului," *Transilvania* 65, no. 5, (Sept.–Oct. 1934): 312–13.

77. Moldovan, *Statul etnic*, 18.

78. Moldovan et al., *Tratat*, 8.

79. Făcăoaru, *Curs de Eugenie*, 64.

80. Făcăoaru, *Curs de Eugenie*, 64

81. Făcăoaru, *Curs de Eugenie*, 65.

82. Făcăoaru, *Curs de Eugenie*, 67.

83. "Troisième Section—Eugénique: Discussions," in *XVIIe Congres International d'Anthropologie et d'Archéologie Préhistorique: VIIe session de l'Institut International d'Anthropologie Bucarest 1–8 septembre, 1937* (Bucharest, 1939), 681–82.

84. Făcăoaru, *Curs de Eugenie*, 69–70.

85. I. Vailescu-Buciumi, "Tendances eugéniques dans le nouveau Code penal roumain Carol II," in *XVIIe Congres*, 682. Unfortunately, there are no specific statistics on the total number or ethnicity of participants voting on this issue to show clearly how many Romanian participants voted against Făcăoaru.

86. Recently Diane Paul has also emphasized the ambiguous attitude of many supporters of eugenics in the United States, Great Britain, and Germany. See *Controlling Human Heredity*, 83–85. Also see Weindling, *Health, Race and German Politics*.

87. I. Făcăoaru, "Norme eugenice în organizațiile legionare," *Cuvântul* 17, serie nouă, no. 69 (21 Dec. 1940): 1–2.

88. Corneliu Zelea-Codreanu, *Pentru legionari*, vol. 1 (Sibiu: Ed. Totul pentru țară 1936).

89. Nicola Iorga's criticism of the legionary movement cost him his life. His assassination became imbedded in the memory of all Romanians throughout the war as a warning against any potential opposition to the Iron Guard.

90. I would like to thank an anonymous reader of my manuscript for pointing out this issue. See Constantin Rădulescu-Motru, "Rasa, cultura și naționalitatea în filosofia istoriei," *Arhiva pentru Reforma și Știința Socială* 4, no. 1 (1922): 18–34; or Garabet Ibrăileanu, "'Caracterul specific' în literatură," in *Opere*, vol. 5 (Bucharest: Ed. Minerva, 1977), 92–94. See also Ornea, *Anii treizeci*.

91. Făcăoaru, letter to Petre Râmneanțu, 1 Jan. 1978.

92. Manliu, *Crâmpeie*, 9, 15.

93. Manliu, *Crâmpeie*, 34–5.

94. Manliu, *Crâmpeie*, 25, 26.

95. Manliu, *Crâmpeie*, 26.

96. Manliu, *Crâmpeie*, 29.

97. See chapter 1.

98. Banu, *Sănătatea*, 18.

99. Gheorghe Banu, "Mari probleme actuale de igienă socială," *Revista de Igienă Socială* 5, no. 2 (1935): 96, 99.

100. Banu, "Mari probleme," 99.

101. Banu, *Sănătatea*, 55–56. A more thorough discussion of this legislation follows in chapter 5.

102. Banu, "Principes," 566.

103. Banu, "Principes," 594.

104. Banu, "Principes," 588.

105. The difference in styles is a matter of personal choice. However, it is also tied to the authors' visions of their audience. While Moldovan wrote *Biopolitica* for educated readers who were not necessarily specialists, Banu addressed himself to doctors, biologists, anthropologists, and others who were already involved in a debate about developing a system of public health.

106. Banu, *L'Hygiène*, 290–94.

107. Banu, *L'Hygiène*, 206.

108. The writings of Cuza had long made explicit reference to some of the race theories critiqued by Banu. See also chapter 1.

109. Banu, *Tratat*, vol. 1, 138.

110. Banu, "Principes," 567.

111. Banu, *Sănătatea*, 519.

CHAPTER 4

1. In the United States the focus on social relations was often shaped by local interests such as anti-immigration or race relations, while in Great Britain class issues prevailed over other social relations. For the United States see Larson, *Sex, Race, and Science*; for Great Britain, see Mazdumar, *Eugenics and Human Failings*. In Germany there was more diversity in the focus of eugenicists on social relations before 1933, but racist prerogatives prevailed over all others after the Nazi takeover; see Weindling, *Health, Race and German Politics*. The Romanians showed local particularities as well, most importantly the obsession with miscegenation between Romanians and Hungarians in Transylvania. Proponents of eugenics from the Regat did not dispute the argument that marriages needed to be kept unaltered by potential "dysgenic" populations, such as ethnically inferior individuals. But they were not quite as preoccupied with identifying in the most precise manner the particularities that rendered ethnic Hungarians inferior. See, for instance, the works of Râmneanțu discussed in this chapter versus Banu's discussion of ethnicity in "Eugenie, ereditate, rasă: Conferință ținută în 29 ianuarie 1935," *Revista de Igienă Socială* 5, no. 2 (1935): 102–7.

2. Ioachim Crăciun, "Les classes sociales en Transylvanie," *Révue de Transylvanie* 5, no. 4 (1939): 448–67; Love, *Crafting the Third World*; Andrew C. Janos, "Modernization and Decay in Historical Perspective: The Case of Romania," in Jowitt, *Social Change*, 72–116.

3. David Blackbourn and Geoff Eley, *The Peculiarities of German History: Bourgeois Society and Politics in Nineteenth-Century Germany* (Oxford: Oxford University Press, 1984).

4. For discussions of similar developments elsewhere in Eastern Europe, see Gary Cohen, *Education and Middle-Class Society in Imperial Austria* (West Lafayette, Ind.: Purdue University Press, 1996); Harley D. Balzer, ed., *Russia's Missing Middle Class: The Professions in Russian History* (Armonk, N.Y.: M. E. Sharpe, 1996); András Gerö, *Modern Hungarian Society in the Making: The Unfinished Experience* (Budapest: Central European University Press, 1995).

5. George Marinescu, *Laboratoriile și intelectualii* (Bucharest, 1920), 6.

6. Some British Socialist (Fabian) eugenicists raised similar criticisms of the development of capitalism at that time. See Paul, *Controlling Human Heredity*, chapter 3.

7. Paul, *Controlling Human Heredity*, 9.

8. Iuliu Hațiegan and Aurel Voina, "Astra medicală și biopolitică: Planul de activitate," *Societatea de Mâine* 2, nos. 46–47 (15–22 Nov. 1925): 813–14.

9. Crăciun, "Les classes sociales."

10. Livezeanu, *Cultural Politics*, chapter 4.

11. See chapter 6.

12. Bucur, "Private Philanthropy."

13. George Strat, *T. R. Malthus şi principiul poporaţiei* (Bucharest, 1934); I. Făcăoaru, "Pagina eugenică: Selecţiunea socială negativă prin denatalitatea elementelor superioare," *Transilvania* 68, no. 3 (May–June 1937): 193–96.

14. P. Râmneanţu, "Soluţiuni în legatură cu problema declinului etnic al populaţiei româneşti din Banat," *Revista Institutului Social Banat–Crişana* 4, no. 14 (1936): 1–40; C. Grosforeanu, "Femeia la răscruce," *Revista Institutului Social Banat–Crişana* 6, no. 22–23 (Apr.–Sept. 1938): 96–98.

15. This was a phenomenon described by many eugenicists abroad, especially in Great Britain, where fear that the poor would outreproduce the middle classes was a constant in eugenic debates. See Mazdumar, *Eugenics and Human Failings;* Paul, *Controlling Human Heredity.*

16. Florin Ştefănescu-Goangă, *Selecţiunea capacităţilor şi orientarea profesională* (Cluj, 1929), 2.

17. Volovici, *Nationalist Ideology,* chapter 1.

18. Agârbiceanu, *Preotul,* 153.

19. Agârbiceanu, *Preotul,* 153.

20. Ornea, *Anii treizeci.* See also chapter 2.

21. Paul, *Controlling Human Heredity;* Weiss, "Race Hygiene Movement."

22. Agârbiceanu, *Preotul.*

23. Moldovan, *Biopolitica,* 13–14.

24. Ioan Agârbiceanu, "Necesitatea culturalizării masselor: Technica culturală," *Transilvania* 64, no. 2 (Mar.–Apr. 1934): 78.

25. Ioan Agârbiceanu, "Astra şi Serviciul Social," *Transilvania* 70, no. 1 (Jan.–Feb. 1939): 16.

26. Gheorghe Banu, *Şomajul intelectual în România* (Bucharest, 1933), 4.

27. Banu, *Şomajul intelectual,* 4.

28. Banu, *Şomajul intelectual,* 44.

29. Sabin Manuilă, "Suprapopularea universităţilor şi şomaj intelectual?" *Sociologie Românească* 3, nos. 4–6 (Apr.–June 1938): 229.

30. P. P. Negulescu, *Destinul omenirii,* vol. 1 (Bucharest: Bucharest: Fundaţia pentru Literatură şi Artă "Regele Carol II," 1938), 57. Negulescu was a prominent philosopher who critiqued the fledgling Romanian democracy while remaining a supporter of parliamentary pluralism and democracy. He spoke out against the totalitarian ideologies of the left and the right from a staunchly positivist-rationalist position, openly criticizing racism. See P. P. Negulescu, *Geneza formelor culturii* (Bucharest: Ed. Minerva, 1993).

31. Dimitrie Gusti, "Echipa şi fiii satului," *Curierul Echipelor Studenţeşti* 2, no. 7 (16 Aug. 1936): 1.

32. Gheorghe Banu, "Biologia satelor," *Arhiva pentru Reforma şi Ştiinţa Socială* 7, nos. 1–2 (1927): 87–121.

33. Banu, *Sănătatea.*

34. Nicolae Iorga, *O viață de om, așa cum a fost* (Bucharest, 1934); Crainic, *Ortodoxie.*

35. Moldovan, *Amintiri;* Petre Râmneanțu, "Visuri de pe Semenic," unpublished ms. Courtesy of the Romeo Lăzărescu personal archive, Bucharest.

36. See chapter 6.

37. G. Retezeanu, "La o răspîntie: (Capitalul uman de mâine)," *Buletin Eugenic și Biopolitic* 4, nos. 3–4 (Mar.–Apr. 1930): 66.

38. The communist regime got around this issue by creating internal passports that firmly grounded each individual in the place where he or she was born. An individual could change residence permanently only by marrying someone from another locality or obtaining a permanent position in a particular workplace.

39. Sabin Manuilă, *Evoluția demografică a orașelor și minoritățile etnice din Transilvania* (Bucharest: Cultura națională, 1929), 15.

40. Sabin Manuilă, *Evoluția demografică,* 16.

41. Sabin Manuilă, *Evoluția demografică,* 115.

42. This was a fear shared by many eugenicists abroad, from Germany to the United States. Individuals like Margaret Sanger, who celebrated women's newfound sense of economic and personal independence, were in a small fringe minority among proponents of eugenics. Paul, *Controlling Human Heredity.*

43. Veturia Manuilă, "Situația femeii în societatea modernă și feminismul," *Buletin Eugenic și Biopolitic* 2, no. 6 (June 1928): 189–92; Strat, *T. R. Malthus;* Traian Brăileanu, "Feminizare și efeminare," in *Sociologia și artă guvernării: Articole politice* (Cernăuți: Ed. Însemnari sociologice, 1937).

44. Veturia Manuilă, "Rolul femeilor în asistența socială a familiei," *Buletin Eugenic și Biopolitic* 1, no. 1 (Jan. 1927): 24–26; Brăileanu, "Feminizare."

45. For a classic discussion of the separation of the private and the public spheres and the gendered aspects of both, see Mary Ryan, *Cradle of the Middle Class: The Family in Oneida County, New York, 1790–1865* (Cambridge: Cambridge University Press, 1983). See also Nancy F. Cott, *The Bonds of Womanhood: "Woman's Sphere" in New England, 1780–1835,* 2d ed. (New Haven, Conn.: Yale University Press, 1997).

46. Câncea, *Mișcarea;* Elena Bogdan, *Feminismul* (Timișoara: Tip. Huniadi, 1926); Calypso Botez, "Problema feminismului–o sistematizare a elementelor ei," *Arhiva pentru Știința și Reforma Socială* 2, no. 1–3 (Apr.–Oct. 1920): 25–84.

47. See the discussion of Mary Stopes and Margaret Sanger in Paul, *Controlling Human Heredity,* 91–96.

48. Davidoff and Hall, *Family Fortunes.*

49. Valeria Căliman, *Mama generatoare de viață românească* (Sibiu: Ed. subsecției eugenice și biopolitice a Astrei, 1942).

50. For a discussion of the impact of these civil codes on women's rights in the family and society, see Botez, "Problema."

51. Linda K. Kerber, *Women of the Republic: Intellect and Ideology in Revolutionary America* (New York: W. W. Norton, 1986).

52. "Dare de seamă despre activitatea Secţiei femenine-biopolitice a 'Astrei,' pe anul 1931 pînă la iunie 1932," *Transilvania* 63, nos. 1–8 (Jan.–Aug. 1932): 36.

53. See chapter 5.

54. Bucur, "In Praise."

55. Petre Râmneanţu, "Problema căsătoriilor mixte în oraşele din Transilvania în perioada dela 1920–1937," *Buletin Eugenic şi Biopolitic* 8, nos. 10–12 (Oct.–Dec. 1937): 317–38.

56. Petre Râmneanţu, "Influenţa căsătoriei asupra fertilităţii şi etnicului unui neam," *Transilvania* 68, no. 5 (Sept.–Oct. 1937): 400.

57. Ovidiu Comşia, "Biologia familiei. II. Familie şi ereditate," *Buletin Eugenic şi Biopolitic* 5, nos. 11–12 (Nov.–Dec. 1934): 301–8.

58. Sara Friedrichsmeyer, Sara Lennox, and Susanne Zantop, eds., *The Imperialist Imagination: German Colonialism and Its Legacy* (Ann Arbor: University of Michigan Press, 1998); Elizabeth Hallam and Brian V. Street, eds., *Cultural Encounters: Representing Otherness* (New York: Routledge, 2000).

59. Dominic Stanca, "Lupta contra prostituţiei," *Societatea de Mâine* 2, no. 32–33 (9–16 Aug. 1925): 573.

60. Râmneanţu and David, "Cercetări asupra."

61. Petre Râmneanţu, *Expunere de titluri şi lucrări ştiinţifice* (Cluj, 1942), 5.

62. Iordache Făcăoaru, "Amestecul rasial şi etnic în România," *Buletin Eugenic şi Biopolitic* 9, nos. 9–10 (Sept.–Oct. 1938): 282.

63. Făcăoaru, "Norme eugenice."

64. Sabin Manuilă, "Comandamentele rassiale şi politică de populaţie," *România Nouă* 7, no. 17 (26 Oct. 1940): 3.

65. Almost all historical analyses of his work that I have come across depict Manuilă as a tolerant, rational, and balanced thinker, in refreshing contrast to other interwar commentators on the question of minorities. See the introduction by Larry Watts to Sabin Manuilă and Wilhelm Filderman, *The Jewish Population in Romania during World War II* (Iaşi: Fundaţia Culturală Română, 1994); Sorina Bolovan and Ioan Bolovan, eds., *Sabin Manuilă: Istorie şi demografie* (Cluj: Fundaţia Culturală Română, 1995).

66. Sabin Manuilă, "Problema rassială a României," *România Nouă* 7, no. 41 (22 Nov. 1940): 5.

67. Simion Mehedinţi, *Întrebări* (Bucharest, 1942), 255–56.

68. Nicole Hahn Rafter, *Creating Born Criminals* (Urbana: University of Illinois Press, 1997).

69. Mostly eugenicists with a neo-Lamarckian outlook had this view. See Paul, *Controlling Human Heredity*, chapter 3.

70. Ovidiu Comşia, "Semnificaţia socială a veneriilor," *Buletin Eugenic şi Biopolitic* 3, nos. 7–8 (July–Aug. 1929): 232–43, esp. 237.

71. Judith Walkowitz, *Prostitution and Victorian Society: Women, Class, and the State* (Cambridge: Cambridge University Press, 1980).

72. Ovidiu Comşia, "Consideraţii generale asupra cauzelor prostituţiei," *Buletin Eugenic şi Biopolitic* 4, nos. 1–2 (Jan.–Feb. 1930): 53.

73. Stanca, "Lupta contra prostituției," 572.

74. Iuliu Moldovan, "Combaterea boalelor venerice," *Buletin Eugenic și Biopolitic* 1, no. 1 (Jan. 1927): 16–18.

75. Veturia Manuilă, "Studiul a 100 delicvenți minori din penitenciarul Văcărești," *Asistența Socială* 5, no. 1 (1936): 14–32.

76. Iordache Făcăoaru, *Devalorizarea patrimoniului ereditar întrō familie de intelectuali* (Bucharest, 1938); and "Pagina eugenică: Înzestrarea inferioară ca fenomen ereditar," *Transilvania* 68, no. 2 (Mar.–Apr. 1937): 116–17. The Kallikak family case had become infamous in eugenic research, publications, and textbooks, popularized by American eugenicists as the archetype of how a dysgenic strand of a family could overpower the healthy hereditary baggage of those whom they married. The case illustrated how, in spite of the presence of many "normal" and even exceptionally gifted individuals, the dysgenic heredity among some of this family's members eventually reduced the genetic capital of the Kallikaks over several generations. This example provided the proof eugenicists sought for arguing on behalf of greater control over the bodies of the (apparently) healthy population and not just obviously dysgenic individuals. See Kevles, *In the Name*, 78–79.

CHAPTER 5

1. Emilian Dimitriu et al., *A Concise History of Education in Romania* (Bucharest: Ed. științifică și enciclopedică, 1981), 22–31.

2. Livezeanu, *Cultural Politics.*

3. For a discussion of Astra's role in pre-1918 Transylvania and its place in the history of eugenics see chapter 1.

4. Livezeanu's work also focuses on this issue, but does so by examining the implementation of enrollment, examination, employment in state-funded schools, and reactions to violent acts of extremist nationalism.

5. Petre Râmneanțu, "The Classical Blood Groups and the M, N Properties in the Nations from Transylvania," in *XVIIe Congres*, 325–32. Also see Petre Râmneanțu and Iordache Făcăoaru, "The Blood Groups and the Facial Index in the Population from Transylvania," in *XVIIe Congres*, 333–36.

6. Aurel Voina, *Igienă pentru clasa VIII secundară de băeți și fete* (Bucharest, [1936]), 73.

7. Gheorghe Preda, *Câteva date biologice și psihologice, necesare unei educațiuni moderne* (Sibiu, 1926), 10.

8. Gheorghe Preda, *Câteva date,* 13.

9. See chapter 2.

10. Paul, *Controlling Human Heredity.*

11. Iordache Făcăoaru, *Instituțiile educative de azi: Originea lor raționalistă și fundamentarea biologică a reformei lor* (Cluj, 1941), 41, 43.

12. Gheorghe Preda, *Câteva date,* 14.

13. Cupcea, *Probleme,* 60.

14. Hitchins, *Rumania*, 56–59.

15. Bârsănescu, *Politică culturală*, 130–31.

16. As quoted in P. P. Negulescu, *Reforma învăţământului*, 2d ed. (Bucharest: Ed. Casei şcoalelor, 1927), 41.

17. Negulescu, *Reforma*, 41–42.

18. Bârsănescu, *Politică culturală*, 118–22.

19. The term in Romanian is "*şcoala muncii*"—one that Mehedinţi coined and that became overused during the communist period.

20. For a brief discussion of his ideas, especially with regard to rural education, see Livezeanu, *Cultural Politics*, 204–5; Dimitriu et al., *Concise History*.

21. Mehedinţi, *Trilogii*, 337.

22. Simion Mehedinţi, "Şcoala română şi capitalul biologic al poporului român," *Buletin Eugenic şi Biopolitic* 1, nos. 9–10 (Sept.–Oct. 1927): 266–67.

23. Florin Ştefănescu-Goangă was at one time the rector (i.e., president) of the University of Cluj. In the late 1930s he became an object of violence by student members of the Iron Guard, including an attempt to assassinate him. This ordeal is discussed briefly in Nicolae Mărgineanu, *Amfiteatre şi închisori: Mărturii asupra unui veac zbuciumat* (Cluj-Napoca: Ed. Dacia, 1991).

24. Ştefănescu-Goangă, *Selecţiunea capacităţilor*, 8.

25. Donald Mackenzie, "Eugenics in Britain," *Social Studies of Science* 6 (1976): 501–2.

26. Their attempt to identify the intelligentsia as a socially distinct group vis-à-vis the entrepreneurial bourgeoisie was also related to this inconsistent view of the middle classes. See also chapter 4.

27. Iordache Făcăoaru, "Pagina biopolitică, demografică şi eugenică: Inteligenţa naturală în raport cu clasele sociale [part 2]," *Transilvania* 70, no. 1 (Jan.–Feb. 1939): 39.

28. Most eugenicists used the model of the bell curve to discuss both notions of hereditary intelligence and strategies for reforming education in accordance with the varied intellectual and social potential registered by the slopes of the curve. See Ştefănescu-Goangă, *Selecţiunea capacităţilor*, 14.

29. Moldovan, *Biopolitica*, 36–37.

30. Ovidiu Comşia, "Pagina biopolitică: Biopolitică şi invăţămănt," *Transilvania* 69, no. 2 (Mar.–Apr. 1938): 102. The term Comşia uses for "mission" is "*menire*," which carries a very strong determinist connotation in Romanian.

31. Comşia, "Biologia familiei. VI."

32. Ştefănescu-Goangă, *Selecţiunea capacităţilor*, 30.

33. Alexandru Roşca, *Copiii superior înzestraţi* (Cluj, 1941), 114.

34. Roşca, *Copiii superior*, 114–15.

35. Ştefănescu-Goangă, *Selecţiunea capacităţilor*, 368–69.

36. Vasile Ilea, "Desvoltarea intelectuală a copilului," *Transilvania* 57, no. 4 (Apr. 1926): 196.

37. Ilea, "Desvoltarea intelectuală," 197.

38. Făcăoaru, *Devalorizarea*, 10.

39. Iuliu Moldovan, Petre Râmneanțu, and Iordache Făcăoaru, "Înregistrarea etno-biologică a populației," *Buletin Eugenic și Biopolitic* 10, nos. 1–2 (Jan.–Feb. 1939): 1–9; Petre Râmneanțu, "La methode biotypologique dans l'étude du village," *Arhiva pentru Reforma și Știința Socială* 16, nos. 1–4 (1943): 172–77.

40. Cupcea, *Probleme*, 37.

41. Mihai Zolog, "Inteligența copiilor de școală," *Buletin Eugenic și Biopolitic* 1, no. 2 (Feb. 1927): 50–53.

42. Dominic Stanca, "O anchetă sanitară la un liceu [part 1]," *Societatea de Mâine* 1, no. 32 (23 Nov. 1924): 641–44.

43. Comșia, "Biologia familiei. VI," 35.

44. Ovidiu Comșia, "Biologia familiei. IV. Biologia sexelor," *Buletin Eugenic și Biopolitic* 6, nos. 4–6 (Apr.–June 1936): 127–35.

45. Ovidiu Comșia, "Biologia familiei. V. Problema intersexualității," *Buletin Eugenic și Biopolitic* 6, nos. 10–12 (Oct.–Dec. 1935): 372–73.

46. Dominic Stanca, "O anchetă sanitară la un liceu [part 2]," *Societatea de Mâine* 1, no. 33 (30 Nov. 1924): 660–63.

47. Alexandru Roșca, *Selecția valorilor* (Sibiu: Ed. secției biopolitice a Astrei, 1943), 24–25. Carol II also created a similar small-scale experiment in shaping the education of his son, Michael I. There is no indication, however, that a direct link existed between Carol II's school and the kind of broad comprehensive reform discussed by eugenicists. See Paul Quinlan, *The Playboy King: Carol II of Romania* (Westport, Conn.: Greenwood Press, 1995).

48. Liviu Rusu, "Drum liber celor înzestrați," *Societatea de Mâine* 6, nos. 1–2 (15 Jan.–1 Feb. 1929): 3–4.

49. "Norme bugetare de alcătuire a bugetului Ministrerului Instrucțiunii: Declarațiile d'lui ministru Gusti," *Dreptatea* 7, no. 1633 (5 Mar. 1933): 4.

50. Livezeanu, *Cultural Politics*.

51. Maria Bucur, "Awakening or Constructing Biological Consciousness?: 'Astra' and Biopolitics in Interwar Romania," *Colloquia: Journal of Central European History* 2, nos. 1–2 (Jan.–Dec. 1995): 172–85.

52. Hațiegan, "Ce este," 36–38.

53. Aurel Voina, "Datoria mamelor față de neam," in *Calendarul Asociațiunii 1927*, 174–76.

54. *"Astra" în anii*, 57.

55. For a complete list of all the participants in this series and the titles of their papers see *Buletin Eugenic și Biopolitic* 1, no. 1 (Jan. 1927), back cover. The *Buletin* published some of these conferences.

56. Racoviță, *Evoluția*, 7.

57. See *Transilvania* 68, no. 4 (July–Aug. 1937): 238, and 69, nos. 3–4 (May–Aug. 1938): 147.

58. In 1933 Vasile Ilea, the Astra leader for the Reghin territory, published a study entitled *Şcoala superioară ţărănească* at the same time that he organized a series of conferences on the subject of hygiene, public health, and the biology of the Romanian nation. Iuliu Moldovan wrote the preface to this work. The setting of the book, as well as its expressed goal of being a model for organizing such peasant schools in the future as means of spreading biopolitical principles, exemplifies very well the relationship that developed over time between the leadership of the Medical and Biopolitical Section— its ideas and directives—and other intellectuals at the local level. People like Ilea became virtual spokespersons for the hereditary determinism that dominated the section's rhetoric and concepts of public programs.

59. Iuliu Moldovan, preface to Ilea, *Şcoala superioară*, 3. My italics.

60. Moldovan, preface, 4.

61. Moldovan, preface, 6.

62. Moldovan, preface, 17.

63. Preda, *Activitatea;* Gheorghe Preda, *Ziua Astrei* (Sibiu, 1937).

64. These lectures were called "*şezători*" in Romanian. Traditionally, they had been informal get-togethers at which the group would usually spin and weave cloth together or embroider holiday costumes and chat. They would take place mostly during the winter season and provided essential spaces where women could socialize in a female-defined atmosphere, much like village taverns represented a space for male socialization.

65. Iuliu Moldovan, "Colaborarea între Astra şi Uniunea Femeilor Române," *Buletin Eugenic şi Biopolitic* 1, no. 4 (Apr. 1927): 119–22.

66. N. Căliman, "Şcoala ţărănească pentru femei," *Transilvania* 67, nos. 2–3, (Mar.–Apr. 1936): 511–24.

67. Moldovan, "Colaborarea."

68. Moldovan, "Colaborarea," 515.

69. Moldovan, "Colaborarea," 515.

70. See Hitchins, *Rumania,* 356–58; Roberts, *Rumania,* esp. chapter 8.

71. See Milovan Gavazzi, "The Extended Family in Southeast Europe," *Journal of Family History* 7, no. 1 (1982): 89–102, for a general look at European developments. See also Louise Tilly and Joan W. Scott, *Women, Work, and Family* (New York: Routledge, 1987).

72. N. Căliman, "Şcoala ţărănească," 515.

73. N. Căliman, "Şcoala ţărănească," 515.

74. "Din activitatea Secţiei feminine," in *Calendarul Asociaţiunii pe anul comun 1938,* 126–31 (Sibiu: Ed. Asociaţiunii, 1938).

75. Valentin Puşcariu, "Selecţia sexuala la om," *Buletin Eugenic şi Biopolitic* 2, nos. 11–12 (Nov.–Dec. 1928): 323.

76. For a complete list of the school's patrons and faculty see *Asistenţa Socială* 1, no. 1 (1929): 1.

77. Veturia Manuilă, "Evoluţia ideii de asistenţa socială," *Buletin Eugenic şi Biopolitic* 1, nos. 7–8 (July–Aug. 1927): 242–44.

78. "Cuvânt înainte," *Asistenţa Socială* 1, no. 1 (1929): 10.

79. "Asociația pentru progresul asistenței sociale," *Asistența Socială* 5, no. 1 (1936): 38–41.

80. Veturia Manuilă, "Femenismul și familia," *Buletin Eugenic și Biopolitic* 2, no. 3 (Mar. 1928): 92–96.

81. Mihai Zolog, "Baza biologică a instrucției școlare," *Buletin Eugenic și Biopolitic* 6, nos. 1–3 (Jan.–Mar. 1935): 9.

82. Voina, *Igienă*, 68–69.

83. Voina, *Igienă*, 225.

84. Ministerul Instrucțiunii, comp., *Programa analitică a învățământului primar: Sancționată cu Înaltul Decret Regal no. 578 din 26 martie 1936* (Craiova: Scrisul românesc, 1936), 104.

85. Ștefan Bârsănescu, *Pedagogia și didactica pentru școlile normale, școale profesionale și învățători*, 7th rev. ed. (Craiova, [1943?]), 34, 43; quote from 34. For a similar earlier formulation, see Alexandru Roșca, *Igienă mintală școlara* (Cluj: Ed. Institutului de psihologie al Universității din Cluj, 1939). See, for example, the Roșca epigraph at the beginning of chapter 5.

86. Vulcănescu et al., *Dimitrie Gusti*.

87. Făcăoaru, letter to Petre Râmneanțu, 1 Jan. 1978, 5.

88. Gheorghe Banu, "La science de la medecine sociale," *Revista de Igienă Socială* 9, nos. 11–12 (1939): 686–87.

89. See chapter 2.

90. Bădina, *Cercetarea sociologică concretă*, 131.

91. "Legea sanitară și de ocrotire," *Monitorul Oficial*, no. 154 (14 July 1930): 5357.

92. "Legea sanitară," 5346.

93. The law made this point in emphatically eugenic terms. See Iuliu Moldovan, "Expunere de motive," Moldovan, fond personal, dos. 22, 13.

94. "Legea sanitară," 5358.

95. "Legea sanitară," 5345–55.

96. George Mosse, *Nationalism and Sexuality* (Madison: University of Wisconsin Press, 1988).

97. V. Christodorescu, "Educația fizică. Factor de progres și regenerare națională," *Porunca Vremii* 2, no. 35 (11 Oct. 1932): 2.

98. The pre-Pioneer youth organization set up by the communist regime had a similar name, "The Fatherland's Falcons." I have been unable to discover whether this was a simple coincidence or a decision made by someone who at one time had been a "Carpathian Falcon." There were also other groups in East-Central Europe with similar names, such as the Czech "Sokol" and the German "Wanderfogel." I would like to thank Nancy Wingfield for pointing out these similar names.

99. "Proiect de statute pentru organizațiunea de educație fizică și eugenică sub auspiciile 'Astrei,'" *Buletin Eugenic și Biopolitic* 2, nos. 9-10 (Sept.–Oct. 1928): 279.

100. "Proiect de statute," 281.

101. T. B., "Semnificația activității Astrei în anii din urmă," *Transilvania* 71, nos. 5–6 (Sept.–Dec. 1940): 196–201. A study by Iuliu Moldovan from 1937, entitled *Ziua Astrei*,

puts the figure at fifteen thousand. I cite the larger one here because it is subsequent to Moldovan's article. Neither of these sources makes any explicit remark about the ethnic makeup of the membership.

102. "Discurs rostit de Simion Mehedinți la adunarea generală a Societății Regale Române de Geografie," *Timpul* 5, no. 1473 (16 June 1941): 11.

103. Nicolae Roșu, "Școala caracterului," *Cuvântul* 17, serie nouă, no. 2 (15 Oct. 1940): 1.

104. Iordache Făcăoaru, "Valoarea biorasială a națiunilor europene și a provinciilor românești," *Buletin Eugenic și Biopolitic* 14, nos. 9–10 (Sept.–Oct. 1943): 352.

CHAPTER 6

1. Moldovan, "Expunere de Motive," 6.

2. Felix, *Despre progresele*, 19.

3. Eidelberg, *Great Rumanian Peasant Revolt*.

4. Banu, *Sănătatea*, 51–53; Bologa et al., *Istoria*.

5. Victor Babeș, "Considerațiuni asupra conducerii și organizării luptei noastre sanitare," *Arhiva pentru Reforma și Știința Socială* 3, nos. 2–3 (1921): 220.

6. See chapter 1.

7. Râmneanțu, "Iuliu Moldovan," 49–52.

8. Moldovan, "Expunere de Motive."

9. "Congresul extraordinar al medicilor funcționari asistați de medicii practicieni," *Sănătatea Publică* 1, no. 4 (Apr. 1921): 13–14.

10. The reasons why these two politicians supported Moldovan might have differed, however, for Vaida-Voevod's and Maniu's Peasantist factions parted ways early on in the postwar period. Both considered themselves spokesmen for the peasant constituency, but while Maniu's faction embraced a more democratic pluralist outlook, Vaida-Voevod became a supporter of populist politics with rightist leanings. Hitchins, *Rumania*, 417; Ioan Scurtu, *Istoria Partidului Național Țărănesc* (Bucharest: Ed. enciclopedică, 1994).

11. See chapter 1.

12. Ion I. C. Brătianu, *Activitatea corpurilor legiuitoare și a guvernului de la ianuarie 1922 până la 27 martie 1926: Dare de seamă* (Bucharest: Cartea românească, s.a., 1926), 340.

13. This is a term with no equivalent in modern medical practice in the West. These individuals received limited training in basic health care matters, such as administering shots and giving routine checkups. Like nurses, in the eugenic vision, they were to become the main presence in overseeing day-to-day developments of "social plagues" and in educating the rural population about their eugenic responsibilities.

14. Brătianu, *Activitatea corpurilor*, 339.

15. Brătianu, *Activitatea corpurilor*, 340. The amounts I quote are the budget sums for the following categories: schools for sanitary agents, midwives, and nurses; social disease campaigns; and tuberculosis.

16. Brătianu, *Activitatea corpurilor*, 346.

17. Moldovan, *Amintiri*, 62–84.

18. Aurel Voina, "Organizarea sanitară a Transilvaniei în primul deceniu al unirii," in *Transilvania, Banatul, Crişana, Maramureşul: 1918–1928*, vol. 1 (Bucharest: Cultura naţională, 1929), 745.

19. Moldovan, *Amintri;* Voina, "Organizarea sanitară"; Brătescu, *Biological and Medical Sciences.*

20. Moldovan, fond personal, dos. 1.

21. "Roumania [Report]," 3, folder 18, box 3, record group 1.1, series 783C, Rockefeller Foundation Archives, RAC, 3.

22. "Rumania—Approval of Program: 4 March 1929 [Report]," 2, folder 28, box 3, record group 1.1, series 783J, Rockefeller Foundation Archives, RAC, 2. My italics.

23. "Roumania," folder 416, box 34, record group 6.1, series 1.1, Rockefeller Foundation Archives, RAC.

24. In 1926, 50,000 dollars represented 8 million lei, which was a little under one-fourth of the 33.5 million lei spent on preventive health in 1925. The exchange rate did not improve for the lei in the next fifteen years.

25. "Diary of F. Elisabeth Crowell," 1929–38, esp. 11 Nov. 1935 and 31 Jan. 1936, folder 404, box 33, record group 6.1, series 1.1, Rockefeller Foundation Archives, RAC.

26. Some of the prominent figures taking part in these discussions held by the Superior Health Council of the Ministry of Health were Ioan Cantacuzino, Iuliu Iacobovici, C. I. Parhon, and Gheorghe Banu. Moldovan, fond personal, dos. 19.

27. The Moldovan Law was published in its entirety as "Legea sanitară." See chapter 5, note 91.

28. "Legea sanitară," 5367–69.

29. "Legea sanitară," 5369–74; quote from 5369–70.

30. "Legea sanitară," 5393.

31. "Legea sanitară," 5373.

32. Fond Ministerul Sănătăţii, 1930, dos. 282, 1939, dos. 6.

33. Fond Ministerul Sănătăţii, 1933, dos. 339–342. This is an estimate based on the number of pages in these files. Each page represents one decision.

34. Matei, *Asociaţiunea transilvană*, 64–66.

35. "Legea sanitară," 5393.

36. Fond Ministerul Sănătăţii, 1932, dos. 262.

37. Gheorghe Banu, "Necesitatea reorganizării statului sub raportul sanitar şi al igienei sociale," *Revista de Igienă Socială* 7, no. 1 (Jan. 1937): 10.

38. Iuliu Moldovan, "Modificarea legii sanitare şi de ocrotire," *Buletin Eugenic şi Biopolitic* 5, no. 7 (July 1934): 134–39. My italics.

39. I. Pupeza et al., "Sănătatea publică în România," in *Enciclopedia României*, vol. 1, ed. Dimitrie Gusti et al. (Bucharest: Imprimeria naţională, 1938), 515–17.

40. *Universul* was the most popular mainstream daily paper with liberal political inclinations. *Adevărul* was a left-wing newspaper, not as popular as *Universul* but with its own significance, since it stimulated lively debates with papers situated to its right on the political spectrum.

41. Doctorul Ygrec, "Căsătorii cu certificat medical şi . . . 'montă' cu permisiunea

Statului," *Adevărul* 36, no. 12098 (10 July 1923): 1–2; quote from 1. "Doctorul Ygrec" was a pseudonym used by the doctor with a regular medical advice column in *Adevărul.*

42. Doctorul Ygrec, "Iarăşi despre avorturi provocate şi medicii avortori," *Adevărul* 36, no. 12152 (8 Sept. 1923): 1–2.

43. G. Manicatide, "Certificatul de sănătate pentru contractarea căsătoriei," *Revista de Igienă Socială* 2, no. 1 (1932): 9.

44. Banu, "Mari probleme," 105.

45. Râmneanţu, "Problema."

46. Râmneanţu, "Problema," 336.

47. *Codul Penal "Regele Carol II" din 18 martie 1936* (Bucharest: Ed. librăriei "Universala," 1936), 74.

48. *Codul Penal 1936,* art. 376.

49. Basile Stanesco, *La capacité civile de la femme mariée en Roumanie après la nouvelle loi du 20 avril 1932* (Paris: Domat-Montchrestien, 1937).

50. Aurel Tiniş, "Examenul prenupţial obligator în mediul rural," *Ardealul Medical* 2, no. 10 (Oct. 1942): 451.

51. Gheorghe Cosma, "Mişcarea populaţiei dela 1930–1944 în Plasa sanitară Haţeg şi activitatea acesteia pe anul 1944," *Sora de Ocrotire* 4, nos. 4–6 (1946): 34.

52. Doctorul Ygrec, "Medicii avortori şi 'făcătoarele de îngeri,'" *Adevărul* 36, no. 12125 (6 Aug. 1923): 1.

53. Ygrec, "Medicii avortori," 1.

54. Sabin Manuilă, "Reglementarea avortului," *Asistenţa Socială* 5, no. 1 (1936): 33.

55. I. Manliu, "Un pericol social: Discuţii," *Adevărul* 36, no. 12135 (18 Aug. 1923): 1–2.

56. Manliu, "Un pericol," 2.

57. Banu, "Mari probleme," 106, 107.

58. *Codul Penal 1936,* art. 484, 89–90. The law did not make explicit how to determine the certainty of hereditary illnesses, leaving it to doctors to determine this factor.

59. Selskar M. Gunn and W. Leland Mitchell, "Public Health in Rumania [Report]: July, 1925," folder 4, box 1, series 1.1, Rockefeller Foundation Archives, RAC.

60. C. Georgesco, "La fertilité differentielle en Roumanie," in *XVIIe Congres,* 644.

61. Romanian eugenicists did not employ this terminology. I use it because of the similarity between fears expressed by Romanian eugenicists during this period and the speeches of Theodore Roosevelt on regulating immigration and abortion.

62. Banu, "Mari probleme," 100.

63. For the 1933 figure see Banu, "Mari probleme," 101; for 1940 see "Raport lunar demografic-sanitar, judetul Braşov, pe luna februarie 1940, comune rurale," fond Ministerul Sănătăţii, 1939, dos. 872, 1. The last figure is for a specific region rather than the entire country. However, because it is a report for a rural area, it most likely comes close to the upper figures for the mortality rate.

64. Banu, "Mari probleme," 100.

65. Iordache Făcăoaru, "Legiuirile recente pentru sterilizarea eugenică," *Buletin Eugenic şi Biopolitic* 5, nos. 8–10 (Aug.–Oct. 1934): 236.

66. Gheorghe Banu, "L'orientation moderne de l'eugénique," in *XVIIe Congres*, 639.

67. Banu, "L'orientation moderne," 638.

68. Banu, "Necesitatea."

69. Mitchell, "Roumania: Observations," 11.

70. "Jurnal de călătorie în America," Moldovan, fond personal, dos. 2a, 27.

71. "Numirea membrilor."

72. Ministerul Sănătății și al Asigurărilor Sociale, comp., *Probleme și realizări*, vol. 1 (Bucharest, 1939), 108. Two little-known documents from Carol II's archives also suggest that he was somewhat familiar with eugenics. In 1937, Liviu Câmpeanu, one of the main doctors at the Gheorghe Mârzescu hospital in Brașov, sent two enthusiastic and insistent letters to Carol II, urging him to turn his scouts' organization, the Cercetași, into a tool for pushing a eugenic agenda, calling it "biotypology." However, the two letters do not show any familiarity between this doctor and other eugenicists in Romania or any knowledge of the Carpathian Falcons. See fond Casa Regală, 1937, dos. 11, 2–6. 12–22, Arhivele Naționale, Bucharest.

73. "Decret-lege pentru organizarea Ministerului Sănătății și Ocrotirilor Sociale," *Monitorul Oficial* 57, no. 269 (20 Nov. 1939): 6752–77.

74. See chapter 5.

75. "Regulamentul pentru organizarea și funcționarea Serviciului Social (partea privitoare la Căminele Culturale)," *Buletinul Serviciului Social* 1, no. 2 (Apr. 1939): 1–20.

76. *Buletinul Serviciului Social* 1, no. 4 (Aug. 1939).

77. "Regulamentul," art. 109, 4.

78. V. Pantelimonescu, comp., *Statutul Evreilor din România* (Bucharest: Ed. ziarului "Universul," 1941).

79. Pantelimonescu, *Statutul Evreilor*, 71.

80. Pantelimonescu, *Statutul Evreilor*, 71. The preamble to the law makes a direct reference to the 1935 laws in Germany as an inspiration, claiming apologetically that "the German people is and must be a racist entity."

81. "Regimul medicilor: Extras din Decretul Lege no. 3789/1940 pentru organizarea și funcționarea Colegiului medicilor (dispozițiunile referitoare la medicii evrei)," in Pantelimonescu, *Statutul Evreilor*, 121–32.

82. Al. Popovici, "Problema sănătății în statul legionar," *Cuvântul* 17, serie nouă, no. 71 (23 Dec. 1940): 11.

83. Ștefan Anghelescu, "Fascismul și familia," *Porunca Vremii* 11, no. 2333 (19 Sept. 1942): 1.

84. Al. Popovici, "Problema sănătății," 11.

85. "Comisiunea de igienă socială," *Cuvântul* 17, serie nouă, no. 34 (16 Nov. 1940): 12.

86. "Decret-lege pentru înființarea Institutului de boli ereditare și tumorale," *Monitorul Oficial* 58, no. 250 (25 Oct. 1940): 6091; Leon Prodan, "Problema ocrotirei și asistenței," *Buletin Eugenic și Biopolitic* 11, nos. 1–4 (Jan.–Apr. 1941): 35–40.

87. Mihai Antonescu, "Înfăptuirile regimului Antonescu," *Porunca Vremii* 11, no. 2323 (6 Sept. 1942): 1–4.

88. "Decret-lege pentru organizarea sanitară a statului," *Monitorul Oficial* 71, no. 1 (25 Mar. 1943): 2653–81.

89. Iuliu Moldovan, "Instituții sanitare și de ocrotire," *Buletin Eugenic și Biopolitic* 14, nos. 3–4 (Mar.–Apr. 1943): 87.

90. "Decret-lege pentru organizarea sanitară," 2653.

91. Gheorghe Banu, "Organizarea medicinei asigurărilor sociale din România," *Revista de Igienă Socială* 13, nos. 1–3 (Jan.–Mar. 1943): 3–46.

92. "Regulament nr. 24 pentru combaterea boalelor venerice," *Monitorul Oficial* 71, no. 246, (Oct. 1943): 9528.

93. "Regulament nr. 24," 9529.

94. Ancel, *Transnistria;* Ioanid, *Holocaust in Romania.*

95. Ancel, *Transnistria,* vol. 3, chapter 6; Ioanid, *Holocaust in Romania,* chapter 6.

96. Ancel, *Transnistria,* vol. 3, 21–31.

97. Ancel, *Transnistria,* vol. 3, 104, 125.

98. Ioanid, *Holocaust in Romania,* 224. See also Ioanid's concluding remarks, 289–95.

99. Ioanid, *Holocaust in Romania,* 291.

100. See Făcăoaru, "Valoarea biorasială," esp. 279.

101. Făcăoaru, "Valoarea biorasială," esp. 279.

102. P. Vlad, "Organizația asistenței în Capitală în concepția Consiliului de Patronaj," *Buletin Eugenic și Biopolitic* 14, no. 1 (Jan. 1943): 44–50.

103. Ancel, *Transnistria,* vol. 3, 58.

104. Ancel, *Transnistria,* vol. 3, 58. See also Ioanid, *Holocaust in Romania,* 286.

105. Iosif Stoichiția, "Principiile călăuzitoare ale organizației sanitare," *Buletin Eugenic și Biopolitic* 15, nos. 3–4 (Mar.–Apr. 1944): 67.

106. For his early ideas see Mihai Kernbach, "Biologia crimei," *Buletin Eugenic și Biopolitic* 15, nos. 1–2 (Jan.–Feb. 1944): 1–10; for his later opinions see Mihai Kernbach, *Medicina în procesul socializării* (Sibiu: Ed. Dacia Traiană, 1944), 7.

107. Iosif Stoichiția, "Organizația sanitară în Rusia Sovietică," *Buletin Eugenic și Biopolitic* 15, nos. 9–12 (Sept.–Dec. 1944): 232. My italics.

108. Fond Ministerul Sănătății, 1946, dos. 1.

109. Fond Ministerul Sănătății, 1947, dos. 11.

110. "Boli venerice: Referat de D-l consilier venerolog Dr. N. Vătămanu, la 6 iunie, 1946, către ministru," fond Ministerul Sănătății, 1946, dos. 14, 2.

111. Moldovan, *Amintiri,* 108. The sentence was not directly related to his work in eugenics but rather to his having served as General Secretary at the Ministry of Health in 1929–30.

CONCLUSION

1. Ioanid, *Holocaust in Romania;* Randolf Braham, ed., *The Destruction of Romanian and Hungarian Jews During the Antonescu Era* (Boulder, Colo.: Social Science Monographs, 1997).

2. Făcăoaru, "Cercetări," 1–3.

3. Moldovan, fond personal, Iuliu Moldovan, dos. 3, 15–17, 19–29.

4. Moldovan, fond personal, Iuliu Moldovan, dos. 3, 15.

5. See chapter 6.

6. Viorel Achim, *Țiganii în istoria României* (Bucharest: Ed. enciclopedică, 1998), esp. 133–142. The author does identify Moldovan with the racist view of Roma and Jews but uses only quotes from Iordache Făcăoaru's writings to substantiate this claim.

7. Ioanid, *Holocaust in Romania,* chapter 7.

8. Săhleanu, *Începuturile medicinii sociale,* 78–79.

9. Romeo Lăzărescu, interview with author, Bucharest, Apr. 1995.

10. Dr. Crişan Mircioiu, interview with author, Cluj, Apr. 1995.

11. Andrei's work *Sociologie generală* was reprinted in 1970 by the publishing house of the Romanian Academy as an important textbook of sociology. Although this revised edition omits several sections from the initial one, it still includes Andrei's discussion of eugenics and his positive evaluation of this theory's scientific soundness.

12. Săhleanu, *Începuturile medicinii sociale,* 78–79.

13. See Ernö Gáll, *Sociologia burgheză din Romînia: Studii critice* (Bucharest, 1958), esp. 206–215, for a typical treatment of these issues.

14. Victor Preda, *Din istoria luptei dintre materialism şi idealism în biologie* (Bucharest, 1960).

15. The topic of Romania's communist pronatalist policies has drawn increasing interest among historians, anthropologists, and psychologists. The most important work to date is Gail Kligman, *The Politics of Duplicity: Controlling Reproduction in Ceauşescu's Romania* (Berkeley: University of California Press, 1998).

16. Kligman, *Politics of Duplicity,* 46–49.

17. Petre Râmneanţu, letter to Prof. Dr. Ioan Morariu, General Secretary at the M.S.P.S., 20 July 1965, 10. Courtesy of the Romeo Lăzărescu personal archive, Bucharest.

18. Râmneanţu, letter to Prof. Dr. Ioan Morariu, 20 July 1965, 3.

19. Râmneanţu, letter to Prof. Dr. Ioan Morariu, 20 July 1965, 4.

20. At one point, Râmneanţu identified Ceauşescu's pronatalist policies with Iuliu Moldovan's ideas. A statement like this, when eugenics was still officially vilified as a fascist ideology, represented a bold move on his part. He was never reprimanded for it. See his letter to the publishing house of the Academy of the Socialist Republic of Romania, 23 Jan. 1978. Courtesy of the Romeo Lăzărescu personal archive, Bucharest.

21. Kligman, *Politics of Duplicity.*

22. "Decretul nr. 770 pentru reglementarea întreruperii cursului sarcinii. Publicat în Buletinul Oficial al R.S.R. nr. 60 din 1 oct. 1966," in *Colecţie de Legi, Decrete, Hotătîri şi alte acte normative, nr. 5 (1 septembrie–31 octombrie 1966),* comp. Ministerul Justiţiei (Bucharest: Ed. ştiinţifică, 1967), 30–31. My italics.

23. Kligman, *Politics of Duplicity.*

24. Kligman, *Politics of Duplicity.*

25. Kligman, *Politics of Duplicity,* 127.

26. Vera Sokolova, "In the Name of the Nation: Gypsies, Sterilization, and the Discourse on Race and Sexuality in Socialist Czechoslovakia, 1972–1989" (paper presented at the AAASS Annual Convention, Boca Raton, Fla., Sept. 1998).

27. Achim, *Țiganii în istoria României*, 62.

28. Hugo Strauss, "Iuliu Moldovan," in *Figuri reprezentative ale medicinii și farmaciei clujene*, vol. 1 (Cluj-Napoca: Institutul de medicină și farmacie, [1980]), 31–46.

29. Strauss, "Iuliu Moldovan," 38.

30. Gáll, *Sociologia burgheză*, 206–15.

31. Săhleanu, *Începuturile medicinii sociale*, 83.

32. Săhleanu, *Începuturile medicinii sociale*, 83.

33. Brătescu, "Viziunea biosociomedicală," 136.

34. Iorga's National Democratic Party was, after all, openly anti-Semitic.

35. Michael Shafir, "Radical Politics In Post Communist East Central Europe: Part I: 'Reds,' 'Pinks,' 'Blacks,' and 'Blues,'" *RFE/RL East European Perspectives* 1, no. 1 (3 Nov. 1999); Michael Shafir, "X-Raying Post-Communist 'Radical Minds,'" *RFE/RL East European Perspectives* 1, nos. 3–4 (1–15 Dec. 1999) and 2, nos. 1–2 (12–26 Jan. 2000). Available at <http://www.rferl.org/eereport>.

36. Vladimir Tismăneanu, *Fantasies of Salvation: Democracy, Nationalism, and Myth in Post-Communist Europe* (Princeton: Princeton University Press, 1998), esp. chapter 4.

37. In fact, some publications have made a real effort to expose this type of extremism. See *Dilema* 7, nos. 314, 325, 334, 349 (1999)—four special issues that focus on clichés about the Roma, Hungarians, Germans, and Jews.

38. Gail Kligman and Susan Gal, "Gendering Postsocialism: Reproduction as Politics in East Central Europe," in *Between Past and Future: The Revolutions of 1989 and Their Aftermath*, ed. Sorin Antohi and Vladimir Tismăneanu (Budapest: Central European University, 2000), 207.

SELECT BIBLIOGRAPHY

PRIMARY SOURCES

Archival Sources

Arhivele Ministerului Sănătății. Arhivele Naționale, Filiala București, 1923–40, 1944–48.*
Fond Personal Iuliu Moldovan. Arhivele Naționale, Filiala Cluj.
Fond Personal Sabin Manuilă. Arhivele Naționale, Filiala București.
Lăzărescu, Romeo. Personal Archive. Bucharest.
Rockefeller Foundation Archives. Rockefeller Archive Center, North Tarrytown, N.Y.
United States Holocaust Memorial Museum Institute. RG-31 (Ukraine). Washington, D.C.

Manuscripts

Făcăoaru, Iordache. "Cercetări antropologice în patru sate din Transnistria." Unpublished ms. 1943. Odessa State Archives, fond 2242, file 1, 1942. Microfilm, United States Holocaust Memorial Museum Institute, RG-31 (Ukraine) / 004 m, Reel 2.
Râmneanțu, Petre. "Iuliu Moldovan: Viața, realizările și epoca sa." Unpublished ms. Bucharest, 1977.
———. "Visuri de pe Semenic." Unpublished ms. Bucharest., n.d.

Essays and Monographs

"Activitatea Secțiunilor literare-științifice ale Astrei. 5. Secțiunea medicală și biopolitică." *Transilvania* 69, nos. 3–4 (May–Aug. 1938): 147–48.

* The archives of the Ministry of Health for the wartime period were not made available to me. The personnel at the National Archives explained that these years had not been catalogued and therefore could not be examined.

Agârbiceanu, Ioan. *Asociațiunea transilvană pentru literatură și cultura poporului român—"Astra." Ce a fost? Ce este? Ce vrea sa fie?* Sibiu: Ed. Asociațiunii, 1936.

———. "Astra și Serviciul Social." *Transilvania* 70, no. 1 (Jan.–Feb. 1939): 15–19.

———. "Necesitatea culturalizării masselor: Technica culturală." *Transilvania* 64, no. 2 (Mar.–Apr. 1934): 78.

———. *Preotul și familia preoțească: Rostul lor etnic în satul românesc.* Sibiu: Ed. subsecției eugenice și biopolitice a Astrei, 1942.

Andrei, Petre. *Sociologie generală.* Craiova: Ed. Scrisul românesc, 1936.

Anghelescu, Ștefan. "Fascismul și familia." *Porunca Vremii* 11, no. 2333 (19 Sept. 1942): 1.

———. "Natalitatea și spațiul vital." *Porunca Vremii* 12, no. 2490 (6 Apr. 1943): 1, 3.

———. "Națiune și natalitate." *Porunca Vremii* 8, no. 1377 (15 June 1939): 1–2.

Antipa, Grigore. *Problemele evoluției poporului român.* Bucharest: Cartea românească, 1919.

Antonescu, Daniela. "Asistența delicvenților." *Sănătatea Publică* 42, nos. 3–4 (Mar.–Apr. 1930): 309–18.

Antonescu, Ion. "Apel către femeia română." In *Către români . . . Chemări—Cuvântări—Documente: La o răscruce a istoriei,* compiled by Admiral Dan Zaharia, 44–47. Bucharest: Ed. Socec and Co., 1941.

———. "Un apel al d-lui General Antonescu." *Timpul* 5, no. 1464 (6 June 1941): 1.

Antonescu, Mihai. "Înfăptuirile regimului Antonescu." *Porunca Vremii* 11, no. 2323 (6 Sept. 1942): 1–4.

———. "Principiile nouei reforme a Statului Român (Despre statul biologic și funcțional)." *Societatea de Mâine* 18 (Oct.–Dec. 1941): 85–86.

Aronovici, A. *Omul și sociologia dupe Darvin, Lamark, Herbert Spencer, Letourneau, Buchner, etc.* Galați: Lib. G. D. Nebuneli și Fii, n.d.

"Asistența socială." In *Trei ani de guvernare. 6 septemvrie 1940–6 septemvrie 1943,* 399–414. Bucharest: Monitorul oficial și imprimeriile statului, 1943.

"Asociația pentru progresul asistenței sociale." *Asistența Socială* 5, no. 1 (1936): 38–41.

"Astra" în anii de după răsboi (1918–1928). Sibiu: Ed. "Asociațiunii," [1928?].

Babeș, Victor. "Considerațiuni asupra conducerii și organizării luptei noastre sanitare." *Arhiva pentru Reforma și Știința Socială* 3, nos. 2–3 (1921): 210–22.

Bagdasar, D. "Sterilizarea." *Adevărul* 36, no. 12170 (29 Sept. 1923): 1.

Banu, George. *See* Gheorghe Banu.

Banu, Gheorghe. "Biologia satelor." *Arhiva pentru Reforma și Știința Socială* 7, nos. 1–2 (1927): 87–121.

———. "Eugenia poporului românesc." *Revista de Igienă Socială* 11, nos. 11–12 (Nov.–Dec. 1941): 341–97.

———. "Eugenie, ereditate, rasă: Conferință ținută în 29 ianuarie 1935." *Revista de Igienă Socială* 5, no. 2 (1935): 102–7.

———. *L'Hygiène de la race: Étude de biologie héréditaire et de normalisation de la race.* Bucharest and Paris, 1939.

————. "Mari probleme actuale de medicină socială." *Revista de Igienă Socială* 5, no. 2 (1935): 97–102.

————. "Necesitatea reorganizării statului sub raportul sanitar și al igienei sociale." *Revista de Igienă Socială* 7, no. 1 (1937): 23–26.

————. "Organizarea medicinei asigurărilor sociale în România." *Revista de Igienă Socială* 13, nos. 1–3 (Jan.–Mar. 1943): 3–46.

————. "L'orientation moderne de l'eugenique." In *XVIIe Congres International d'Anthropologie et d'Archéologie Préhistorique: VIIe session de l'Institut International d'Anthropologie Bucarest 1–8 Septembre, 1937*, 635–40. Bucharest, 1939.

————. "Principes d'un programme d'hygiene de la race." *Revista de Igienă Socială* 6, no. 10 (1936): 565–98.

————. *Sănătatea poporului român*. Bucharest: Fundația pentru literatură și artă "Regele Carol II," 1935.

————. "La science de la médecine sociale." *Revista de Igienă Socială* 9, nos. 11–12 (1939): 686–87.

————. *Șomajul intelectual în România*. Bucharest, 1933.

————. *Tratat de medicină socială*. Vol. 1. *Medicina socială ca știință: Eugenia—Demografia*. Bucharest: Casa școalelor, 1944.

Bârsănescu, Ștefan. *Pedagogia și didactica pentru școlile normale, școale profesionale și învățători*. 7th rev. ed. Craiova, [1943?].

————. *Politică culturală în România contemporană: Studiu de pedagogie*. Iași, 1937.

Bogdan, Elena. *Feminismul*. Timișoara: Tip. Huniadi, 1926.

Boilă, R. "Capitalul uman și organizația constituțională a Statelor (23 martie)." *Buletin Eugenic și Biopolitic* 1, no. 4 (Apr. 1927): 124.

Bologa, Valeriu. "Eugenezia." *Revista Sănătății* 1, no. 3 (June 1921): 79–84.

Botez, Calypso. "Drepturile femeii în constituția viitoare." In *Constituția din 1923 în dezbaterile contemporanilor*, compiled by Institutul Social Român. Bucharest: Humanitas, 1990.

————. "Problema feminismului–o sistematizare a elementelor ei." *Arhiva pentru Știința și Reforma Socială* 2, no. 1–3 (Apr.–Oct. 1920): 25–84.

Brăileanu, Traian. "Desăvîrșirea structurii elitei legionare." In *Sociologia și arta guvernării: Articole politice*. Cernăuți: Ed. Însemnări sociologice, 1937.

————. *Elemente de sociologie pentru clasa VIII secundară*. Bucharest: Ed. Națională-Ciornei, [1935].

————. "Feminizare și efeminare." In *Sociologia și arta guvernării: Articole politice*. Cernăuți: Ed. Însemnări sociologice, 1937.

————. *Fundamentarea biologică a sociologiei și importanța ei pentru teoria și practica pedagogică*. Cernăuți, 1934.

Brătianu, Ion I. C. *Activitatea corpurilor legiuitoare și a guvernului de la ianuarie 1922 până la 27 martie 1926: Dare de seamă*. Bucharest: Cartea românească, s.a., 1926.

Căliman, N. "Școala și sănătatea publică." *Transilvania* 57, no. 4 (Apr. 1926): 192–96.

————. "Şcoala ţărănească pentru femei." *Transilvania* 67, nos. 2–3, (Mar.–Apr. 1936): 511–24.

Căliman, Valeria. *Mama generatoare de vieaţă românească.* Sibiu: Ed. subsecţiei eugenice şi biopolitice a Astrei, 1942.

Carol II. "Idei călăuzitoare." *Curierul Echipelor Studenţeşti* 3, no. 3 (20 June 1937): 3.

Clopoţel, Ion. "Biopolitică aplicată." *Societatea de Mâine* 20, no. 2 (Feb. 1943): 23–24.

————. "Biopolitică şi democraţie." *Societatea de Mâine* 3, no. 10 (7 Mar. 1926): 171.

————. "Elanul vital." *Societatea de Mâine* 18, no. 4 (Oct.–Dec. 1941): 63–64.

————. "Primatul vitalităţii româneşti. Programul jubiliar al "Societăţii de Mâine." *Societatea de Mâine* 20, no. 12/400 (Dec. 1943): 175–76.

Codul Penal Carol al II-lea din 18 martie 1938, cu modificările din 22 ianuarie 1938, 24 septemvrie 1938, 7 octomvrie 1939, 2 martie 1940 şi 30 mai 1940. 5th ed. Bucharest: Ed librăriei "Universala," 1940.

Codul Penal "Regele Carol II" din 18 martie 1936. Bucharest: Ed. librăriei "Universala," 1936.

Codul Penal "Regele Mihai I." 8th ed. Bucharest: Ed. R. Cioflec, 1945.

Comicescu, Gh. "Orientarea biologică a educaţiei." *Buletin Eugenic şi Biopolitic* 4, nos. 1–2 (Jan.–Feb. 1930): 1–7.

"Comisiunea de igienă socială." *Cuvântul* 17, serie nouă, no. 34 (16 Nov. 1940): 12.

Comşa, Ovidiu. See Ovidiu Comşia.

Comşia, Ovidiu. "Biologia familiei. II. Familie şi ereditate." *Buletin Eugenic şi Biopolitic* 5, nos. 11–12 (Nov.–Dec. 1934): 301–8.

————. "Biologia familiei. III. Familie şi ereditate." *Buletin Eugenic şi Biopolitic* 6, nos. 1–3 (Jan.–Mar. 1935): 28–35.

————. "Biologia familiei. IV. Biologia sexelor." *Buletin Eugenic şi Biopolitic* 6, nos. 4–6 (Apr.–June 1935): 127–35.

————. "Biologia familiei. V. Problema intersexualităţii." *Buletin Eugenic şi Biopolitic* 6, nos. 10–12 (Oct.–Dec. 1935): 369–78.

————. "Biologia familiei. VI. Din biotipologia femeii." *Buletin Eugenic şi Biopolitic* 7, nos. 1–2 (Jan.–Feb. 1936): 32–37.

————. "Biologia în interpretarea istoriei." *Buletin Eugenic şi Biopolitic* 9, nos. 9–10 (Sept.–Oct. 1938): 257–64.

————. "Biologie şi istorie." *Buletin Eugenic şi Biopolitic* 9, nos. 5–6 (May–June 1935): 164–80.

————. "Consideratii generale asupra cauzelor prostituţiei." *Buletin Eugenic şi Biopolitic* 4, nos. 1–2 (Jan.–Feb. 1930): 53.

————. "Neamul regenerat." *Buletin Eugenic şi Biopolitic* 8, nos. 10–12 (Oct.–Dec. 1937): 304–16.

————. "Pagina biopolitică: Biopolitică şi învăţământ." *Transilvania* 69, no. 2 (Mar.–Apr. 1938): 102.

————. "Politica şi biopolitica: Pagina biopolitică." *Transilvania* 68, no. 2 (Mar.–Apr. 1937): 113.

———. "Semnificația socială a veneriilor." *Buletin Eugenic și Biopolitic* 3, nos. 7–8 (July–Aug. 1929): 232–43.

Conta, Vasile. *Teoria ondulațiunii universale.* Iași, [1876–78].

Cosma, Gheorghe. "Mișcarea populației dela 1930–1944 în Plasa sanitară Hațeg și activitatea acesteia pe anul 1944." *Sora de Ocrotire* 4, nos. 4–6 (1946): 28–36.

Costres, Eugenia. "Familia germană." *Sora de Ocrotire* 1, nos. 3–4 (1943): 36–39.

Crăciun, Ioachim. "Les classes sociales en Transylvanie." *Révue de Transylvanie* 5, no. 4 (1939): 448–67.

Crainic, Nichifor. *Ortodoxie și etnocrație.* 1938. Bucharest: Ed. Albatros, 1997.

———. *Puncte cardinale în haos.* 1936. Iași: Ed. Timpul, 1996.

Critescu, Grigore. "Cultul competenței și organizarea elitelor sociale." *Transilvana* 59, no. 4 (Apr. 1928): 302–13.

Cupcea, Salvator. "Biologia teoretică și aplicată în U.R.S.S." *Buletin Eugenic și Biopolitic* 15, nos. 9–12 (Sept.–Dec. 1944): 299–318.

———. *Probleme de eredobiologie.* Sibiu, 1944.

"Cuvânt înainte." *Asistența Socială* 1, no. 1 (1929): 10.

Cuza, A. C. *Despre poporație: Statistica, teoria, politica ei: Studiu economic-politic.* 2d rev. ed. Bucharest, 1929.

———. *Doctrina Naționalistă Creștină: Programul Ligii Apărării Naționale Creștine.* Cluj, 1934.

———. *Meseriașul român.* Bucharest, 1893.

Daniel, Dinu C. *Les Élites psychobiologiques et leurs rapports avec l'ethnographie.* Bucharest, [1940]. First published in *Revista de Medicină Legală* 3, nos. 3–4 (1939–40).

"Dare de seamă despre activitatea Secției femenine-biopolitice a 'Astrei,' pe anul 1931 pînă la iunie 1932." *Transilvania* 63, nos. 1–8 (Jan.–Aug. 1932): 35–38.

"Dare de seamă despre activitatea Secției medicale și biopolitice a 'Astrei,' dela 30 iunie 1930–30 iunie 1931." *Transilvania* 62, nos. 1–8 (Jan.–Aug. 1931): 36–37.

"Dare de seamă despre activitatea Secției medicale și biopolitice a 'Astrei,' dela 1 iunie 1931–1 iunie 1932." *Transilvania* 63, nos. 1–8 (Jan.–Aug. 1932): 34–35.

"Decret-lege no. 189 pentru organizarea sanitară a statului." *Monitorul Oficial* 62, no. 71, no. 1 (25 Mar. 1943): 2653–82.

"Decret-lege pentru combaterea boalelor venerice [no. 604]." *Buletinul Sănătății și Ocrotirilor Sociale* 48, nos. 8–9 (Aug.–Sept. 1943): 659–66. First published in *Monitorul Oficial*, no. 212 (10 Oct. 1943).

"Decret-lege pentru înființarea Institutului de boli ereditare și tumorale." *Monitorul Oficial* 58, no. 250 (25 Oct. 1940): 6091.

"Decret-lege pentru organizarea Ministerului Sănătății și Ocrotirilor Sociale." *Monitorul Oficial* 57, no. 269 (20 Nov. 1939): 6752–77.

"Decret-lege pentru organizarea sanitară a statului." *Monitorul Oficial* 71, no. 1 (25 Mar. 1943): 2653–81.

"Decret-lege pentru organizarea și funcționarea Colegiului medicilor." *Monitorul Oficial* 58, no. 269 (15 Nov. 1940): 6455–60.

"Decretul nr. 770 pentru reglementarea întreruperii cursului sarcinii. Publicat în Buletinul Oficial al R.S.R. nr. 60 din 1 oct. 1966." In *Colecție de Legi, Decrete, Hotărîri și alte acte normative, nr. 5 (1 septembrie–31 octombrie 1966)*, compiled by Ministerul Justiției, 30–31. Bucharest: Ed. științifică, 1967.

"Denatalitate în Oltenia?" *Revista Institutului Social Banat–Crișana* 10 (May–Aug. 1942): 529–30.

"Din activitatea Secției femenine." In *Calendarul Asociațiunii pe anul comun 1938*, 126–31. Sibiu: Ed. Asociațiunii, 1938.

"Discurs rostit de Simion Mehedinți la adunarea generală a Societății Regale Române de Geografie." *Timpul* 5, no. 1473 (16 June 1941): 11.

"Discursul d-lui Iuliu Maniu." *Dreptatea* 7, no. 1878 (19 Dec. 1933): 1.

Dobrogeanu-Gherea, Constantin. "Neoiobăgia." In *Opere complete*, vol. 4. 1910. Reprint, Bucharest: Ed. Academiei R.S.R., 1977.

Enăchescu, S. D. "Sterilizarea eugenică." *Revista de Medicină Legală* 1, no. 2 (1936): 273–79.

Făcăoaru, Iordache. "Amestecul rasial și etnic în România." *Buletin Eugenic și Biopolitic* 9, nos. 9–10 (Sept.–Oct. 1938): 276–87.

———. "Compoziția rasială la români, săcui și unguri." *Buletin Eugenic și Biopolitic* 8, nos. 4–5 (Apr.–May 1937): 124–42.

———. *Curs de eugenie*. Cluj, 1935.

———. *Devalorizarea patrimoniului ereditar întrô familie de intelectuali*. Bucharest, 1938. First published in *Revista de Medicină Legală* 2, nos. 3–4 (1938).

———. "Din problematica și metodologia cercetărilor genetice în cadrul monografiilor sociale." *Arhiva pentru Reforma și Știința Socială* 15, nos. 1–2 (1937): 162–72.

———. "Eugénique et biopolitique—Hérédité.—Selection sociale." In *XVIIe Congres International d'Anthropologie et d'Archéologie Préhistorique: VIIe session de l'Institut International d'Anthropologie Bucarest 1–8 Septembre, 1937*, 718–99. Bucharest, 1939.

———. "Familii degenerate și costul lor pentru societate și stat." *Buletin Eugenic și Biopolitic* 7, nos. 5–7 (May–June 1936): 214–21.

———. "Înmulțirea disgenicilor și costul lor pentru societate și stat." *Buletin Eugenic și Biopolitic* 6, nos. 4–5 (Apr.–June 1935): 169–83.

———. *Instituțiile educative de azi: Originea lor raționalistă și fundamentarea biologică a reformei lor*. Cluj, 1941. First published in *Buletin Eugenic și Biopolitic* 11, nos. 1–3 (Jan.–Mar. 1940): 25–44.

———. "Introducerea eugeniei în învățământul german." *Buletin Eugenic și Biopolitic* 7, nos. 8–10 (Aug.–Oct. 1936): 270–77.

———. "Legea pentru apărarea sănătății ereditare a populației Germane." *Buletin Eugenic și Biopolitic* 7, nos. 1–2 (Jan.–Feb. 1936): 49–53.

———. "Legiferarea avortului din indicații eugenice în Germania." *Buletin Eugenic și Biopolitic* 7, nos. 1–2 (Jan.–Feb. 1936): 57–59.

———. "Legiuirile recente pentru sterilizarea eugenică." *Buletin Eugenic și Biopolitic* 5, nos. 8–10 (Aug.–Oct. 1934): 231–39.

————. "Norme eugenice în organizațiile legionare." *Cuvântul* 17, serie nouă, no. 69 (21 Dec. 1940): 1–2.

————. "Pagina biopolitică, demografică și eugenică: Inteligența naturală în raport cu clasele sociale [part 2]." *Transilvania* 70, no. 1 (Jan.–Feb. 1939): 36–39.

————. "Pagina eugenică: Înzestrarea inferioară ca fenomen ereditar." *Transilvania* 68, no. 2 (Mar.–Apr. 1937): 116–17.

————. "Pagina eugenică: Selecțiunea socială negativă prin denatalitatea elementelor superioare." *Transilvania* 68, no. 3 (May–June 1937): 193–96.

————. "Privire critică asupra legii finlandeze de sterilizare în comparație cu legea germană." *Buletin Eugenic și Biopolitic* 8, nos. 10–12 (Oct.–Dec. 1937): 33–54.

————. *Știința omului și concepția antibiologică în educația tineretului. Discuții în jurul reformei învățământului secundar.* Cluj, 1939. First published in *Buletin Eugenic și Biopolitic* 11, nos. 1–3 (Jan.–Mar. 1940): 1–22.

————. "Valoarea biorasială a națiunilor europene și a provinciilor românești." *Buletin Eugenic și Biopolitic* 14, nos. 9–10 (Sept.–Oct. 1943): 352.

Felix, Iacob. *Despre progresele igienei din cei din urmă ani.* Bucharest, 1885.

Georgesco, C. "La fertilité differentielle en Roumanie." In *XVIIe Congres International d'Anthropologie et d'Archéologie Préhistorique: VIIe session de l'Institut International d'Anthropologie Bucarest 1–8 Septembre, 1937,* 323–25. Bucharest, 1939.

Georgescu, D. C. *Cercetarea cadrului biologic al satului: Îndreptar extras din: Îndrumări pentru monografiile sociologice.* Bucharest, 1940.

————. "Secția de demografie, antropologie și eugenie a Institutului Social Român." *Sociologie Românească* 1, no. 1 (Jan. 1936): 56–57.

Gheorghiu, C. C. "Demofilia și eugenia ca principii divergente în doctrina populației." *Revista de Igienă Socială* 3, no. 4 (1937): 211–17.

Gomoiu, V. "Preoțimea în slujba operelor de ocrotire și medicină socială." *Analele Ministerului Sănătățiiși Ocrotirilor Sociale* 4 (40), nos. 4–9 (Apr.–Sept. 1927): 82–101.

Goșteanu, Iosif. "Schița unui program initial de muncă pentru Căminele Culturale ale Astrei." *Transilvania* 70, no. 3 (May–June 1939): 150–60.

Grosforeanu, C. "Femeia la răscruce." *Revista Institutului Social Banat–Crișana* 6, no. 22–23 (Apr.–Sept. 1938): 96–98.

————. "Rasismul și problema minoritară." *Revista Institutului Social Banat–Crișana* 4, no. 16 (Oct.–Dec. 1936): 81–82.

Gusti, Dimitrie. "Echipa și fiii satului." *Curierul Echipelor Studențești* 2, no. 7 (16 Aug. 1936): 1.

————. *Opere alese.* 3 vols. Edited by Ovidiu Bădina and Octavian Neamțu. Bucharest: Ed. Academiei R.S.R., 1968.

Gusti, Dimitrie, and Traian Herseni. *Elemente de sociologie cu aplicări la cunoașterea țării și a neamului nostru: Clasa VIII-a secundară.* 8th rev. ed. Bucharest: Ed. Cartea românească, 1943.

Gusti, Dimitrie, et al., eds. *Enciclopedia României.* Vol. 1. *Statul.* Bucharest: Imprimeria națională, 1938.

Hațiegan, Iuliu. "Ce este secția medicală și biopolitică a Astrei?" In *Calendarul Asociațiunii pe anul comun 1927*, compiled by Horia Petra-Petrescu, 36–38. Sibiu: Ed. Asociațiunii, 1926.

———. "Rolul social al medicului român în opera de consolidare a statului național." *Transilvania* 54 (Nov.–Dec. 1925): 587–91.

Hațiegan, Iuliu, and Aurel Voina. "Astra medicală și biopolitică: Planul de activitate." *Societatea de Mâine* 2, nos. 46–47 (15–22 Nov. 1925): 813–14.

Hațieganu, Iuliu. *See* Iuliu Hațiegan.

Herseni, Traian. "Anchetă bio-socială." *Buletin Eugenic și Biopolitic* 18, nos. 9–12 (Sept.–Dec. 1947): 184–96.

———. "Rasă și destin național." *Cuvântul* 18, serie nouă, no. 91 (16 Jan. 1941): 1, 7.

———. "Selecționarea elitelor." *Cuvântul* 17, serie nouă, no. 40 (22 Nov. 1940): 1–2.

Ibrăileanu, Garabet. "Caracterul specific în literatură." In *Opere*, vol. 5. Bucharest: Ed. Minerva, 1977. First published in *Viața Românească* 2 (1923).

Ilea, Vasile. "Biopolitică românească." *Societatea de Mâine* 20, no. 11 (Nov. 1943): 160–61.

———. "Desvoltarea intelectuală a copilului." *Transilvania* 57, no. 4 (Apr. 1926): 196.

———. *Școala superioară țărănească.* Sighet, 1933.

"Instituțiunile sanitare și de ocrotire din Ardeal." *Sănătatea Publică* 1, nos. 7–8 (July 1921): 11–16.

Institutul Social Român, comp. *Doctrinele partidelor politice.* Bucharest, [1923].

Ionescu, Tiberiu. "Dr. Casian Topa: Monografia sanitară a circumscripției Văscăuți (Storojineț), pe anii: 1931–35." *Sociologie Românească* 3, nos. 4–6 (Apr.–June 1938): 272–74.

———. "Problema sănătății satului și acțiunea sanitară preventivă." *Curierul Echipelor Studențești* 4, no. 9 (15 July 1938): 2.

Iorgulescu, Nicolae. "Neavenirea avortului preventiv: Imoralitatea 'Avortului moral' și antieugenia celui eugenetic." *Curierul Judiciar* (24 Mar. 1935).

Kernbach, Mihai. "Biologia crimei." *Buletin Eugenic și Biopolitic* 15, nos. 1–2 (Jan.–Feb. 1944): 1–10.

———. "Ereditatea și criminalitatea." *Buletin Eugenic și Biopolitic* 1, no. 6 (June 1927): 166–68.

———. *Medicina în procesul socializării.* Sibiu: Ed. Dacia Traiană, 1944.

"Legea sanitară și de ocrotire." *Monitorul Oficial*, no. 154 (14 July 1930): 5338–98.

"Legea Serviciului Social." *Buletinul Serviciului Social* 1, no. 1 (Mar. 1939): 3–10.

Leon, N. "Generațiunea spontanee și darvinismul." *Convorbiri Literare* 37, no. 4 (1903).

Leonida, Iosif. "Ce poate realiza practic eugenia la noi?" *Mișcarea Medicală Română* 8, nos. 5–6 (May–June 1935): 366–71.

Lepși, I. *Eugenia.* Chișinău, [1938?].

Lovinescu, Eugen. *Istoria civilizației române moderne.* 3 vols. Bucharest: Ed. Minerva, 1992.

Manicatide, G. "Certificatul de sănătate pentru contractarea căsătoriei." *Revista de Igienă Socială* 2, no. 1 (1932): 8–13.

"Manifestul PNȚ." *Dreptatea* 7, no. 1865 (4 Dec. 1933): 1, 6.

Manliu, I. *Crâmpeie de eugenie și igienă socială.* Bucharest: Tip. Jockey Club, 1921.

———. "Un pericol social: Discuții." *Adevărul* 36, no. 12135 (18 Aug. 1923): 1–2.

M[anoilescu], M[ihail]. "Date rasiale românești." *Lumea Nouă* 10, nos. 5–8 (May–Aug. 1941): 282–83.

Manuilă, Sabin. "Acțiunea eugenică ca factor de politică de populație." *Buletin Eugenic și Biopolitic* 11, nos. 1–4 (Jan.–Apr. 1941): 1–4.

———. "Comandamentele rassiale și politică de populație." *România Nouă* 7, no. 17 (26 Oct. 1940): 3.

———. "Decadența demografică și expansiune politică." *România Nouă* 7, no. 37 (18 Nov. 1940): 1.

———. *Evoluția demografică a orașelor și minorită țile etnice din Transilvania.* Bucharest: Cultura națională, 1929. First published in *Arhiva pentru Știința și Reforma Socială* 8, nos. 1–3 (1929).

———. "Problema rassială a României." *România Nouă* 7, no. 41 (22 Nov. 1940): 5.

———. "Les Problèmes démographiques en Transylvanie." *Révue de Transylvanie* 1, no. 1 (May 1934): 45–60.

———. "Reglementarea avortului." *Asistența Socială* 5, no. 1 (1936): 33.

———. "Societatea Regală Română de Eugenie și studiul eredității." *Sociologie Românească* 1, no. 5 (May 1936): 31–32.

———. *Structure et évolution de la population rurale.* Bucharest: Institut central de statistique, 1940. First published in *La Vie rurale en Roumanie.*

———. "Suprapopularea universităților și șomaj intelectual?" *Sociologie Românească* 3, nos. 4–6 (Apr.–June 1938): 227–29.

Manuilă, Sabin, and Wilhelm Filderman. *The Jewish Population in Romania during World War II.* Bilingual ed. Introduced by Larry Watts. Iași: Fundația Culturală Română, 1994.

Manuilă, Veturia. "Asistență socială." *Buletin Eugenic și Biopolitic* 1, no. 1 (Jan. 1927): 22–24.

———. "Evoluția ideii de asistență socială." *Buletin Eugenic și Biopolitic* 1, nos. 7–8 (July–Aug. 1927): 242–44.

———. "Femenismul și familia." *Buletin Eugenic și Biopolitic* 2, no. 3 (Mar. 1928): 92–96.

———. "Importanța cunoașterii factorilor sociali și biologici criminologeni în asistența delicvenților minori." *Sociologie Românească* 1, no. 4 (Apr. 1936): 7–10.

———. "Rolul femeilor în asistența socială a familiei." *Buletin Eugenic și Biopolitic* 1, no. 1 (Jan. 1927): 24–26.

———. "Situația femeii în societatea modernă și feminismul." *Buletin Eugenic și Biopolitic* 2, no. 6 (June 1928): 189–92.

———. "Studiul a 100 delicvenți minori din penitenciarul Văcărești." *Asistența Socială* 5, no. 1 (1936): 14–32.

Mărgineanu, Nicolae. *Amfiteatre și închisori: Mărturii asupra unui veac zbuciumat.* Cluj-Napoca: Ed. Dacia, 1991.

Marinescu, G. *Despre hereditatea normală și patologică și raporturile ei cu eugenia.* Academia Română. Memoriile secțiunii științifice, seria III, vol. 13, mem. 7. Bucharest, 1936.

———. *Determinism și cauzalitate în domeniul biologiei.* Academia Română. Memoriile secțiunii științifice, seria III, vol. 13, mem. 7. Bucharest, 1938.

———. *Laboratoriile și intelectualii.* Bucharest: 1920. First published in *Revista Renașterea Română* 3, no. 3 (Sept.–Nov. 1920).

Mehedinți, Simion. *Antropogeografia pentru clasa VI-a secundară.* 2d ed. Bucharest: Ed. Librăriei Socec and Co., 1938.

———. *Întrebări.* Bucharest, 1942. First published in *Revista Fundației Regale,* no. 2 (Feb. 1942): 243–57.

———. "Școala română și capitalul biologic al poporului român." *Buletin Eugenic și Biopolitic* 1, nos. 9–10 (Sept.–Oct. 1927): 266–81.

———. *Trilogii: Știința—școala—viața: Cu aplicări la poporul român.* Bucharest, [1940?].

Ministerul Instrucțiunii, comp. *Programa analitică a învățământului primar: Sancționată cu Înaltul Decret Regal no. 578 din 26 martie 1936.* Craiova: Scrisul românesc, 1936.

Ministerul Instrucțiunii, Cultelor și Artelor. Direcția educației poporului. *Program de lucru pentru acțiunea culturală.* [Bucharest], 1933.

Moldovan, Iuliu. *Amintiri și reflexiuni.* Bucharest: Ed. universitară Carol Davilla, 1996.

———. *Biopolitica.* Cluj: Ed. Asociațiunii, 1926.

———. "Circulara no. 2, nos. 1667/1939: Instrucțiuni, privind aplicarea prin Astra a Legii Serviciului Social în Ținuturile Someș, Mureș, și Timiș." *Transilvania* 70, no. 2 (Mar.–Apr. 1939): 3.

———. "Colaborarea între Astra și Uniunea Femeilor Române." *Buletin Eugenic și Biopolitic* 1, no. 4 (Apr. 1927): 119–22.

———. "Combaterea boalelor venerice." *Buletin Eugenic și Biopolitic* 1, no. 1 (Jan. 1927): 16–18.

———. "Cuvânt de deschidere a Adunării Generale a 'Astrei' din Timișoara." *Transilvania* 68, no. 5 (Sept.–Oct. 1937): 365–72.

———. "Cuvânt înainte!" *Transilvania* 65, no. 1 (Jan.–Feb. 1934): 1–2.

———. "Cuvânt inaugural la Adunarea Generală a 'Astrei' (5 noemvrie 1944)." *Transilvania* 75, nos. 10–12 (Oct.–Dec. 1944): 743–46.

———. "Cuvânt la deschiderea Adunării generale din Tîrgu-Mureșului." *Transilvania* 65, no. 5, (Sept.–Oct. 1934): 312–13.

———. "Cuvântul Președintelui 'Astrei.'" *Transilvania* 67, no. 5 (Sept.–Oct. 1936): 489.

———. "Educația fizică și morală în cadrele 'Astrei.'" *Buletin Eugenic și Biopolitic* 2, nos. 1–2 (Jan.–Feb. 1928): 38–46.

———. "Familia ca unitate biologică." *Sora de Ocrotire* 2, nos. 3–4 (1944): 25–31.

———. "Familia țărănească și familia burgheză: Biologia lor." *Transilvania* 73, no. 10 (Oct. 1942): 735–41.

———. *Igienă națiunii.* Cluj: Ed. Asociațiunii, 1925.

————. "Instrucţiuni pentru ambulatoarele policlinice. Nr. 10992/1921." *Sănătatea Publică*, Cluj 1, no. 5 (May 1921): 3–7.

————. *Introducere în etnobiologie şi biopolitică*. Sibiu, 1944.

————. "Modificarea legii sanitare şi de ocrotire." *Buletin Eugenic şi Biopolitic* 5, no. 7 (July 1934): 134–39.

————. "Motive pentru înfiinţarea Ministerului Sănătăţii Publice." *Sănătatea Publică* 1, no. 1 (Jan. 1921): 10–11.

————. *Neamul*. Sibiu, 1942. First published in *Buletin Eugenic şi Biopolitic* 13, nos. 1–4 (Jan.–Apr. 1942): 1–9.

————. "Un program biopolitic." *Societatea de Mâine* 1, no. 3 (27 Apr. 1924): 69–70.

————. *Statul etnic*. Cluj, 1943.

Moldovan, Iuliu, Petre Râmneanţu, and Iordache Făcăoaru. "Înregistrarea etno-biologică a populaţiei." *Buletin Eugenic şi Biopolitic* 10, nos. 1–2 (Jan.–Feb. 1939): 1–9.

Moldovan, Iuliu, et al., eds. *Tratat de medicină socială*. Vol. 1. 2d ed. Cluj, 1947.

Moldovanu, Iuliu. *See* Iuliu Moldovan.

Negulescu, P. P. *Destinul omenirii*. 2 vols. Bucharest: Fundaţia pentru literatură şi artă "Regele Carol II," 1938.

————. *Geneza formelor culturii*. Bucharest: Ed. Minerva, 1993.

————. *Reforma învăţământului*. 2d ed. Bucharest: Ed. Casei şcoalelor, 1927.

Noveanu, V. "Consideraţiuni eugenice asupra căsătoriei şi originei familiei." *Buletin Eugenic şi Biopolitic* 3, nos. 3–4 (Mar.–Apr. 1929): 75–80.

————. "Mişcarea eugenică în Franţa." *Buletin Eugenic şi Biopolitic* 3, nos. 1–2 (Jan.–Feb. 1929): 26–31.

"Numirea membrilor directoratului Frontului Renaşterii Naţionale." *Lumea Românească* 3, no. 591 (22 Jan. 1939): 3.

Odobescu, Grigore I. *Politică eugenică*. Bucharest, 1936. First published in *România Medicală*, no. 22 (15 Nov. 1936).

Pantelimonescu, V., comp. *Statutul Evreilor din România*. Bucharest: Ed. ziarului "Universul," 1941.

"Partidul Naţional şi cazul Iuliu Moldovan." *Infrăţirea* (28 Apr. 1922).

Pârvan, Vasile. *Idei şi forme istorice: Patru lecţii inaugurale*. Bucharest: Ed. Cartea românească, 1920.

Petrini (de Galatz). *Filosofia medicală: Despre ameliorarea rasei umane*. Bucharest: Tipografia D. A. Laurian, 1876.

Poenaru-Căplescu, C. "Medicii avortori şi făcătoarele de îngeri: Răspuns d'lui dr. Ygrec." *Adevărul* 36, no. 12144 (30 Aug. 1923): 1–2.

Popazolu, C. *Ereditatea*. Bucharest: Tipografia ziarului "Universul," 1915. First published in *Ziarul Ştiinţelor Populare şi al Călătoriilor*, nos. 6 and 7 (10 Feb. 1915).

Popovici, Al. "Problem sănătăţii în statul legionar. *Cuvântul* 17, serie nouă, no. 71 (23 Dec. 1940): 11.

Popovici, George. "Biopolitica, puericultura şi schimbarea sistemului în conducerea statului." *Societatea de Mâine* 5, nos. 22–24 (1–5 Dec. 1928): 443–44.

———. "L problème des populations de la Roumanie, vu á la lumière des recherches sur les races d'ápres le sang." *Révue de Transylvanie* 69, nos. 1–4 (1938): 15–27.

———. "Recherches serologiques sur les races en Roumanie." *Révue Anthropologique* 35, nos. 4–6 (Apr.–June 1925): 152–64.

Popoviciu, Gheorghe. *See* George Popovici.

Preda, George. *See* Gheorghe Preda.

Preda, Gheorghe. *Activitatea "Astrei" în 25 ani dela Unire (1918–1943)*. Sibiu, 1944.

———. "Biologie și biopolitică: O apropiere între nouile descoperiri fizice și științele biologice medicale." *Societatea de Mâine* 1, no. 1 (12 Apr. 1924): 20–21.

———. *Câteva date biologice și psihologice, necesare unei educațiuni moderne.* Sibiu, 1926.

———. "E periclitată intelectualitatea?" *Societatea de Mâine* 8, nos. 16–17 (1–15 Sept. 1931): 316.

———. "Ereditatea și educațiunea." *Buletin Eugenic și Biopolitic* 3, nos. 9–10 (Sept.–Oct. 1929): 316–20.

———. *O încercare de apropriere a raporturilor între știință și religie.* Sibiu, 1925. First published in *Transilvania* 11–12 (1925).

———. *Ziua Astrei.* Sibiu, 1937.

Preda, Victor. "Legatură dintre embriologie, ereditate și antropologie în cadrul problemei evoluției etnice." *Buletin Eugenic și Biopolitic* 9, nos. 1–2 (Jan.–Feb. 1938): 52–56.

"Problema natalității,—la noi și aiurea." *Universul* 41, no. 213 (13 Aug. 1923): 1.

Prodan, Leon. "Problema ocrotirei și asistenței." *Buletin Eugenic și Biopolitic* 11, nos. 1–4 (Jan.–Apr. 1941): 35–40.

"Programul Partidului Național-Țărănesc." *Aurora* 6, no. 1481 (13 Oct. 1926): 4.

"Proiect de statute pentru organizațiunea de educație fizică și eugenică sub auspiciile 'Astrei.'" *Buletin Eugenic și Biopolitic* 2, nos. 9–10 (Sept.–Oct. 1928): 279.

Pupeza, I., Virgiliu Leonte, C. Gheorghiu, and D. Mezincescu. "Sănătatea publică în România." In *Enciclopedia României*, vol. 1, edited by Dimitrie Gusti et al., 490–518. Bucharest: Imprimeria națională, 1938.

Pușcariu, Valentin. "Mendelismul la om: Ereditatea caracterelor fiziologice." *Buletin Eugenic și Biopolitic* 1, no. 3 (Mar. 1927): 66–71.

———. "Problema eredității—Legile lui Mendel." *Buletin Eugenic și Biopolitic* 1, no. 2 (Feb. 1927): 31–34.

———. Selecția sexuală la om." *Buletin Eugenic și Biopolitic* 11–12 (Nov.–Dec. 1928): 320–24.

———. "Teoriile evoluției: Lamarck și Lamarckismul: Geoffrey Saint-Hilaire." *Buletin Eugenic și Biopolitic* 1, no. 2 (Feb. 1927): 35–37.

Racoviță, Emil. *Evoluția și problemele ei.* Cluj: Ed. Asociațiunii, 1929.

———. "Valoarea științei." *Revista de Filosofie și Pedagogie* 1, fasc. 1 (Jan. 1906): 33.

Rădulescu-Motru, Constantin. "Rasa, cultura și naționalitatea în filosofia istoriei." *Arhiva pentru Reforma și Știința Socială* 4, no. 1 (1922): 18–34.

Rainer, Francisc. "Amendamentul unui om de știința: Scrisoare deschisă d-lui Ion Mihalache, Ministru al Agriculturii." *Adevărul* 42, no. 13954 (21 June 1929): 1–2.

———. *Enquêtes anthropologiques dans trois villages roumains des Carpathes.* Bucharest: Monitorul Oficial, 1937.

———. "Rasele umane: Conferință." *România Medicală* 12, no. 10 (15 Mar. 1934): 142.

Râmneanțu, Petre. "Activitatea lui Iuliu Moldovan în medicină socială." *Clujul Medical* 56, no. 3 (1973): 623–25.

———. "Bărbatul român medionormal." *Buletin Eugenic și Biopolitic* 13, nos. 1–4 (Jan.– Apr. 1942): 9–35.

———. "The Classical Blood Groups and the M, N Properties in the Nations from Transylvania." In *XVIIe Congres International d'Anthropologie et d'Archéologie Préhistorique: VIIe session de l'Institut International d'Anthropologie Bucarest 1–8 Septembre, 1937,* 325–32. Bucharest, 1939.

———. "Consecințele amestecului de populație." *Transilvania* 71, nos. 5–6 (Sept.–Dec. 1940): 186–92.

———. "Efectul exodului populației noastre dela sate la orașe." *Buletin Eugenic și Biopolitic* 5, nos. 11–12 (Nov.–Dec. 1934): 295–301.

———. *Expunere de titluri și lucrări științifice.* Cluj, 1942.

———. "Influența căsătoriei asupra fertilității și etnicului unui neam." *Transilvania* 68, no. 5 (Sept.–Oct. 1937): 302–404.

———. "La méthode biotypologique dans l'étude du village." *Arhiva pentru Reforma și Știința Socială* 16, nos. 1–4 (1943): 172–77.

———. "Origine éthnique des Szeklers de Transylvanie." *Révue de Transylvanie* 2, no. 1 (Aug.–Sept. 1935): 45–59.

———. "Pagina biopolitică, demografică și eugenică: Problema căsătoriilor mixte în orașele din Transilvania în perioada dela 1920–1937." *Transilvania* 70, no. 2 (Mar.– Apr. 1939): 91–94.

———. "Problema căsătoriilor mixte în orașele din Transilvania în perioada dela 1920–1937." *Buletin Eugenic și Biopolitic* 8, nos. 10–12 (Oct.–Dec. 1937): 317–38.

———. "Soluțiuni în legatură cu problema declinului etnic al populației românești din Banat." *Revista Institutului Social Banat–Crișana* 4, no. 14 (1936): 1–40.

———. "Studiul natalității și efectul reproducerii diferențiale a populației asupra calităților ei viitoare." *Buletin Eugenic și Biopolitic* 13, nos. 9–12 (Sept.–Dec. 1942): 381–411.

Râmneanțu, Petre, and Petre David. "Cercetări asupra originii etnice a populației din Sud-Estul Transilvaniei pe baza compoziției serologice a sângelui." *Buletin Eugenic și Biopolitic* 6, nos. 1–3 (Jan.–Mar. 1935): 36–66.

Râmneanțu, Petre, and Iordache Făcăoaru. "The Blood Groups and the Facial Index in the Population from Transylvania." In *XVIIe Congres International d'Anthropologie et d'Archéologie Préhistorique: VIIe session de l'Institut International d'Anthropologie Bucarest 1–8 Septembre, 1937,* 333–37. Bucharest, 1939.

Ramneantzu, Pierre. *See* Petre Râmneanțu.

"Regulament nr. 24 pentru combaterea boalelor venerice." *Monitorul Oficial* 71, no. 246, (Oct. 1943): 9528.

"Regulamentul pentru organizarea și funcționarea Serviciului Social (partea privitoare la Căminele Culturale)." *Buletinul Serviciului Social* 1, no. 2 (Apr. 1939): 1–20.

Relgis, Eugen. *Umanitarism și eugenism.* Bucharest: Ed. Vegetarismul, [1934].

Retezeanu, G. "La o răspîntie: (Capitalul uman de mâine)." *Buletin Eugenic și Biopolitic* 4, nos. 3–4 (Mar.–Apr. 1930): 65–69.

Roșca, Alexandru. *Copiii superior înzestrați.* Cluj: Ed. Institutului de psihologie al Universității din Cluj la Sibiu, 1941.

———. *Igienă mintală școlară.* Cluj: Ed. Institutului de psihologie al Universității din Cluj, 1939.

———. *Selecția valorilor.* Sibiu: Ed. secției biopolitice a Astrei, 1943.

Rosenblatt, Hawa. "Certificatul medical prenupțial." Medical Thesis in Surgery, Bucharest Medical School, 1936.

Roșu, Nicolae. "Școala caracterului." *Cuvântul* 17, serie nouă, no. 2 (15 Oct. 1940): 1.

Rotman-Cerna, I. "Sifilisul și căsătoria." *Universul* 41, no. 173 (3 July 1923): 6.

Rusu, Liviu. "Drum liber celor înzestrați." *Societatea de Mâine* 6, nos. 1–2 (15 Jan.–1 Feb. 1929): 3–4.

Sadoveanu, Izabela. "Feminismul și familia." *Buletin Eugenic și Biopolitic* 2, no. 5 (May 1928): 150–55.

———. "Rolul social al femeii." *Buletin Eugenic și Biopolitic* 2, nos. 7–8 (July–Aug. 1928): 220–31.

Șapira, B. "Eugenie cantitativă și calitativă." *Revista de Igienă Socială* 2, no. 7 (July 1932): 569–72.

Scraba, G. D. "Legea Sanitară din punct de vedere social." *Revista de Studii Sociale* 1, no. 1 (1 Feb. 1911): 30–32.

Soma, Sorin. "Politică demografică în Italia," *Preocupări Universitare* 1, no. 1 (Dec. 1943): 106–7.

Spârchez, Tiberiu. "Astra medicală la sate." *Societatea de Mâine* 4, no. 19 (15 May 1927): 256–57.

Stanca, Dominic. "Ambulatorul policlinic ca organ special în combaterea plăgilor sociale." *Societatea de Mâine* 6, nos. 9–10 (15 May–1 June 1929): 163–65.

———. "Lupta contra prostituției." *Societatea de Mâine* 2, nos. 32–33 (9–16 Aug. 1925): 571–73.

———. "O anchetă sanitară la un liceu [part 1]." *Societatea de Mâine* 1, no. 32 (23 Nov. 1924): 641–44.

———. "O anchetă sanitară la un liceu [part 2]." *Societatea de Mâine* 1, no. 33 (30 Nov. 1924): 660–63.

Stănescu, C., and Elisabeta Constante. "Asistența socială în România." In *Enciclopedia României,* vol. 1, *Statul,* edited by Dimitrie Gusti et al., 519–33. Bucharest: Imprimeria națională, 1938.

Statistica învăţămîntului în România pe anii 1921–22, 1928–29. Bucharest, 1931.

Ştefănescu-Goangă, Florin. *Selecţiunea capacităţilor şi orientarea profesională*. Cluj, 1929.

Stînc, Ştefan. *Mediul social ca factor patologic*. Iaşi: Tip. H. Goldner, 1897.

Stoichiţia, Iosif. "Casa culturală şi de sănătate." *Transilvania* 68, no. 2 (Mar.–Apr. 1937): 108–11.

————. "Evoluţia şi perspectivele igienei aplicate în România." *Buletin Eugenic şi Biopolitic* 16, nos. 1–3 (Jan.–Mar. 1945): 1–39.

————. "Organizaţia sanitară în Rusia Sovietică." *Buletin Eugenic şi Biopolitic* 15, nos. 9–12 (Sept.–Dec. 1944): 213–41.

————. "Principiile călăuzitoare ale organizaţiei sanitare." *Buletin Eugenic şi Biopolitic* 15, nos. 3–4 (Mar.–Apr. 1944): 65–78.

————. "Referat asupra călătoriei pentru studiul organizaţiei sanitare din Germania." *Analele Ministerului Sănătăţii şi Ocrotirilor Sociale* 46, no. 7 (July 1941): 334–44.

Strat, George. *T. R. Malthus şi principiul poporaţiei*. Bucharest, 1934.

Suţu, Al. "Eugenica şi hereditatea." *Gazeta de Medicină Chirurgicală a Spitalelor* 5, no. 12 (15 Sept. 1874): 186.

Teodorescu C., and Traian Topliceanu. "Darea de seamă asupra anchetei monografice din comuna Belint, jud. Timiş-Torontal (15 august–2 septembrie 1934)." *Revista Institutului Social Banat–Crişana* 2, nos. 10–12 (July–Dec. 1934): 89–93.

Tiniş, Aurel. "Examenul prenupţial obligator în mediul rural." *Ardealul Medical* 2, no. 10 (Oct. 1942): 451–52.

Tipărescu, P. *Rasă şi degenerare. Cu un studiu statistic asupra jidanilor*. Bucharest, 1941.

Trei ani de guvernare: 6 septemvrie 1940–6 septemvrie 1943. Bucharest: Monitorul oficial şi imprimeriile statului, 1943.

"Troisieme Section—Eugénique. Discussions." In *XVIIe Congres International d'Anthropologie et d'Archéologie Préhistorique: VIIe session de l'Institut International d'Anthropologie Bucarest 1–8 Septembre, 1937*, 681–82. Bucharest, 1939.

Vaida-Voevod, Alexandru. "Politică naţională şi capitalul biologic naţional." *Buletin Eugenic şi Biopolitic* 1, nos. 7–8 (July–Aug. 1927): 199–211.

Vasilescu-Buciumi, Ioan. "Criminologia şi eugenia." *Revista de Medicină Legală* 1, no. 1 (1936): 84–90.

————. "Eugenia şi înoirile codului penal." *Mişcarea Medicală Română* 8, nos. 5–6 (May–June 1935): 363–65.

————. "Tendances eugéniques dans le nouveau Code penal roumain Carol II." In *XVIIe Congres International d'Anthropologie et d'Archéologie Préhistorique: VIIe session de l'Institut International d'Anthropologie Bucarest 1–8 Septembre, 1937*, 678–82. Bucharest, 1939.

————. "Tendinţe eugenice în noul cod penal." *Revista Penală* 2, no. 5 (May 1936): 212–14.

Vlad, P. "Organizarea asistenţei Capitalei în conceptia Consiliului de Patronaj." *Buletin Eugenic şi Biopolitic* 14, nos. 1–2 (Jan.–Feb. 1943): 44–50.

Voina, Aurel. "Datoria mamelor faţă de neam." In *Calendarul Asociaţiunii pe anul comun 1927*, compiled by Horia Petra-Petrescu, 174–76. Sibiu: Ed. Asociaţiunii, 1926.

———. "Doi factori de progres: Igiena şi Eugenia." *Societatea de Mâine* 1, no. 8 (1 June 1924): 183–84.

———. *Igienă pentru clasa VIII secundară de băeţi şi fete.* Bucharest, [1936].

———. "Organizarea sanitară a Transilvaniei în primul deceniu al unirii." In *Transilvania, Banatul, Crişana, Maramureşul: 1918–1928,* vol. 1, 739–49. Bucharest: Cultura naţională, 1929.

Vornic, Tiberiu. "Criza intelectuală şi morală." *Societatea de Mâine* 3, no. 12 (21 Mar. 1926): 216–17.

Vornica, Gheorghe. "Concepţia de rasă în Italia fascistă." *Buletin Eugenic şi Biopolitic* 11, nos. 9–12 (Sept.–Dec. 1941): 179–83.

———. "Studii eugenice." *Transilvania* 73, nos. 2–3 (Feb.–Mar. 1942): 221–24.

Ygrec, Doctorul. "Căsătorii cu certificat medical şi . . . 'montă' cu permisiunea Statului." *Adevărul* 36, no. 12098 (10 July 1923): 1–2.

———. "Cum vor nemţii să-şi îmbunătăţească rasa?" *Adevărul* 36, no. 12143 (28 Aug. 1923): 1–2.

———. "Iarăşi despre avorturi provocate şi medicii avortori." *Adevărul* 36, no. 12152 (8 Sept. 1923): 1–2.

———. "Medicii avortori şi 'făcătoarele de îngeri'." *Adevărul* 36, no. 12125 (6 Aug. 1923): 1–2.

———. *Problema sifilisului în faţa budgetului ţării.* Bucharest, 1930.

———. *Rasa şi rasismul: Cea mai mare escrocherie ştiinţifică a secolului.* Bucharest: Ed. Adam, [1935?].

Zelea-Codreanu, Corneliu. *Pentru legionari.* Vol. 1. Sibiu: Ed. Totul pentru ţară, 1936.

Zeletin, Ştefan. *Burghezia română: Originea şi rolul ei istoric.* Bucharest, 1925.

Zolog, Mihai. "Baza biologică a instrucţiei şcolare." *Buletin Eugenic şi Biopolitic* 6, nos. 1–3 (Jan.–Mar. 1935): 5–15.

———. "Un caz indicat pentru sterilizare eugenică." *Buletin Eugenic şi Biopolitic* 1, no. 11 (Nov. 1927): 326–33.

———. "Influenţa mediului social şi a sexului asupra capacitaţii intelectuale." *Buletin Eugenic şi Biopolitic* 1, no. 4 (Apr. 1927): 113–18.

———. "Inteligenţa copiilor de şcoală." *Buletin Eugenic şi Biopolitic* 1, no. 2 (Feb. 1927): 50–53.

Zolog, Mihai, and Ovidiu Comşia. "Consultaţiunile prenupţiale şi certificatul prenupţial." *Buletin Eugenic şi Biopolitic* 5, no 7 (July 1934): 129–34.

———. "Indicaţiile eugenice ale avortului artificial." *Buletin Eugenic şi Biopolitic* 5, nos. 8–10 (Aug.–Oct. 1934): 165–72.

Zolog, Mihai, and Iordache Făcăoaru. "Indicaţia şi legislatia eugenică a sterilizării." *Buletin Eugenic şi Biopolitic* 5, nos. 8–10 (Aug.–Oct. 1934): 186–92.

Zosin, Panaite. *Determinismul.* [Bucharest]: Lito-Tipografia Motatzeanu şi Lambru, 1895.

SECONDARY SOURCES

Achim, Viorel. *Ţiganii în istoria României.* Bucharest: Ed. enciclopedică, 1998.

Adams, Mark B. "Eugenics in Russia, 1900–1940." In *The Wellborn Science: Eugenics in Germany, France, Brazil, and Russia,* edited by Mark B. Adams, 153–216. New York: Oxford University Press, 1990.

————, ed. *The Wellborn Science: Eugenics in Germany, France, Brazil, and Russia.* New York: Oxford University Press, 1990.

Ancel, Jean. *Transnistria.* 3 vols. Bucharest: DU Style, 1998.

Bădina, Ovidiu. *Cercetarea sociologică concretă: Tradiţii româneşti.* Bucharest: Ed. politică, 1966.

Bădina, Ovidiu, and Octavian Neamţu. *Dimitre Gusti: Contribuţii la cunoaşterea operei şi activităţiisale.* Bucharest: Ed. ştiinţifică, 1965.

Banac, Ivo, and Katherine Verdery, eds. *National Character and National Ideology in Interwar Eastern Europe.* New Haven, Conn: Yale Center for International and Area Studies, 1995.

Berman, Marshall. *All That Is Solid Melts Into Air.* New York: Penguin, 1988.

Bock, Gisela. "Racism and Sexism in Nazi Germany: Motherhood, Compulsory Sterilization, and the State." In *When Biology Became Destiny: Women in Weimar and Nazi Germany,* edited by Renate Bridenthal, Atina Grossmann, and Marion Kaplan, 271–96. New York: Monthly Review Press, 1984.

Bologa, Valeriu, et al. *Istoria medicinii româneşti.* Bucharest: Ed. medicală, 1972.

Bolovan, Sorina, and Ioan Bolovan, eds. *Sabin Manuilă: Istorie şi demografie.* Cluj: Fundaţia Culturală Română, 1995.

Braham, Randolf, ed. *The Destruction of Romanian and Hungarian Jews During the Antonescu Era.* Boulder, Colo.: Social Science Monographs, 1997.

Brătescu, Gheorghe. *Biological and Medical Sciences in Romania.* Bucharest: Ed. ştiinţifică şi enciclopedică, 1989.

————. *Istoria sănătăţii publice în România: Sinteză.* Bucharest, 1981.

————. "Viziunea biosociomedicală a lui Iuliu Moldovan." In *Amintiri şi reflexiuni,* edited by Iuliu Moldovan, 133–39. Bucharest: Ed. universitară Carol Davilla, 1996.

————, ed. *Din tradiţiile medicinii şi ale educaţiei sanitare: Studii şi note.* Bucharest: Ed. medicală, 1978.

————, ed. *Trecut şi viitor în medicină: Studii şi note.* Bucharest: Ed. medicală, 1981.

Breuilly, John. *Nationalism and the State.* Manchester: Manchester University Press, 1982.

Bridenthal, Renate, Atina Grossmann, and Marion Kaplan. *When Biology Became Destiny: Women in Weimar and Nazi Germany.* New York: Monthly Review Press, 1984.

Broberg, Gunnar, and Nils Roll-Hansen, eds. *Eugenics and the Welfare State: Sterilization Policy in Denmark, Sweden, Norway, and Finland.* East Lansing: Michigan State University Press, 1996.

Bucur, Maria. "Awakening or Constructing Biological Consciousness?: 'Astra' and Biopolitics in Interwar Romania." *Colloquia: Journal of Central European History* 2, nos. 1–2 (Jan.–Dec. 1995): 172–85.

———. "From Private Philanthropy to Public Institutions: The Rockefeller Foundation and Public Health in Interwar Romania." *Romanian Civilization* 4, no. 2 (summer 1995): 47–60.

———. "In Praise of Wellborn Mothers: On Eugenicist Gender Roles in Interwar Romania." *East European Politics and Societies* 9, no. 1 (winter 1995): 123–42.

———. "Philanthropy, Nationalism, and the Growth of Civil Society in Romania." Working Papers of the Johns Hopkins Comparative Nonprofit Sector Project, no. 31. Edited by Lester M. Salamon and Helmut K. Anheier. Baltimore: The Johns Hopkins Institute for Policy Studies, 1998.

Călinescu, George. *Istoria literaturii române de la origini pînă în prezent.* 2d rev. ed. Bucharest: Ed. Minerva, 1982.

Câncea, Paraschiva. *Mișcarea pentru emanciparea femeii în România.* Bucharest: Ed. politică, 1976.

Canning, Kathleen. *Languages of Labor and Gender: Female Factory Work in Germany, 1850–1914.* Ithaca: Cornell University Press, 1996.

Carol, Anne. *Histoire de l'eugénisme en France: Les médecins et la procréation, XIX-e–XXe siècle.* Paris: Seuil, 1995.

Chirot, Daniel. "Ideology, Reality and Competing Models of Development in Eastern Europe Between the Two World Wars." *East European Politics and Societies* 3, no. 3 (fall 1989): 378–411.

Clay, Cathrine, and Michael Leapman. *Master Race: The Lebensborn Experiment in Nazi Germany.* London: Hodder and Stoughton, 1995.

Costea, Ștefan, and Ion Ungureanu. *A Concise History of Romanian Sociology.* Bucharest: Ed. științifică și enciclopedică, 1981.

Cott, Nancy F. *The Bonds of Womanhood: "Woman's Sphere" in New England, 1780–1835.* 2d ed. New Haven, Conn.: Yale University Press, 1997.

Davidoff, Eleonore, and Catherine Hall. *Family Fortunes: Men and Women of the English Middle Class, 1780–1850.* Chicago: Chicago University Press, 1987.

Degler, Carl N. *In Search of Human Nature: The Decline and Revival of Darwinism in American Social Thought.* New York: Oxford University Press, 1991.

Desmond, Adrian. *The Politics of Evolution: Morphology, Medicine, and Reform in Radical London.* Chicago: University of Chicago Press, 1989.

Dikötter, Frank. *Imperfect Conceptions: Medical Knowledge, Birth Defects, and Eugenics in China.* New York: Columbia University Press, 1998.

———. "Race Culture: Recent Perspectives on the History of Eugenics." *American Historical Review* 103, no. 2 (Apr. 1998): 467–78.

Dimitriu, Emilian, et al. *A Concise History of Education in Romania.* Bucharest: Ed. științifică și enciclopedică, 1981.

Eidelberg, Philip G. *The Great Rumanian Peasant Revolt of 1907.* Leiden: Brill, 1974.

Enăchescu, Th. "Contribuțiile profesorului Francisc J. Rainer la dezvoltarea antropologiei românești." *Studii și Cercetări Antropologice* 7, no. 2 (1970): 165–79.

Farrall, Lyndsay A. "A History of Eugenics: A Bibliographic Review." *Annals of Science* 36 (1979): 111–23.

Figuri reprezentative ale medicinii și farmaciei clujene. 2 vols. Cluj-Napoca: Institutul de medicină și farmacie, [1980].

Foucault, Michel. *The Archaeology of Knowledge.* London: Tavistock, 1972.

———. *Discipline and Punish: The Birth of the Prison.* New York: Vintage Books, 1979.

Freeden, Michael. "Eugenics and Progressive Thought: A Study of Ideological Affinity." *Historical Journal* 22, no. 3 (1976): 645–71.

Gáll, Ernö. *Sociologia burgheză din Romînia: Studii critice.* Bucharest, 1958.

Georgescu, Vlad. *The Romanians: A History.* Columbus: Ohio University Press, 1991.

Ghișe, Dumitru, and Pompiliu Teodor. *Fragmentarium Iluminist.* Cluj: Ed. Dacia, 1972.

Gleason, Abbott. *Totalitarianism: An Inner History of the Cold War.* Oxford: Oxford University Press, 1995.

Gordon, Linda. *Woman's Body, Woman's Right: Birth Control in America.* New York: Penguin Books, 1986.

Gotz, Aly, Peter Chroust, and Christian Pross. *Cleansing the Fatherland: Nazi Medicine and Racial Hygiene.* Baltimore: Johns Hopkins University Press, 1994.

Graham, Loren R. *Between Science and Values.* New York: Columbia University Press, 1986.

———. "Science and Values: The Eugenics Movement in Germany and Russia in the 1920s." *American Historical Review* 82, no. 5 (Dec. 1977): 1133–64.

———. *Science in Russia and the Soviet Union: A Short History* (New York: Cambridge University Press, 1993).

Grossmann, Atina. *Reforming Sex: The German Movement for Birth Control and Abortion Reform, 1920–1950.* New York: Oxford University Press, 1995.

Haller, Mark H. *Eugenics: Hereditarian Attitudes in American Thought.* New Brunswick, N.J.: Rutgers University Press, 1963.

Heinen, Armin. *Die Legion "Erzengel Michael" in Rumänien.* Munich: Oldenbourg, 1986.

Hitchins, Keith. "*Gândirea*": Nationalism in Spiritual Guise." In *Social Change in Romania, 1860–1940: A Debate on Development in a European Nation,* edited by Kenneth Jowitt, 140–73. Berkeley: University of California Press, 1978.

———. *L'Idée de nation chez les Roumains de Transylvanie, 1691–1848.* Bucharest: Ed. științifică și enciclopedică, 1987.

———. *Mit și realitate în istoriografia României.* Bucharest: Ed. enciclopedică, 1997.

———. *Rumania 1866–1947.* Oxford: Clarendon Press, 1994.

Hobsbawm, Eric J. *Nations and Nationalism since 1780.* Cambridge: Cambridge University Press, 1990.

Hutchinson, John. *The Dynamics of Cultural Nationalism.* London: Allen and Unwin, 1987.

Iancu, Gheorghe. *Contribuția consiliului dirigent la consolidarea statului național unitar român (1918–1920)*. Cluj-Napoca: Ed. Dacia, 1985.

Ioanid, Radu. *The Holocaust in Romania: The Destruction of Jews and Gypsies Under the Antonescu Regime, 1940–1944*. Chicago: Ivan R. Dee, 2000.

———. *The Sword of the Archangel*. Boulder, Colo.: Columbia University Press, East European Monographs, 1989.

Izsak, Samuel, ed. *Cetatea de medicină și farmacie clujeană*. Cluj, 1983.

Janos, Andrew C. "Modernization and Decay in Historical Perspective: The Case of Romania." In *Social Change in Romania, 1860–1940: A Debate on Development in a European Nation*, edited by Kenneth Jowitt, 72–116. Berkeley: University of California Press, 1978.

Jowitt, Kenneth, ed. *Social Change in Romania, 1860–1940: A Debate on Development in a European Nation*. Berkeley: University of California Press, 1978.

Kaplan, Marion. *The Making of the Jewish Middle Class: Women, Family, and Identity in Imperial Germany*. New York: Oxford University Press, 1991.

Kerber, Linda K. *Women of the Republic: Intellect and Ideology in Revolutionary America*. New York: W. W. Norton, 1986.

Kevles, Paul. *In the Name of Eugenics: Genetics and the Uses of Human Heredity*. New York: Knopf, 1985.

Kligman, Gail. *The Politics of Duplicity: Controlling Reproduction in Ceaușescu's Romania*. Berkeley: University of California Press, 1998.

———. "The Politics of Reproduction in Ceaușescu's Romania: A Case Study in Political Rule." *East European Politics and Societies* 6, no. 3 (1992): 364–418.

Kligman, Gail, and Susan Gal. "Gendering Postsocialism: Reproduction as Politics in East Central Europe." In *Between Past and Future: The Revolutions of 1989 and Their Aftermath*, edited by Sorin Antohi and Vladimir Tismăneanu, 198–215. Budapest: Central European University, 2000.

Kohn, Hans. *The Idea of Nationalism: Its Origins and Background*. 2d ed. New York: Macmillan, 1961.

Kovacs, Maria. *Liberal Professions and Illiberal Politics: Hungary from the Habsburgs to the Holocaust*. Washington, D.C.: Wilson Center Press and Oxford University Press, 1994.

Kuhl, Stefan. *The Nazi Connection: Eugenics, American Racism, and German National Socialism*. New York: Oxford University Press, 1994.

LaCapra, Dominique. *Rethinking Intellectual History: Texts, Contexts, Language*. Ithaca: Cornell University Press, 1983.

Laqueur, Thomas. *Making Sex: Body and Gender from the Greeks to Freud*. Cambridge: Harvard University Press, 1990.

Larson, Edward. "The Rhetoric of Eugenics: Expert Authority and the Mental Deficiency Bill." *British Journal of the History of Science* 24, part 1, no. 80 (Mar. 1991): 45–60.

———. *Sex, Race, and Science: Eugenics in the Deep South*. Baltimore: Johns Hopkins University Press, 1995.

Livezeanu, Irina. *Cultural Politics in Greater Romania: Regionalism, Nation Building and Ethnic Struggle, 1918–1930*. Ithaca: Cornell University Press, 1995.

Love, Joseph. *Crafting the Third World: Theorizing Underdevelopment in Rumania and Brazil*. Stanford, Calif.: Stanford University Press, 1996.

Mackenzie, Donald. "Eugenics in Britain." *Social Studies of Science* 6 (1976): 499–532.

Matei, Pamfil. *"Asociaţiunea transilvană pentru literatură şi cultura poporului român" (Astra) şi rolul ei în cultura naţională (1861–1950)*. Cluj-Napoca: Ed. Dacia, 1986.

Mazdumar, Pauline M. H. *Eugenics, Human Genetics and Human Failings: The Eugenics Society, Its Sources and Its Critics in Britain*. New York: Routledge, 1992.

Micu, Dumitru. *"Gîndirea" şi gîndirismul*. Bucharest: Ed. Minerva, 1975.

Mitrany, David. *The Land and the Peasant in Rumania*. London: H. Milford, Oxford University Press, 1930.

Mosse, George. *Nationalism and Sexuality*. Madison: University of Wisconsin Press, 1988.

Nagy-Talavera, Nicholas. *The Green Shirts and Others: A History of Fascism in Hungary and Rumania*. Stanford, Calif.: Hoover Institution Press, 1970.

Nemoianu, Virgil. "Variable Sociopolitical Functions of Aesthetic Doctrine: Lovinescu vs. Western Aestheticism." In *Social Change in Romania, 1860–1940: A Debate on Development in a European Nation*, edited by Kenneth Jowitt, 174–207. Berkeley: University of California Press, 1978.

Oldson, William. *A Providential Antisemitism: Nationalism and Polity in Nineteenth Century Romania*. Philadelphia: American Philosophical Society, 1991.

Ornea, Z. *Anii treizeci: Extrema dreaptă românească*. Bucharest: Ed. Fundaţiei Culturale Române, 1995.

———. *Ţărănismul. Studiu sociologic*. Bucharest: Ed. politică, 1969.

———. *Tradiţionalism şi modernitate în deceniul al treilea*. Bucharest: Ed. Eminescu, 1980.

Paul, Diane. *Controlling Human Heredity, 1865 to the Present*. Atlantic Highlands, N.J.: Humanities Press, 1995.

———. "Eugenics and the Left." *Journal of the History of Ideas* 45, no. 4 (Oct.–Dec. 1984): 567–90.

Pauly, Phillip J. "Essay Review: The Eugenics Industry—Growth or Restructuring?" *Journal of the History of Biology* 26, no. 1 (spring 1993): 131–45.

Pernick, Martin S. *The Black Stork: Eugenics and the Death of "Defective" Babies in American Medicine and Motion Pictures Since 1915*. New York: Oxford University Press, 1996.

Preda, Victor. *Din istoria luptei dintre materialism şi idealism în biologie*. Bucharest, 1960.

Provine, William B. *The Origins of Theoretical Population Genetics*. Chicago: University of Chicago Press, 1971.

Rabinow, Paul. *French Modern*. Cambridge: MIT Press, 1989.

Rafter, Nicole Hahn. *Creating Born Criminals*. Urbana: University of Illinois Press, 1997.

Roberts, Henry. *Rumania: Political Problems of an Agrarian State.* Hamden, Conn.: Archon Books, 1969.

Romanescu, Constantin, and Cristina Ionescu, eds. *Pagini medico-istorice.* Iaşi: Institutul de medicină şi farmacie Iaşi, 1973.

Rosenberg, Charles. *No Other Gods: On Science and American Social Thought.* Baltimore: Johns Hopkins University Press, 1976.

Rusenescu, M., and Ion Saizu. *Viaţa politică în România, 1922–1928.* Bucharest: Ed. politică, 1979.

Rusu, Vasile. "Figuri celebre de medici români." *Tribuna Sibiului* 35, no. 7958 (27 Feb. 1983): 2.

Ryan, Mary. *Cradle of the Middle Class: The Family in Oneida County, New York, 1790–1865.* Cambridge: Cambridge University Press, 1983.

Sǎhleanu, Victor. *Începuturile medicinii sociale în România: George Banu.* Bucharest, 1979.

Saizu, Ioan. "Dezbateri interbelice privind 'raţionalizarea' culturii româneşti." In *Dezvoltare şi modernizare în România interbelică: 1919–1939,* edited by Vasile Puşcaş and Vasile Vesa, 236–54. Bucharest: Ed. politică, 1988.

———. "Relatia ştiinţă-societate în gîndirea românească interbelică." *Revista de Istorie* 34, no. 5 (1981): 799–819.

Sandache, Cristian. *Doctrina naţional creştină în România.* Bucharest: Paideia, 1997.

Savu, Al. Gh. *Sistemul partidelor politice din România, 1919–1940.* Bucharest: Ed. ştiinţifică şi enciclopedică, 1976.

Schneider, William. *Quality and Quantity: The Quest for Biological Regeneration in Twentieth-Century France.* Cambridge: Cambridge University Press, 1991.

Scurtu, Ioan. *Istoria Partidului Naţional Ţărănesc.* Bucharest: Ed. enciclopedică, 1994.

———. *Din viaţapolitică a României, 1926–1947.* Bucharest: Ed. ştiinţifică şi enciclopedică, 1983.

Searle, G.R. "Eugenics and Politics in Britain in the 1930s." *Annals of Science* 36 (1979): 159–69.

Shafir, Michael. "Radical Politics in Post Communist East Central Europe: Part I: 'Reds,' 'Pinks,' 'Blacks,' and 'Blues.'" *RFE/RL East European Perspectives* 1, no. 1 (3 Nov. 1999). Available at <http://www.rferl.org/eepreport>.

———. "X-Raying Post-Communist 'Radical Minds.'" *RFE/RL East European Perspectives* 1, nos. 3–4 (1–15 Dec. 1999), and 2, nos. 1–2 (12–26 Jan. 2000). Available at <http://www.rferl.org/eepreport>.

Shoemaker, Robert. *Gender and English Society, 1650–1850: The Emergence of Separate Spheres.* New York: Longman, 1998.

Smith, Anthony D. *Theories of Nationalism.* Rev. ed. New York: Holmes and Meier, 1983.

Sokolova, Vera. "In the Name of the Nation: Gypsies, Sterilization, and the Discourse on Race and Sexuality in Socialist Czechoslovakia, 1972–1989." Paper presented at the AAASS Annual Convention, Boca Raton, Fla., Sept. 1998.

Stahl, Henri H. *Amintiri și gînduri din vechea școală a "monografiilor sociologice."* Bucharest: Ed. Minerva, 1981.

Stepan, Nancy Leys. *"The Hour of Eugenics": Race, Gender and Nation in Latin America.* Ithaca: Cornell University Press, 1991.

Strauss, Hugo. "Iuliu Moldovan." In *Figuri reprezentative ale medicinii și farmaciei clujene,* vol. 1, 20–46. Cluj-Napoca: Institutul de medicină și farmacie, [1980].

———. "Salvator Cupcea." In *Figuri reprezentative ale medicinii și farmaciei clujene,* vol. 2, 108–15. Cluj-Napoca: Institutul de medicină și farmacie, [1980].

Tismăneanu, Vladimir. *Fantasies of Salvation: Democracy, Nationalism, and Myth in Post-Communist Europe.* Princeton: Princeton University Press, 1998.

Turner, Henry Ashby, Jr. "Fascism and Modernization." *World Politics* 24, no. 4 (July 1972).

Vlaicu, Roman. "Iuliu Hațieganu." In *Figuri reprezentative ale medicinii și farmaciei clujene,* vol. 1, 1–19. Cluj-Napoca: Institutul de medicină și farmacie, [1980].

Volovici, Leon. *Nationalist Ideology and Antisemitism: The Case of Romanian Intellectuals in the 1930s.* Oxford: Pergamon Press, 1991.

Vulcănescu, Mircea, et al., eds. *Dimitrie Gusti și Școala Sociologică dela București.* Bucharest, 1937.

Walkowitz, Judith. *City of Dreadful Delight: Narratives of Sexual Danger in Late-Victorian London.* Chicago: University of Chicago Press, 1992.

———. *Prostitution and Victorian Society: Women, Class, and the State.* Cambridge: Cambridge University Press, 1980.

Weber, Eugen. *Varieties of Fascism.* New York: Vintage Books, 1964.

Weindling, Paul. *Health, Race and German Politics Between National Unification and Nazism, 1870–1945.* Cambridge: Cambridge University Press, 1989.

Weiss, Sheila Faith. *Race Hygiene and National Efficiency: The Eugenics of Wilhelm Schallmayer.* Berkeley: University of California Press, 1987.

———. "The Race Hygiene Movement in Germany, 1904–1945." In *The Wellborn Science: Eugenics in Germany, France, Brazil, and Russia,* edited by Mark B. Adams, 8–68. New York: Oxford University Press, 1990.

INDEX